Contemporary Security Management

Second Edition

Contemporary Security Management

Second Edition

John J. Fay

ELSEVIER

BUTTERWORTH
HEINEMANN

Amsterdam • Boston • Heidelberg • London
New York • Oxford • Paris • San Diego
San Francisco • Singapore • Sydney • Tokyo

Elsevier Butterworth–Heinemann
30 Corporate Drive, Suite 400, Burlington, MA 01803, USA
Linacre House, Jordan Hill, Oxford OX2 8DP, UK

Library of Congress Cataloging-in-Publication Data
Application submitted

British Library Cataloguing-in-Publication Data
A catalogue record for this book is available from the British Library.

ISBN-13: 978-0-7506-7928-X
ISBN-10: 0-7506-7928-X

For information on all Elsevier Butterworth–Heinemann publications
visit our Web site at www.books.elsevier.com

Printed in the United States of America
06 07 08 09 10   10 9 8 7 6 5 4 3 2

For Barbara, my beautiful and persevering wife

Contents

Contents

1. Historical Roots

That men do not learn very much from the lessons of history is the most important of all the lessons that history has to teach.
—Aldous Huxley

INTRODUCTION

Efforts to organize human work have existed at least since people started living in tribes, but few descriptions of managed work were recorded prior to about 200 years ago. Before then, work activities were fairly simple and involved relatively small groups. Typically, the workplace was a single room containing raw materials, simple tools, a craftsman, and an apprentice. The craftsman was the equivalent of today's line supervisor, a skilled and knowledgeable practitioner of a trade. The apprentice was not difficult to manage because the tasks he performed relied on low levels of technology. The apprentice learned mainly by observing the craftsman and by accepting direct supervision.

INDUSTRIAL REVOLUTION

The Industrial Revolution changed that arrangement. It began in Europe in the late eighteenth century and spread quickly to the United States. In his classic book *The Wealth of Nations*, Adam Smith stole a glance into the future when he recognized the great increase in work output offered by the use of machines.

Fertile Ground

The United States provided fertile ground for cultivating a system of mechanized factories. Funds needed to form large manufacturing companies were willingly provided by the affluent. The lack of tariff barriers between the states, coupled with an expanding network of roadways and waterways, facilitated large-scale movements of mass-produced goods. Nature's generous endowment ensured a large and dependable supply of raw materials. The advent of the steel plow opened the West to agricultural production, and the factories that produced farm equipment and other work-enhancing machines provided jobs that attracted large numbers of people to urban industrial centers.

Growth of Factories

The growth of the factory system led to mass employment, which in turn provided incomes that made mass consumption possible. Consumer demand enabled mass production to prosper. At the same time, improvements made in agricultural techniques freed a large part of the workforce from food production. With abundant farmland and industrial raw materials, the young American republic developed a balance of agriculture and industry.

Mass Production

As the production of goods migrated from small workshops to large factories, many more people were engaged, each working on only one part of the manufactured product and having little contact with those who were making the other parts. This marked the beginning of specialization of labor, which introduced new requirements for managing production. Coordination of separate work efforts was essential and at the same time difficult to achieve.

The absence of recorded references to management practices cloud the Industrial Revolution and the ensuing changes it fostered. Although managers likely discussed common problems among themselves, few or no exchanges of ideas in writing were circulated or passed on to succeeding managers. Later, however, descriptions of management practices began to appear mainly in the professional journals of management societies. The faint outlines of a management movement began to unfold.

SCIENTIFIC MANAGEMENT

Frederick W. Taylor observed that workers were pretty much free to carry out their job assignments at their own paces by their own methods. In search of better ways of performing jobs, he used the scientific method of logical inquiry to experiment with work methods .

Although not all of the principles that came to be known as scientific management originated with Taylor, he brought the standard principles of his time into a comprehensible whole, put them into operation, and verified that they worked. Taylor published his findings in *Principles of Scientific Management*. He stressed that his concepts provided a method for labor and management to work together. Taylor's pioneering efforts, however, were widely misunderstood at the time [1].

Taylor is often referred to as the Father of Scientific Management, but he was not the only expert in this area. Among others, Frank and Lillian Gilbreth developed the principles of motion study, through which jobs were broken into component movements and studied so that wasted motions and fatigue could be reduced [2].

Similar management research was taking place in Europe. For example, Henri Fayol — chief executive of a large French mining and metallurgical firm — studied management from the top down, with emphasis on overall administration. He published widely on management practices applicable to industrial and governmental organizations.

HUMAN RELATIONS

The pioneers of scientific management, although clearly oriented to efficiency in production, recognized the human element in management. Elton Mayo's study of workers' social needs at the Hawthorne plant of the Western Electric Company emphasized the need to take workers' attitudes into account (see Figure 1-1) and to recognize them as important contributors to production [3].

The emphasis by Mayo and others did not downplay the prevailing interest in efficiency. It simply added a new dimension; that is, that management's legitimate interest in getting the work done has to be tempered with an interest in the people who do the work. Technical systems for performing work through social interactions of workers quickly evolved, and the term *sociotechnical systems* came into use to describe the merger.

Figure 1-1 The "human relations" era ushered in an emphasis on relationships among employees.

OPERATIONS RESEARCH

Efforts to apply hard science to management led in 1937 to the development in the United Kingdom of a separate discipline called operations research. By 1942, spurred by the pressing demands of World War II, all three of Britain's military services were engaged in operations research. Learning from the British experience, the United States committed heavily to the use of the approach in the industrial environment — and with the advent of the computer in the early 1950s it took on an entirely new dimension.

Operations research has three pillars: a systems approach to problem solving, the use of teams from many disciplines, and the application of scientific methods. The systems approach recognizes that an effect on one part of a system will have an effect on the behavior of the system as a whole. It is the interaction between and among parts, not the actions of one or a few parts, that determines how well or how poorly the system performs. The use of interdisciplinary teams brings expertise to the work, much of which involves the application of highly technical analyses and mathematical modeling (e.g., see Figure 1-2).

Operations research brought about significant change in problem-solving techniques. Computers and other scientific tools capable of dealing with large and complex problems are routinely used for business purposes, requiring the modern manager to have strong quantitative skills.

Program Evaluation and Review Technique

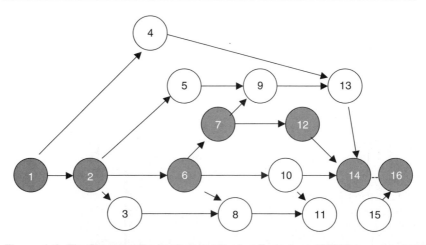

Figure 1-2 The Program Evaluation and Review Technique (PERT) is commonly used to track progress in large and complicated projects. The critical path is the sequence of activities and events that takes the greatest amount of time to complete and that has the least slack in activity [4].

AGE OF TECHNOLOGY

In the early craft shop environment, tasks were performed with humans controlling the process and providing the energy to perform the work. In the transition to mass production, people controlled the operation of machines directly but the energy was provided by another source. The next improvement was automatic control in which the machine could sense its manipulations, compare them to preset requirements, and adjust accordingly. Today's automated systems provide instructions to machines that comply and provide feedback. Sophisticated systems make use of such technologies as the Global Positioning System (GPS), as indicated in Figure 1-3.

Without question, one of the greatest triumphs of technology was the electronic computer, and business was profoundly changed as a result. Many of the early applications were to mechanize routine clerical operations such as payroll and accounting. As software advanced, so did the use of computers in performing more difficult work tasks.

Computer-controlled equipment can make decisions based on signals generated at the points of production. For example, automatic material-handling equipment can move objects to locations depending on the signals they receive, robots can perform operations on the items being produced, and machines equipped with racks of tools and automatic tool changers can carry out commands — all without human intervention.

In addition to the use of technology to improve efficiency and productivity, much can be gained from new management practices. The concept of just-in-time (JIT) production, which originated in Japan, is an example. JIT is founded on the simple notion that costs can be avoided by employing a

Figure 1-3 Satellite technology has led to many new security applications, such as use of the Global Positioning System.

Figure 1-4 Manufacturing components shipments are timed to support just-in-time production. *(Photo courtesy of Burns International Security Services.)*

minimum of inventories to make products. Companies operating in this way coordinate their operations so that one work center produces only what is required by subsequent work centers. Production is timed so that it occurs at the moment the necessary components arrive (see Figure 1-4). Successful implementation of JIT requires reliable sources of supplies and effective preventive maintenance to avoid line breakdowns.

BUSINESS TODAY

The management landscape continues to evolve. Business activities are global, made so by intense competition and the lure of profits in emerging markets overseas. Mergers and acquisitions have created super-giant companies that sometimes wield more economic and political power than the governments under which they operate. Businesses are operating with higher standards of conduct and accepting added social responsibility.

Business plays a vital role in the life and culture of countries with free-market systems (i.e., systems in which prices and wages are determined by competition). In the United States, for example, many businesses purchase and sell goods and services as their primary sources of revenue. Except when a law is violated, prices and wages are determined by the competing demands in a marketplace free of government intervention. Nearly all companies in a free-market system are driven by the profit motive [5].

Figure 1-5 Manufactured goods move to retailers via wholesalers.

Firms that manufacture goods for the security industry include large companies that make complete, finished products — such as access control systems, computer systems, locks, safes, and furniture — and smaller companies that make only parts and components of systems. Other firms manufacture supplies and low-cost end-user products.

Merchandisers help move goods through channels of distribution. As indicated in Figure 1-5, wholesale merchandisers purchase goods in large amounts from manufacturers, mark up the prices, and sell to retailers. Retail merchandisers sell goods to consumers. The separation between wholesaling and retailing is increasingly narrowed by new technologies. Telephone and computer communications allow retailers to make purchases directly from the manufacturers while simultaneously servicing large numbers of customers.

The Internet permits an almost unlimited capacity for sales because the retailer and customer are not required to meet physically. For example, a clerk at a security guard company can sit at a desktop computer (see Figure 1-6), browse a manufacturer's on-line catalog, punch in an order, and be assured of next-day delivery.

SECURITY INDUSTRY

Today's security practices have roots going back thousands of years. Protection of personal property and life were left up to the individual, later to tribes, and then to cities. Security of one sort or another consisted of personal

Figure 1-6 The desktop personal computer revolutionized clerical operations. *(Photo courtesy of Burns International Security Services.)*

weapons, and of natural and man-made barriers, walls, moats, and fortifications. The rise of kings and their lords lent organization to security, even if only to protect the possessions of kings and their loyal protectors.

English Roots

The greatest influence on American security came out of England [6]. In 1655, Oliver Cromwell set up in England and Wales a police force that operated along military lines. Its principal duty was to capture and punish criminals. In 1748, London magistrate Henry Fielding introduced the concept of crime prevention. Instead of waiting for crime to occur, Fielding wanted to prevent crime ahead of time. He organized citizen patrols that came to be known as "runners" because they often chased criminals through back alleys. Fifty years later, English Home Secretary Sir Robert Peel formed the first formal police department. His name lives on in "bobby," the name given to police officers in England.

The British approach to police work came to American shores with vast numbers of immigrants from England, Ireland, and Scotland. Faced with rampant crime in U.S. cities, law enforcement had little time and resources to give to the protection of private property. The owners of such property turned to private individuals, some of whom came to the job armed and prepared to deal with criminals, and some whose duty was to watch for trouble and to give a "hue and cry" when it appeared. The watchman form of security was an earlier version of security practices that endure to this day.

Law Enforcement and Security

It was inevitable that law enforcement and security, although evolving from the same roots, went in different directions. Each developed its own constituency: the police serving the public's interest, and security serving private interests. As crime mounted in the latter half of the nineteenth century, police departments that had previously looked down their noses at private security began to see the benefits of a partnership. Police jobs that did not involve enforcement, arrest, and the use of force were turned over to security. Many government buildings once protected by police are now under the protection of security officers, traffic control on and around commercial properties such as office buildings is often provided by security officers, and it is not unusual to see security patrols operating in neighborhoods that were once patrolled by the police.

Terrorism

The advent of terrorism has shown the need for greater collaboration between law enforcement and security. Police and security leaders are coordinating their respective plans, establishing and testing mutual arrangements — not only between themselves but with leaders in other first-response agencies such as firefighting, safety, emergency management, emergency medical treatment, public health, government administration, and with specialists in biology, chemistry, and radiology. In the trenches are the police officers who respond to terrorist acts wherever they occur and the security officers who respond on the private premises they protect. The current view on police/security collaboration generally agrees on the following principles.

- Leaders of major law enforcement and private security organizations must make a formal commitment to cooperation.
- The federal government must fund research and training to facilitate cooperation between law enforcement and security.
- The federal government must create an advisory council to oversee implementation of an overall partnership.
- Individual partnerships must be formed at city to federal levels and must identify key problems facing them, agree on solutions, and set priorities.

Security Marketplace

The security industry abounds with a wide variety of service providers, many of which are small and fill particular niches. Investigation firms and consultancies tend to be local or regional and limited in the number of customers that can be accommodated at one time.

Guard Services

In the guard business, a handful of companies dominates in size and revenue but controls a relatively small piece of the overall market. Increasingly, European guard companies are purchasing or merging with U.S. companies. Pinkerton's, Burns, Wackenhut, and others are now owned by non-U.S. groups.

The service sector continues to grow very rapidly and now constitutes a significant percentage of all security-related spending. In the United States and other countries of wealth, a chief driver of security spending is the concern of property owners for the protection of their assets.

Professionalism

Accompanying the industry's rapid growth is recognition of the need for professionalism. More than 20,000 security supervisors, managers, students, and vendors hold membership in the American Society for Industrial Security International. Members can obtain certification as experts in security management, physical security, and investigations. The primary organization of chief security officers is the International Security Management Association, and that of consultants and small independents is the International Society of Professional Security Consultants. Investigators, polygraph examiners, fraud examiners, and forensic specialists hold membership in professional groups such as the National Association of Licensed Investigators, National Council of Investigation and Security Services, Association of Certified Fraud Examiners, American Polygraph Association, National Forensic Center, American Academy of Forensic Sciences, and American Society of Questioned Document Examiners.

In the defense sector is the National Defense Association, which forms a link between industrial security and the government. The largest group of owners and operators of watch, guard, and patrol companies belong to the National Association of Security Companies. In the equipment and installation business are the American Fire Sprinkler Association, National Burglar and Fire Alarm Association, American Fire Sprinkler Association, National Fire Sprinkler Association, Electronic Industries Alliance, and the American Hardware Manufacturers Association. Proponents of standards for security-related equipment are the Security Industry Association and the American Society for Testing Materials International.

Other factors are impacting the security industry. Although the security industry has remained largely unaffected, permanent and full-time employees are decreasing as a percentage of the total work population. Many companies are employing contractors and temporary employment agencies to fill line, staff, managerial, and professional positions (see Figure 1-7).

A Sample of Positions in the Security Industry

Chief Security Officer. An organization's senior security person. Operates one or two levels below the chief executive officer. Develops policy and plans and oversees the development of procedures that guide subordinates, security officers, and others holding responsibilities in various security-related responses. Negotiates contracts with security-related vendors such as owners/operators of companies that provide security services. Procures security-related equipment such as access control and intrusion detection systems, information technology and communications equipment, and materials and equipment that support security group functions. Acts as advisor to the CEO, the executive team, and department-level managers.

Physical Security Specialist. Reports to the chief security officer. Performs inspections of physical security safeguards in place at the organization's major physical assets such as office buildings, plants, warehouses, and construction projects. Identifies physical security weaknesses and makes recommendations for correction. Is knowledgeable concerning fences, lighting, lock and key systems, CCTV systems, intrusion and alarm sensors, access control and intrusion detection systems, and security control panels.

Corporate Investigator. Reports to the chief security officer. Conducts investigations of matters in which the organization is a party of interest. Collects evidence, conducts surveillances and interviews, prepares reports, testifies at hearings and trials, and liaises with law enforcement counterparts and others in the criminal justice system.

Technical Services Countermeasures Technician. Reports to the chief security officer either as a direct subordinate or outside contractor. Using sophisticated electronic equipment, searches for signals indicative of surreptitious surveillance. Conducts examinations of telephones, telephone rooms, fax machines, ceilings, duct work, conference rooms, and other items or places involving discussion of sensitive organizational matters.

Polygraph Examiner. Most often an outside contractor reporting to the chief security officer and/or the corporate investigator. Conducts polygraph examinations of persons suspected of committing a crime against the organization. If the organization is exempt from the provisions of the Employee Polygraph Protect Act, conducts polygraph examinations of the organization's job applicants.

Forensics Technician. Reports to the chief security officer either as a direct subordinate or outside contractor. Examines fraudulent documents, interviews people, collects evidence, coordinates with in-house and outside auditors and attorneys, retains outside experts such as questioned documents and fingerprint examiners, testifies at hearings and trials, liaises with law enforcement counterparts and others in the criminal justice system.

Investigative Photographer. Most often an outside contractor reporting to the chief security officer and/or the corporate investigator. Takes photographs, normally during surveillance of persons suspected of committing crimes against the organization and of the physical activities of employees that have filed workers' compensation claims.

Owner and/or Operator of a Security Services Company. Submits bids for security-related services, such as guard services, investigations, and security assessments. Liaises with the chief security officer concerning services provided to the organization. Negotiates contracts, ensures that contract specifications are met, and intervenes as necessary with subordinates to ensure proper delivery of contracted services.

Account Manager of a Security Services Company. Sells and inspects security services provided to clients and performs a quality control function. Liaises with the users of services, and

Figure 1-7 The chief duties of persons working in the security industry.

manages a city or regional office where guard applicants are hired and trained. The office maintains employee dossiers and payroll records and performs other administrative functions.

Supervisor of Security Operations. Supervises security guard operations at a client's site. Maintains a work schedule and hours worked, inspects posts, and serves as a day-to-day contact with the client's representative concerning the delivery of guard services. Conducts on-the-job training of security officers, issues to them their needed equipment, and accounts for the employer's property. This person is usually uniformed and may carry a military-style rank such as sergeant, lieutenant, or captain.

Security Officer. Checks identification at stationary posts, opens and locks doors, performs walk-through inspections looking for fire and safety hazards, rides patrol on the client's premises, escorts client employees to their automobiles after dark, escorts client employees carrying valuables, such as cash to a bank, and serves as a first responder in emergency situations such as major accidents and fire, serious injury or illness to the client's employees, criminal acts, workplace violence, civil disorder, unauthorized intrusion, and evacuation of the premises. Operates a security console that registers fire, duress, and intrusion alarms, dispatches security guards to make inquiries and respond as needed, notifies the security supervisor and others such as client representatives, law enforcement officers, and firefighters. Writes reports and maintains daily logs.

Security Consultant. Provides expert guidance in one or two areas of expertise, which can include soliciting and negotiating security-related contracts, reducing criminal opportunities, selecting and overseeing the installation and testing of various security systems, reducing potential liability that arises from inadequate security or failure to provide reasonable security, conducting studies of liability issues, and testifying as an expert witness at hearings and civil trials.

Figure 1-7 *continued*

Technology

New technology, principally the computer, is replacing people. Human labor is profoundly affected. Like millions of farmers displaced by machines at the beginning of the previous century, millions of factory and office workers are now being displaced by computer-assisted technologies. A new labor class of technologists has arisen to meet the need for operating and maintaining this new technology. They are often allowed to set their own working hours and work from home or wherever they happen to be.

The Future

If the past 200 years can serve as an indicator of challenges to security management, lively times lie ahead. Leaders in the field of security can look forward to even greater changes and greater opportunities for reward.

NOTES

1. Frederick Winslow Taylor's system of industrial management influenced the development of mass production. At age 25, he introduced time study, a technique that later became

the basis of his theories of management science. Taylor argued that production efficiency in a shop or factory could be greatly enhanced by close observation of the individual worker and elimination of wasted time and motion.

2. Frank and Lillian Gilbreth and their 12 children were the subject of the 1950 movie comedy *Cheaper By the Dozen*. This true-to-life film was based on humor resulting from the father using the children in motion studies.

3. Elton Mayo was an early leader in the field of industrial sociology. He initiated a pioneering industrial research project at the Western Electric Company's Hawthorne Works in Chicago. His study findings concerning labor/management relations and informal interaction among factory employees continue to be influential. Mayo also advocated employee counseling programs to meet the needs of workers unable to derive satisfaction from factory employment.

4. Russell D. Archibald and Richard L. Villoria, *Network-Based Management Systems (PERT/CPM)*, pp. 435, New York: John Wiley and Sons, 1967.

5. The profit motive is the will to operate profitably. It is an essential competitive feature of buying and selling in a free-market system. Profit is the monetary difference between the cost of producing and marketing goods or services and the price subsequently received.

6. *Understanding Crime Prevention*, pp. 2–3, Louisville, KY: National Crime Prevention Institute Press, 1978.

2. Strategy

I like the dreams of the future better than the history of the past.
—Thomas Jefferson

BUSINESS STRATEGY

Three observations about security management are in order. First, the chief security officer (CSO) operates in a rapidly changing business world. The fast-paced and highly competitive nature of business is forcing companies to continually find new ways to be productive at lower cost. The new ways of doing business bring new security risks. Second, every important decision made by the CSO depends on technical knowledge. Important security decisions are never risk free, and technical knowledge is often a critical factor in arriving at the best possible decision. Third, international terrorism is on the scene in a very serious way (see Figure 2-1). It can take many forms, is shrouded in secrecy, and threatens critical assets essential to the operation and viability of national infrastructures.

CORE AND SUPPORT ACTIVITIES

Nearly every business of size is organized along lines that permit simultaneous management of two main activities: the core activities at the heart of the enterprise and the support activities that contribute to the core. The core work, being essential to the business and having value that demands protection, is usually assigned to proven and trusted employees. The support work, although important to some degree, usually does not produce a significant or sustainable advantage to the business. The support staff tends to be varied, running the gamut from unskilled to highly skilled.

OUTSOURCING

The manner of staffing in large companies has always been driven by economic imperatives. Company leaders endlessly look for ways to cut costs,

Figure 2-1 The terrorist attack on the World Trade Center towers impacted the nation's financial infrastructure.

and in recent years outsourcing has been a principal cost-cutting tool in the management of human resources. A main theme of outsourcing is to lower labor costs by replacing higher-paid permanent employees with lower-paid contract employees.

Business leaders that opt for outsourcing embrace the notion that support work is mainly done in-house for reasons of convenience and that transferring support work to vendors will not affect the critical core of the enterprise. They wish to realize the full value of essential activities at a lower overall cost and at the same time attain greater flexibility and a sharper focus on improving the core.

In a fast-evolving market in which new technologies are emerging, the knowledge and skills of individuals are very limited. The technologies themselves may be proprietary and not available on the open market. If organizations can attract the knowledge and skills base of technologies, they have an advantage [1].

Beginning in the early 1980s, one major company after another fell head-over-heels in love with outsourcing. A few hold regrets; many do not.

By transferring noncritical work to outside providers, managers believed their valuable time was freed up to concentrate on generating revenues. Added advantages included transferring frontline supervisory responsibilities to vendors and holding them to high service standards. The really big incentive to outsourcing was cost reduction.

A management often seeks to link the outsourcing process to the aims and success factors of the business. The idea is to take into account the company's drivers and market position, commercial and customer values, and the culture of the workforce. Decisions about retaining functions versus outsourcing them involve considerations as to efficiency and effectiveness, as well as to cost. Also considered are opportunities to regroup functional tasks in lieu of outsourcing and to unbundle tasks so that some can be kept and some outsourced. After those decisions have been made, the management identifies potential providers, tenders, negotiates, and awards bids, and manages the transition.

OUTSOURCING AND THE SECURITY GROUP

Protecting Assets Under Altered Circumstances

The CSO's duty in outsourcing involves developing and implementing new procedures for protecting assets under the altered circumstances. The duty is not easily fulfilled. The company's most valuable assets (such as entire computer systems and sensitive databases) are frequently placed into the direct and unrestricted control of vendors. Although happy to accept assets, vendors are not always enthusiastic about following the CSO's asset-protecting guidance, even when the outsourcing contract calls for the vendor to safeguard the entrusted assets. Adding to the general misery of the CSO can be the unwillingness of the company's managers to intercede. They may see security as counterproductive, at least in the short term as it relates to making outsourcing succeed. Problems encountered in an early stage of outsourcing can be difficult to solve. The CSO's warning that assets may be at risk is often muted by the day-to-day bustle of launching the project. The following case study points out some of the problems involved.

CASE STUDY

The XYZ Company sold merchandise on the Internet and by catalog. The critical core of the business had always been marketing, processing orders and payments, and paying attention to customers. Receiving goods from manufacturers, storing them in a warehouse, and shipping orders to customers from the warehouse were considered noncritical support functions. After hard negotiations that were kept secret from employees, including the CSO, XYZ outsourced the support functions to a low-bidding vendor. The XYZ inventory was transferred to the vendor's warehouse — a much larger facility at which orders were shipped for numerous mail-order companies, some of which were in direct competition with XYZ. Nearly 90 percent of the XYZ receiving, warehousing, and shipping employees were let go and the warehouse sold. Near the end of one year, XYZ was not happy with the vendor.

Orders had been consistently lost, misaddressed, and filled improperly; large quantities of goods in storage were missing and not accounted for; and there were indications that the vendor had released an XYZ customer list to an XYZ competitor. The XYZ CSO went to the vendor's warehouse to make recommendations for improving the security of XYZ goods and information. He was turned away. XYZ announced to the vendor the intent at the end of 90 days to cancel the contract. The vendor demanded to be paid in advance for the final 90 days. When XYZ refused, the vendor closed its doors to XYZ representatives and stopped all work in support of XYZ. Not able to fill orders and not having access to its own inventory, XYZ was effectively put out of business.

A civil court restored XYZ's rights but the business had been badly damaged. The vendor's defense to the judge was that XYZ had made unreasonable demands, insulted the vendor's employees by telling them how to do their jobs, overstated how much the vendor would earn in the contract, and offered only criticism in the resolution of problems.

Due Diligence

A number of lessons can be found in the story. First is to learn all that can be learned about the vendor before awarding the contract. A particularly good learning device is the due diligence inquiry conducted by the CSO. (Note: A due diligence inquiry is an investigation conducted by a company contemplating doing business with another company. The company conducting the inquiry seeks to verify representations made by the other company and to generally assess suitability, integrity, and financial strength. The inquiry, which is usually conducted under the supervision of the CSO, includes gathering credit reports, searching records of criminal and civil courts, and making background checks of principal officers.)

Ambiguous Specifications

Ambiguous specifications can lead to problems. An example is, "Vendor will provide a reasonable level of security for client assets entrusted to the Vendor." A clear definition has to be made as to what is meant by "reasonable level of security."

EFFECT OF STRATEGY ON SECURITY MANAGEMENT

Anticipate

An often underappreciated skill is the anticipation of the effect a particular management strategy will have on the provision of security services. In the development of a company strategy, the CSO can be a key contributor by proposing measures to close security-related exposures that may arise when the strategy is implemented. For example, if the strategy includes outsourcing the company's electronic data-processing function the CSO may see a possible compromise of sensitive proprietary data. Identifying the exposure is important, but is much less than half the chore. The difficult work comes in developing a countermeasure that will offset the risk and not sidetrack the strategy.

Exposures

Although potential exposures are not easy to detect and even more difficult to prevent or mitigate, the CSO can at least rely on the common sense observation that security risks rise when adjustments are made to the manner of work performance. A shift in strategy can move through the organization like a slow-moving earthquake. Formal and informal controls on people performance that have been set in place by tested practice can be broken. Tiny fissures on the surface signal large disturbances below, foretelling eruptions that carry high risk. Loss events are waiting to happen, and it is the CSO's function to anticipate and prevent them.

Magnitude

The magnitude of potential loss tends to rise relative to the nature of the work affected. Think, for example, of the potential loss linked to a strategy shift that brings temporary filing clerks into the accounts receivable department. Now compare that shift to one in which the secret formula for the company's best-selling product is placed in the custody of a vendor.

Complexity

Complexity of the work is also a factor. The opportunity to prevent a security-related loss or to detect its early occurrence decreases relative to the complexity of the work. A CSO (or anyone in an organization, for that matter) cannot be an expert in every area of the company's total operations. Information technology (IT) is a good example. In an outsourced situation there may be few, if any, individuals remaining in the core workforce who have a level of IT expertise sufficient to notice an exposure in a complex operation. Even after a loss occurs, the company may not have in-house resources capable of properly diagnosing the exposure and prescribing the correct remedy.

TECHNICAL KNOWLEDGE

Although it is unreasonable to expect the CSO to possess a comprehensive range of technical knowledge, it is quite reasonable to expect him/her to know where to find it and to have it available on demand. Technical knowledge can be viewed as a dimension of business, and operating in three human competencies: access, quality, and teamwork.

Access

Access refers to knowing where to find the right information, service, or product at the best price. It often means building sound relationships with actual and potential vendors and networking with peers. The transfer of "best practices" among security practitioners in different companies and industries is an example of accessing technical knowledge.

Quality

Quality is the optimal balance between cost and technical excellence. It includes quality control and quality assurance. Quality control is the responsibility of the supplier; quality assurance derives naturally from confidence in the relationship. In a mature connection between client and vendor, cost and quality will occur together, to the advantage of both parties.

Teamwork

Teamwork is the bringing together of people who contribute from complementary specialties. It is a competency that also gives to the players the right information, service, or product. A team or teams may be the security group or the security group in tandem with various product suppliers and consultants. Team composition will vary according to the mission, with each member contributing a different set of skills and abilities. Teamwork calls for sustained leadership and goal orientation. These three competencies operate to obtain access to the essential information, services, and products that fuel the security function, ensuring their quality and integrating them through teamwork.

STRATEGY AND RISK

The ability to predict and quantify a full menu of risks is the CSO's highest mark of excellence.

Predict

To predict risk, an ability restricted by the limitations of human understanding and available technology, is to identify the nature of threats confronting the organization and assess the probability of their occurrence.

Quantify

To quantify risk is to measure potential consequences through the application of science and experience. To control risk is to logically and flexibly manage resources in ways that offset threats. The genuinely competent CSO will obtain through continuous self-development an ability to deal with evolving threats, know where to find the technical assistance sufficient to counter them, and be positioned to acquire that assistance when it is needed.

IMPERATIVES

The reader may detect the outlines of a security strategy taking shape. Integral to it are the following six mutually reinforcing imperatives.

- Improve on quality and cost.
- Forge close links with customers.
- Establish close relationships with suppliers.
- Make effective use of technology.
- Operate with minimum layers of management.
- Continuously improve the security staff.

Improve on Quality

The measuring stick of security performance is high quality at reasonable cost. The facets of quality are excellence, reliability, and speedy delivery of services. The successful security operations are those that strive to be the "best in class" in all main performance activities. A characteristic of the leading performers is an emphasis on competitive benchmarking (i.e., comparing personal and unit performance with the industry's leaders, and setting goals to measure progress).

Forge Close Links with Customers

Successful CSOs make a concerted effort to develop close ties with their customers. A customer is the user of security services. Who are the users? They are all of the persons within the organization that employs the CSO—a fact that too many CSOs lose sight of.

Forging a link is less like making friends through public relations and more like "getting into the mind" of the customer. It can happen that the CSO will know what should be in the customer's mind even before the customer becomes aware of it. Having that mental connection allows the CSO to respond rapidly and appropriately to the users of security services.

Strategy in any business context is meaningless without reference to customers. The dominant aim of strategy is to deliver superior value to customers. A persistent and unavoidable challenge of the CSO in the battle to enhance and sustain superior value is to stay one or more steps ahead of security groups that support competitors. Simply emulating what others do cannot lead to superior performance [2].

Establish Close Relationships with Suppliers

Too often, cooperation with suppliers is achieved through the coercive power of the buyer. The alternative described here, however, is the creation of partner relationships in which price is not always the single most important factor. Coordination with external vendors is crucial to a CSO in acquiring technical assistance in whatever form that assistance might take (e.g., electronic countermeasures, forensic examinations, surveillance, undercover operations, and so on).

If a key element of strategy is to position the in-house security staff to be a leader in using technical advances in support of the mission, it follows that the CSO will be active in developing partnerships with the suppliers of technology. The idea is to select a small number of capable suppliers and work with them. A partnership arrangement has little room for second-guessing and beating suppliers down to the last penny.

When a vendor provides contracted guard services, the CSO should forge a positive working relationship with the guard company's account manager. An understanding between them can help both parties find a balance between ensuring high guard performance and recognizing the guard firm's right to supervise its own employees. If guard performance is inadequate, the CSO has a duty to offer constructive direction and the account manager has an obligation to listen and respond within reasonable limits. None of this is possible without a solid working relationship.

Make Effective Use of Technology

A security strategy linked to technology will demand of the CSO knowledge of work-enhancing technologies available in the marketplace and skill in using them wisely. Being wise about technology involves recognizing that newer is not always better, and even when a technology is in fact superior the final payoff has to exceed the costs of applying it. In short, technology must earn its way.

In looking for a technological solution, the CSO should not try to reinvent the wheel but at the same time not have a closed mind to a technology simply because it does not perfectly match the situation. Common mistakes are to reject a technology that is not totally applicable but is workable in important respects and to expect more than a technology can deliver. Very important also is to get the solution right the first time, because retrofitting can be costly.

Another consideration is the working relationship between the security employees and the equipment or routines that make up the technology. This is not so much a matter of ergonomics but of the symbiotic linkage of man and machine. In companies in which technology is routinely applied, the security employees are better able to adjust when a new or more complicated technology is acquired for their use.

Operate with Minimum Layers of Management

Organizational structure (i.e., the horizontal distribution of departments and the vertical arrangement of managerial layers) varies considerably from company to company. Today's trends favor greater functional integration and fewer layers of management, both of which promote speedy delivery of services and a strong responsiveness to customer needs. These are virtues to be cherished by any prudent CSO.

Execution of the security strategy will in most cases rely on a small yet well-rounded staff of the highest quality, working in partnership with suppliers who bring to the arrangement a broad array of technical competencies. The competencies that stand out are in the job domains of computer security specialists, anti-surveillance technicians, auditors, questioned document examiners, architects, access control specialists, and so on. The security profession, although very broad and mature, is surprisingly innovative when it comes to harnessing special talent.

Continuously Improve the Security Staff

The first five strategy elements require departures from the conventional way of dealing with employees. The changes call for developing a new mind set, a new commitment, and strong leadership. Progress will seldom be comfortable as old ideas are cast off and refashioned.

The improvement of security staff depends on the infusion of large doses of meaningful, useful knowledge. The modes of teaching can include counseling, formal classroom instruction, and on-the-job coaching. The constant in the process is unending development of employees, not merely development to get the strategy up and going but development throughout employees' working lifetimes. The outcome of staff development will be technical competency, quality output, teamwork, and a flexibility that permits the acceptance of daunting challenges.

STRATEGIC PLANNING

In most of the previous century, planning carried out by senior management was called long-range planning. In today's high-tech environment, it is deserving of a fancier name: strategic planning. Large companies everywhere plan strategically, and smaller companies in increasing numbers are following suit. Indeed, it can be said that in the fast-paced and intensely competitive marketplace of the new millennium any corporation worth its salt cannot afford to operate without strategic planning. According to Christopher Hoenig, a leadership guru, an organization has no choice but to engage in strategic planning. The real issues are how much planning to do, how to do it well, and when to do it [3].

Murphy's Law

Nothing is as easy as it looks.
Everything takes longer than you think.
Anything that can go wrong will go wrong.
If there is a possibility of several things going wrong, the one that will cause the most damage will be the one to go wrong.
If there is a worse time for something to go wrong, it will happen then.
If anything simply cannot go wrong, it will anyway.
If you perceive that there are four possible ways a procedure can go wrong, and circumvent these, then a fifth way, unprepared for, will promptly develop.
Left alone, things tend to go from bad to worse.
If everything seems to be going well, you have obviously overlooked something.
Nature always sides with the hidden flaw.
It is impossible to make anything foolproof because fools are ingenious.
Whenever you set out to do something, something else must be done first.
Every solution breeds a new problem.

Figure 2-2 A tongue-in-cheek guide for security planners.

Strategic planning underscores a point sometimes forgotten: a business organization has two types of management. That which is done at the top is called strategic management. Everything else is operational management. Planning done at the top is strategic in nature, and planning below the top is tactical in nature. The CSO is always a developer of operating plans, but is only sometimes involved in the development of strategic plans (see Figure 2-2).

The proposition that a CSO should have a basic understanding of strategic planning rests on a number of simple observations. One is that strategic planning (see Figure 2-3) is a consistent element in companies that are successful. Another is that strategic planning is clearly a part of managing. Every leader is expected to understand the nature of planning and to be comfortable in its design and execution. Yet it is a fact that some leaders either have a fuzzy understanding of planning or feel threatened by it. The gains to be made to a leader personally and to his/her subordinates can be lost when the leader is excluded from strategic planning. A leader who shies away is apt to be viewed as a non-player, particularly when the planning involves the leader's sphere of operations.

Policy and Planning

The relationship between policy development and strategic planning can be described as totally intimate. You can't have one without the other, and although the functions are distinguishable they are at the same time inseparable.

A policy establishes the arena in which the actions of the business are to occur. It provides a vision for the business and, as such, serves as a guide

---

Strategic Planning Elements

Measurable Goals

Specific tasks that lead to measurable goals and assign personal accountability.

Incentives

Rewards that make people want to carry out the plan.

Realistic Estimates

Ambitious outcomes grounded in reality.

Incremental Efforts

A division of work that organizes a big plan into achievable chunks.

Landmarks

Results-oriented milestones that signify progress according to plan.

Flexibility

A forward view that allows alternative paths and modified expectations.

Focus

A keen eye on the course and a steady hand at the wheel.

Value Perspective

A view that looks at the cost of plan execution as an investment.

Figure 2-3 These elements characterize effective strategic planning [4].

for action. Planning, on the other hand, is the architecture of the arena; it is specific and detailed. To illustrate the difference, the chief executive officer in a petroleum company might say: "It is our policy to be profitable in the petroleum industry." One tier down in the organization, the vice president of exploration might say of his operation: "Our objective is to meet projections each year of our five-year plan to find exploitable quantities of oil and gas." The production manager might say: "Our objective for the current year is to produce five hundred thousand barrels of crude and twenty million cubic feet of natural gas." The CSO might say: "Our number one job is to protect the company's exploration and production assets." All of these statements are likely to include modifiers such as "at least possible cost," "with maximum assurance of the safety of persons and the ecology," and so forth. However, the main point here is that a policy broadly defines the universe of action, whereas planning is concerned with what happens inside.

The reader at this point may want to thump these pages and vigorously point out that a CEO's policy-making function involves more than just issuing a simple pronouncement. And the reader would be right. Policy making is more complicated than that. Policies virtually abound in the corporate environment. They cover staffing, growth, planning, managerial authority, conflicts of interest, marketing, production, finance, facilities, and many more areas. Then, too, there are the qualitative differences in policies. Some are simply more important than others, giving credence to the term *high-level policy*.

The badge of honor in the corporate environment is often the extent to which a leader is involved in policy development. The higher the policy and the more the leader decides it, either entirely or by contribution, is a determinant of status in the formal, corporate organization. In the security field, we see evidences of this concern for status in the large number of surveys mailed to CSOs. Surveyors interested in selling products and services seem to believe that policy decisions go hand in hand with purchasing power, and that leaders who set policy earn more money than those who do not. These assumptions are not always true, but true often enough for them to be widely held.

It may help to think of policies as many trees in an orchard. The gardener is the CEO. The roots of the security tree spread deep into the organization. Each root is a separate element such as security officer operations, physical security, and investigations. All roots collectively draw nutrients from the soil in the form of funding for labor and equipment. The gardener is ever watchful for blooms that produce the fruit. If the security tree does not bear fruit, the gardener will investigate and where appropriate change the composition of the soil, prune the unproductive limbs, or remove the tree and plant another. The gardener may also decide that a security tree is not needed at all.

The CSO and Strategic Planning

Strategic plans send ripples throughout the whole of the organization. Negative ripples impacting the CSO can be lessened to the extent that the CSO participated in developing the plan. The degree of involvement by a CSO tends to be determined by three factors. First is where the CSO sits on the organizational chart. If at the lower end of the pecking order, he/she won't have much input. Second is the shape of the organization. If it is a flat organization with only a few levels separating the chairman from the frontline workers, the chance for a lower-level manager to contribute is increased. Third is the personality of the CSO. If perceived as being inept or uncaring about strategic planning, he/she won't be invited to participate, no matter where located on the organizational chart and no matter the shape of the organization. If perceived as having something meaningful to contribute and willing to contribute, the CSO may be invited into the upper, upper realm. The following anecdote is instructive.

CASE STUDY

Eighteen months ago, Patrick was hired to be the manager of loss prevention for a computer store chain. The first objective of the job was to reduce warehouse thefts. At first, Patrick was the major player in developing and implementing security plans. But as the warehouse theft rate began to decline, the chief operations officer (COO) began to complain. The new security measures, he said, were cumbersome and costly. Unfortunately for Patrick, his direct boss was the COO. For the past six months, Patrick has not been invited to planning meetings and learns of security-related decisions only after they have been made. Patrick decides to document his achievements so far and take them to the top, dragging along the COO if he must.

Business Is Like War

A critical duty of senior management is to decide how to use efficiently the company's resources in producing goods or services at competitive prices. This duty is not easily discharged under any circumstances, and is especially fraught with difficulty in turbulent times. In one respect, business is like war. If the general's grand strategy is correct, any number of tactical errors can be made, yet in the end the war is won. A tactical error, such as the inefficient use of a company resource, can hurt the war effort but won't necessarily result in the other side winning. But if the grand strategy is faulty to begin with, even the most efficient use of internal resources will not keep the war from being lost. The ideal situation is to have a correct strategy and to implement it with tactics that are efficient and effective.

If we carry the war analogy a little further, we can say that the general's first order of business is to decide the mission. Are we going to destroy the enemy entirely or do we hurt the enemy to a certain level? What resources do we have at our disposal? This thinking process leads to the setting of objectives, the development of a strategy and a plan, the making of immediate decisions, and the evaluation of earlier decisions. These are not matters for the troops to handle; they can only be decided at the top. In the theater of operations, the field commanders carry out the general's orders. Occasionally, the field commanders are called to the general's command post and asked to provide their input. The parallels between war and business are clear.

No Absolutes in Strategic Planning

Strategic planning has elements common to all competitive human endeavors, yet there is no such thing as a standard or universal system for strategic planning. It is not possible to transfer the strategic planning mechanism of one company to another and expect it to work properly. Business organizations, even when in the same line of work, will be different in many key respects, including differences in the nature and the how of planning.

Neither is it sensible to expect that CEO Smith and CEO Jones, given the same premises, will develop closely similar strategic plans. Differences apply here as well, but in a special sense. It is no accident that geniuses often occupy senior executive chairs. These are leaders whose intuition and intelligence bring them like cream to the top. Their success is seldom the result of developing a written plan and sticking to it without deviation. They tend to fly on the seat of their pants and make snap decisions intuitively, often relying on a past experience, a gut feeling, or a flash of brilliant insight. If an organization is managed by a genius — and there are many examples in today's high-tech businesses — formal strategic planning will likely suffer, and that may be just as well. But if the CEO is not the intuitive type, strategic planning can be "set in stone." This is not altogether bad, and can be very appropriate for mature organizations. Planning will be formalized, highly documented, based on research and input from many sources, and involve the participation of many people.

Strategy and Change

A change in strategy precipitates changes in policy, which precipitate changes in plans, which precipitate changes in work practices. The strategy change begins as a snowball that gets larger and larger as it rolls downhill, producing change all along the way. (Note: managing change is addressed in a later chapter.)

The CSO must anticipate resistance to change in the security group. "But we've always done it this way" is a common cry heard when work practices change. The old ways of doing things may be so entrenched that even the best-laid preparation will falter. Engineering change even under the best of circumstances is hard work. It requires imagination, analytical ability, and fortitude.

To sum up, every company has a strategic management at the top and operational management below. Strategic plans are extensions of policy. Policy and plans should be, but are not always, created with input from the CSO, but without exception the CSO is impacted by strategic plans.

NOTES

1. Maurice F. Greaver II, *Strategic Outsourcing: A Structured Approach to Outsourcing Decisions and Initiatives*, pp. 16, New York: American Management Association, 1999.

2. Liam Fahey, *Competitors*, pp. vii, New York: John Wiley and Sons, 1999.

3. Christopher Hoenig, "The Master Planner," *CIO*, May 1, 2000, pp. 76.

4. Ibid., pp. 78.

3. Leading

A good leader can't get too far ahead of his followers.
—Franklin D. Roosevelt

INTRODUCTION

The experienced CSO knows that when threats to security increase it inevitably follows that demands on the security group will increase proportionally. The demands can vary, yet they all require for satisfactory response a trait we call leadership.

Build a Vision

The CSO is expected to build within the security group a vision corresponding to the primary mission of the larger organization.

Enlist Followers

The CSO has to persuade peers from other functions to accept the what, how, and why of security operations. For this last demand, persuasiveness is a crucial skill. In the persuading mode, a CSO can be likened to a minister pleading with a congregation to live by a universal truth. Everyone will agree on the truth but not everyone will agree on how it is to be lived. The same is true for the concept of security: everyone will agree that security is important but not everyone will agree on how it is to be done.

LEADERSHIP DEFINITIONS VARY

Some CSOs are relatively new to cross-functional leadership, and feel inadequate because historically they haven't needed to exercise leadership skills outside the boundaries of the security group. Although leadership is difficult to define, most people agree that a leader has a focus on the future; that is, a CSO prescribes the means and methods for reaching group goals. Agreement on leadership starts to fragment when discussion moves to the question of how a leader is made. Yet, when the shouting has ended widespread support will remain for the proposition that the head of security has to exercise strong leadership skills when setting the vision for the security group and obtaining approval throughout the organization.

Complex and Subtle

Leadership in the security domain is complex and subtle. It involves thinking strategically, transforming strategy into results, working well with myriad personalities and groups, managing conflict, and directing the day-to-day operations of the security group. Functional expertise, which has always been important to effective security management, is a narrow part of a much broader picture. Setting up an access control system is functionally focused and narrow; formulating a vision and moving others toward its attainment is diffuse and broad. The wide horizon also encompasses an understanding of the nature of the company's business, the industry, the marketplace, and the constraints acting upon the company, both internally and externally.

Manager Versus Leader

The top security person is always a manager but not always a leader. A significant distinction exists between managing and leading. A manager does things right; a leader does the right things. Each role is critical to the success of the organization, yet the roles differ greatly in execution and impact.

Peter Principle

A common problem in many security groups is that the person at the top spends too much time managing and not enough time leading. Some of the fault lies in a Peter Principle (see Figure 3-1) holding that an employee who excels technically be moved up to a supervisory or managerial position, even when it is apparent the employee lacks leadership skills. Partly to blame may be an absence in the organization of education and training systems that teach leadership skills.

General George S. Patton, one of the great teachers of leadership, said, "You young lieutenants have to realize that your platoon is like a piece of spaghetti. You can't push it. You've got to get out in front and pull it. [1]"

COMPETENCIES

Gain Attention

Gaining attention is a first step in creating a reason for others to accept a vision and to follow it. A leader is able to draw the attention of others through an

---

A Peter Principle

In a hierarchy, every employee tends to rise to his or her level of incompetence. Therefore:

In time, every post tends to be occupied by an employee who is incompetent to carry out the duties.

Work is accomplished by employees who have not yet reached their individual levels of incompetence.

Figure 3-1 The Peter Principle is characteristic of hierarchical organizations.

uncommon expression (e.g., Martin Luther King Jr.'s "I Have a Dream") and a prescription for change. The leader communicates a powerful commitment to break new ground and to go where others have feared to tread.

Set a Goal

An outcome, a goal, a sense of direction is articulated. Attention is shifted to the leader, and people are drawn to the vision and are consequently enrolled. The vision is imprinted in the minds of followers, which involves one percent explicating and 99 percent creating a mental picture. The leader will be adept at using metaphors to transform words into tangible ideas and at reducing complexities with phrases, slogans, and models. The meaning of the vision is molded into a form that can be understood by all.

Communicate the Message

The techniques for communicating a message are limited only by imagination. People who would be leaders, such as candidates for elected office, look for innovative ways of getting their messages into the public psyche. A sign on Harry Truman's desk said, "The Buck Stops Here." That simple slogan conveyed a great deal about Truman and what he stood for, helping him to retain the presidency in spite of the odds against him.

Cultivate Trust

Cultivating trust is another competency. The chief component of trust is reliability. "You know where he stands" is a statement pointing to reliability. "That's not what he said yesterday" is also an indicator of reliability, although in the negative sense. People will follow an individual who can be counted on to stay the course. Reliability in the pursuit of a goal will gather followers even among people who disagree with the goal. Other components of reliability include honesty, integrity, and faithfulness. Figure 3-2 points out the desirable traits of a leader.

Leadership Attributes

Leaders say that leaders are:

  Achievement oriented

  Charismatic

  Confident

  Empathic

  Open-minded

  Passionate

  Persuasive

  Philosophical

  Tenacious

Figure 3-2 At a symposium sponsored by *CIO* (a magazine for IT executives), the leaders in attendance shared their thoughts on the attributes to look for in potential leaders [2].

Develop Oneself

Deploying a correct mix of relevant knowledge and skills is a key competency. Included is the leader's nurturing and strengthening of personally held knowledge and skills, an activity carried out for the most part in the realm of experience. Leaders learn by doing, and because the doing is never perfect, mistakes occur. The pertinent point is that leaders learn from their mistakes. A mistake is often viewed as a lesson learned, as an option that proved to be less successful than another option, as an inevitable step on the way to achieving a goal. The leader's focus is on progressing, not on losing ground. An example is the coach with a team on a long winning streak. He or she will influence the team to play to win, not play to keep from losing.

EMPOWERMENT

Contributing

An effect of leadership is each employee's belief in contributing to the success of the organization. For various reasons some employees make large contributions and others do not, yet all employees need to feel they are making a positive difference. The outcome of effective leadership is empowerment, a kinship that exists at all levels. The guard in the parking garage has the same feeling of belonging as the CSO on the executive floor. An interesting aspect of empowerment is a sense of community even among warring factions. It is quite possible for some people to dislike each other yet share a feeling of unity.

Sharing Accomplishments

The new millennium is marking a dramatic transformation of leadership. Tarnish is forming on the time-honored belief that a great organization is the work of one person. The shining new belief holds high the importance of leadership at all levels and is characterized by comradeship grounded in shared accomplishment. It is demonstrated and energized by small teams working toward common goals, and performing challenging tasks collaboratively. Understanding and managing these multiple relationships as essential partnerships is a must.

The greatest factor in the empowerment of a workforce and the ultimate determiner of which organizations succeed or fail is leadership. For as long as strategies, processes, and cultures change, the key to success remains leadership.

Energizing and Motivating

A CSO can bring excitement, challenge, and enjoyment to security jobs. These attributes develop out of vision and ideals that energize and motivate with little or no impetus from the promise of material reward or the threat of discipline. A pat on the back at the right moment can be more valuable, both to the security group and to the individual, than a raise in pay. An encouragement to improve performance can sometimes yield better results than a written admonishment.

Conflicting Values

When the CSO's vision fails to inspire, the reason is likely to result from a conflict of values. If the CSO adds or changes tasks, and as a result reduces the quality of a service, some task performers will not want to follow because their core values prevent them from delivering a shoddy service.

Quantity Versus Quality

Interestingly, quantity is viewed objectively — such as the number of security guard hours sold per month — whereas quality is viewed subjectively, such as the morale of the security guards providing the services. A good leader understands both dimensions and is aware of the interplay between the definitive bottom line and the amorphous human soul.

Love of Work

Intimately connected with the concept of quality is love of work. A person who loves work will not be motivated by the desire for reward or the fear of rebuke. Love of work may lead the employee to improve output without prodding. The employee may discover a better way to perform a task, which can be the exact opposite of (and a great improvement to) the work system mandated by management. The following anecdote is instructive in this regard.

CASE STUDY

One morning while passing through the lobby of the corporate headquarters where he worked as CSO, Andy observed a long line of impatient people waiting to be issued visitor passes. A few hours later, after the morning rush had subsided, Andy made it a point to stop at the visitors counter to ask the security officer why the early morning processing of visitors had taken so long. The security officer put his finger on a memo in his post orders and replied, "My supervisor told me to exactly follow this memo—the one you wrote."

Andy went back to his office and read his copy of the memo he had recently sent to the guard supervisor. It prescribed in great detail the procedure for issuing a visitor pass. Although long, Andy could see nothing wrong with the procedure. He called the officer on the phone and asked him what he had been doing before the new procedure went into effect.

"I was doing it my way," the security officer replied, and then he described his way. The officer's way was faster and made perfect sense, Andy realized. He thanked the security officer for doing a good job and rescinded the memo.

FOLLOWERS

It is inescapably true that a leader cannot exist without followers, and writings on leadership give the impression that good leaders create good followers. Although a leader may attract and recruit people who are willing to follow, the followers may not be good at following.

Taking Directions

Becoming an effective subordinate is not all that easy. A first requirement for the follower is to take direction. A second may be to suspend an opposing belief or abandon a personal principle. Abstaining from dissent may also be an expectation. Over a period of time, small divergences can become large holes in the fabric of the group.

Telling the Truth

The most important characteristic of a follower may well be a willingness to tell the truth. As work accelerates and complexities multiply, a leader is increasingly dependent on subordinates for good information. Followers who tell the truth and a leader who listens can be a formidable combination.

Providing Feedback

An effective CSO looks for good people from many backgrounds with different points of view, and encourages thoughtful dissent when decisions are due. Disagreement forces the CSO to closely examine a wide range of options that can lead to improved choices and better results. A leader is poorly served when his or her ideas are the only ideas or when the ideas are met with a unanimous yes or an acquiescent silence. A good leader will understand that dissent in the decision-making process, when cultivated and usefully channeled, is very healthful. Whatever annoyance a leader may experience at the moment of receiving contradictory feedback can be outweighed by the value of having made the best calculation possible. The soothing balm to the leader's damaged ego can be the expectation of group success and personal advancement.

LEADERS ADD VALUE

A leader's greatest contribution may be to add value. Imagine that the head of marketing in a national contract guard company develops a unique method for selling services over the Internet. The method succeeds so well that the company improves its market share by 20 percent and raises profits to an all-time high. The head of marketing has added value by enabling the company to excel in a crucial aspect of the business.

It may be well to note that interesting things can happen in the aftermath of the event described previously. The head of marketing might be seen from the top as a brilliant and well-rounded leader who deserves admittance to the company's inner sanctum. On the other hand, the innovative marketer might be labeled a narrowly skilled specialist lacking the vision required to perform at a higher level of management. The manner in which the head of marketing engineers the innovation and handles the success will affect his or her personal career.

COMPETITION AMONG LEADERS

A CSO is invariably in competition with other leaders, all of whom may have the same upward mobility aspirations. An organization can benefit greatly from competition among co-leaders seeking to impress the powers that be. In the contract guard company described previously, a long-standing accession practice was to move the head of operations into the next higher position on the totem pole. The success of the marketer, however, altered the script. Faced with a threat to advancement, the operations man shifted into high gear and found opportunities to reduce the company's turnover ratio, which in turn helped fill new jobs created by the marketer's innovation.

Ambition

Do not doubt for an instant the ambitious nature of the CSO. Although hard work behind the scenes may be a condition of the job, it is in the natural order of things for the CSO to aspire to a higher position. The lure of advancement and status is a powerful narcotic that draws people to positions of power and leadership.

Loyalty

There is an irony in the truth that a leader in the making is a follower and that following requires loyalty. Loyalty is steadfastness, a trait that is often called "hanging in there." Steadfastness is not blind devotion and fawning adulation. Loyalty the follower shows the leader can be justifiably withdrawn when the leader takes a seriously wrong turn. For example, a CSO's loyalty to the CEO can entirely disappear when it is clear that a serious crime — personal or corporate — has been committed, and that the CEO is a guilty party and actively engaged in its concealment. The CSO is no longer a willing follower and may have just one option: blow the whistle and move on.

A CSO will move on for other reasons as well. He or she may decide that the time is right to advance, either by hiring on with another organization or by creating an organization. The decision to leave may also result from a realization that advancement in the current organization is simply not attainable or not worth continuing the effort. Behind such a decision may be the deterioration of the relationship between the CSO and the boss. More than a few talented people have said adios because of "philosophical differences."

PRICE OF LEADERSHIP

Then there is the price of leadership. The demands of a top position can cause a CSO to sacrifice family, friends, and the simple pleasures of life. Staying at or moving toward the top can have price tags: divorce, alienation, physical breakdown, and mental aberration.

A society that adulates and disproportionately rewards athletes is also a society that focuses on organizational leaders. Just as a premium athlete can quickly fall from grace, so can a CSO. The head of a security group will be removed from the helm with the same speed as the manager of a cellar-dwelling baseball team.

LEADING IN THE TWENTY-FIRST CENTURY

The reader by now should have grasped a key point; that is, that the hero form of leadership has given way to a new form in which the leader is a catalyst and facilitator [3].

Build and Manage

The CSO is expected to build and manage a network of personal relationships that goes beyond direct reports and subordinates. The CSO has to initiate and cultivate relationships throughout the organization and in the external environment. This personal network cannot tolerate dead wood. Relationships that do not work out or are heading nowhere have to be abandoned and replaced with new relationships. Associates inside and outside the organization belong in the CSO's personal network to the extent that they contribute to the security group's goals, and the vendors of security products and services who are long on promise and short on delivery need to be weeded out.

Know the Landscape

The CSO has to know where true power resides in the organization, understand the nuts and bolts of the organization's business, and understand where the organization fits into the larger picture such as the industry or the regional and national economy. Very demanding and essential is the perception of patterns and trends occurring in the organization, in the customer and supplier bases, and in the political and legislative arenas. What do the trends mean to the security mission now or in the future? How can these insights be turned to good advantage? Knowing the landscape requires face-to-face exposure to insiders and outsiders, hence reinforcing the importance of building and managing a personal network.

Expect the Best

The CSO in pursuit of exemplary achievement is self-challenging. He or she sets personal goals that are higher than prior achievements, yet attainable. This attribute is conveyed by example to subordinates.

Do Not Micromanage

A common failing is to be personally active in every facet of security group activity. Subordinates lose interest in their work when the boss is continually looking over their shoulders and telling them how to cross the *T*s and dot the *I*s. A command-and-control approach may have value in military and training settings but not in a fast-paced business setting, especially in a security group staffed with capable people.

Be Accessible

Staying out of the way of people at work is one thing; being available to help is another. Accessibility can be as simple as inviting questions, giving prompt answers, listening, and letting subordinates know that "the door is always open" or giving them a contact telephone number or e-mail address.

Focus on What Is Important

Certain of a security group's activities will be more important than others. Important activities are those that have high relevance to company goals and those of an exigent nature. Sometimes the exigencies occur with such great frequency that the CSO is forced to focus almost exclusively on putting out brush fires. Part of being properly focused is choosing the correct yardsticks for measuring security group performance. To illustrate, a traditional focal point of a cost-conscious CSO is the amount of money spent on guard services, especially for overtime. In being overly concerned with controlling overtime, the CSO may miss the more important issue of providing adequate protection. A better measure of performance might be dollars saved through reduction of loss.

Point the Way

The ability to communicate a clear direction is essential. Every person in the security group should be able to articulate exactly what they do and why. The CSO has to help subordinates understand their individual roles and how those roles contribute to the goals of the group and to the larger organization. This is essential for the same reason it is essential for the CSO to know his or her landscape.

CONCLUSIONS

Effective leaders are persons who get things done. They become leaders by attaining knowledge, gaining experience, and learning from mistakes. They remain leaders by inspiring their followers to work together in pursuit of common goals. For some people leadership is elusive; for others it comes naturally. It may appear that some people are born to be leaders, but the truth is that leaders are made, and by their own efforts. Figure 3-3 points out aspects central to the effective CSO.

NOTES

1. Alan Axelrod, *Patton on Leadership*, pp. 33, Paramus, New Jersey: Prentice Hall Press, 1999.

2. Mindy Blodgett, "Teaching Johnny To Lead," *CIO*, November 15, 1999, p. 81.

3. The remainder of the chapter on leading is based on views expressed by William E. Fulmer in "Shaping the Adaptive Organization," *CIO*, May 1, 2000, pp. 203–212. The full text of Fulmer's views can be found in *Shaping the Adaptive Organization: Landscapes, Learning and Leadership in Volatile Times*, New York: AMACOM, 2000.

A Credo for the Security Leader

Decide what you do best and then do it. Identify your strengths and apply them where they are likely to yield the greatest return. Look for opportunities that correspond to your strengths; improve your ability to do work you presently cannot do well.

Anticipate change. Know the business of your employer. Anticipate that the business will evolve and be prepared to evolve with it. Don't be content to merely hold your job; look for ways to become better. You can be certain that the way your business operates today will not be the way it will operate a year from now.

Self-assess continually. Never stop asking, "What are my goals and am I on the right track? How can I improve the services I provide? Do I have operating costs that can be reduced or eliminated?"

Maintain a dialogue with the users of security services. Deliberately and actively strive for open communications with the employees at all levels. Ask them what they want; pay attention to the answers; deliver what they want, if you can. If you can't deliver, say so. Be honest, even when there's a risk that the listener will be unhappy with what you have to say.

Think partnership. Be more than just another manager. Get into the employees' minds to learn needs, wants, and expectations. Devise new ways to deliver. Be proactive in suggesting better ways to do the job.

Act like a winner. Display confidence. Emphasize the positives and don't hide behind excuses. Be determined to do what it takes. A good motto is "I will not fail." The flip side of deciding not to fail is making business decisions unemotionally. When a course of action under your control shows signs of certain failure, have the courage to shut it down quickly.

Think long-term but concentrate on today. People have concerns about what you are doing for them today, not what you think you will be able to do for them next year.

Show the value. People are willing to buy into security programs when they understand the value derived. Demonstrate how security programs contribute to the bottom line. For example, a new access control system will enhance control of entry and reduce the cost of guard services. Explain these advantages. Use real-life examples to drive home your points.

Figure 3-3 Many skills are required to be an effective CSO.

4. Organizing

We trained hard — but it seemed that every time we were beginning to form up into teams we were reorganized. I was to learn later in life that we tend to meet any new situation by reorganizing, and what a wonderful method it can be for creating the illusion of progress while actually producing confusion, inefficiency, and demoralization.
—Petronius Arbiter, 210 B.C.

STAFFING

The hiring process in a mature organization is almost always under the exclusive ownership of the human resources (HR) group. Hiring tends to be more formal than flexible and moves through stages arranged and monitored by HR staff. (Note: Here we are not discussing the hiring process for security guards employed under contract. The CSO can specify in the contract that certain preemployment standards must be met for guards assigned to the contract, but the CSO has no direct part to play in hiring the guards.) Although HR controls the hiring process, many administrative tasks must be performed by the CSO. The sections that follow describe how the process works.

Justify the Position

A position opening occurs when a new position is created or when a job incumbent leaves an existing position. In either event, the CSO prepares a job description that incorporates the following.

- Names the major tasks, duties, and functions of the position. The principal duties of the chief investigator are presented in a series of statements such as the following.
  - Conduct investigations of felony crimes committed against the company, and workplace violations involving theft, drug trafficking and abuse, assault, harassment, and other matters selected by the chief security officer.

- ○ Collect physical evidence.
- ○ Interview witnesses and suspects.
- ○ Prepare investigative reports.
- ○ Testify at administrative and legal proceedings.
- ○ Coordinate with legal entities concerning restitution.
- ○ Advise the CSO on weaknesses in the organization that contribute to crime and/or violations of workplace rules.
- ○ Establish and maintain working relationships with industry peers and persons in the criminal justice system.
- States where the job fits into the organization's formal hierarchy; that is, the position to which the incumbent reports, the positions that report to the incumbent, and the positions that are equivalent to the incumbent. For example, a job description may state that the chief investigator in the corporate security group reports to the CSO, supervises two investigators, and is at the same organizational level as the chief of physical security in the corporate security group.
- Names the grade level, spending authority, and size of budget commanded (e.g., that the incumbent is at grade level 9, can spend up to $1,000 without prior approval, and manages the investigation office's annual budget of $250,000).
- Sets forth required experience, education, and training. This might read as follows: The job incumbent must have worked in a responsible investigative position for at least five years and possess at least a baccalaureate degree, preferably in business management, accounting, criminal justice, or similar major area of study.

When the vacant position is an already-established position, the CSO updates the existing job description. When the position is new, the CSO starts from scratch.

Identify Relevant Skills and Knowledge

A thoughtful examination of a job's tasks will reveal the skills and knowledge that must be applied by the incumbent to operate at the desired level of performance. If the incumbent's job includes conducting investigations of felony crimes, he or she must be skilled at collecting evidence, interviewing witnesses and suspects, writing reports, and testifying at judicial proceedings. These particular skills require, among others, knowledge of forensic sciences, criminal psychology, rules of writing, and criminal trial procedures.

If the task is to network with peers in security and law enforcement, a relevant skill is verbal communication. The supporting knowledge includes understanding the structure and workings of the criminal justice system. Unfortunately, and damaging to the hiring process, it only rarely happens that a job description will define skill and knowledge requirements to the level of specificity needed to search for and sift through qualified candidates.

Search for Qualified Candidates

Four avenues of search are available to the CSO and HR staff. First is the help-wanted sections of newspapers. For hourly wage employee positions, local newspapers suffice, but for salaried security management positions the scope of the search broadens. *The Wall Street Journal*, for example, is an appropriate source for seeking upper-level CSOs. A second search avenue is position-open notices in publications that can range from newsletters of security association chapters to nationally distributed security magazines and journals.

The third avenue, and often the most productive, is the word-of-mouth search that begins with the CSO and spreads throughout the industry's grapevine. "I hear that Widgets International is looking for an investigator," is the type of comment often made over the phone and at cocktail parties. The fourth avenue is employment placement agencies (i.e., professional head-hunters). This method is almost always limited to searching for management candidates.

Choosing a search avenue is not nearly as complicated as traveling the avenue. Complications arise in the way the job and the qualifications of the candidate are described. Help-wanted ads that contain descriptors such as "Ivy League type," "recent high school graduate," and "energetic individual" imply discrimination on the basis of class and age. Sex-biased descriptors include "gal Friday" and "salesman." Other discriminatory references might be "former military officer" and "retiree."

Legal challenge can be avoided by explicitly describing the required job skills and knowledge. A security investigator, for example, writes reports, testifies, and respects Constitutional rights. The appropriate descriptors could be "capable writer," "good verbal communicator," and "knowledge of Constitutional law [1]."

Compare Candidates Against Job Requirements

This stage in hiring is not as simple as it sounds. Valid comparisons rely on having two sets of data that can be matched one against the other. The data sets are well-defined job requirements and clear evidence of qualifications that correspond to the requirements. The matching process becomes unworkable when one data set is apples and the other is oranges, and complicated when minor job requirements are included. The idea is to make the data sets fit nicely with each other and to not bother with lesser job requirements. An example of a good match between a key job requirement and a clear qualification (see Figure 4-1) is "knowledge of criminal investigative methods" and a certificate showing completion of a course in criminal investigation.

INTERVIEW SUMMARY OF JOB APPLICANT

Applicant: _____   Interview Date: _____

Position: _____   Salary Requested: _____

Interviewer: _____   Date Available: _____

EVALUATION	EXCELLENT	GOOD	FAIR	POOR
Enthusiasm	☐	☐	☐	☐
Experience	☐	☐	☐	☐
Education	☐	☐	☐	☐
Required Skills	☐	☐	☐	☐
Attitude	☐	☐	☐	☐
Appearance	☐	☐	☐	☐

Other:

_____	☐	☐	☐	☐
_____	☐	☐	☐	☐
_____	☐	☐	☐	☐

Comments: _____

_____

_____

_____

_____

Recommendation: _____

_____

_____

Interviewer's Signature: _____

Figure 4-1 Key data are recorded during the interview of a job applicant.

Identify the Apparent Best Candidate

At this point, the search has been narrowed considerably. The candidates still in the running are on what is called the "short list." The candidate that looks the best is selected from the list. This is not the moment to tell a candidate that he or she appears to be the best candidate. It is a decision-making moment to be shared by a select few, such as the CSO and the HR representative. The next step is to ensure that the best candidate has honestly presented the facts.

Conduct a Background Inquiry

A background inquiry is said to be confirmatory when the employer seeks only to confirm that the job candidate has been truthful in providing information. The confirmatory inquiry is almost always limited to information requested on a job application form such as previous employment, education and training achievements, and criminal history. A background inquiry is said to be investigative when the employer looks for information that a candidate may be concealing such information as a cause for termination from a previous job or the commission of a serious crime. An investigative background inquiry will often be initiated when a confirmatory inquiry revealed possible deception by the candidate [2].

Test the Apparent Best Candidate

Alcohol and drug testing are common procedures for evaluating a candidate for a security job, or for that matter any job that involves protection of human life or sensitive assets such as nuclear material and secret information. The negative effects of alcohol and drugs on human performance in the workplace are widely known. They include lost productivity, absenteeism, high accident rates and medical costs, theft, and violence [3]. (Note: A detailed discussion of alcohol and drug testing can be found in the chapter dealing with substance abuse prevention.)

Human behavior can be assessed also through psychological testing. Test content may be directed to almost any facet of intellectual or emotional functioning. Among the aspects of greatest concern to a CSO are honesty, propensity for violence, personal traits, values, and attitude. Test results are obtained by comparing the individual's responses against standard responses, with the standard responses having been developed previously by commonly accepted scientific methods. A test score can predict an individual's behavior in a narrowly defined set of circumstances, and is said to have predictive validity when it yields consistent, reliable measurements. For example, an honesty test has predictive validity if persons who score high are later shown by their behaviors to be honest. When accurate in predicting a job applicant's future behavior, psychological tests can be valuable hiring tools.

Proficiency tests can be used to select job candidates and to determine their suitability for particular jobs. Aptitude tests predict future performance in a job for which the individual is not currently trained. If a person's score is similar to scores of others already working in a given job, likelihood of success in that job is predicted. Some aptitude tests cover a broad range of skills pertinent to many different occupations. The General Aptitude Test Battery is an example. It not only measures general reasoning ability but includes measures of perception, motor coordination, and finger and manual dexterity.

Intelligence tests measure the global capacity of an individual to cope with the environment. Test scores are generally known as intelligence quotients, or IQs. Objective personality tests measure social and emotional adjustment. Responses that briefly describe feelings, attitudes, and behaviors provide a profile of the personality as a whole. The most popular of these tests are the Minnesota Multiphasic Inventory and the California Psychological Inventory.

One cannot discuss preemployment testing without reference to their critics. The major criticisms stem from two interrelated issues. The first is technical shortcomings in test design. Because technical weakness to some degree is inescapably present in all forms of preemployment testing, the sharpest of critics demand that such testing not be used at all. The mainstream view is that test results represent only one piece of information about an individual, and as such should not be used as the sole criterion for selection or rejection.

The second criticism deals with interpretation and application of results. Opponents argue that testing can under- and over-valuate job candidates, and employers who use testing often place an inappropriate reliance on tests. These arguments have been particularly loud in the case of intelligence testing. Psychologists generally agree that using intelligence tests to bar individuals from job opportunities, without careful consideration of other relevant factors, is unethical. Critics have taken their views to the courtroom. A chief argument is that certain tests emphasize skills associated with white, middle-class functioning, resulting in discrimination against disadvantaged and minority groups.

Offer the Job

At this point, the final stage of the hiring process, the job is offered. If accepted, the new hire may be required to sign a confidentiality agreement. In the following anecdote, the new hire is a security group employee. The CSO will likely require the new hire to undergo an orientation that identifies prohibited behaviors, penalties for violations, and the methods used to assess and enforce compliance with rules.

CASE STUDY

Larry's search for a security group investigator narrowed to two candidates: Cynthia Castillo and Brendan Murphy. Details in the job applications for both candidates had been verified. Cynthia had a degree in business management and seven years of work experience as a credit card fraud investigator. Brendan had a degree in criminal justice and 22 years as an agent in the Bureau of Alcohol, Tobacco and Firearms. Although Larry was careful in final job interviews to ask each candidate the same set of questions, the conversation tended to stray. With Brendan, for example, the matter of his age came up, as did his Irish descent and Catholic upbringing. Cynthia mentioned that she had a child by a previous marriage and was engaged.

Larry selected Cynthia. He was sold on her education, her prior work experience, and her enthusiasm. A month later, Larry was informed that Brendan had filed a discrimination complaint. Brendan alleged that he had been denied the position because of responses he made to questions that were illegal to ask. He also alleged that Cynthia had been preferred over him because she was female and Hispanic.

The Independent Contractor

Independent contractors or consultants typically work for more than one client, operate out of their own offices, set their own hours, and work according to their own methodologies. Unlike regular employees, consultants are not entitled to overtime, vacation pay, and time off to deal with family and medical emergencies. Consultants may or may not be accorded protections against discrimination based on race, gender, religion, disability, or age. The legal obligations of a client to a consultant are not nearly as demanding as those that apply to regular employees. CSOs employ consultants when

- The work to be performed requires technical expertise not available in the security group or not readily available in the larger organization. An example is the use of a so-called "tiger team" to conduct computer penetration tests.
- The need for the work is occasional or periodic. For example, a risk management consultant may be hired once per year when annual security audits are conducted.
- The cost of the consultant is less than the cost of performing the work in-house.
- Contingencies arise that make it impossible or difficult for the security group to effectively carry out its mission. The CSO, for example, may engage the services of freelance investigators to augment security group staff during a major investigation.

ORGANIZING ACTIVITIES

In the routine course of business, the CSO engages in a variety of practices loosely called organizing. The following are examples.

- Establish job positions
- Hire people to fill the jobs
- Assign work
- Delegate responsibilities
- Acquire materials and tools

Ten Commandments of Good Organization

1. Definite and clear-cut responsibilities should be assigned to each executive, leader, supervisor, and foreman.
2. Responsibility should always be coupled with corresponding authority.
3. No change should be made in the scope or responsibility of a position without a definite understanding to that effect on the part of all persons concerned.
4. No executive or employee, occupying a single position in the organization, should be subject to definite orders from more than one source.
5. Orders should never be given to subordinates over the head of a responsible executive. Rather than do this, the officer in question should be supplanted.
6. Criticisms of subordinates should be made privately. In no case should a subordinate be criticized in the presence of executives or employees of equal or lower rank.
7. No dispute or difference between executives or employees as to authority or responsibility should be considered too trivial for prompt and careful adjudication.
8. Promotions, wage changes, and disciplinary action should always be approved by the executive immediately superior to the one directly responsible.
9. No executive or employee should be assistant to and at the same time a critic of the person he is assistant to.
10. Any executive whose work is subject to regular inspection should, whenever practicable, be given the assistance and facilities necessary to enable him to maintain an independent check of the quality of his work.

Figure 4-2 These ideas were expressed in the early 1930s by M. C. Rorty, a vice president of International Telephone & Telegraph Corporation.

- Manage time
- Counsel and guide employees

The organizing activities of the CSO (see Figure 4-2) reflect the business processes of the company. A manufacturing company will work differently than a company in lending, banking, retailing, or mining, as will a government agency in educating, regulating, or enforcing. The CSO will of necessity operate in harmony with the processes of the company no matter what they are. Although the CSO might incorporate practices found reliable through personal knowledge and experience, the overriding imperative is to meld group operations with the needs of the larger organization. For this to succeed, the security group must operate in harmony with itself and with other groups. The CSO understands that security operations are but one part of a large and complex mosaic.

ESTABLISHING OBJECTIVES

The organizing function operates at two levels: group and individual.

Group Objectives

Group objectives are subparts of a goal or a mission. If the company's mission is to be a profitable competitor in the mining of silver, one of the objectives of the security group will be to prevent theft of silver extracted from ore. Group objectives, then, are consistent with the needs and nature of the company's business. The fulfillment of group objectives is a major consideration when senior management rates the CSO's performance.

Individual Objectives

The objectives of individuals working in the security group are employee performance targets that are set annually, monitored periodically throughout the year, and evaluated impartially at the end of the year. The targets are sometimes negotiated between the CSO and the subordinate. Once agreed upon or set, performance begins or continues from the previous target period. From time to time, such as monthly or quarterly, the CSO and subordinate meet to discuss progress.

Individual objectives fall under group objectives. They are extensions of the major tasks, duties, and functions defined in an individual's job description. These objectives state what the individual is expected to do in his/her job and establish measurable criteria as to volume and quality. Imagine that it's the duty of the security group's physical security specialist to conduct security vulnerability assessments of the company's six manufacturing plants. The CSO establishes an objective for this duty: perform one security vulnerability assessment every quarter of the calendar year and produce from each assessment a written report that meets established criteria for content, format, and readability.

The outcomes of group and individual objectives are often measured with a yardstick called "value derived versus cost," a fancy name for a concept that poses a simple question: Was the delivered service worth the expenditure? Organizing by objectives allows an answer that is rational and impersonal.

ORGANIZING CONSISTENT WITH POLICIES

The company's statements of missions and goals are found in its policy or policy set, and security is one of the matters addressed. A company's management may choose to express its security philosophy in an overarching policy that addresses a range of issues such as preemployment screening, substance abuse, and workplace violence. In addition or alternatively, the company may choose to create a number of standalone policies, each covering a fairly discrete issue such as preemployment screening only. In the latter arrangement, the security group would likely own a policy of its own and share ownership in other policies. In whatever form, the ideal security policy is endorsed by management at the highest level and understood by all parties affected by it.

The point here is that security policy carries with it commitments that must be met. It is the difference between effectiveness and efficiency, as pointed out

Effectiveness

The extent to which objectives are met, considering the resources employed.

Efficiency

The capacity to produce results in proportion to the effort expended.

Figure 4-3 Effectiveness and efficiency have different meanings.

Goals and Objectives

Protect human assets

In this reporting period, increase by 10 percent the number of security escorts of employees from the office building to the parking garage.
In each quarter of the reporting period, conduct at least one crime prevention presentation on a crime topic of current concern.

Control access

Before June 30, install a CCTV camera at the side entrance of the office building.
Before March 31, install aesthetically acceptable physical boundaries to control visitors waiting to be processed by the lobby receptionist.

Prevent property theft

Before February 1, revise the property removal pass system.
Before February 15, train the security officers in the use of the system.
At least three times in the next reporting period, post notices of the system on the company's bulletin boards and intranet.
In the next reporting period, increase by 10 percent the number of rounds made by the roving patrol.

Protect proprietary information

Hire a qualified contractor to perform an electronic countermeasures inspection at least twice in the next reporting period.
In each month of the next reporting period, conduct at least one after-hours inspection to assess compliance with the company's clean desk policy.
Assign a security group representative to show the proprietary information video at employee meetings three or more times in the next reporting period.

Upgrade the competency of security group staff

Use the annual employee performance appraisal as an opportunity to identify needed and missing skills. Security staff will be scheduled to attend improvement courses as needed.
Before May 1, meet with each direct report to discuss individual self-development plans, and make recommendations

Figure 4-4 This is an example of objectives within goals.

in Figure 4-3. If the policy pledges to obey laws, respect the rights of people, and establish a safe work setting, the CSO must ensure that the manner of protecting company assets must not violate the law, must not violate anyone's rights, and must not create safety risks. This is an example of "objectives within goals," as represented by Figure 4-4.

Obtaining Resources

Ideally, resources are determined by objectives but the reality is that objectives conform to resources. A security group objective can make perfect sense, but if the resources are not available it makes no sense at all.

It is accurate to say that resources entrusted to the CSO derive from the dictates of senior management. If the CEO issues a policy that requires the security group to prevent unauthorized entry to a manufacturing plant, funding must be made available to meet the policy's requirement. The CSO may judge that fencing, lighting, and access control equipment will need to be installed and more guards hired. The plant superintendent, however, may disagree with the CSO's thinking. He may say, "A fence and guards checking passes will slow people down when they come to work. Plant productivity will drop. I don't like it." The financial officer at the plant may say, "Since we're providing the funds for this project, we think we can get by without access control equipment and with three new guards instead of five." If the CSO cannot negotiate a level of funding adequate to meet the policy requirement, he/she may have to appeal to the CEO (and in the process alienate the plant superintendent and financial officer).

Perception is also a determinant in the allocation of resources. When senior management perceives that the CSO and the security group are effective at what they do, there is a greater chance that security operations will be adequately funded. This is a fickle reality because the perceptions of senior managers are based on "snapshot" views of security: "The guard at the main entrance was alert and smiled as I drove by," or "The moron at the security desk didn't even know my name." Sadly, resource allocations can be based on such perceptions.

The People Resource

The resource most important to the CSO is competent people. A security group can have a state-of-the-art assemblage of equipment and a full complement of personnel yet be incapable of meeting group objectives when human competence is lacking. Competence is a mix of knowledge, skill, and attitude. The first two can be taught and learned without much difficulty. The last of the mix, attitude, can be taught but for some people not easily learned. Consider the following scenario.

CASE STUDY

A motorist driving on a lonely country road sees ahead of him a red octagonal sign bearing in the center large white letters that spell STOP. The driver understands that motor vehicle law requires motorists to come to a complete and full stop at the intersection where the sign is posted. The driver has just demonstrated knowledge. The driver removes his foot from the accelerator, applies the brakes, and maintains steering. The driver has just demonstrated a skill. The driver notices that the intersection ahead of him is clear. There's no other vehicle in sight. The driver proceeds through the intersection without stopping. The driver has just demonstrated an attitude.

A CSO's efforts to organize the security group can be successful only if the group possesses and applies a correct mix of knowledge and skill, accompanied by a positive attitude.

ORGANIZING BEYOND BOUNDARIES

The security group supports and works in concert with other company groups. Although it can serve important support functions, it cannot do everything related to security. For protection to prevail, every employee must pull his/her own weight: the executive secretary locks the safe before going home, the scientist removes data maps from the conference room wall, the janitor locks doors, the chief of operations does not discuss sensitive matters over the telephone. The catalyst is the CSO.

Some employees hold more responsibilities than others. This is especially true of employees in line management. Company assets, such as vehicles and desktop equipment, are signed out to managers and supervisors. Even though a group's assets are in the custody of subordinates, the group leader is responsible for their care. The responsibility is often spelled out in a policy statement such as the following.

CASE STUDY

Managers and supervisors at all levels are responsible for protecting the assets entrusted to them, ensuring that subordinates do likewise, and meeting security standards and practices necessary to maintaining a secure, safe, and productive work environment for our employees, guests, and the customers we serve. The matter of assets protection will be an element in the annual evaluation of managers and supervisors and may be a factor in determining individual pay raises, bonuses, and promotions.

A policy statement that links security responsibilities with pay and advancement can be a powerful motivating tool. Because few managers and supervisors have a firm understanding of protective measures, they must turn to the CSO for guidance. It is in this regard that the CSO plays an organizing role outside the boundaries of the security group.

The CSO does not *provide* security but rather helps others discharge their security responsibilities by offering expert counsel. Counsel can take many forms: face-to-face discussions, presentations at line management meetings, alerts and advisories by e-mail, and memoranda. The arrangement can work very well, provided the CSO is not stretched thin. This can happen when the company is very large, operates in many geographical areas, and works in partnership with other organizations.

Assigning Tasks

The total work in a security group is the sum of all tasks. A single task can be thought of as a combination of elements: a physical or mental action (e.g., directing vehicle traffic), the place of action (e.g., the exit gate from

Examples of Task Statements

For a job advertisement:
> The candidate for this position will be able to direct vehicle traffic; patrol floors; etc.

For a training curriculum:
> The student will learn to direct vehicle traffic; perform roving patrol; etc.

For a job description:
> The incumbent directs vehicle traffic; patrols floors; etc.

For a performance evaluation:
> In this reporting period, this employee did an outstanding job at directing vehicle traffic.

Request for a purchase of equipment:
> The equipment requested is needed by the security officer who directs vehicle traffic.

For a standard operating procedure:
> From 1 to 6 PM, daily, the security officer assigned to this post will direct vehicle traffic at the exit driveway of the company parking lot.

Figure 4-5 Tasks are basic building blocks for organizing human performance.

the company's parking lot), conditions affecting the action (e.g., inclement weather), and equipment needed to perform the action (e.g., a traffic vest, traffic baton, and rain slicker). Two other elements are highly determinative of task performance. First is the importance or criticality of the task. Some tasks have greater impact and consequences than do others. The task of directing traffic is less critical than the task of preventing unauthorized entry. A second determinant of performance is the training that precedes and facilitates task execution.

Tasks are arranged in groups according to jobs. The security officer holding the job called console operator will perform a set of tasks unlike the set of tasks performed by a gate guard. Tasks in written form are seen in many venues (see Figure 4-5).

Monitoring Performance

Inside the CSO's organizing tool kit is a practice called monitoring. The following are examples of monitoring.

- Looking at tasks as they are being performed to detect mistakes, small and large, that can lead to problems
- Examining the output of task performance such as general correspondence and incident reports
- Visiting guard posts
- Observing tests of fire detection and suppression equipment, backup power supplies, and other equipment kept in readiness for emergency responses

Many will liken the process to "management by walking around," whereas a few may call it "making a nuisance of oneself." Whatever the label, monitoring is an indispensable part of organizing. Monitoring in the sense used here is essentially inward (i.e., it is focused on security operations). Monitoring that is focused on operations outside the security group is discussed later, particularly in the chapter dealing with risk management. The following anecdote makes the point that routine monitoring can identify the need for change.

CASE STUDY

The CSO for a minerals extraction company made it a point to monitor daily reports of security incidents. He noted an upward trend in the number of incidents that appeared to be drug related. He visited the HR director and the company's head physician. The HR director pointed out that the company had a workplace rule that prohibited use of illegal drugs on company property. The CSO pointed out that the rule had no teeth because without drug testing there was no way to determine if a given incident resulted from a violation of the no-drug-use rule. The physician suggested starting a random drug testing program, with testing by a certified lab using the urinalysis method. Agreement was reached and approval given by the CEO.

On the first day of urine collection, the CSO appeared at the collection site to monitor how things were going. He observed a worker in line who appeared to be intoxicated. The CSO confronted the worker, and after smelling alcohol on his breath asked him if he had been drinking. The worker affirmed that he had been drinking and admitted he was under the influence, and then said, "But I'm here for a drug test. I don't do drugs. I only do whiskey."

The CSO sent a report to the CEO, with copies to the HR director and the head physician. The CEO ordered that the new random testing program be changed to include testing for alcohol as well as drugs.

TERMINATING AN EMPLOYEE

For two reasons the CSO needs to be knowledgeable about termination interviews. First is the need to personally inform a subordinate that his or her services are no longer required. Second, the CSO is often asked to be present when trouble is expected at a termination interview of someone else's subordinate.

The sagacity of Solomon is required to anticipate the range of potential reactions in a termination interview. Certain typical responses, however, can be expected. These include stunned reaction, psychological trauma, sorrow, and belligerence.

Stunned Reaction

In this case, the termination notice is received as almost good news, the employee seems to be fully composed and in control, the session is proceeding well, and the CSO is gaining confidence there will be no problems. The fact may be that the employee is stunned by the news and unable to respond in a manner that reflects true inner feelings. People who react this way may lack the capacity to vent, and if they hold back the stress — which tends to build over time — they can explode hours, days, or weeks later. To the CSO, this is a concern because the explosion can be directed at the company.

It can also happen that the employee will be so taken aback by the termination notice that he/she will not mentally process the implications and, in effect, act is if the interview is nothing more than a routine meeting. The employee simply chooses not to hear the bad news.

Psychological Trauma

Employees who react to termination with uncontrolled weeping, absolute silence, or what appears to be shock are probably incapable of reacting. It can be very unnerving when the employee clearly appears to need help and the CSO, who would like to give help, lacks the capacity to do so.

It occasionally happens that the CSO, motivated by a desire to help, will hint at or promise to assist the employee in some way that is not permitted by the terms of the discharge. This is clearly not a good move for the employee because the offered help cannot be delivered, and for the CSO the result may be a complaint on the grounds of a breach of promise.

When the employee cannot be returned to a normal state, the CSO should bring a treatment professional into the picture. A company, especially when multiple terminations are involved, would be wise to have counselors available when interviews are being held.

Sorrow

Many employees will respond initially with expressions of disappointment and hurt. A lesser number will express anger, betrayal, and resentment. These are all natural reactions that can be healthy because they are venting mechanisms. The CSO can expect the employee to move from normal expressions of sorrow to practical questions about what happens next.

Belligerence

The CSO will be apprehensive about encountering an employee who overreacts when informed of termination. Although it is true that violence is possible, experience indicates that the odds are low that it will occur. Experience also indicates that when the CSO approaches the situation primed to respond with stiff resistance, the odds change greatly in favor of a confrontation.

The critical factor, then, when confronted with a potentially belligerent employee is to maintain self-control and not escalate the hostility. On the other hand, the CSO should not be defensive to the point of agreeing with the employee. Calmative gestures — such as a smile, a shrug, an open posture, and soft silence — may be useful in helping a belligerent person regain composure. A positive outcome is enhanced when the CSO proves to be an empathetic listener.

Disparaging comments against the CSO and the company are in the realm of normal behavior and to be expected. But certainly there are limits to the abuse the CSO should tolerate. Threats of harm and intimidating physical contact are unacceptable, and should they occur the CSO has three options: (1) warn the employee that the behavior must cease immediately, (2) call for assistance, or (3) conclude the interview.

Managing the Termination Interview

Preparing for the termination interview increases the probability of producing the desired results, reduces the stress placed on the CSO, and helps keep the process on a professional level. Preparation means reviewing the reasons for terminating the employee, anticipating the range of reactions that may be exhibited, and determining a strategy and a set of tactics for controlling the reactions. As indicated in Figure 4-6, preparation also means the following.

- Scheduling the interview at a suitable place and time
- Ensuring that the employee will appear, even to the extent of personally escorting the employee to the interview

Tips for the Termination Interview

Write and memorize the key points of a script.

Anticipate problems and be ready with appropriate responses.

State the purpose early in the interview. Avoid small talk; get to the point in a business-like (but not necessarily cold) fashion.

Maintain direct eye contact in a manner that projects openness and honesty.

Be sure the employee understands that he or she has been terminated; that certain rights and benefits apply; that certain follow-up steps will be taken by the company; and that the employee will be expected to do certain things, such as turn-in assigned keys and equipment and pick up personal items at the work station.

Allow the employee to vent emotions but stay with the script.

Say only what is necessary.

Avoid words, terms, or phrases that are open to interpretation.

Don't promise or give any hint of help that can't be delivered.

Don't imply or remotely suggest discrimination.

Don't suggest that the employee has an opportunity to change the decision to discharge or to negotiate a change in the terms of the discharge.

Avoid platitudes, homilies, and philosophical discussions.

Avoid comments suggesting that the discharge decision was based on anything other than job-related factors.

Don't give the impression that the discharge is retaliation for something that the employee may have done against the wishes of the company.

Don't be defensive or admit in any way that the termination is unjustified or improperly administered.

Keep the meeting as brief as possible, and close the meeting on a positive note.

Figure 4-6 Doing the right things at a termination interview can avoid problems.

- Knowing what should be collected (e.g., keys, credit cards, files, portable laptop, and so on)
- Arranging for security officer assistance that may be needed to counter a belligerent reaction
- Arranging for HR counseling to deal with an emotional reaction
- Setting up a procedure for the employee to leave the work site with personal property in hand

ORGANIZATIONAL STRUCTURES

Organization theory is an attempt to explicate and predict human behavior in an organization [4]. The theory presupposes that the design or shape of a business organization will influence human activities. In the vertical organization, work processes are directly influenced by instructions passed down from bosses to subordinates and by lateral coordination among the bosses and the subordinates.

Vertical Model

The vertical organization is sometimes called the classic or pyramidal organization. At the top of the pyramid is the head of the organization and at the bottom level are the least influential of the rank-and-file employees. Status and authority increase as one moves up. Closely related functions are tied together in vertical chains, and hence the term "chain of command." A single chain might start one or two levels from the top, beginning with the CSO. One level below might be positions for the head of investigations and the head of guard operations. Below each of those might be three or four positions representing the functions of preemployment screening, credit card fraud, and physical security inspections.

At the top of the vertical organization is the senior executive and/or an executive team, typically consisting of the CEO, COO, chief financial officer (CFO), chief information officer (CIO), and CSO. As an organization grows in size and complexity, the chains multiply and lengthen. Figure 4-7 indicates the pyramidal shape of a vertical hierarchy.

Another in the variety of organizational form has pyramids on top of pyramids. The pyramid at the very top is corporate management. It is here that goals are established and major decisions made that affect operations in all of the underlying pyramids.

Below corporate management are pyramids that can represent subsidiaries, major functions, business streams, or geographical locations. Each of these second-level pyramids has a senior management team that directs its enterprise in accord with the dictates of corporate management. The very lowest level of pyramids is operational management. These pyramids are arranged in sets that correspond to and support a senior management team.

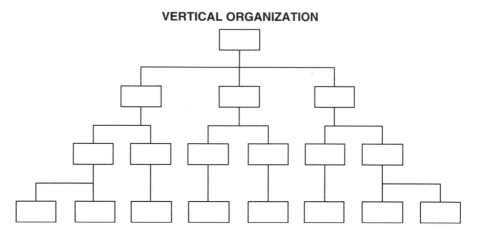

Figure 4-7 The vertical organization has a pyramidal shape.

Network Model

Humanity seems always to have organized its practices in hierarchies. Systems of top-to-bottom control have not been restricted to business but are found in the practices of religion, education, and the military. The notion of hierarchies has been enduring because it is orderly, efficient, and amenable to control. Many of us enjoy ranking things and don't feel comfortable without being ranked and knowing where they fit in the scheme of things.

The questions of today are "Does the hierarchical or vertical business model work as well or better than other models?" and "Does the vertical model fit rapidly changing world markets?" The answers are often no. Markets can suddenly rearrange in new and exciting patterns, calling for new business practices and human skills. The vertical model is slow to react to rapid change.

Many organizations now believe that the vertical hierarchy no longer functions effectively as a universal model. In its place has come a model that goes by several names: flat, horizontal, open, and network. For our purposes, we will call it the network model. The network model features clusters of employees grouped according to the sets of multiple skills they possess and which are needed to meet the organization's performance objectives. Teams, not individuals, constitute the fundamental units of the organization and are encouraged to be self-managing [5].

Fewer layers of management are necessary because many of the managers and supervisors are either team leaders or almost "inside" the work process. In this arrangement, horizontal does not mean flat as in "flat as a pancake." Horizontal refers to work flowing horizontally. The work is performed by teams, each possessing skill sets that correspond to the nature of the work.

The network model is rooted in a plain observation that business practices based on price and economies of scale have lost their magic. Success in the

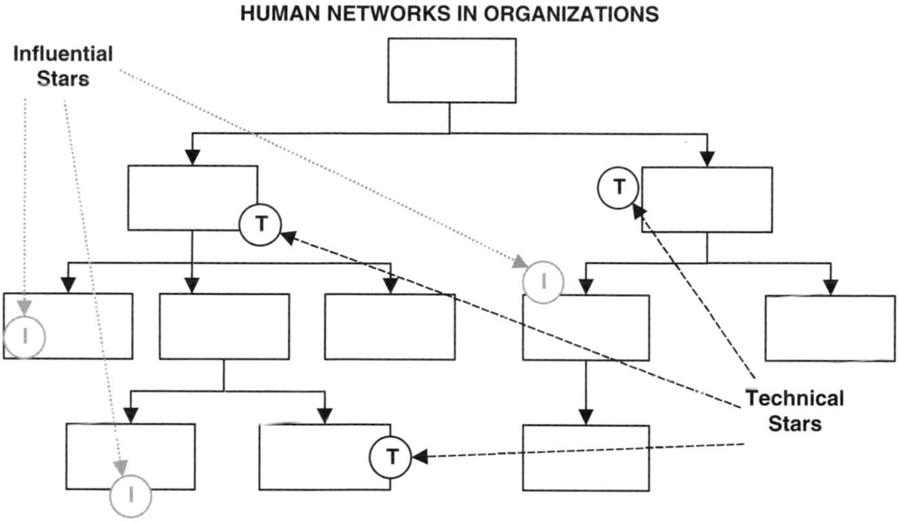

HUMAN NETWORKS IN ORGANIZATIONS

Figure 4-8 The formal network in a large organization will be supplemented with informal networks consisting of employees with influence and technical talent.

new competitive environment is now believed to proceed from the possession and use of knowledge and rapid technological development. As a result, massive organizational changes are common, hierarchical organizations are flattening and opening up, and work is shifting from individual efforts to team efforts. Team success is often made possible by tapping into unique talent, inside or outside the organization. Human networks often form of their own accord to supplement networks of the formal organization (see Figure 4-8). "Stars" of influence and technical know-how become contributors with or without management intervention.

Security Group Fit

To the CSO, the type of organizational model may not be as important as the work processes influenced by the model. The practices of control, downward supervision, and upward feedback that are part and parcel of the vertical organization diminish or disappear in the network organization. The CSO's attempts to retain and apply traditional controls are not always welcome in a company that believes in empowerment.

The mandate for the CSO is to achieve the same or higher level of results in a different manner (see Figure 4-9). This is neither simple nor easy. On the one hand, the organization's management wants the CSO to embrace bold new concepts, yet on the other hand wants no dilution in the protection of assets. Whether the CSO likes it or not, he/she is caught up in a process of learning and adapting to organizational change [6].

Traditional Hierarchy v. Open Network

Traditional	Open Network
Formal and rationalized	Informal and evolving
Closed to outsiders	Open to the world
Collects capital and properties	Collects human talent and information
Static and stable	Dynamic and fast moving
Prizes its managers	Prizes its technical stars
Motivates by reward and punishment	Motivates by opportunity and challenge
Manages by command	Promotes self-management
Control from the top	Empowerment below
Make the boss happy	Make the team happy
Specific skills for specific jobs	Sets of related skills and broad competencies
Compensation is the status symbol	Accomplishment is the status symbol
Stay off my turf	It's our turf
It's a job	It's my life
Look before you leap	Leap. You can always pick yourself up
Lifers	What can you do for me today?
Employees find it hard to move to other firms	Employees bounce at will
I want a bigger office	I want a better computer
I'm happy doing what I'm doing	What's the next project?

Figure 4-9 Sharp comparisons can be made between the traditional (i.e., vertical) model and the network model.

NOTES

1. Deborah L. Jacobs, *Small Business Legal Smarts*, pp. 100–101, Princeton: Bloomberg Press, 1998.

2. Carl E. King, "Background Checks: Record Searches," in *Encyclopedia of Security Management*, John J. Fay (ed.), pp. 67, Boston: Butterworth-Heinemann, 1993.

3. John J. Fay, *The Drug-Free Workplace*, pp. 1–4, Boston: Butterworth-Heinemann, 2000.

4. Albert H. Rubenstein, "Organization Theory," in *Encyclopedia of Management*, Carl Heyel (ed.), pp. 799, New York: Van Nostrand Rheinhold, 1982.

5. Frank Ostroff, *The Horizontal Organization*, pp. 59, New York: Oxford University Press, 1999.

6. John J. Fay, "Corporate Security: Protecting Assets in an Evolving Shamrock-Like Organization," pp. 2–3, *Security Journal*, October 1992.

5. Managing People

Success is just a matter of attitude.
—Darcy E. Gibbons

WORKING THROUGH PEOPLE

Success at managing people rests on interpersonal skills that take the leader far beyond the issue of being liked. Motivating others is not a matter of earning admiration but of inspiring them to work individually and as a team. The leader's principal task is to create a climate for work in which team efforts are organized and directed toward the attainment of agreed-upon and well-understood goals. But to effectively discharge that task the leader must comprehend the human needs, differences, and emotions of those being managed.

The willingness of subordinates to apply themselves to productive work activities is linked to how much personal value they find in the work itself. The leader's challenge is to discover the rewards people find in their jobs and to integrate the rewards with work processes. This merging of personal desires with organizational needs is at once tricky and difficult. An understanding of motivational theory can help.

MASLOW'S THEORY

Maslow's theory holds that motivation is the cause of an organism's behavior, or the reason an organism carries out a particular activity. In the human organism, motivation involves both conscious and unconscious drives. Psychological theories hold that a primary level of motivation satisfies basic needs such as those for food, oxygen, and water. A secondary level of motivation meets social needs such as companionship and achievement. The primary needs must be satisfied before a person can attend to secondary drives [1] (see Figure 5-1).

The American psychologist Abraham Maslow devised a six-level hierarchy of motives that determine human behavior. According to Maslow, human needs operate in an ascending hierarchy that begins with a natural striving

Figure 5-1 To the extent lower-level needs are met, higher needs come into play.

to satisfy the physiological imperatives. In this hierarchy, which can be abstracted as a pyramid, a higher need does not provide motivation until all lower, more basic, needs are satisfied. When a need is satisfied, it ceases to be a motivator.

Physiological

The physiological needs are man's basic requirements for nourishment, water, air, and rest. A person's focus will be entirely on these needs for as long as they continue to be unmet. Once met, the individual's focus shifts upward.

Survival

At the next level is the requirement to be free from harm. The safety and security of the individual dominates. Like the underlying physiological needs, this level is concerned with survival and self-preservation.

Love

At the third level, the individual strives for love and belonging. Affection and human relationships are the focal points.

Self-esteem

Competence and prestige wrapped in self-esteem come next. These needs are satisfied through personal achievement, independence, status, and recognition, and are similar to love needs because both are social in orientation.

Self-fulfillment

The fifth order of needs is self-fulfillment or self-actualization. At this level, the individual self-expresses through the exercise of personal capabilities. Satisfaction is derived through the development of one's own potential and the expression of creative urge.

Curiosity

The highest and most abstract in Maslow's order of needs is curiosity. At this level, the individual is highly curious and strives to satisfy a thirst for understanding. The individual, for example, may find satisfaction delving into the mysteries of religion, life, or the origins of the universe.

Key Tenets

The key tenets of Maslow's theory can be summed up in the following observations.

- Man is a continuously wanting animal. When fulfilled in one need, he develops desires in another.
- When a person's needs have been satisfied they cease to motivate. A person must be confronted with a need before being moved to initiate, change, or sustain behavior.
- A need can be satisfied in different ways. A person who needs money will be motivated to acquire it. The method of acquisition in extreme cases can be irrelevant. For example, a person might meet the need for money by going so far as stealing.
- One style of behavior may satisfy more than one need. A person who works hard to earn money may want the money to buy food (physiological), pay the mortgage (security), or gain prestige (self-esteem).

Maslow in the Security Environment

A person's natural striving to establish human relationships and to experience self-esteem are present as much in the workplace as in any other setting. A security employee, whether working at the line level or in management, has social needs that include friendship with co-workers and acceptance within the work group. The extent and intensity of individual efforts will vary, however. An individual who satisfies social needs outside the workplace may exhibit less striving than someone whose entire social experience is dependent on co-workers.

Attempts to satisfy the higher needs of self-esteem are often expressed by seeking recognition as a standout performer or as a valued contributor to the attainment of group goals. Most of us never stop looking for assurance that we are held in high regard by our peers, and even when we obtain that assurance today we will seek it tomorrow and every day thereafter. Consider the following situation.

CASE STUDY

Jason was young, competent, and newly promoted as head of the security group's credit card fraud unit. He loved his work and admired his boss. One day he got into a heated dispute with a peer, the head of the physical security unit. Jason took the matter to the CSO hoping for a positive intervention. When the CSO seemed reluctant to intervene, Jason remarked, "What's a person supposed to do around here?" Without thinking, the CSO answered, "A man should do what he has to do."

Jason went back to his desk in anger. The anger festered for a week. A call came in for him from a headhunter. Before the month ended, Jason had resigned and relocated to another city, and the CSO never knew why.

Did the CSO err in the way he responded to Jason's request for intervention? Yes. Does the error prove poor leadership? Not necessarily. What the incident shows is how easy a good worker can be lost.

Basic to an understanding of human needs is the recognition that people respond to leaders, co-workers, and situations as perceived, not as they are in reality. Retention studies show that 70 to 80 percent of the reasons people leave companies are related to bosses [2].

The ambitious employee working for an unsupportive boss will look at the options: stay with the company and get nowhere, or leave the company and continue to pursue the personal dream. Of course, not all employees are ambitious or highly motivated. An employee may not have a personal goal or may see the job as absolutely essential to personal happiness. At the other extreme is the employee who has a goal so lofty that the job is viewed as inconsequential.

It is not enough for a leader to simply assign work. The work has to be organized in ways that facilitate needs. If an employee has a need to belong, he or she may find reward working alongside others; if the need is for self-esteem, reward may be found in having an important job title; and if ego satisfaction is the reward, the employee may find job happiness in being recognized. The leader in some respects acts as a broker who helps parties of differing aspirations reach a mutually satisfying agreement.

The leader who grasps Maslow's theory will appreciate that different employees have different needs and that their needs affect their output. The leader looks for the signs of needs and supervises accordingly.

PEOPLE DEVELOPMENT

Excellence in managing people is founded on a belief that group performance is a reflection of the people comprising the group, the point being that the effective CSO will help group members be the best they can be.

Encourage

Although a member's development is largely the result of personal effort, the leader plays a key role by encouraging the effort and offering opportunities (see also Figure 5-2). Encouragement is often a matter of letting people know where they stand at the moment, giving them a clear sense of a future that includes them, and showing that the company will help them develop so that they can participate in that future. Encouragement is also given by making decisions about people fairly, equitably, and in the context of performance. It involves communicating openly and honestly and rewarding those who excel. Subordinates worth keeping usually want to know the following.

- Where is this train going?
- What risks will I encounter along the way?
- When will we get there?
- What rewards will be mine personally?

Expect Excellence

Generating momentum for the development of subordinates is often achieved when the CSO expects excellence, is intolerant of substandard work, gives credit where it is due, and shoots for the highest star. The development of

---

You Know You Are A Poor Leader When...

You get more fun out of working a crossword than asking your employees how they're doing.

Your idea of freedom to work is not requiring employees to clock in on holidays.

Your top reward for an employee's outstanding work is a coupon for a Big Whopper.

An interviewee for a job learns your life story but you forget to ask why he wants the job.

An assistant says he can't get time to talk with you, and you tell him the world wasn't built in a day.

You invite subordinates and the CEO to a party at a posh restaurant and no one shows up.

An employee asks to know the long-range plan, and you send him to a fortune teller.

At a departmental meeting you show slides taken at your daughter's high school graduation.

You tell a subordinate to rate his own performance and then you argue with him about it.

You show up at the job, your card key doesn't work, and a stranger is sitting at your desk.

Figure 5-2 It sometimes helps to use humor when being self-critical.

people is a basic ingredient in the recipe for enhancing group performance. Some employees will seek self-development; others will avoid it. Some employees will merit development opportunities by demonstrating enthusiasm and exceptional performance; those with low enthusiasm and poor performance will not. Consider also the points made in Figure 5-3.

APPRAISING PERFORMANCE

Performance appraisal is the ongoing process of setting objectives and assessing individual and collective achievements during a finite period of time. It is primarily about counseling and feedback on ways to improve performance at an individual and team level and the quality of work relationships. Performance improvement results from people being clear about priorities and objectives, what skills need to be enhanced, and which types of behavior can help to this end. Clarity of purpose relies on open, positive, and constructive discussion between leaders and individuals, and agreement on how to do the job better.

In the appraisal process, a CSO evaluates, coaches, counsels, and develops subordinates on a continuing basis throughout the reporting period, usually one year. In the conduct of these activities, the leader's performance is subject to appraisal as well.

Setting Targets

Near the close or at the very beginning of the reporting period, the leader and his direct subordinates — individually or as a team — meet for the purpose of setting performance targets. Target setting ensures that the leader and the people to be rated are in agreement as to what should be achieved.

Target Qualities

The targets are specific, measurable, relevant, and time related. Although firm when formulated, they can be amended and supplemented throughout the reporting period. Although targets will consistently correspond with business results and expected standards of performance, they can vary according to the type of work involved. They can also relate to personal development. For example, the CSO may encourage a subordinate to attain the Certified Protection Professional (CPP) designation. Although attainment of this target may not directly relate to a specific work output, few can dispute the job relatedness of skills and knowledge acquired in pursuit of CPP status.

To the uninitiated, target setting may appear to be more trouble than it's worth. Targets can be difficult to formulate and sometimes impossible to agree upon. They cause problems when the leader and subordinates can't come to terms because the targets are irrelevant, unchallenging, or overly demanding.

People Management Standards

All employees must be taught the business context and their individual roles as team members.
The leader will:
- Have primary accountability and authority for leading, deploying, developing, coaching, and rewarding people.
- Show commitment and competence through active and visible participation in teamwork, openly communicating with employees, and networking with others.
- Continually build personal capabilities.

The company will have a bias toward retention of skills and protecting its investment in people.
The leader will:
- Systematically select and place competent employees.
- Use a variety of practices and methods to transfer skills and experience.
- Advertise employment opportunities.
- Utilize external re-sourcing after internal re-sourcing has been exhausted.
- Build relationships with, and maintain access to, external suppliers of specialized support and expertise.

Development of people is essential for improving business performance.
The leader will:
- Describe the performance contract and competitive position to individuals and teams with clear and agreed-upon objectives.
- Ensure sharing and learning from others including those outside the company.
- Assess individual and team performance. Provide clear feedback on performance delivery and improvement actions.
- Seek feedback from subordinates and peers via upward appraisal. Prioritize individual development objectives that improve skills and enable better performance and delivery through people.
- Identify employees with management and senior management potential early in their careers and participate in their development and deployment.
- Encourage personal development planning by individuals and coach them in their development and reality-check their plans.

The company will benefit to the extent that employees share in success.
The leader will:
- Provide a competitive base compensation and benefits package.
- Demonstrate the relationship between business, team, and individual performance and reward, and ensure understanding by all employees.
- Quantify annual reward to reflect business performance: for example, pay top bonuses for top performance.

People are an asset and an investment.
The leader will:
- Identify people risks, assess their consequences and probabilities, and set processes in place to address them.
- Audit the execution of people management standards to enable sharing of better practices and lessons learned and improve business performance.
- Ensure legal requirements are met.
- Support common systems to allow information to be shared and utilized.
- Identify responsibility for maintaining personnel records and systems that demand protection against unauthorized access.

Figure 5-3 This document is an example of senior management's direction to organizational leaders.

The leader might reject a subordinate's suggested targets on the grounds they lack sufficient work value, are not in line with business goals, or are simply too easy. The subordinate may resist the leader's targets when they are passed down from above like Moses' tablets and when they appear inflexible or laden with the risk of failure. Posing questions such as the following may be helpful to leader and subordinate alike in formulating a target.

- Does the target make good sense? Is it important to the subordinate, the leader, and the company?
- Does it mesh with group or company goals?
- Does the target fall within the CSO's area of responsibility and authority?
- Does it carry risks operationally? Financially?
- If questioned, will top management support the target?
- Is the subordinate capable of meeting the target?
- Can attainment of the target be verified in a measurable way?

For most jobs, six to 10 targets will be sufficient, and it is possible that some or all will change or evolve as work progresses. Targets will sometimes be contingent upon factors beyond the leader's ability to control, such as higher-level approval of a planned project, availability of funds or equipment, and a dependence upon the work of others outside the leader's supervision.

Focus on Action Steps

In determining targets, it is useful to focus on the action steps required for achievement. A single target can incorporate several action steps. If the target is to "develop and administer a training module for entry-level security officers," the action steps could include writing a lesson plan, preparing or acquiring audiovisuals, constructing a test to measure learning, setting a training schedule, arranging for the place of training and needed training equipment, preparing certificates of completion, and making a record of attendance and scores. Time frames or deadline dates can be established for each action step, can be programmed to occur in a particular sequence, and can be assigned to several individuals in a team effort.

Base and Stretch

Targets can be of two types: base and stretch. A base target involves tasks that are integral to the job and sometimes routine in nature. Writing a report of investigation is an integral part of a security investigator's job and is fairly routine, at least to the investigator. A productivity gain might be possible by performing this task in a different manner. The leader and his investigator may agree on a target calling for the investigator to revise the group's report writing method.

A stretch target goes beyond the norms of job expectations. It typically addresses a major problem, challenge, or opportunity, and its achievement

EMPLOYEE REVIEW

Employee Name: _____ Date: _____

Department: _____ Period of Review: _____

Reviewer: _____ Reviewer's Title: _____

	EXCELLENT	GOOD	FAIR	POOR
Honesty	☐	☐	☐	☐
Productivity	☐	☐	☐	☐
Work Quality	☐	☐	☐	☐
Technical Skills	☐	☐	☐	☐
Work Consistency	☐	☐	☐	☐
Enthusiasm	☐	☐	☐	☐
Cooperation	☐	☐	☐	☐
Attitude	☐	☐	☐	☐
Initiative	☐	☐	☐	☐
Working Relations	☐	☐	☐	☐
Creativity	☐	☐	☐	☐
Punctuality	☐	☐	☐	☐
Attendance	☐	☐	☐	☐
Dependability	☐	☐	☐	☐
Communication Skills	☐	☐	☐	☐

Comments: _____

_____

_____

Employee's Signature: _____ Reviewer's Signature: _____

Figure 5-4 A form such as this can be helpful in considering the pertinent aspects of an employee's performance.

can bring substantial reward to the organization. It may seek to raise quality, increase productivity, reduce costs, create new markets, and so on. Once the targets are set they need to be put into writing, and any later changes should be written down and acknowledged by the leader and subordinates with signatures or initials.

Reviewing Performance

At preestablished intervals, the CSO and the subordinate meet to review progress. The subordinate is invited to comment on performance with respect to the agreed-upon targets, highlighting areas of success, improvement, and difficulties encountered. A form such as that shown in Figure 5-4 might be used for this purpose.

A review meeting can be a time for revising, canceling, or creating targets in light of experience. The meeting is often documented, sometimes with the use of a form. The subordinate may be invited to comment (see Figure 5-5), such as offering suggestions about how performance on particular targets could be improved. The documentation can serve as a discussion point at the next review meeting. The usual practice is to not make any formal rating of the subordinate until the final review meeting of the reporting period.

Self-appraisal

Self-appraisal is often a standard element in an organization's system for performance evaluation. The benefits of asking for a self-appraisal in most cases outweigh any disadvantages produced by the requirement [3]. The following are advantages of a self-appraisal.

- The employee may be the best source of information about the quality of job performance.
- Self-appraisal increases the perception of fairness.
- Areas over which the rater and employee disagree can be highlighted.
- The process may help the employee gain personal insights as to success or failure.

The following are disadvantages of a self-appraisal.

- The employee may deliberately give a low rating in order to avoid disagreement with the rater.
- The employee may deliberately give a high rating in order to put pressure on the rater.
- When the employee and the rater disagree, bad feelings can result.
- The employee may dislike the idea of self-disclosure.

EMPLOYEE SELF-EVALUATION

Employee Name: _____   I.D. No: _____

Department: _____   Date: _____

List objectives you met or exceeded during this performance review period.

1. _____
2. _____
3. _____
4. _____

List objectives that you did not meet during this performance review period.

1. _____
2. _____
3. _____
4. _____

List your key strengths.

1. _____
2. _____
3. _____

List skills you need to develop further.

1. _____
2. _____
3. _____

List your primary goals and objectives for the next performance review period.

1. _____
2. _____
3. _____
4. _____

Figure 5-5 In appraising an employee's performance, the supervisor may see value in asking the employee to make a self-appraisal.

Performance Appraisal Cycle

Evaluation of performance is a process that continues uninterrupted. Although significant events relating to performance may occur at points over time and are certainly worthy of consideration, they are not the only criteria for making an overall judgment. The process described here operates cyclically; that is, it transitions to a starting point from the ending point of a previous period, passes through one or more phases marked by preestablished time intervals, and moves to the starting point of the next cycle.

Starting Point

The starting point for appraisal involves leader and subordinate agreeing on targets for the upcoming cycle, measures that will be used to evaluate performance, and meeting dates for the purpose of reviewing progress. Between quarterly reviews, the leader observes the subordinate's performance, obtains feedback from the subordinate, and provides appropriate guidance or assistance.

Quarterly Reviews

On specified dates — usually at the end of the first, second, and third quarters of the reporting period — leader and subordinate meet to compare performance against the targets. The targets are revised, if needed, and the subordinate is coached and counseled, if needed. During the final progress review, the subordinate's overall performance is considered, forming a foundation for a written performance rating.

Ending Point

The end of one cycle and the start of the next tend to blur. Between the final progress review and the end of the cycle, the leader selects a performance rating; writes the performance report and obtains the subordinate's comments and signature on the report; determines the subordinate's merit pay increase or bonus, if any; and begins to develop with the subordinate a new set of targets for the upcoming cycle.

Rating on Merit

A chief purpose of performance appraisal is to administer pay in a manner that takes into account the separate contributions of individual employees. Through a systematic rating procedure, usually called merit rating, a leader is able to make equitable decisions regarding monetary awards based on appraisal records. Despite recurring complaints about the imperfections of procedures that link performance to pay, such procedures are usually objective and provide information that often cannot be obtained any other way.

Objective and Quantitative

Merit ratings are designed to replace subjective general impressions with judgments that are formed from empirically derived evidence. Generally, the evidence is quantitative in nature, capable of analysis, and collected over a period of time such as one year. When soundly developed and systematically administered, merit ratings can stimulate the person being rated, particularly when the rating methodology provides opportunities for leader and subordinate to discuss ways and means for focusing performance on meaningful work outputs. This aspect of appraising is in the nature of making a "reality check."

A merit rating system requires the rater to make objective judgments and present supporting evidence. The rater is confronted with two questions: What is the standing of the rated person, relative to others, in terms of receiving a financial reward for work contributions? and, What proof is there to support that standing?

Unfortunately, the appraisal process is sometimes used only as a tool for making merit, salary, and promotion determinations, as opposed to harnessing the process to the larger issue of improving productivity. In some organizations, supervisors have come to view the appraisal process as a necessary evil to be endured. They admit the process may have some value to the human resources staff, but believe it has little value to the tasks of supervision or to the enhancement of work output. Appraising for some leaders becomes nothing more than filling out forms.

Conducted casually, performance appraisal can be destructive. Without a clear focus and a commitment at all levels, the process can poison leader/subordinate relationships and seriously detract from optimum productivity. The rater and the rated person can be soured on the process and management's credibility can be damaged.

EVALUATION IS ESSENTIAL

Evaluating human performance in the workplace is both essential and difficult. Evaluating is essential because it provides the data for making decisions that affect the profitability of the organization and the aspirations of employees. Evaluating is difficult because it is continuous, complex, and fraught with hazards at every turn. The negative outcomes of an imperfectly administered program can be substantial, but so also are the positive outcomes.

Upward Feedback

Upward feedback is a mechanism for communicating between leaders and their subordinates. The process is intended to be mutually beneficial and has

Figure 5-6 Upward feedback requires friendly collaboration.

the following four aims.

- Improve communication between the leader and his or her team
- Improve teamwork
- Identify management practices where change will result in managing people more effectively
- Create an action plan to which all members of the team can commit

Upward feedback (see Figure 5-6) is marked by open thinking, personal impact, empowerment, and networking, and can help a leader improve personal performance by obtaining a better understanding of how to lead others.

Upward feedback (see Figure 5-7) is sometimes called the 360-degree process when it evaluates the leader with input obtained from the leader's subordinates and peers. Management and communications skills are the primary performance factors assessed. A chief feedback criterion in the 360-degree review addresses whether subordinates are satisfied with their access to information about, and opportunities for, career advancement [4].

A leader's natural instinct may be to react to what at first appears to be personal criticism. After getting past the initial surprise, annoyance, and rationalization, the leader may be ready to listen to the feedback and accept help.

Obtain Subordinates' Ratings

The process usually begins by distributing a questionnaire to the leader's direct reports. The questionnaire is anonymous and contains questions relating to

UPWARD FEEDBACK QUESTIONNAIRE

Notice to person completing this questionnaire: Upward feedback plays an important part in the Company's performance appraisal process. The Company is now asking you to provide constructive feedback on your manager's leadership skills and abilities. Please be honest and confidential in your answers. Directly forward the completed form to the Human Resources Department.

Name of Manager: _____

Rating Scale

Strongly Agree	Agree	Disagree	Strongly Disagree
1	2	3	4

My manager:

____ Encourages me to suggest improvements in the way work is performed.
____ Obtains my reactions and suggestions before making a major change that may affect me.
____ Encourages me to express my concerns or doubts about a proposal under consideration.
____ Empowers me to do my job.
____ Identifies clear, attainable goals and objectives by stating what needs to be done and how.
____ Provides an environment that motivates me to achieve my goals and objectives.
____ Provides challenging opportunities that maximize the use of my skills.
____ Acts as a sounding board for ideas.
____ Recognizes and rewards innovation and creativity.
____ Enables good performance by clearing roadblocks and providing support.
____ Gives me opportunities for professional development and improvement of my skills.
____ Is flexible in management style.
____ Communicates corporate and departmental goals and objectives.
____ Acts as coach and mentor.
____ Builds a cohesive team.
____ Provides honest and constructive feedback about my performance.
____ Delegates effectively.
____ Conducts regular one-to-one feedback meetings.

Comments:

_____

_____

_____

_____

_____

_____

_____

_____

_____

_____

Figure 5-7 The upward feedback process focuses on leadership skills important to the business.

management practices that are widely held to be supportive of effective team-work. The person filling out the questionnaire is asked to rate each practice in certain dimensions; for example, the relative importance that the respondent places upon the practice and the degree to which the leader uses the practice.

The completed questionnaires are sent to an upward feedback adviser, who is usually a third party such as an outside consultant or a specialist within the organization's HR group. The questionnaires are scored, with significant variances noted. An example of a significant variance might be that the respondent considered conflict resolution within the team to be highly important but rated the leader very low in effectively resolving conflict. A report is generated in the scoring process. Such a report might present findings as numerical data such as bar charts and as short narratives describing outstanding strengths and weaknesses.

Upward Feedback Report

The report, which provides a snapshot of team members' perceptions, is the central topic of a one-on-one meeting between the leader and an upward feedback adviser. The leader sizes up the report's information, raises issues and questions with the adviser, identifies areas that need to be clarified, and develops an agenda and a plan to meet with the team to review the report.

The follow-up meeting with the team is chaired by the leader, with the adviser present to ease the comfort level of the attendees. The leader actively solicits observations and examples pertinent to the feedback report, listens carefully, and probes for understanding. The desired outcomes are for the leader to gain a true understanding of the feedback and determine a foundation for action.

Immediately following the team meeting, the leader and the adviser confer privately. They review and obtain clarity on what was said. The adviser provides objective commentary and assists the leader in "reading between the lines." The leader is led to explore areas in which change is appropriate and to make a personal commitment for improvement steps. The leader develops a draft of a realistic action plan that incorporates personal and team objectives.

Objectives for the Leader

Finally, the leader sets up a meeting with his or her boss to identify ways to fully support achievement of the objectives in the action plan. Included on the agenda is a discussion of the training, education, or other resources that may be needed to carry out the plan. The leader circulates the agreed-upon action plan to team members. This helps confirm that the feedback has been heard at a level higher than the leader and that commitments have been made to act on the key areas. Consider, for example, the following anecdote.

CASE STUDY

Sally is the chief security officer at a major hospital. She was accepted into the hospital's management development program consisting of formal instruction followed by a period of applied learning on the job. She filled out a pre-entry survey that asked her to rate her leadership ability. She considered herself reasonably skilled as a leader and thus gave herself an 8 on a 10-point rating scale. During the formal instruction, she was required to ask for feedback from her boss, peers, and direct reports. The feedback indicated she had significant leadership weaknesses to overcome. In light of what the development program taught her and what the feedback told her, Sally concluded that leadership was more difficult and complicated than she originally thought it to be. She finished the formal instruction, and per the requirements of the program set personal development goals. In the ensuing months, she noticed improvements in her working relationships and the overall performance of the security group. Then came her annual performance appraisal. A self-appraisal form asked her to rate herself on a 10-point scale. Sally gave herself a 7.

In a nutshell, upward feedback works best when [5]

- It is business driven.
- The organization needs the behaviors that are measured.
- The process reliably measures the leader's behaviors and matches them against the needed behaviors.
- Conditions exist for developing the behaviors.

EVALUATING POSITIONS

Position evaluation is the determination of an appropriate grade level for a specific position or job. Evaluation is focused on the nature of the job, not on the qualities of the job incumbent. Because grade level is the chief determinant of salary or wage and other job benefits, the process of position evaluation is both critical and sensitive. Certain key pieces of information are necessary to make an accurate evaluation. These include the following.

- The nature and function of the job
- How the job fits into the organization
- The extent of accountability built into the job, including the dimensions and quantity of accountability

Grade Level Determination

Grade level determination is an attempt to systematize or make objective what would otherwise be a subjective endeavor. Management, in trying to sort out and make sense of the comparative values of different work functions, recognizes that the best that can be done is to introduce a sense of order into making what are essentially human judgments. Although many evaluation schemes use numbers and other seemingly objective criteria (see Figure 5-8), the process is more art than science.

POSITION DESCRIPTION

Position Title: _____

Name of Incumbent: _____

Department: _____

Location: _____

Supervisor: _____

Position Number	_____
Approved By	_____
Date Approved	_____

MAJOR DUTIES

1. _____

_____

2. _____

_____

3. _____

_____

4. _____

_____

5. _____

_____

ORGANIZATIONAL RELATIONSHIPS

This position reports to: _____

The direct reports for this position are: _____

The organizational peers for this position are: _____

COMPLEXITIES OF THE POSITION

(Circle One)   Very Simple   Simple   Complex   Very Complex   Highly Complex

IMPACT OF THE POSITION ON THE ORGANIZATION'S MISSION

(Circle One)   Very Low   Low   Average   High   Very High

POSITION DATA

Number of Employees Supervised: _____   Annual Budget: _____

Education Required: _____   Years of Experience Required: _____

Training and/or Certifications Required: _____

COMMENTS

_____

_____

_____

Figure 5-8 A position description form describes the essential characteristics of a job.

Position Description

A position description will usually contain the following.

- Identifying details such as job title, department, location, and so forth
- A description of the overall purpose and chief objectives of the position and the nature of activities such as production, maintenance, sales, or special projects
- Organizational relationships that identify the person to whom the position reports and those reporting to the position
- The annual budget of the activity performed, the number of employees supervised, the nature and amount of funds that are affected by the incumbent, licensing, education and experience requirements, and the extent and nature of contacts maintained by the incumbent
- Principal accountabilities performed in accomplishing the overall purpose and chief objectives of the job

Position evaluation is the process of comparing, ranking, and evaluating jobs by the use of specific qualitative and quantitative factors that include mental and physical skills, degrees of responsibility, and working conditions. It is the job that is evaluated, not the person performing it. An evaluation acceptable to an employer and an employee is used as a basis for determining pay and terms of employment.

NOTES

1. Maslow's propositions were offered in an article titled "A Theory of Human Motivation," which appeared in *Psychological Review*, pp. 370–396, 1943.

2. Polly Schneider, "Are You a Bad Boss?," *CIO*, April 1, 2000, pp. 142.

3. Dick Grote, *The Complete Guide to Performance Appraisal*, pp. 236, New York: AMACOM, 1996.

4. Mindy Blodgett, "Teaching Johnny To Lead," *CIO*, November 15, 1999, pp. 80.

5. Walter W. Tornow, *Maximizing the Value of 360-Degree Feedback*, pp. 76, San Francisco: Jossey-Bass Publishers, 1998.

6. Budget Management

Trust, but verify.
—Ronald Reagan

THE BUDGET

A budget is a forecast of expenditures and revenues for a specific period of time. Because a budget sets priorities and monitors progress toward selected goals, it is a basic planning tool. A budget helps a CSO make informed decisions on the management of people and assets in the security group. Typically, the CSO prepares the budget on the basis of estimates to meet priorities for the next fiscal year. The estimates reflect inflationary pressure and current year spending.

The budget is presented to the CSO's supervisor, who may modify the estimates and rearrange priorities. The supervisor delegates to the CSO formal authority to enter into financial obligations at certain agreed dollar levels. An independent body within the company, such as a financial control group, generally monitors security expenditures to ensure they are consistent with organizational objectives. In any operation of size and complexity, budgeting will be a routine, yet essential, element of planning from year to year. The following three purposes stand out.

- Estimate the costs of planned activities.
- Provide a warning mechanism when variances occur in actual costs.
- Exercise uniformity in the matter of fiscal control.

The budgeting process has four distinct stages: preparation, authorization, execution, and audit.

Preparation

An annual budget places on the CSO the responsibility of preparing security group estimates and coordinating them with overall company planning. The CSO and his/her supervisor meet, sometimes with key security group staff present, to discuss planned activities. It is not unusual to begin as early as six months in advance of the next fiscal year.

Security budget preparation begins with targets and ends with binding commitments. Outlays and spending authority are usually categorized by functions such as security officer operations, investigations, and physical security inspections. New spending requests, even when approved at the next higher level, tend to be very critically examined.

Preparation includes obtaining buy-in from groups dependent on or affected by security group activities. Garnering buy-in is typically informal: phone calls, e-mails, memoranda, and one-on-one meetings. The CSO's primary aim is to identify essential security services that have not already been addressed. A secondary aim is to identify objections that may surface later, when the time for patching up has passed.

Authorization

Authorization begins by obtaining supervisory approval. Preceding approval may be meetings with peers. Peers head up groups and report to the same supervisor. It is very likely that a peer will be a security services customer and therefore will have a stake in the security enterprise and a right to offer input.

The next step is to present the proposed budget to a budget review committee composed of specialists from the company's finance group. The review committee typically asks to receive the proposed budget for study in advance of one or more discussion meetings to follow. The CSO's budget proposal is detailed item by item and thoroughly documented. Details address projected activities, purposes and benefits, and likely consequences if activities are not funded adequately.

When the CSO presents the proposed budget in person, he/she uses a mild combination of negotiation and persuasion. Several such meetings ensue before the budget review committee sends the proposed budget to a higher level for final decision. The decision will certainly involve the chief financial officer (CFO) and possibly others on the executive team.

Execution

The budget begins at the start of the fiscal year. The CSO's responsibility is to ensure effective and efficient performance of security group functions while at the same time keeping costs in line with the budget.

At one point or another, the CSO may find it necessary to amend the budget; for example, when an unanticipated event requires the expenditure of unbudgeted funds. In the business of security, unanticipated events are the norm rather than the exception. The CSO will send a funding request up the chain of command.

Other amendments can occur. Unspent funds in one account can be moved to another account short of funds, not unlike a shopper that moves money from one pocket to another. In some cases in some organizations, the CSO can make such transfers on his/her authority. They must, however, be documented. Although formal and closely managed, a budget is in a constant state of change, and not all changes bring added funds. In times of economic stress, the CSO may be required to cut spending.

Audit

A budget is audited during execution by the CSO and the company's accounting group. The CSO keeps track of spending almost as it occurs. Every invoice or bill signed by the CSO is copied and placed in a file. Auditing by the accounting group is largely a matter of recording payments made to fund security group activities. A record is prepared monthly. When significant variances appear, the accounting group informs the CSO. When variances increase or are not corrected, the accounting group notifies the CSO's supervisor. The security group's budget can also be examined by the company's audit office for one or two reasons: as a routine control measure or as a formal investigation of suspicious irregularities.

THE BUDGET DIRECTOR

A budget director brings all group budgets into a comprehensible whole called the master budget. It is an overall forecast of transactions within a given period, set up in a manner that delivers to senior management timely reports of financial results. The master budget enables the preparation of financial statements such as the income statement and balance sheet [1].

The process of budget preparation at the group level adheres to a methodology specified by the budget director. Group leaders identify and justify their planned activities and estimate costs. The format and dollar figures of proposed budgets are developed according to a common framework. Without it, the auditing function would be hampered and the master budget difficult to comprehend.

The prescribed methodology of the common framework and the actual budget are two different things: the first is a tool and the second is the object crafted by the tool. A budget is purpose driven and function conscious. The form of budgeting specified by the budget director will correspond to organizational goals and the functions necessary to reach them. Selection of the budgeting approach can be influenced also by history and experience ("the way we've always done it"), tax implications, and the preferences of the executive team and the board of directors. Major spending decisions can be made at the board level but are most often made by the executive team. The budget director reports to the CFO, a member of the executive team.

ZERO-BASED BUDGETING

Zero-based budgeting starts with an assumption that zero dollars are available. Dollars become available when proof is presented that an activity is necessary to the business. Implied in the approach is a requirement to explore alternatives for achieving the same or similar results at a lower cost. Group leaders, including the CSO, make their case by answering three questions: What is the purpose of the activity? What will it cost? What is the added value? Benefits that can be derived from the activity are weighed against cost. The CSO makes the argument that benefits will be lost or that undesirable consequences will come about if an activity is not funded or funded at a lesser level.

Zero-based budgeting forces the CSO to look at different levels of effect associated with carrying out an activity. The levels may range from minimum to optimum. At each spending level, the CSO would show the costs of the activity, the predicted value, and the effects likely to be experienced by increases or decreases in spending. The CSO could be required to describe the probable outcomes of operating a guard force at different spending levels. The manager's description to the budget committee might appear as follows.

GUARD FORCE OPERATIONS

Option 1: Operate at an Optimum Level of Security

This level of activity for guard service at the Corporate Tower includes coverage on a 24-hour basis with guard positions as follows.

- Security supervisor
- Console operator
- Front desk officer
- Office area patrol
- Garage patrol
- Cleaning patrol

Guard service functions at the optimum level of activity include the following.

- Immediate response by an experienced supervisor to serious incidents such as fire, bomb threats, injurious accidents, illness, and violence
- Uninterrupted monitoring of console equipment (such as CCTV monitors, access control and intrusion detection alarm systems, and fire alarm systems) and the initiation of immediate requests for assistance from fire and law enforcement departments and emergency medical treatment agencies
- Prompt processing of visitors to the Tower

- Prompt opening of locked offices and conference rooms with use of the security officer master key
- Identification and immediate correction of safety and security hazards in the offices areas, such as electric heaters and coffee makers left on and access control doors propped open
- In building evacuation situations, assistance to fire wardens such as directing employees down stairwells, carrying incapacitated or injured occupants to safety, and directing street traffic to allow deployment of fire trucks around the Tower
- Prevention of assault, theft, and vandalism in the Tower garage
- Escorting contract janitors while they work on floors containing sensitive information

The total annual cost for this level of activity is $1,500,000. [Note: At this point the CSO would make reference to an attached document reflecting a breakdown of the total annual cost, such as salaries, benefits, and equipment. The same note would follow Options 2 through 4.] The effects of operating at the optimum level are as follows.

- Security officer manpower will be sufficient to meet increasing security demands such as those now being made by the recently formed Research and Development Group.
- The company will be in compliance with City Fire Code in respect to emergency evacuation of the Tower.
- Employee complaints alleging lack of security in the garage will be reduced if not eliminated.
- The risk to sensitive information posed by unaccompanied janitors will be eliminated.

Option 2: Operate at the Current Level of Security

This level of activity for guard service at the Corporate Tower includes coverage with guard positions as follows.

- Console operator
- Front desk officer
- Office area patrol

Guard service functions at the current level of activity include the following.

- On-and-off monitoring of console equipment
- Processing of visitors to the Tower, with occasional delay
- Opening of locked offices and conference rooms with use of the security officer master key; some delays must be expected
- Identification and immediate correction of safety and security hazards in the offices

continued

The total annual cost for this level of activity is $85,000. The effects of operating at the current level are as follows.

- Security officer manpower is not able to meet increasing security.
- The company is not in full compliance with City Fire Code in respect to emergency evacuation of the Tower.
- Employee complaints of poor security in the garage will continue. Assault, theft, and vandalism are possible.
- The risk to sensitive information posed by unaccompanied janitors is possible. The cost for offsetting the risk is considerably less than the loss that will be experienced if sensitive information is damaged, destroyed, or compromised.

Option 3: Operate at a Lower Level of Security

This level of activity for guard service at the Tower includes coverage on a 10-hours-per-day basis, normal working days only, with guard positions as follows.

- Console operator
- Front desk officer
- Office area patrol

Guard service functions at this level of activity include the following.

- On-and-off monitoring of console equipment
- Processing of visitors to the Tower, with occasional delays expected
- Opening of locked offices and conference rooms with use of the security officer master key; delays expected
- Identification but not immediate correction of safety and security hazards in the offices

The total annual cost for this level of activity is $65,000. The effects of operating below the current level are as follows.

- Security officer manpower will not be able to maintain a reasonable level of security. Given the number and nature of security reports made in the past year concerning breaches of security (i.e., an assault in the garage, auto theft, auto vandalism, unauthorized entry, and theft of equipment), it is possible to foresee the occurrence of similar crimes, and a failure to address crime with preventive measures can result in civil liability.
- The company will not be in full compliance with City Fire Code in respect to emergency evacuation of the Tower.
- A 10-hour day for security operations will very likely result in contract janitors being on the premises with no oversight except

that provided by their employer. Theft of assets, including information and equipment, is a possibility.

WARNING: The differential in costs between Options 2 and 3 is insignificant in comparison to losses that would very probably result under Option 3. Also, in the opinion of the CSO, any reduction in security below Option 3 would have nearly the same effect as having no security at all.

Not shown in this example is an option to eliminate the security program entirely, an option that the executive team could very well direct the CSO to consider and reply to in writing (not a pleasant chore for a CSO that values the job).

Directions Flow Down

Directions on major budget issues flow from the top down and requests for funding flow upward. Directions passed downward tend to deal with both administrative and substantive matters. Administrative matters provide guidance as to the format of the budget document, the placement of particular costs into particular categories, the attachment of supporting documentation, and the deadlines for submitting drafts.

Limitations

Substantive matters can include limitations, such as no new hires, no purchases without prior authority, and no increase of the group budget beyond a certain level (e.g., not more than 5 percent above the total budget of the current year). Figure 6-1 points out the differences between traditional and zero-based budgeting.

A down-and-then-up-again pattern is usually the case before a group's budget is set in stone. The CSO meets multiple times with multiple functionaries. At one meeting, the budget is okay; at the next meeting, it is not okay. At every meeting, the CSO pleads his/her case. Nearly every meeting is called the "final" meeting, which turns out to be not the case. Because the CSO never knows if the next meeting will be the final meeting, he/she has to approach it as if it were a "last chance."

Cost/Benefit Ratio

A request for a major purchase may require approval by a spending authority separate from the budget committee. A major purchase not reflected in a budget is called an "exception to the budget." A preparatory step in considering

Traditional v. Zero-Based Budgeting

Traditional	Zero-Based
Oriented to a function or a department.	Oriented to programs and projects.
How much do you want?	How much do you need for what and why?
Focused on new incremental programs.	All programs, old and new, compete for the same scarce resources.
Extrapolate past spending.	Programs and projects are presented as decision packages.
Increment for inflation.	Inflation is reflected in the decision packages.
Reduce spending by trimming across the board.	Eliminate low-ranked packages.
Fuzzy linkages to the organization's goals and objectives.	Decision packages clearly reflect organizational goals and objectives.
The end product is an aggregated set of numbers difficult to understand.	The end product is a lean set of ranked priorities that can be changed as circumstances warrant.
Internal politics, gamesmanship, selling, and negotiating adversely influence approval.	The decision packages speak for themselves.
Needed trimming can be offset by deliberately inflating numbers that are difficult to verify.	Inflated numbers stand out.
In the scramble for scarce resources, the cogency of requests is blurred by emotions.	The options are laid open for discussion and evaluation in a businesslike atmosphere.
At the end, the management decides who gets how much.	The end is determined by the persuasiveness of the decision packages.
Corporate infighting leads to low morale, turnover, decreased productivity, etc.	Personal feelings can be put to the side when decision packages correspond to the organization's goals and resource limitations.
Spending is easily monitored and controlled.	Spending is easily monitored and controlled. More importantly, decision packages can be evaluated according to results achieved.

Figure 6-1 Note the differences between traditional budgeting and zero-based budgeting.

a large expenditure is to determine the cost/benefit ratio, a figure computed by dividing costs by benefits. To illustrate:

- An access control system costs $500,000 to purchase.
- The service life of the system is 10 years.
- Guards replaced by the system result in a saving of $100,000 per year.
- The cost/benefit ratio is therefore 0.5:1, meaning that the cost of the purchase is half the benefits or that the benefits are twice as great as the costs.

The ratio was arrived at by multiplying the annual guard cost savings by the number of years of useful service of the access control system. This figure

($1,000,000) represents the benefit, and is divided into the cost of the system ($500,000). Benefit versus cost is 0.5. When the ratio is less than 1, it is favorable, and unfavorable when it is higher than 1.

CONTROLLING COSTS

Apart from the process of budget preparation and approval is the day-to-day task of maintaining a budget folder. This folder is informal and a device of convenience. Placed into the folder are invoices, statements, price quotes, purchase orders, sales receipts, notes and memos concerning expenditures, and like items. Monthly, the accounting group sends to the CSO a computer-prepared summary that (1) reflects spending for the previous month and year-to-date, (2) compares those figures against the budget's planned expenditures, and (3) highlights variances. The CSO is expected to take action when actual spending exceeds planned spending by a significant amount. The action is to put a brake on spending, if possible; if not possible, the CSO submits a request to increase the budget, a request that is never warmly received.

OVERSPENDING

Overspending is frequently the result of poor planning. Failing to anticipate rises in the costs of essential products and services or incorrectly calculating how many and how much of each will be needed is somewhat forgivable. Underspending for a budget item is rarely a problem; overspending is an indication of poor money-managing skills. Figures 6-2 through 6-5 show various forms used to track and control spending.

NOTES

1. The income statement summarizes the company's revenues, expenses, gains, and losses. The balance sheet shows the value of a company's assets, liabilities, and equity as of a certain date. The value of the assets is equal to the combined value of the liabilities and equity.

BUSINESS EXPENSE REPORT

Employee Name: _____   Title: _____   Department: _____   Building: _____

Phone/Extension: _____   Supervisor: _____   Purpose of trip: _____

Date	Description	Tickets	Hotel	B'fast	Lunch	Dinner	Trans.	Entertain	Misc.	TOTAL
SUBTOTALS										

LESS EXPENSE ADVANCE AND CHARGES TO COMPANY

TOTAL DUE ME (COMPANY)

Employee Signature: _____   Title: _____   Date: _____

Approval Signature: _____   Title: _____   Date: _____

Figure 6-2 The business expense report is a means of keeping track of expenses related to travel.

AUTO EXPENSE REPORT

Employee Name: _____ Title: _____

Phone/Extension: _____ Supervisor: _____ Month of: _____

DATE	ODOMETER		MILEAGE X .35	GAS/OIL	PKG/ TOLLS	MISC.	TOTAL
	START	STOP					
	TOTALS						

LESS CASH ADVANCE & CHARGES TO COMPANY ☐

BALANCE DUE ME (COMPANY) ☐

IF SUBMITTED AS AN EXPENSE REPORT, ATTACH RECEIPTS AND SIGN BELOW		
Employee Signature:	Title:	Date:
Approval Signature:	Title:	Date:

Figure 6-3 The auto expense report is a means of monitoring expenses related to business travel by automobile.

WEEKLY TIME SHEET

WEEK ENDING:

Employee Name: Title:

I.D. No: Status (Temporary, non-exempt):

Department: Supervisor:

DATE	START TIME	END TIME	REGULAR HRS.	OVERTIME HRS.	TOTAL HRS.
		WEEKLY TOTALS			

Employee Signature: Date:

Supervisor Signature: Date

Figure 6-4 The weekly time sheet is a record of hours worked by an employee.

MONTHLY BUDGET REPORT

Spending By Category	Actual This Month	Projected This Month	Actual Year-to-Date	Projected Year-to-Date
Salaries/Benefits/Payroll Tax/Overtime				
Temporary Labor				
Contract Labor				
Monetary Awards				
Travel Expenses				
Rent				
Personnel Development and Training				
Moving Expenses				
Office Supplies				
Office Furniture and Equipment Purchases				
Furniture and Equipment Rentals				
Software Purchases and Maintenance				
Computer Supplies				
Computer Services (Vendor)				
Freight and Express				
Telephone				
Philanthropic and Miscellaneous Contributions				
Professional Memberships and Certifications				
Subscriptions and Publications				
Professional Meetings				
Recruiting and Relocation				
Totals				

Figure 6-5 A report of this type, including actual numbers, is computer-generated—with copies sent to the responsible manager and others holding budget oversight and management responsibilities.

7. Managing Change

Change is the progress by which the future invades our lives.
—Alvin Toffler

CHARACTERISTICS OF CHANGE

The pace and magnitude of change in the security industry can be overwhelming at times. Demands on CSOs to transition to new ways of getting the job done seem to arrive unexpectedly, often with short deadlines and high expectations of success. Change, like the redesign of the organization's structure and the adoption of advanced technology, also seems to arrive during periods of constrained resources. Although natural and inevitable, change has taken on dimensions of size and complexity not seen before. To manage change effectively, the CSO has to recognize certain truths inherent to change. Among these are the following [1].

- Change defies the status quo and creates dynamics that have to be managed.
- The processes of change are predictable and transferable as knowledge.
- Change in work practices cannot be achieved without the commitment and willingness of those who perform the work.
- Consultation and collaboration are more effective in carrying out change than is the case with traditional approaches such as issuing directives and monitoring for compliance.
- Change must not be judged by occurrence but by consequences.
- Change is a permanent feature of modern management.

Impact and Context

Although these truths stand firm, change varies in impact and context. When the Justice Department ordered the breakup of AT&T into "baby Bells," a great shock rippled through the organization, the communications industry, Wall Street, and telephone customers. In contrast, a barely perceptible ripple would follow a decision to switch from employing personal secretaries to employing secretarial pools. Both actions represent change, but change of markedly different magnitudes. The contexts in the two examples are also very different. In the first case, the rules of the game were altered; in the second case, the manner of work was altered. Varying impacts and contexts call for varying approaches. An analytical question-and-answer drill for finding an approach might work as follows [2].

- What is the problem that is to be solved by the change? What is the change exactly? What are its dimensions, how amenable is it to implementation and control, and what impact will it have on work processes?
- Who are the significant people? Who will do the implementing and controlling and who will be most affected by it? Who will be the willing participants? Who will oppose the change? Who are the organization's gatekeepers?
- What other changes are in progress that will impact this change? Will the impacts be positive or negative? Can other changes be incorporated by or linked to this change?

Analysis along these lines can be very helpful in mapping out action steps to engineer the change. The map, or plan of action, is updated as the change evolves. This is because the goal of change is not to attain change for the sake of change but to solve problems. This explains why change is not a one-time event but a process of constant improvement. Rarely can we perfectly solve a problem. Just getting to the 80-percent level of improvement can be a marvelous reward. But the change process does not stop there; it evolves in form, striving to attain the last 20 percent.

Working Through People

Change can occur only through people willing to accept it and make it work well. The CSO, who is constantly affected by change and who is sometimes the engineer of it, works by necessity through people at all levels of the organization. Today it might be a physical security safeguard installed here and a planning idea planted there; tomorrow it might be counseling caution at one place and recommending action at another. The CSO's influence in the organization is deep and broad, yet at the same time sharply focused on the security group. Discussion with team members (e.g., direct reports and supervisors of key functions) and within teams (e.g., security officer operations, investigations, and physical security) is essential to building a consensus. A meeting typically begins with arguments for and against, moves to a common ground for agreement, and ends with clearly understood objectives and individually accepted responsibilities. The outcomes of the meeting are understood by all to be group owned. Consider, for example, the following anecdote.

CASE STUDY

CSO Jim Smithers listened carefully as Alex Harcourt, the company's head lawyer, complained that reports prepared by security group investigators were just not good enough.

Harcourt said, "The reports are entirely narrative, filled with opinion, and lack a consistent format. Also, my secretary has to search through each report to find discrete facts, like dollar loss and date of occurrence."

"I'll take care of it," Smithers replied. He went back to his office and drew up an investigative report form he believed would satisfy Harcourt, a key organizational player and end user of the security group's investigative output. Smithers shared the new report form with Terry Allen, head of the security group's investigations unit. The form was disseminated from Allen to the investigators, along with a memo ordering the change.

A week later, Harcourt told Smithers, "The report form you made is not what I had in mind. The problem remains the same, except that the investigators are now making errors in spelling and punctuation. You've got to find a solution."

Smithers went to Allen's office. Allen defended his investigators, saying they were unhappy with the change and offended by not being consulted. In addition, he said they placed blame on the security officer unit. In too many cases, faulty data contained in guard reports led to poor investigative reports.

Smithers went back to his office and began making notes. "Who are most affected by the problem? Harcourt and his secretary for sure. Who else? Probably other recipients of investigative reports such as the head of the human resources department and the head auditor. I'll have to check on that. Who is able to solve the problem? Again, Harcourt and his secretary. Their views are essential to defining a report. Then there is Allen and his investigators, plus the head of the security officer unit. Who will oppose the change? Don't know yet, but one or a few investigators are likely to resist change. Who are the gatekeepers? Harcourt and the head of human resources are gatekeepers and have the muscle to push through a change, provided I can come up with a solution they can agree on.

"Can and should this change be linked to other changes in progress? Hey, the company has just announced an electronic forms system designed to cut back on paperwork. Maybe I can tie the investigator's report form into that system. Maybe tie in the security officer report form as well. Have to be concerned about confidentiality, though. Still, it's worth checking into. Need to talk with the head of information technology. Add her to the list of people involved in effecting a solution."

A confident smile tugged at the corners of the CSO's face as he placed a call to the legal department. "Alex? Jim Smithers here. Concerning the report problem, I'd like to get some people together to brainstorm this thing. I wonder if you and your secretary would. . ." Smithers was on a new track to managing change and he felt confident about it.

TEAMWORK IN EFFECTING CHANGE

Teamwork is essential to managing change, and the CSO engenders it via the following.

- Creating an atmosphere that encourages open discussion
- Persuading, listening, reflecting, and demonstrating flexibility
- Ensuring that the people who have accepted change-creating tasks possess the requisite knowledge and skills
- Empowering people to act, giving them trust and encouragement, and supporting them logistically
- Helping people improve performance of their change-creating tasks by affording developmental opportunities
- Addressing conflicts fairly and openly and resolving them with integrity
- Allowing people to learn from their mistakes without fear of punishment

Team confidence is a natural by-product of the constructive exchange of ideas and assurance that conflicts can be raised and resolved fairly. High confidence and high morale are not by themselves guarantors of good results, however.

Success in managing change requires three attributes. First is the ability to create a sense of teamwork and functionality. This involves helping team members do their individual jobs well and in harmony with one another. It also means delegating authority to make task-related decisions. A second attribute is the ability to create within the team a high expectation of service delivery. Excellence is the sole criterion; good work is not good enough. Third is an ability to correctly evaluate team performance. Note also that feedback from the team to the CSO is useful. Security officers, for example, are superb conduits for obtaining evaluations from the users of security officer services. "How are we doing?" is an easy-to-ask question that can produce valuable insights.

Familiar But Not Understood

CSOs as a class are quite familiar with change. Outsourcing, downsizing, and terrorism are but a few of the major changes that in the past three decades have impacted security operations, and the pressure for change continues unabated. Yet for all of their experience in dealing with change, CSOs do not commonly share an understanding of it and have not developed a uniform approach to managing it.

In some cases, very necessary change is avoided. For example, the public's demands for high standards in the selection and training of security officers are largely unheeded. A majority of the major companies in the security officer industry resist standards despite the success of initiatives to establish standards. Upgrades in security officer standards have been minor, long in coming, and driven for the most part by exasperated legislatures. Even when change is crucial, it is often resisted, and for wrong reasons.

Change driven by professional values can enjoy wide acceptance, whereas change driven by forces external to the profession — such as law-making bodies and regulatory agencies — is apt to be regarded as impossible to reconcile with professionalism. Whatever the source and however regarded, change demands an understanding of how to make things work for the better.

Poor Approaches

Not knowing how to manage change, the human inclination is to use rewards and punishment. In this approach, the change is announced, implemented with operating procedures, periodically evaluated, revised, and driven by a system of rewards and punishment. This approach rarely works because it ignores the need for workers to understand why the change is needed and how it can impact them personally.

Change is sometimes attempted by running a pilot project. After the bugs have been worked out, the project is launched and propelled at full speed.

Tips on Managing Change

Don't try to control everything all the time.

Focus on the purpose of change.

Avoid changing more than necessary and changing the wrong things. Unnecessary change increases the probability of unintended consequences.

Expend more effort working through cooperative people and less effort overcoming resistance.

Do not rely on structural change to obtain practice change.

Change has value only to the extent that it solves a problem.

Figure 7-1 The dos and don'ts of managing change.

Scant attention is given to collateral effects; all that matters is to move forward. The occurrence of change is evidence of success. The consequences of change are forgotten.

Another poor attempt is the copycat approach, which is to replicate change processes used by like organizations. This essentially quick-fix approach overlooks the complexities of change management. Figure 7-1 points out some dos and don'ts of managing change.

TECHNOLOGY AND CHANGE

Technology has always been a primary driving force of business change. An organization's market, mode of operation, and competitive climate can be radically altered by the emergence of a new technology. As an agent of change, technology can be called disruptive because it disturbs the status quo, in some cases to the point of threatening an organization's survival [3]. The printing press, steam engine, horseless carriage, flying machine, and personal computer are examples of technologies that were highly disruptive when first introduced.

It is also evident that a technology can be affected by the way in which an organization uses it. Assume, for example, that the CSO purchases a software application that tracks the status and makes a record of each incident handled by the security group. The application works well except that it does not categorize incidents by type, frequency, and amount of loss per category. The CSO learns that other security groups have the same need. The CSO communicates the need to the software manufacturer. The application is modified. This is an example of an organization affecting a technology (see Figure 7-2).

POLITICS AND CHANGE

Change at the front end is not like change at the back end. What was first contemplated may bear little resemblance to the final result. The cause can

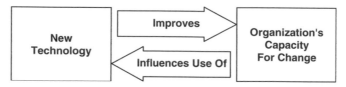

Figure 7-2 New technology and the organization interact with one another.

be politics, the process by which people exercise and resist power. We tend to think of politics as an adversarial game played between democrats and republicans, which it is, and are unmindful of politics in the business venue. Politics inside a business organization can be invisible yet enormous in effect. It can be a force for driving change, as well as thwarting it. The practice of politics is not limited to the corporate boardroom. It is practiced by people and groups throughout the entire organization. The following is a case in point.

CASE STUDY

Mike Cascio is the chief security officer of Kwal-Buy, a company that owns and operates a thousand convenience stores in a 10-state area. The stores are located in urban areas and are open for business 18 hours a day. In the previous five years, more than two-thirds of the stores were burglarized, robbed, or had an assault incident on the premises. Inventory shrinkage by reason of employee and customer theft was a loss producer in all stores. Before Mike was hired as CSO, Kwal-Buy had urged store operators to install anti-crime equipment such as drop safes, CCTV, and alarms for duress, robbery, and burglary. Kwal-Buy treated each store as an independent profit center, meaning that if a store chose to purchase security equipment and services the costs came out of the pocket of the store operator.

In Mike's periodic visits to stores, he noted that many had no robbery and burglary alarms at all, many had partial systems, and some had inoperable or faulty systems. Some stores had overpaid for the equipment and almost all were being charged higher-than-average fees for alarm monitoring services. Mike also noted problems in lighting, obstructed views, and security training of store employees. A common sentiment of the store operator was, "I know that security is important but I don't feel like I should pick up the tab for it."

After comparing security-related loss numbers against security-related costs, Mike was convinced that even a modest improvement in security would more than pay for itself. He consulted with alarm equipment manufacturers and learned that by purchasing a standard system (CCTV/robbery alarm/burglary alarm) in a quantity of not less than 250, the per-system price would be half the average price being paid by store operators. Mike also priced the cost of purchasing, installing, and operating alarm monitoring equipment, for which there was plenty of room in the security center at Kwal-Buy's corporate offices. Quotes obtained from three major alarm installation and maintenance firms revealed that the security center and every store could be serviced uniformly and cost effectively.

The plan that unfolded in Mike's head involved a change outside Kwal-Buy's experience. It went like this. Kwal-Buy would make an initial purchase of 250 alarm systems plus one central alarm monitoring system. Kwal-Buy would hire a firm to install the central alarm monitoring system at the corporate offices and to install the alarm systems at stores that wished to have them. Annual troubleshooting and service would be included. Store operators would not pay for the equipment, installation, or service. They would, however, pay a monthly fee to Kwal-Buy for alarm monitoring.

Mike's calculations showed that if he could institute his program (i.e., the change) in 150 stores in the first year and 100 more stores in the second year he would generate revenues from alarm monitoring services equal to the costs of the equipment, the installation, and the labor involved in manning the central alarm monitoring system. In the third year, the program would generate revenues sufficient to begin returning added value to store operators in various forms, such as purchases of drop safes, improvements to security lighting, security signage, counsel on security practices, and training store employees in loss prevention techniques. Before the end of eight years, accumulated revenues would be sufficient to update/replace existing equipment. Best of all, Mike concluded, Kwal-Buy and the store operators would reduce losses linked to robbery, burglary, assault, and theft.

How will Mike make the change happen? He has had no experience as a change maker but he has watched others engineer change, particularly in the political arena. Mike decides to proceed as if he were a candidate for public office [4]. Winning the office will be his metaphor for effecting the change.

Mike's platform for election is his vision to provide security to stores in a way that rewards everybody. He describes a new practice that will reduce costs and therefore enhance profits. His campaign is the combined efforts he makes to sell the vision. He sells by conferring one-on-one with store operators and corporate managers, making presentations at company meetings, forming and steering a task force, and taking advantage of every opportunity to explain his vision. He develops a standard speech, a highly focused bulleted points memo, overhead transparencies, slides, posters, newsletters, and e-mail messages.

Mike's campaign identifies the supporters and the detractors. He concentrates on eliciting the help of people who are willing and in a position to champion his cause. He gets people involved to a degree that they take a proprietary interest.

Mike has to overcome a natural tendency of people and organizations to cling to the past. The unproven nature of Mike's vision is unsettling to some and downright heresy to others. Election day is around the corner and Mike is concerned. He conducts a poll by talking personally to his constituents, many of whom he has calculatedly pursued from the start. They were targeted early on because they held authority, either formally or informally. These are the movers and shakers and influence makers. Mike worries some will lose their enthusiasm.

Election day arrives and, hallelujah, Mike gets the nod to move ahead. He has planned for this day. Potential problems in execution have been anticipated and put to rest. Mike knows, however, that a single misstep can be fatal to the attainment of his vision and thus treads carefully. Contingency options are in place to sidestep obstacles. He worries most of all about the candidates he has defeated. Will they continue to oppose him? Mike knows he will be watched and that some of his opponents may be looking for opportunities to sabotage his efforts, but he takes none of this personally.

He decides to move slowly at first and pick up speed gradually. He will know when the time has passed for the go-ahead to be canceled. He wants to get to the point of no return quickly, but not at the risk of losing the support that has brought him this far. He will need to enlist more allies and not be stalled by detractors.

Delivering change is the same as delivering on campaign promises. The electorate wants to see results. Mike wades in, determined to deliver success. He realizes that other campaigns are on his horizon.

CHANGE ON A PERSONAL LEVEL

A CSO deals with change on a personal level by first recognizing three immutable characteristics of change: it is a fact of life, unpredictable, and not controllable by any one individual [5]. An understanding of these characteristics should prompt the CSO to conclude that getting in the way of change can be dangerous to one's career. Getting out of the way of change may be the CSO's best or only choice. In other cases, there may be opportunities to be a part of the change by influencing it. If the change involves changing the way a security group operates, the CSO has (or should have) an opportunity to influence the nature of the change and how it will be implemented. This is certainly better than watching from the sidelines.

Reality Check

The CSO should make a serious reality check when faced with change. He or she has to know the answers to questions such as "What do I believe in?"; Does this change impact my belief system?"; and "How do I fit into this change and do I have a positive part to play?" Coming to grips with the personal implications of change can be traumatic.

When not able to substantively control the personal consequences of change, the CSO can at least control his or her personal reaction to it. A career-damaging change can occur despite the best efforts to the contrary. A change perceived incorrectly as career damaging may turn out to be career damaging simply because of the perception. When looked at free of exaggerated fear, change may look more like a bump in the road than the end of the road. The message here is to take control of the things that can be controlled, such as one's personal response.

Blame-shifters

The people most affected by change on a personal level seem in many cases to be blame-shifters. The usual laments include, "The boss had it in for me. The company deceived me. Lady Luck was against me." They are self-doubters who end up failing because they fear success. They tend to undervalue their talents and destroy their chances of getting ahead. The losers in change are sometimes people who are so locked into their own identity they cannot tolerate working differently. Change to the job is unacceptable because the job and the person are one and the same. "They wanted me to be the fleet manager when I was already the head of security. They can't do that to me." Unfortunately, they did.

Survivors

The survivors are people who have come to grips with change in a healthy way. They see it as a discovery, a renewal, and a challenge. They manage to retain their visions of personal success while accommodating the demands of the new situation.

Action Coaching

A means of bringing individual talents and skills into harmony with change is action coaching [6]. What differentiates action coaching from other forms of coaching is its emphasis on behavior modification. Performing below expectations and interacting poorly with team members are examples of behavioral problems that can be addressed by action coaching. The broad objectives in action coaching are as follows.

- Bring personal goals into line with company goals.
- Help employees adapt to changes in work procedures.
- Encourage employees to achieve their full potential.

A beginning step for the action coach is to determine the modification needed and to assess how the modification fits into the big picture. In shorthand, determine the change and the context. Assume, for example, that Harry Blake works for you and supervises five people. You detect a tension between Blake and his subordinates. The tension results in the main from Blake's lack of skill in dealing with people generally. That is the problem. You know that the CEO is committed to establishing and maintaining harmony in the workforce. That is the context.

Questions naturally pop into your mind: What is it that needs to be done to modify Blake's behavior? How long will it take? How difficult will it be? Will the modification be worth the effort? What opportunities are available to make the modification?

You decide you need more information, and therefore meet with the manager of the HR department. You learn that the company offers an intermediate-level supervisor course that includes training in team-building. Blake is eligible to attend and you have the funds in your budget to pay the attendance fee. The HR manager urges you to confer with Blake, inform him that he is not meeting the company's expectation in respect to working in harmony with others, obtain his feedback, and then develop with him a plan for correcting the problem. You are advised to insist that Blake take personal responsibility for improvement, which would include successful completion of the training course. Be sure also to document everything the HR manager counsels, including details in Blake's performance that first brought the problem to your attention.

Back at your office, you work up a script you intend using when you meet with Blake. Included in the bulleted points are the following.

- Ask him to state the personal goals he hopes to achieve through his employment with the company.
- Ask him if he feels the company has helped him in the pursuit of those goals.
- Ask him if he feels the company has given him the training and coaching he needs to be effective in working with other people.
- Ask him what he has done personally to develop his people skills.
- Be open-minded. Listen carefully. Think before talking.
- Get in touch with his mood and tone. Get him to restate his responses. Use phrases such as "I guess what you are saying is. . ."
- Keep the focus on him. Make sure he understands he has a problem and that the solution belongs entirely to him. Offer help, such as the training course.

- Get him to commit to modifying his behavior. Use phrases such as "What are you going to do to turn this situation around?"
- Establish milestones and a deadline for correcting the problem.
- Look for red flags such as the following.
  - ○ Reluctance to commit to a plan of action
  - ○ Insistence that the problem does not exist or is minor or will go away of its own accord
  - ○ Blaming others

The meeting with Blake turns out to be nonconfrontational. He is shocked at first and then mildly angry with himself for not recognizing the problem. He agrees to self-evaluate during and after transactions with co-workers, readily agrees to attend the training, and expresses confidence that he will do better. An action plan is developed and he commits to it.

After Blake leaves, the CSO considers the need for involving other people. He asks himself: "Will it be helpful to Blake and to the correction of the problem if I brief the boss?" The CSO thinks yes. "If a complaint is lodged against Blake over my head, the boss will understand that the problem is in a correction stage." The CSO decides that the action plan does not require coordination with any other persons or groups.

The CSO is pleased overall. He prepares a file folder on the matter and adds to it a reminder to monitor Blake's performance to ensure that the plan is carried out. He will look for specific changes in Blake's behavior that indicate improvement and decide as events move along if further counseling and motivation will be needed.

NOTES

1. These ideas were borrowed from "Managing Social Work," *National Institute of Social Work Briefing Number 14*, Tavistock, England, January 1996, pp. 1.

2. *Ibid.*, pp. 3.

3. Dennis Dalton, *The Art of Successful Security Management*, pp. 166, Boston: Butterworth and Heinemann, 1998.

4. The idea for analogizing change to politics was taken from a Patricia M. Wallington article titled "Total Leadership: Making Change." The article appeared on pages 68 through 73 in the April 1, 2000 issue of *CIO*.

5. John Fay, "The Winds of Change," *Security Technology and Design*, September 1996, pp. 100.

6. These ideas can be found in *Action Coaching: How to Leverage Individual Performance for Company Success* by David L. Dotlich and Peter C. Cairo, San Francisco: Jossey Bass, 1999.

8. Making Decisions

When you are right, you cannot be too radical; when you are wrong, you cannot be too conservative.
　　　　　　　　—Martin Luther King, Jr.

LEADERSHIP

Leadership, certainly effective leadership, is all about good choices. When the stakes are high and a consequential decision required, business leaders place a greater reliance on logical processes than on instinct and intuition. Flying from the seat of one's pants fits the leader-hero image but is rarely practiced in modern business. A more accurate image may be the jet liner pilot who relies on a standard process involving flight charts, electronic instrumentation, a co-pilot, and a navigator. When the consequences of a decision are high, a good business leader will set aside personal judgments in favor of a process utilizing the analysis of facts. Many such processes exist in the modern business world, yet all of them include six basic stages: frame the issue, collect information, analyze information, decide, implement, and examine feedback (see Figure 8-1).

Frame the Issue

The process begins with defining what must be decided. If the decision involves solving a problem, one starts by investigating the essential nature of the problem. The questions to be preliminarily answered include the following.

- Does a decision need to be made at all?
- What is the crux of the issue? What are its dimensions?
- What impact will a decision have on other issues?
- Is the issue real or imagined?
- Who are the persons or groups best able to contribute to the best decision?
- How long will it take and what will it cost to arrive at and implement a decision?

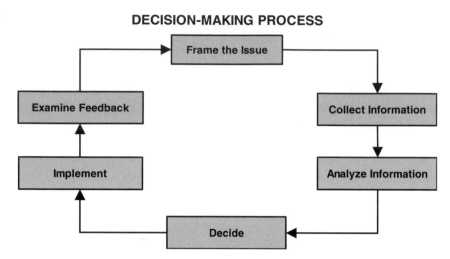

Figure 8-1 The process of making decisions can be seen to move in six stages.

Plunging in and trying to solve the wrong problem is a common error, and one that can be avoided by taking time to look at the issue from several angles and through the eyes of people positioned to understand the facts. The first stage of the decision-making process is not too early to be creative; for example, by brainstorming the issue and encouraging oppositional views. Putting innovative and contrarian minds to work can help clear away the fog of uncertainty.

Collect Information

The second stage of the process involves gathering information, including the hard facts and the best estimates. The good decision maker will draw a clear line between what is known and not known, and seek to obtain the missing information.

Decision trees and hypothetical scenarios can be used to identify missing data and search for mental blind spots. Estimates of variables can be made and then challenged, such as estimating a cost and then critically examining it. Tabletop exercises and hands-on practical exercises can be used to surface information that is needed but missing.

All avenues are explored for collecting relevant information. If relevancy is in question, the information is obtained; if irrelevancy is proved later, the information can be shelved or discarded. The collected information is correlated (i.e., grouped according to subject matter, source, reliability, or other criteria).

Analyze the Information

At this stage, all of the obtainable relevant information will be on hand and ready for analysis. For analysis to be accurate, the information has to be

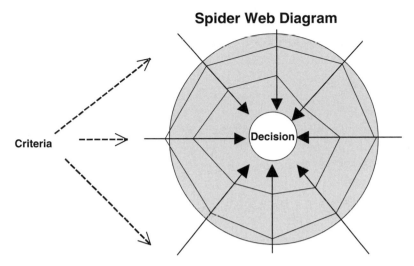

Figure 8-2 Criteria at several levels are weighed and balanced against each other as the decision maker moves closer to a choice.

in a common data set. The most common data set is dollar values. With a common data set established, the data are quantified and then systematically evaluated.

The methods of evaluation vary according to the nature of the information and the practices and resources of the decision maker. Analytical tools include linear modeling, sensitivity analysis to highlight uncertainty, value and probability analysis, decision trees to structure the relationships between alternatives and outcomes, and ranking of probable outcomes. Mistakes at this stage of the process typically include the following.

- Taking mental shortcuts such as giving greater credence to the most recent or most loudly voiced opinions or accepting numbers (e.g., cost projections) at face value.
- Wasting valuable time by considering irrelevant information.
- Being overly confident about the quality of information.
- Relying on information that confirms predetermined expectations.

Emerging from the results of the analyses are the outlines of alternatives, singly and in combinations, which if carried out correctly can achieve the decision maker's objectives. Said another way, the problem is described by its solution (see Figure 8-2).

Decide

In this stage, the solution is described by the corrective actions (i.e., options deemed capable of solving the problem). An option consisting of corrective actions is selected, and a decision is made to proceed with implementation.

Implement

The selected option is put into effect. Implementation is rarely made all at once. It typically proceeds in stages, with each stage building on previous stages. The first stage is likely to be preparation, including the following.

- Developing a plan of action
- Establishing milestones and deadlines
- Acquiring and assembling needed equipment and supplies
- Selling the option to employees
- Training employees in the knowledge and skills necessary to smooth implementation

Examine Feedback

Feedback, meaning information arising from the effect of carrying out the option, is carefully examined in light of the anticipated outcomes. In other words, implementation is compared against results. When the results are less than satisfactory, the decision maker can modify implementation or decide to go with an entirely different option.

Assumptions and reasoning are confirmed or invalidated by feedback, allowing new insights. The nature and dimensions of the problem may turn out to be different than first perceived, and the criteria that went into shaping the option may have been off target. Feedback naturally leads to a reexamination of the problem and the facts that were relied upon to solve it.

When the results of implementation are significantly poor, a natural tendency of the decision maker is to transfer guilt by refuting mistakes and rationalizing choices. The decision maker can go into a state of denial that if not overcome will be an obstacle to finding the correct answer.

Another common misstep is to settle for minimally acceptable outcomes instead of returning to the drawing board for another try at getting it right. Frustration of the decision maker and the bellyaching of detractors can make it attractive to put the entire issue aside and move on. Consider, for example, the following anecdote.

CASE STUDY

In a sense, David was a survivor. He had kept his job as CSO after the company was purchased by another company, and he had seen change after change while managing to keep intact a security group that was largely his own creation. The core of David's group was an in-house guard force that provided security services at the corporate headquarters. David had long ago decided that an in-house guard operation was the best choice for the company, and in some respects he was right. The guards performed very well, they were loyal, and turnover was low.

The previous CEO had agreed with David, stating that he wanted the guards to be in the corporate family. The new CEO, however, had reservations. Last week he commented that guard costs were much too high. Today he called David and said he wanted input for a decision he would make concerning the future of the security group. He specifically asked for cost estimates to outsource guard operations. He also suggested that David might want to consider forming his own guard company and making a bid for the contract.

CONCLUSIONS

As a business grows, effective decision making becomes much more difficult. Leaders find it difficult to get all of the information they need. In addition, they consider how their decisions on hiring, firing, purchasing, and other issues will affect their relationships with other employees and business associates. Under these circumstances, leaders cannot always choose strategies that will maximize profit. Instead, they tend to settle for what they consider reasonable gains for the business. This observation contradicts conventional economic analysis, which assumes that a company always tries to maximize profits [1].

NOTES

1. The observation was made by economist Herbert A. Simon in *Administrative Behavior: A Study of Decision-Making Processes in Administrative Organization*, 4th edition, New York, Free Press, 1999.

9. Managing Risk

The power of accurate observation is commonly called cynicism by those who have not got it.
　　　　　　　—George Bernard Shaw

INTRODUCTION

We are now living in a world of rising risk and increasing volatility. Everywhere we seem to encounter increasing and intensifying risk [1]. Risks of concern to security professionals include terrorism, political conflict, military operations, and harm from criminals.

The management of risk is a fundamental responsibility of all managers, especially the CSO. The CSO directly manages risk within the security group, and indirectly manages risk in other groups by setting security standards, educating employees to meet the standards, providing counsel and advice on security matters, and helping develop incident plans and an overall emergency response plan.

RISK ANALYSIS

Performing the previously cited services involves risk management, which incorporates the function of risk analysis. Risk analysis is a multi-utility tool that helps the chief security officer perform the following.

- Identify assets deserving of protection
- Identify threats to the assets
- Estimate the probability that threats will materialize
- Estimate the impact of threat occurrences
- Estimate the probable frequency of occurrences
- Assess the manageability of threats
- Identify countermeasures that prevent or mitigate threat occurrences

Assets

The assets to be protected can include employees, contractors, customers, buildings, equipment, supplies, money, information, and reputation. Another asset is process: a rational combination of people and properties working together to produce an output. Outputs can be products, such as refined sugar and mass-manufactured automobiles, or services such as real estate sales and legal advice.

Criticality

In risk management, criticality is a characteristic of an asset in terms of loss. Loss includes destruction, damage, and loss of use. Loss is often expressed in dollar values. The dimensions of criticality are cost of replacement, availability of replacement, and importance to a process. Consider the following scenarios. A lightning bolt strikes one of thirty tanks in a gasoline tank farm. The tank catches fire, which destroys fifty thousand gallons of gasoline and damages a connected pipeline. The facility is shut down for two days. What we have here is destruction, damage, and loss of use costing several hundred thousand dollars.

Disgruntled workers at a petroleum refinery sabotage the plant's catalytic converter, shutting the refinery down until the catalytic converter can be replaced. Again, we have destruction, damage, and loss of use. The destruction and damage costs are less than fifty thousand dollars because the catalytic converter is not expensive and the cost of repairing damage near the converter is minor. Because the converter is essential to the refining process, loss of use of the entire plant is extended until a replacement converter is acquired and installed.

The tank farm goes back on line in two days. The petroleum refinery does not have a backup converter and has to order one from the manufacturer. The manufacturer promises delivery in two months; installation requires one month. The refinery is out of operation for three months. The cost of destruction and damage at the tank farm is significantly higher than the cost of destruction and damage at the refinery. However, the overall cost for the refinery is much higher than that for the tank farm because the shutdown time is much longer. What we now see are the dimensions of criticality: cost of replacement, availability of replacement, and importance to a process.

Threats

A threat is an indication, circumstance, or event with a potential to cause destruction, damage, or loss of use of an asset [2]. Threats vary and they fall into two categories: acts of nature and acts of mankind. In the scenarios presented previously, the tank farm fire was an event triggered by Mother Nature; the sabotage at the refinery was an event caused by a human act.

Hurricanes, floods, and earthquakes are events caused by the forces of nature; terrorism and crime are caused by people. All of these events are threats because they present indications of possible occurrence. The storm that sent the lightning bolt against the gasoline tank was an indication; sabotage at the refinery was indicated by employee unrest.

Terror-related threats are indicated by the history, intention, and capability of the terrorist group. History is apparent from the group's past activities, intention is shown when the group declares it will assassinate expatriate employees, and capability is demonstrated when the group actually does what it said it would do.

Probability

The essential question seeking an answer is: How likely is it that a particular threat event will take place? Although demanding of mental concentration, estimating the probability of occurrence has no reliance on mathematical models, equations, or formulas. Precise numerical quantification is never possible when the factors under examination are influenced in the main by human behavior. A good deal of the analytical input comes from knowing the current nature of a threat, tapping into one's base of experience, and applying old-fashioned common sense. The CSO estimating probability applies a broad brush to a large canvas.

Impact

The impact or consequence of the threat event is an approximation based on the organization's prior experiences and the experiences of similar companies in similar situations. Dollars are the customary measure of impact. The rater takes into consideration the costs of replacement, repair, lost productivity, forfeit of business opportunity, cleanup, litigation, reputation damage, and degradation of customer goodwill (see Figure 9-1). Even when the impact is upon human life, the yardstick is dollar value.

Frequency

Frequency is different from probability. In frequency, the rater has evidence of event occurrences such as the number of reports filed in one year by employees whose laptops were stolen. Some events will not have a history. For example, in the matter of a trade secret compromise, the event may not ever have happened but the chance of it happening and the extent of loss are sufficiently compelling to regard the event as a real threat and institute preventive safeguards.

A relatively minor threat event, such as the theft of a laptop, can take on a serious dimension when the frequency of the event is high. A very

Incident Probability, Impact, and Frequency for a Convenience Store				

Event	P	I	F	Probability Legend
Robbery or attempted robbery.	C	LI	M	PU — Probability Unknown NL — Not Likely
Burglary or attempted burglary.	L	MI	Y	L — Likely C — Certain
Assault of employee or customer.	L	HI	Y	**Impact Legend** LI — Low Impact (Under $1,000)
Theft by shoplifting.	C	LI	D	MI — Medium Impact ($1,000-$10,000)
Employee pilferage.	C	LI	W	HI — High Impact (Over $10,000)
Theft from till.	L	LI	M	**Frequency Legends**
Theft of bank deposit.	NL	MI	Y	D — Daily
Vandalism.	L	LI	M	W — Weekly M — Monthly
Arson or attempted arson.	NL	HI	Y	Y — Year or Longer
Bomb threat hoax.	NL	LI	Y	

Figure 9-1 The letter codes in the three columns to the right of the event indicate the rater's best judgment as to an event's probability, impact, and frequency. [The legends to the right of the table explain the letter codes and ranges.]

serious event, such as the one-time compromise of a trade secret, can be less damaging in the long run than repeated theft of laptops. The cost of the event times the number of repetitions provides a dollar figure. If the cost of a laptop is $2,000 and 100 are projected to be stolen, the estimated potential loss is $200,000. This figure gives to management a basis for comparing potential loss against the actual cost of countermeasures. Not mentioned in this example, but extremely relevant to analysis, is the dollar loss associated with work output residing on a laptop's hard drive and the possible disclosure of proprietary data.

Manageability

A valuable perspective to management is the relative manageability of a threat. Manageability is the capacity to reduce the probability and/or impact of a risk (i.e., a threat event). The principle methods of managing risk include the following.

- Avoiding the risk by removing the target. Laptop theft can be avoided entirely by choosing to not provide laptops to employees. A trade secret, such as the formula to a popular soft drink, can be kept in a high-security vault. Some businesses avoid crime-related risks by choosing not to operate in high-crime areas.
- Reducing the risk by decreasing the target. A convenience store robbery loss can be reduced by inserting into a floor safe all cash receipts above a designated amount. The store's shoplifting risk can be reduced by placing high-value merchandise in a locked cabinet and by placing easily

BOSTON SQUARE METHOD FOR ASSESSING RISK AND MANAGEABILITY

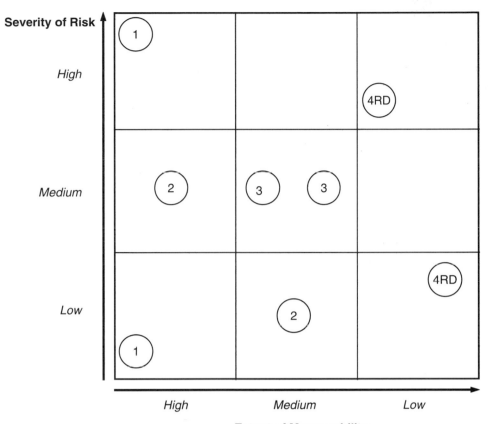

Terms of Reference

Low Severity. An incident at the lowest threshold of dollar loss, e.g., a loss amounting to less than $100,000.

Medium Severity. An incident involving a loss of more than $100,000 but less than $5,000,000.

High Severity. An incident involving a loss of more than $5,000,000.

Reputation Damage. An incident that impairs the company's reputation. This criterion is not always used.

(In this example, dollars have been used as the only measure of loss. Other measures of loss can include injury/death and impact on operations.)

Figure 9-2 This diagram is often called a Boston Square, a simple device for depicting relationships. In this case, it juxtaposes the severity of risks and their manageability.

concealed high-demand items, such as packs of cigarettes, behind the cashier's counter.

- Diffusing the risk involves the use of barrier systems such as perimeter fences; access control and intrusion detection equipment such as card readers and CCTV; locks, safes, and vaults; and standard control procedures such as property removal passes and inventory counts.

- Transferring the risk is possible by purchasing insurance or by raising prices so that the purchasers of the product or service pay for the losses. Another technique is to outsource risk-heavy functions to another party. An example is the transfer of liability when an employer replaces an in-house guard force with a contract guard force. If misconduct by a contract guard causes a serious accident, the employer may be able to escape liability under the terms of the contract.
- Accepting the risk is also an option. A management may decide that a particular risk is worth a gamble or that the cost of loss is not sufficiently large to justify the cost of prevention. Another deciding factor may be the intractability of the risk (i.e., that despite best efforts the risk cannot be controlled to an acceptable degree).

Countermeasures

In this step of risk analysis, security countermeasures are identified and then evaluated according to workability and cost. A countermeasure to laptop theft would be to anchor them to desks. The cost of installing anchors would be negligible compared to the cost of loss, but anchoring the laptops would be objectionable because the countermeasure would cancel out the portability feature of laptops. An alternative might be to install lock-type anchors that can be easily detached with a key or combination dial.

Selection of countermeasures is based on two information sets. First is the information compiled from the risk analysis process (i.e., data derived from identification of assets and threats; estimation of probability, impact, and frequency; and assessment of risk manageability).

The second information set has to do with the nature of the business, goals and operating philosophy of management, and the culture of the organization. The cultural factor can be extremely important and may explain why risk management consultants will in some situations offer unworkable recommendations.

An understanding of the efficacy of countermeasures that require employee cooperation can be found in the theory of social control. The theory holds that people performance is dictated by formal and informal controls. Formal controls consist of rules and laws that coerce human behavior.

Informal controls consist of peer pressures that persuade conformity subtly and powerfully. Informal controls are considered more effective and longer lasting than formal controls [3]. Too often, cultural and social influences will subvert formal controls, which are main components of security safeguards. The examination of countermeasure options can lead management to address relevant questions such as the following.

- Is it always best to prevent the occurrence?
- Is it sensible to take proactive steps to mitigate the effect of the occurrence?
- Is it sensible to combine prevention with mitigation?

- Is it sufficient simply to be aware of the threat and do nothing in advance to prevent or mitigate?
- Is prevention or mitigation cost effective?

A company's potential losses determine the steps taken to avoid or reduce them [4].

SELF-ASSESSMENT

Supervisors, managers, and other persons charged with meeting specific security responsibilities tend to be nervous and run to the CSO when they learn that a peer has been called on the carpet for failing to prevent a security-related loss or when their secretary reminds them that a security audit is on the near horizon. "Tell me what I should do," is the usual plea. A good answer may be, "Find out yourself by making a self-assessment."

A self-assessment is typically a comparison between what is expected in the way of security and what is actually being done. The assessment is usually made of a group by its supervisor or manager. Formalized security expectations are matched against the security behaviors of the group. The assessment might pose questions such as the following.

- What security processes and procedures are in place to meet the requirements of this expectation?
- What are the differences between what we have now and what we need to satisfy the expectation?
- Are people aware of their roles and responsibilities with respect to this expectation?
- Are people aware of their personal responsibilities in meeting this expectation?
- Do employees comply with the security processes and procedures in place to meet this expectation?
- Are security standards in place to meet this expectation? Are they being met?
- Where practice does not meet this expectation, are corrective actions being taken? Are they succeeding?

Self-assessments (see Figure 9-3) have little value in precisely identifying security weaknesses but have some value in raising security awareness.

SECURITY REVIEW

A security review is a loose comparison of security performance against formal, well-understood standards. It is frequently conducted with the use of a checklist (see Figure 9-4). Questions are asked and answers recorded, and not

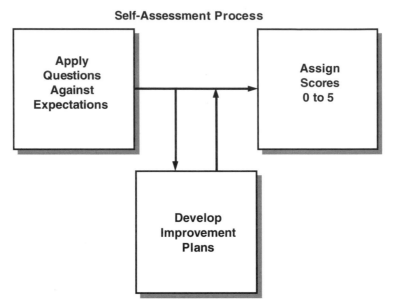

Figure 9-3 Self-assessment can be helpful in preparing for an outside review.

all of the answers are verified. The review points out areas of noncompliance and offers general suggestions for improvement.

The review tends to focus on soft issues. For example, it may look at the organization's programs for overseas travel or employee security awareness but not look at hard issues such as safeguarding very critical assets or preventing and mitigating terrorist attacks. However, when a serious weakness is detected a review can trigger a more penetrating analysis such as an audit or vulnerability assessment.

The security review is conducted at a frequency of about once per year. Each succeeding review examines weaknesses detected in the preceding review. A failure to correct the weaknesses is reflected in a written report, which also describes newly discovered weaknesses. The security review does not typically involve initial and exit interviews with the site's senior management.

SECURITY AUDIT

Where a security review is general, an audit is detailed and systematic, and applies analytical tools such as rating schemes with weighted values, matrices, and formulas. It is often conducted by more than one person. The auditor(s) are experienced professionals with in-depth knowledge of risk analysis. A checklist is appropriate but of minor importance.

Unlike a review, an audit searches intensively for security weaknesses and gives details of corrective actions required. The major focus is on very critical assets such as biological agents studied at a research lab, radioactive material used in a hospital, or sensitive data in an information technology system.

Checklist for Security Review of a Retail Facility

1. Has a prior security review or audit been made of this facility? If so, attach report.
2. Does the facility follow the prescribed automated stock reconciliation procedure?
3. Does the procedure allow transaction audit trails?
4. Does the facility have a copy of the company security manual?
5. Do the employees understand their individual security responsibilities?
6. Does the facility manager have available a source for obtaining professional and objective advice on the installation of CCTV, alarms, safes and related security equipment?
7. Does the facility manager maintain contact with local law enforcement?
8. Are controls in place to prevent employee theft practices such as:
    a. Cash register manipulation (open drawer)?
    b. Short-changing?
    c. Overcharging?
    d. Skimming?
    e. Double imprinting of credit card vouchers?
9. Does the facility manager follow the company's pre-employment screening procedures?
10. Are new hires required to attend a security training program?
11. Does the facility manager:
    a. Enforce strict rules on cash handling and collection?
    b. Monitor cash register transactions?
    c. Pay attention when receiving merchandise from suppliers?
    d. Control keys?
12. Are customer anti-theft procedures in place to prevent:
    a. Shoplifting?
    b. Price switching?
    c. Check and credit card fraud?
    d. Price switching?
13. Are anti-robbery procedures in place such as:
    a. Keeping cash receipts at or below the designated amount?
    b. Using the drop safe?
    c. Making bank deposits daily?
    d. Utilizing a courier service to transport receipts to the bank?
    e. Making the cashier visible from outside the store?
    f. Ensuring that the CCTV taping system and robbery alarm system are functioning properly?
    g. Teaching the employees how to react in a robbery?
14. Is the facility closed after hours? If so:
    a. Is a burglar detection and alarm system in place and does it function properly?
    b. Are surreptitious entry points physically reinforced?
    c. Are high-value items placed in a secure container before closing?
    d. Are procedures being followed in respect to opening and closing of the facility?
15. Are point-of-sale credit card authorization procedures in place?
16. Do point-of-sale clerks understand:
    a. The magnitude of credit card fraud and its impact on profits?
    b. The common techniques of credit card fraud?
    c. The company's policy to vigorously prosecute credit card fraud?

Figure 9-4 A security review can be make of risks associated with operations of a retail facility.

Checklist for a Security Audit

Is the facility security policy:
    In writing?
    Signed by the senior facility manager?
    Does it address the protection of people, property, and processes against loss or compromise?

Does the security policy provide guidance for preventing or mitigating the following?
    Larceny
    Burglary
    Loss or compromise of proprietary information
    Assault on employees and visitors
    Bomb threats
    Arson
    Civil disturbances
    Unethical business conduct
    Alcohol and drug abuse

Is the security policy:
    Communicated in writing to all employees?
    Conspicuously posted throughout the facility?
    Referred to during new employee orientation?
    Referred to at group meetings?
    Contained in a manual?
    Referred to in management and employee training programs?

Does senior management support the security policy:
    By periodic written communications?
    By regular security tours?
    By participating in security program audits?
    Are there written standards for management performance in the security program?

Are security program standards communicated to all levels of management?
    Are security instructions and procedures defined in a program manual?
    Are annual written security program objectives set for the organization?
    What percentage of managers has developed written security program objectives?
    To what degree are program objectives being achieved?

Has a person been designated in writing to coordinate the security program?
    Does this person have direct access to senior management on security program matters?
    Are security responsibilities written into manager job descriptions?
    Is performance to security standards included in manager performance reviews?

Are local law enforcement, intelligence, security, and regulatory agencies contacted regularly for assistance in supporting the security program?

Figure 9-5 A security audit checklist can be quite comprehensive.

Are the people who are selected for sensitive or critical duties and positions screened for suitability and reliability? Does the screening and verification process include:

Criminal record checks?

Credit checks?

Education?

Employment?

Driver's license and driving record?

Professional certification and/or professional licensing?

Personal identity documents?

What percentage of managers receives orientation and induction training to the security program?

Is this orientation and induction training completed within one month of appointment to a management position?

What percentage of managers has had a formal training course on fundamentals of security?

Are written materials used in this formal security management training course?

Is there a program that requires managers to attend formal security-update training at least every three years?

What percentage of managers has had the update training?

What percentage of employees/contractors receives orientation/induction training to security program standards?

Are written materials included in the orientation?

Are security awareness signs and notices posted in appropriate places to reinforce knowledge of security standards?

What percentage of employees holding specific security duties have received formal training in how to perform their duties?

What percentage of contractors who have specific security duties have received formal training in how to perform their duties?

Are training manuals used to aid and reinforce security training?

Are records kept to verify security training and identify employees needing such training?

Has a survey been made to determine the need for security measures, systems, and devices? Did the survey determine the need for:

Perimeter fencing or walls?

Protection of doors, windows, and openings?

Security alarm systems?

Camera surveillance?

Security lighting?

Lock and key control?

Security signs?

Safes, vaults, and protected storage?

Protection of vital utilities?

Communications?

Access control?

Guard force?

Computer protection?

Information security?

Emergency preparedness?

Figure 9-5 *continued*

Which of the needs identified by the survey have been met?

When were the security needs last reviewed and updated?

Are methods taken to control entry and movement of people and vehicles as a security measure? Do these controls include the following categories of personnel?

Visitors

Vendors

Service and delivery personnel

Do these controls include the following categories of vehicles?

Employee

Visitor

Vendor

Contractor

Service and delivery

Is the duplication of keys to buildings, vehicles, and storage areas controlled?

Are procedures in effect to address the following?

Marking of classified information

Control of classified information

Distribution of classified information

Transmission of classified information

Copying of classified information

Storage of classified information

Downgrading of classified information

Destruction of classified information

Is a Clear Desk Policy in effect?

Are all employees/contractors who have access to sensitive information required to sign a nondisclosure agreement?

Are speeches, news releases, presentations, technical papers, and other forms of open information reviewed for sensitivity and protection of trademarks before release?

Is the facility engaged in classified government work or involved in a classified contract?

Do written delegations of financial authority exist?

Are delegations made to and signed at each level of authority?

Are delegations current?

Are delegations routinely followed?

Are adequate controls and written procedures in place to maintain individual accountability for employees with cash-handling responsibilities?

Are approving, purchasing, receiving, and paying functions separated?

Are procedures in place for the disposal of scrap waste and surplus materials?

Are "right to audit" clauses included in vendor and supplier contracts?

Figure 9-5 *continued*

When was the last financial audit conducted?

How often are inventories, accountings, and records checks made to identify security losses?

Are security losses and incidents promptly investigated with the findings and actions reported?

Are loss event reports reviewed for action needed?

Does the security program require a complete investigation of criminal and malicious security losses and incidents that involve:
- Cash and negotiables?
- Irregularities in financial accounts?
- Equipment and materials shortages?
- Expendable supplies and inventory shrinkage?
- Production losses from disturbances?
- Product loss or theft?
- Product extortion or contamination?
- Computer theft?
- Other security losses?

Is there a central facility file of security incident investigation reports?
- Are investigative and incident reports kept in an active file for at least two years?
- Are the appropriate levels of facility management receiving copies of reports and investigative summaries for corrective action?
- Is the appropriate level of specialized security advisor support receiving copies of reports and investigative summaries for information and corrective action?

How often are inspections of facilities and operations made by line management to verify compliance with security standards?
- Are checklists used to guide the security inspections?
- Are the results of security inspections communicated in writing to senior management?
  - Is a copy of the inspection report given to the responsible affected supervisor for follow-up actions?
  - Is there a written follow-up procedure to ensure that appropriate remedial actions have been taken?
  - Is a copy of the inspection report, together with corrective actions, provided to the appropriate level of specialized security advisor support?

Has an overall facility Emergency Plan Coordinator been appointed in writing?
- Are security requirements included in all emergency plans?
- Are emergency response plans reviewed at least annually?
- Do these emergency plans address:
  - Terrorism?
  - Death or serious injury?
  - Kidnapping?
  - Extortion?
  - Bomb threats?
  - Product contamination?
  - Strikes?
  - Civil disorder?

Figure 9-5 *continued*

Failure of alarm and control systems?
Natural catastrophe?
Catastrophic fire or explosion?
Hazardous material discharge or spill?

Are plans coordinated with local law enforcement, fire protection, private security contractors, and emergency response agencies?

How often are drills held to train employees in emergency actions and test their performance?

Does the organization receive security periodicals to update professional knowledge?
   Are security articles or other written materials distributed to managers at least quarterly to update their security management knowledge?

Are there written guidelines on enforcement of security standards to aid supervisors and managers?

How often is an evaluation of key security program indicators made for major units to determine effectiveness of the programs in place?
   Are the results of these program evaluations communicated to senior management?
   Are security promotional materials in use at the facility?
   Are security promotional materials conspicuously posted throughout the facility?

Does security promotion include:
   Posters on bulletin boards?
   Awards that recognize employees who demonstrate exemplary security behavior?
   Presentations at employee meetings?
   Notices on the Company's Email system?

Does the facility have written policies or directives requiring the conduct of security reviews at the concept and design stages of all new developments, construction, and modification projects?

How often are compliance checks of design engineering records made by an unbiased person, with results related management, to determine the percentage of compliance with the engineering policy or directive?

Figure 9-5 *continued*

The auditor(s) meet with and brief senior management prior to, during, and after the audit. The initial briefing covers the audit methodology, the people to be interviewed, and areas at the site that will be of interest. The midpoint briefing covers progress and tentative findings. The exit briefing covers actual findings, recommended corrective actions, and the nature of the audit report. An audit (see Figure 9-6) is conducted at a frequency of one to three years, or sooner when circumstances dictate. Such circumstances include the following.

- Operational changes at the site
- Emergence of a new threat
- A rise in threat level
- Discovery of a serious security breach

PROJECT REVIEW

The purpose of project review is to incorporate security features in the design of new construction projects and major renovations of existing facilities. A secondary purpose is to protect persons, equipment, and materials at the site during the project.

Project review is a team effort, with the CSO playing a central role. Other security professionals on the team can include consultants with know-how in designing, installing, and integrating access control and intrusion detection systems, lighting, and communications equipment. Team membership also will include specialists representing construction or renovation disciplines such as planning, designing, and engineering.

The review can begin prior to the decision that authorizes the project and end when the property is turned over to the user. It would not be unusual for the review period to last two years or more. However, not all members will be actively engaged in the project every day. The CSO, for example, needs to be directly involved when security issues are before the team and when an outside security consultant is at the site. Security at the project site is provided during the project. Every project has a unique set of variables that impact security, and they tend to be external variables such as the following.

- Project location, size, and duration
- Nature and complexity of the construction/renovation work
- Environmental conditions
- Constraints imposed by the public and local government

The CSO's project review responsibilities occur in three stages: security concept, security design and specifications, and pre-acceptance.

Security Concept

In the concept stage the CSO puts on a thinking cap and gets down to serious business. Decisions made at this point can profoundly affect every security issue that follows. To make the best decisions possible, the CSO has to determine the following.

- The core business functions and processes that will take place at the facility
- The critical assets that merit protection and the extent of protection to be afforded
- Actual and potential threats, such as the following:
  - Terrorist acts
  - Sabotage
  - Criminal acts
  - Compromise of sensitive information
  - Internal theft

- ○ Workplace violence
- ○ Acts of nature
- The preferences of senior management as to:
  - ○ Contract versus proprietary guard services
  - ○ Armed versus unarmed guards
  - ○ Guards in uniforms versus subdued clothing
  - ○ Free-moving versus restricted traffic flow onto the site
- Site layout
- Nature of the surrounding neighborhoods and community
- Physical environment within and around the site
- Weather conditions

Two general sources are available to the CSO for making the previously cited determinations: site management and outside agencies that provide services to the facility. The outside agencies might be among the following.

- Law enforcement
- Firefighting
- Emergency medical treatment and public health
- Emergency management
- Contract security services
- Contract property management
- Chamber of Commerce and Better Business Bureau
- Corporate security departments of other organizations

Information can be obtained by interviewing people and examining police call and arrest reports, traffic engineering and demographic studies, security guard incident reports, arson records and fire dispatch reports, emergency medical treatment reports, and hospital admissions related to crime-induced trauma. The mix of data can produce for the CSO a mental snapshot of human activities in and around the place of construction or renovation. A good feel for the data may allow recognition of security risks not immediately apparent. The collected information can answer pertinent questions such as the following.

- Are local response agencies capable of adequately responding to emergencies that are likely to arise during the project period and after the property is turned over to the user?
- Does the local jurisdiction impose any code restrictions that impact security (e.g., a code that prohibits certain types of exit door hardware)?
- Is there a private security force, sufficiently capable and reliable, that can be hired if needed?
- If the project is abroad, are there restrictions as to acquisition of security services and products?

In essence, the CSO ascertains what is needed, what is possible, and what is allowable. The broad outlines of a security system take shape — a shape that is sure to be modified in the design and specifications stage. Consider the following scenario.

CASE STUDY

Barry Wilkes is the CSO for an insurance company planning to build a new office complex on the downtown edge of a major city. Wilkes is the security representative on the construction project team. While attending a luncheon meeting of the local chapter of the Building Owners and Managers Association, Wilkes learns that a shopping mall is planned to be built adjacent to his company's planned office complex.

The project review data he has so far collected indicates that each time a shopping mall had been constructed in or near downtown the crime rate in the surrounding area rose suddenly. Companies near the malls had experienced a sudden upsurge in auto thefts, purse snatchings, vandalism, and trespassing. The reason, Wilkes suspects, had to do with the mall attracting criminal opportunists. He begins to think about this risk, how to offset it proactively, and how to manage it when the new office complex is in operation.

Security Design and Specifications

The CSO now begins to sketch in the details of the scheme formed tentatively in the concept stage. In the matter of physical safeguards, the CSO establishes specifications. In the matter of fencing, for example, the specifications can address length and height, type and gauge of fencing fabric, pounds per square foot of resistance to brute force, size of poles and distances between them, type and alignment of barbed wire topping, and number, size, and type of gates. The specifications are supplemented with details as to cost for materials and labor, availability, and time required for installation. Specifications such as these are drawn up for lighting, closed-circuit television, sensors, doors, and other physical safeguards.

Specifications are also drafted for guards, such as education, certification in first aid and CPR, stamina, proficiency with firearms, absence of felony convictions, and no evidence of alcohol or drug abuse. The cost and availability of guard services are included.

Pre-acceptance

The pre-acceptance stage is reached when the constructed or renovated facility is ready to be turned over to the user. The CSO's main responsibility in this stage is to ensure that physical safeguards are in place and that guard services are ready to commence. Because safeguards and guards complement each other, there needs to be guidance. The CSO provides the guidance in the form of written instructions. Important among them are incident plans and procedures that deal with contingencies such as fire, workplace violence, and terrorist acts.

Project review technically ends on the day the site is turned over to and accepted by site management. Not later than six months following the acceptance date, a comprehensive security audit or a vulnerability assessment is conducted.

SECURITY INCIDENT CAUSATION MODEL

In the immediate aftermath of a serious security-related loss, the CSO can reliably expect anxious questions from people at the top. They will want to know what happened, why it happened, and who was responsible. Later, when the facts are in and the finger pointing finished, management will expect to see corrective actions.

The CSO, one of the principals charged with conceiving and carrying out corrective actions, will be called upon to apply investigative and analytical skills. The investigative skill is applied first (e.g., the scene or venue of the loss is closely examined, evidence collected, and witnesses interviewed). The analytical skill is applied after all of the relevant facts have been assembled. From the analysis will come a guide for remedial action.

A security incident causation model (SICM) [5] can be a valuable tool when investigating and analyzing a security-related loss. More than that, it is a method of identifying potential loss situations before they happen. SICM channels the CSO into giving very careful consideration to every relevant circumstance in a potential or actual security-related loss, and following that into making a thoughtful analysis of the circumstances individually, in combinations, and totally. The analysis discloses the causal factors of a loss.

Incident

An incident is an undesired event that results in harm to people or loss to property or process, and is usually the result of a violation of law, policy, or work rule. As to the harming of people, the violation may be the assault of one employee by another. For property, the violation may be theft, and for process it may be malicious disruption of work such as setting off a false fire alarm or making a bomb threat.

It helps to think of SICM as an active volcano, as shown in Figure 9-6. Coming out of the top is smoke and lava. This is the loss. Inside the volcano, in descending order, are the incident, the hidden causes underlying the incident, and the failures of management to remove the causes.

Loss

The loss is the observable and often measurable impact on people, property, or process. It is the direct and indirect fallout of the security incident and can take many forms. A security incident involving violence will create time lost by employees who are injured or affected as the result of the misconduct. Time will be lost by co-workers who assist the injured and clean up the incident scene, and by supervisors who intervene to restore work activities, prepare reports, and testify at fact-finding proceedings. Then there are losses of time resulting from upset, shock, diverted attention, and lowered morale of employees.

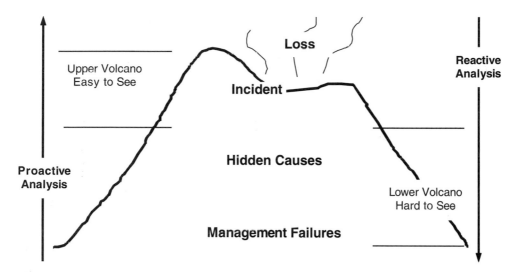

Figure 9-6 SICM can be conceptualized as an active volcano.

Increased operating costs are another form of loss. They result from medical claims and escalated medical insurance premiums; legal expenses associated with hearings and liability claims; penalties, fines and awards; recruiting, selecting, and training people to fill in for employees displaced by the incident; and acquiring interim operating equipment and supplies.

Property losses, which can be substantial, result from numerous violations, such as theft, misappropriation, malicious damage, and destruction. In addition, they often require expenditure of supplies and equipment while dealing with the incident or compensating to overcome the immediate effects. Finally, there is the loss of business (i.e., the missed opportunities during downtime, deterioration of employee and customer goodwill, and adverse publicity).

As stated earlier, loss is precipitated by an incident, which is often rooted in a combination of violations. A theft, for example, is a violation of law, of the employer's policy, and of a work rule, and the same can be said for other violations. In many cases, an incident will consist of conduct that is prohibited in several venues.

Addressing the incident in terms of conduct helps direct thinking to means of controlling unacceptable conduct. Developing control measures that prevent incidents and minimize consequential loss is a fundamental responsibility of the CSO. Implementing the measures is the responsibility of the company's managers and supervisors.

The incident and the loss are amenable to easy examination. Hidden causes and management failures, however, do not stand out. To be seen and understood, the CSO must look deep into the volcano.

Hidden Causes

The hidden causes are the circumstances present in a situation at or immediately prior to the improper conduct. In security parlance, a hidden cause is a nonsecure circumstance. It is very much like the crime prevention equation known as opportunity plus motive equals crime, except that in this case it is hidden cause plus improper behavior equals loss. In managerial parlance, hidden causes are deviations from standards. The term *standard* implies a minimum expectation, a basis for assessing performance against the expectation, and a means of correcting and upgrading unacceptable performance.

STANDARDS

Standards in the workplace have at least two dimensions: practices and conditions. Practices relate to job performance. Conditions are elements of the job environment such as physical setting and job tools.

Practices

When practices are substandard, they appear as human failures (e.g., failure to control access, lock things away, enforce security rules, make proper use of security resources, and recognize and act on the early warning signals of a loss incident in the making). Human failures can result from lack of knowledge, skill, or motivation, and lack of physical mobility, stamina, or mental capability.

Conditions

Conditions pertain to the physical nature of the workplace and of the processes through which the work takes place. Physical aspects include building structure and layout, utilities, machinery, and equipment. Process aspects reflect how the work is carried out. To illustrate, a failure to control access to the company's stock of blank checks occurred when the stock clerk left the blank checks cabinet unattended because no one instructed him to the contrary (a substandard practice resulting from a deficiency in knowledge). The situation held a potential for loss due to the absence of a lock on the cabinet (a substandard condition resulting from poor physical construction) and because the accounting manager did not make access control of blank checks a mandatory step in the routine work processes of the department (a substandard practice resulting from the absence of a policy or directive). Many hidden causes are possible for each substandard practice and condition. Understanding the causes is essential to removing them.

SICM can be applied everywhere in an organization, including the security department. The substandard practices and conditions often found in security operations are poor and infrequent supervision, poor security program and procedures, poor selection of security applicants, poor initial and refresher training, poor assignment and utilization, poor team-building and interpersonal communications, lack of regularly conducted internal assessments, and excessive physical and psychological stresses.

Hidden causes can be tracked down without too much difficulty, but the reasons for them are not always apparent and not always fully understood. More significantly, they tend to be controversial because they point fingers. Patience and persistent probing are needed to get at the root causes and expose them to rational examination. When brought to light, they often suggest the very changes that are needed.

MANAGEMENT FAILURES

The connection between causal factors and the failure of management is analogous to the connection between disease and medicine. The causal factor is the disease that produces the symptoms (hidden causes of further symptoms) that if allowed to persist result in health damage (the loss-producing incident). The disease exists because the patient failed to practice preventive medicine (lack of management control).

In SICM, a basic focal point for analysis and correction is the management. Errors of management underlie all of the deficiencies that lead to loss. The errors tend most often to occur in the setting and enforcing of policies, work rules, and standards.

It does not matter if management attention is directed at production, quality control, accounting, or security, nor does it matter where a manager sits on the organizational totem pole. The simple facts are that every person in a supervisory or managerial position has an obligation to protect the employer's assets and that even the most routine tasks of management involve the utilization of assets.

Another simple fact is that in the rush of meeting other priorities managers tend to push their assets-protecting obligation into the background, and even when not rushed managers often have no idea how to go about meeting the obligation. Many are entirely dependent on the CSO, which in itself is a serious management failure. This is not to suggest ineptitude on the part of the CSO, only that the primary responsibility for the protection of assets belongs to managers and supervisors.

APPLYING THE SICM TECHNIQUE

SICM is a tool for fact finding, both reactively and proactively. If the facts to be found relate to a loss, the CSO starts with an examination of the incident and works downward. The amount of detail increases greatly as the inquiry probes deeper into the volcano. A single incident is likely to result from numerous substandard practices and conditions, and each practice or condition is sure to be rooted in a number of hidden causes.

Proactivity

A proactive use of SICM is to prevent an incident or reduce its negative effects. In this approach, the CSO starts at the bottom of the volcano and works upward. The idea is to identify the causes of an incident and take preventive steps before the incident happens. A logical start is to examine policies that relate to the use and care of assets. One such policy is the security policy. Does such a policy exist? Is it in writing? Has it been communicated throughout the organization? Is it understood, followed, and enforced?

Programs

Next to be examined are the various programs for carrying out policies. Several functional areas of interest come to mind: internal audit, safety, and some aspects of human resources such as preemployment screening and drug testing. Program activities will vary, as will the work groups that create and operate them.

The security program is a legitimate and logical focal point. Program activities worth examining include physical safeguards, security officer operations, protection of proprietary information, investigations, security awareness, and so forth. Each program component is or should be operated according to well-defined standards.

The CSO's Role

The CSO sets the security standards, implements standards that fall within his/her exclusive purview, and communicates security standards to managers for the purpose of helping them carry out their assets-protecting responsibilities. Finally, the CSO evaluates compliance.

The SICM technique can give a new perspective, one that prompts the CSO to ask the right questions and find answers buried below the surface. SICM does not replace good investigative practices and is not a substitute for critical thinking, but it can be a tool for organizing the CSO's approach to risk management.

CONCLUSIONS

Risk management is neither rocket science nor voodoo witchcraft. It is a simple and straightforward process that systematically identifies security-related exposures that affect or arise from the organization's activities. It is not a function to be turned on, such as when a new project is announced, and then turned off when the project is running smoothly. Risk management is in the continuous "on" mode, influencing the CSO's every serious decision.

NOTES

1. Mark Haynes Daniell, *Next Generation Strategy for a Volatile Era*, pp. 3–4, New York: John Wiley and Sons, 2000.

2. Carl A. Roper, *Risk Management for Security Professionals*, pp. 13, Boston: Butterworth-Heinemann, 1999.

3. Sal DePasquale, "Risk Analysis: Development of a Security Program," in *The Security Management Encyclopedia*, John J. Fay (ed.), pp. 637, Boston: Butterworth-Heinemann, 1993.

4. J. Kirk Barefoot, "Risk Management: An Overview," in *The Security Management Encyclopedia*, John J. Fay (ed.), pp. 639, Boston: Butterworth-Heinemann, 1993.

5. John J. Fay, "SICM: A Risk Management Tool," *Security Technology & Design*, August 2000, pp. 23–26.

10. Managing Guard Operations

The real problem is not whether machines think but whether men do.
—B. F. Skinner

PRIVATE POLICING

Private policing arrived in North America with early English settlers. Private police, whose duties were principally to watch for crime during the hours of darkness, supplemented town constables and sheriffs. In today's workplace, private police (i.e., security officers) play a greatly expanded role. They number more than 1.5 million, close to three times the number of public police officers, and have become common sights in many sectors of society, such as shopping malls, department stores, college campuses, office buildings, industrial plants, apartment complexes, and residential gated communities [1]. Organizations and individuals of all types employ security officers to curb trespassing, theft, robbery, and assault.

Security officer services are primarily directed at controlling access, patrolling (see Figure 10-1), escorting, inspecting for fire and safety hazards, and responding to emergencies. In some organizations, they direct traffic, receive supplies, ship goods, process visitors and guests, dispense general information to the public, and deliver mail.

SECURITY OFFICER SELECTION AND TRAINING

States vary according to entry-level requirements for selecting and training security officers. They range from none in states that have no laws regulating security officer work to numerous in states with regulations, and where requirements do exist the variances are not great. Still, there is a need for a single set of standards for all states. The American Society for Industrial Security International (ASIS) has developed selection and training guidelines, which are paraphrased in the following two sections.

Figure 10-1 An electronic wand creates a record of the security officer's patrol tour.

Selection

In the ASIS guidelines, a candidate must:

- Be at least 18 years old for an unarmed security position and 21 years old for an armed security position, with provisions that the candidate be able to perform the duties required of the position.
- Be a citizen or national of the United States, a lawful permanent resident, or an alien authorized to work in the United States.
- Provide to the regulatory authority current and previous residential addresses and phone numbers, and previous employers and their addresses and phone numbers for at least the previous seven years. The regulatory authority should verify the correctness of the candidate's name, social security number, and address and employment history, and should conduct a criminal records check in all jurisdictions where the candidate resided in the immediately previous seven years.
- Possess a high school diploma, the General Education Development (GED) certificate, or an equivalent. The applicant should be able to read, write, and speak English and be proficient in the language(s) appropriate to assigned duties. Aptitude testing is recommended.
- Not have been convicted of or pled *nolo contendere* to a felony during the seven-year period immediately preceding date of hire. If the application is for an armed security position, the candidate must not have been convicted of a state or federal misdemeanor involving the use or attempted use of physical force, or the threatened use of a deadly weapon.

To aid in determining these requirements, the candidate must submit fingerprint impressions.

- Pass a drug test.
- Possess a valid driver's license of the applicable vehicle class if the position applied for involves operation of a motor vehicle.
- Submit supporting documentation if the applicant asserts possession of a registration, certification, license, or other professional qualification related to the position applied for.

Training

The ASIS training guidelines require the employer to give to a security officer 48 hours of training within the first hundred days of employment. The following topics are recommended in the curriculum.

- Nature and Role of Private Security Officers
- Security Awareness
  - Private Security Officers and the Criminal Justice System
  - Information Sharing
  - Crime and Loss Prevention
- Legal Aspects of Private Security
  - Evidence and Evidence Handling
  - Use of Force and Force Continuum
  - Court Testimony
  - Incident Scene Preservation
  - Equal Employment Opportunity (EEO) and Diversity
  - State and Local Laws
- Security Officer Conduct
  - Ethics
  - Honesty
  - Professional Image
- Observation and Incident Reporting
  - Observation Techniques
  - Note Taking
  - Report Writing
- Patrol Techniques
- Principles of Communication
  - Interpersonal Skills
  - Verbal Communication Skills
  - Customer Service and Public Relations
- Principles of Access Control
  - Ingress and Egress Control Procedures
  - Electronic Security Systems
- Principles of Safeguarding Information
  - Proprietary and Confidential Information

- Emergency Response Procedures
  - Critical Incident Response (e.g., natural disasters, accidents, human-caused events)
  - Evacuation Processes
- Life Safety Awareness
  - Safety Hazards in the Workplace/Surroundings
  - Emergency Equipment Placement
  - Fire Prevention Skills
  - Hazardous Materials
  - Occupational Safety and Health Administration Requirments (e.g., OSHA-related training, bloodborne pathogens, and so on)
- Job Assignment and Post Orders

Depending on the requirements and specifications applicable to the assignment, consideration should be given to training that covers the following.

- Employer orientation and policies
- Substance abuse
- Communications modes (e.g., telephones, pagers, radios, computers)
- Workplace violence
- Conflict resolution awareness
- Traffic control and parking lot security
- Crowd control
- Procedures for first aid, cardiopulmonary resuscitation (CPR), and automatic external defibrillators (AEDs)
- Crisis management
- Labor relations (strikes, lockouts, and so on)

The employer should administer written and/or performance examination(s) that demonstrate that the security officer understands the subject matter presented by training and is able to perform the basic duties of a security officer.

SECURITY SCHEME

Deciding if security officer services are appropriate for an organization and determining how services will be performed are matters best dictated by a needs assessment. Conducted or commissioned by the CSO, the needs assessment identifies the assets to be protected and the manner of protection. The assessment considers security techniques such as physical safeguards, access control, and intrusion detection. Assessment findings lead to the development of a protective scheme that combines techniques with trained manpower, allowing also for contingencies such as industrial accidents, natural disasters, and workplace violence. As the protective scheme is fleshed out, the CSO determines the needed:

- Number of officers
- Officer skills
- Job tools and equipment

Staffing

When determining the number of officers required, the CSO looks at the staffing requirements for each post. If the post is to be manned by one security officer 24 hours per day, seven days per week, the number of actual performance hours per year will be 8,736 (i.e., $24 \times 7 \times 52$). If the post operates with three eight hour shifts, the number of hours of actual performance by one guard per year will be 2,912 ($8,736 \div 3$). But the CSO does not want to overwork security officers or pay excessive overtime wages. He operates from an assumption that a security officer will be productive by working eight hours per day, five days per week, for a total of 2,080 hours ($8 \times 5 \times 52$). The difference between the required shift hours (2,912) and the realizable shift hours (2,080) will have to be made up.

Other factors taking a security officer off post include vacation days, paid holidays, sick days, training, and time spent preparing for a day's tour of duty (e.g., checking out a weapon, standing inspection, receiving orders of the day, and traveling to the post). After running numbers on his pocket calculator, the CSO determines that the post in question, although operated 24 hours a day, will actually require 28 hours of labor per day. He determines the post's staffing requirement by multiplying the required person-hours per day (28) with the days per year (365) divided by the realizable shift hours per year (2,080). The result is 4.9 security officers [2].

Skills

Security officer capabilities for each post are also identified. Every post demands a combination of cognitive (knowledge), psychomotor (physical), and affective (attitudinal) skills (see Figure 10-2). Some posts require more of one than others. For example, a security console officer needs to know how to operate the equipment on the console, a post that requires an officer to stand or walk has physical and stamina demands, and a post that brings an officer face to face with people requires tact and a positive attitude.

Equipment

A job that requires the use of equipment cannot be performed properly without it. How simple. If a post is to be manned by an armed officer, the CSO necessarily considers the costs of providing, maintaining, and storing firearms and ammunition. Training in the use of firearms and laws that apply to deadly force is a very important consideration. The CSO gives equal attention to

Figure 10-2 Operating radio equipment is a basic task of a security officer.

equipment needs for access control, emergency medical response, firefighting, mobile patrol, and other security service functions.

PROPRIETARY VERSUS CONTRACT SECURITY

The user of security officer services can choose to employ security officers directly or contract for services with an outside firm. In the first option, called proprietary or in-house security, the officers receive their instructions and supervision from the employer. They are on the employer's payroll and are generally afforded the benefits and privileges of a regular employee. In the second, the security officers are in the direct employ of a contract security firm, and although they provide services to the customer they are supervised and managed by the contract firm.

Proprietary

The proprietary option will appeal to an organization that values loyalty, dislikes turnover, and feels a need to exercise close control over security officer operations. The contract option will appeal to a management that does not want to commit its supervisory resources to the administration of security officer services and wants to distance itself from security officer operations, thus hoping to reduce liability resulting from security officer negligence. In either option, the CSO makes the choice or gives input to it, and is held responsible for ensuring that the services contribute to the organization's overall assets-protecting objective.

When the proprietary option is selected, the CSO works with the organization's HR group. Recruiting, selecting, and hiring are handled in-house, with training provided or directed by the CSO. Going with a proprietary arrangement involves a hiring process unlike the hiring process of a contract security services company.

Contract

The usual procedure is to solicit bids from 10 or so contract security firms, and it is here that the CSO does the homework. He/she looks for bidders with strength in the following three broad areas.

- Quality performance delivered consistently
- Prompt responsiveness to concerns expressed by the customer
- Rates that are competitive but not necessarily low

Coming up with names of contract security firms that meet these simple criteria can be difficult. Helpful information sources include the American Society for Industrial Security International, the Building Owners and Managers Association, the Better Business Bureau, and the local Chamber of Commerce [3].

Bid Solicitation

The bid solicitation will reflect an expectation as to compensation. Although the contract firm may be free (within the limits of employment law and collective bargaining agreements) to offer compensation it believes reasonable and appropriate, the user of the contract service wants assurance that compensation is high enough to attract and retain quality officers. A rule of thumb in the security industry prescribes that an officer receive about 65 percent of the rate paid to the contract firm. The other 35 percent represents fringe benefits, the contract firm's operating costs, and profit. If the contractor offers a rate of $10.00 per hour for an entry-level guard, the customer has to know that the guard will be paid about $6.50 an hour. The question has to be asked: Will compensation at this level attract and hold a quality employee?

Figure 10-3 Security at a nuclear power plant requires knowledge of security and attention to safety.

The solicitation will also describe the nature, place, and conditions of work; the personal qualities the officers must possess in order to perform to minimum expectations (see Figure 10-3); and penalties for failure to deliver the agreed services. Very specific details will be included as to how and when bids are to be submitted and judged.

Scope of Work

A solicitation will refer to the *scope of work*, a term roughly corresponding to a job description. The scope of work might state that the site to be protected requires a security officer to examine badges at an entry point. The task of examining badges is broken down into specifics such as when and where the task is to be performed, the manner of performance, and the environmental conditions that apply (see Figure 10-4). Post orders and other written guidance might be appended.

Officer Standards

The solicitation might include details as to the knowledge, skill, and training required for acceptable officer performance (see Figure 10-5). These might call for knowledge of law, skill in operating certain equipment, or certification in CPR and first aid.

Responding To a Duress Alarm

What you need to know	Duress alarms are in place at several key locations on Company premises, e.g., the receptionist's desk on the executive floor, the credit union teller's station in the lobby, and the operator's desk at the computer center. Also positioned at these locations are CCTV cameras that automatically go into the record mode when the duress button has been pressed.	**Violent emergencies**	If the emergency is of a violent nature, such as a shooting or a robbery in progress, the response will be to take no action that could cause an escalation of violence. In this case, the console operator immediately will take the following actions: ■ Call 911 and ask for police assistance. ■ NOT dispatch the roving patrol. ■ Continue to watch the CCTV monitor and respond appropriately, e.g., relay further details to the police, such as descriptions of the offender, the offender's vehicle, direction of travel from the scene, or make a request for an ambulance if injuries occurred.
What to do when a duress alarm activates	Upon receipt of a duress alarm, the console operator at the security control center will look at the CCTV monitor to learn the nature of the emergency.		
Non-violent emergencies	If the emergency is of a nonviolent nature, such as an injury or sudden illness, the console operator will: ■ Use the base station radio to dispatch the roving patrol to the incident location and provide details as to the nature of the emergency. ■ Call 911 to ask for an ambulance, if one is needed.	**Needed reports**	An activation of a duress alarm will in every case require an entry in the Daily Log and an Incident Report. A verbal report will also be made to the Security Leader.

Figure 10-4 Job instructions are often attached to the solicitation of a contract bid.

Bid Evaluation

Selecting a contractor begins by verifying the bidder's license and insurance certificates. A Dun & Bradstreet report can provide information on the history and ongoing operations of the bidder. Inquiries might include a check of civil court records and criminal histories of the bidder's owners and senior managers. The CSO should obtain written assurance that the bidder will agree to a hold-harmless clause, a stipulation that frees the organization of fault or guilt stemming from improper performance of services. Other considerations include selecting a provider that can document the following.

- A lower-than-average turnover rate.
- A capability to quickly engage competent new hires.

Recommended Hiring Standards for Security Officers

A security officer applicant must:

Be at least 18 years old if applying for an unarmed officer position, and be at least 21 years old if applying for an armed officer position.

Possess a valid driving license if driving is a part of the job.

Submit an application that includes full identification data, citizenship status, and a statement of conviction of crimes. Attach two sets of fingerprints and two passport-size photos.

Furnish information about prior employment during at least the last seven years. Provide three personal references.

Pass a pre-employment drug test.

Never have been convicted or pled guilty or *nolo contendere* to a felony.

Never have been convicted or pled guilty or *nolo contendere* to a misdemeanor involving moral turpitude, acts of dishonesty, or acts against government authority, including the use and/or possession of a controlled substance in the last seven years.

Never have been convicted or pled guilty or *nolo contendere* to any crime involving the sale, delivery, or manufacture of a controlled substance.

Never have been declared by any court to be incompetent by reason of mental disease or defect.

Must have completed training in areas involving the law, security operations, firearms, administrative requirements, electronic technology, armored transport, and the use of force.

Must have completed training specific to the type of license applied for. Examples of licenses include:

> Temporary Permit. Issued by the employer after the applicant has completed training and the license application has been submitted to the state licensing agency.
>
> Class I: Security Officer/Unarmed Alarm Responder. Issued by the state licensing agency after the applicant has met the application criteria.
>
> Class II: Armed Security Officer/Armed Alarm Responder.
>
> Class III: Armored Car Security Officer. This license is issued by the state licensing agency after the applicant has met the application criteria and has successfully completed a state-approved firearms training course.

Figure 10-5 The International Association of Chiefs of Police (IACP), which has for many years collaborated with the security industry, recommends these hiring standards.

- A hiring process that screens out drug and alcohol abusers, felons, and persons with a history of violent conduct. Choosing a security services provider in an overseas area requires addressing the matter of human rights violations. The CSO should take care to not contract with companies whose past or current performance indicates a disregard for human rights. Excessive use of force and cruel or degrading treatment are examples [4].
- Skilled on-site supervision.
- A training program that provides new hires with entry-level knowledge, skill, and on-the-job tutorials (see Figure 10-6).

QUALITY OF SERVICE

Selection of a security services provider should be based first on quality of service. Price, although always important, is secondary to quality. At this

Figure 10-6 Important skills are developed through one-on-one coaching.

point a contractor has been selected. Now begins the CSO's next function: monitoring contractor performance and comparing performance against contract specifications. Two areas of monitoring stand out: guard training and guard supervision.

Guard Training

Quality services are founded on training. Before an officer is assigned to the job, he/she must undergo training. Officers at the entry level usually receive instruction in the laws of search and seizure, arrest and detention, and abuse of authority. Instruction might also stress the importance of courtesy, nonfraternization with employees of the customer, punctuality, and personal appearance. The CSO who oversees the contract might also require preassignment training in CPR, first aid, and operation of oxygen-administering equipment and a defibrillator.

Training should continue after the officer has been placed on the job. On the very first day of work, the officer should begin learning the geography of the site, post orders, procedures for access control and intrusion detection, safety rules, responses to emergencies, and report writing. Within a month or so, the officer should have a working familiarity with the customer's business operations and the key players of the organization. With this familiarity comes an understanding of the organization's culture and values.

The methods of training can vary. These include having the officer read relevant materials, attend formal lectures, watch films or videotapes, observe others as they perform the required tasks, and perform required tasks under the watchful eye of a supervisor. The experiences of skilled trainers indicate that learning by doing yields better results than learning by reading, watching, or listening.

Guard Supervision

Two levels of guard supervision are at play in a contract security operation. First, and most important, is the day-to-day supervision directly exercised on-site. The major duties of the supervisor's job include preparing the work schedule, briefing officers prior to going on post, maintaining and updating post orders, inspecting posts, maintaining documentation related to the work, and mentoring officers. Consider the following anecdote.

CASE STUDY

Joe Palombo, on-site supervisor of the contract security officer services at a large shopping mall, knew he did not have enough security officers to adequately patrol the entire site, and he had made his concern known to his employer. Joe's employer, Iritus Security Services, had not responded, even though aware that Iritus had committed in its contract with the mall "to protect persons on mall property."

At the far end of the mall, away from the anchor stores visited by shoppers, was leased office space. The leaseholder was a county department of human services. A male claimant for assistance got into an argument with a female claims processor. The argument migrated into the hallway of the mall, at which point the claimant punched the processor in the face, breaking her jaw.

The claims processor sued the mall owner and Iritus, claiming negligence plus breach of the security services contract between the mall owner and Iritus. The trial court granted summary judgment to the mall owner but not to Iritus. The court said that the mall owner had met the obligation to provide security when it hired the services of a professional security company but the professional security company had failed to meet a fundamental duty described in the contract, specifically the duty of protecting persons at the mall. Iritus fired Joe two days later. Joe subsequently talked to an attorney about filing a wrongful termination suit.

A second form of supervision is exercised by the management of the contract security services provider. An account manager monitors security officer operations to ensure that performance meets the standards defined in the contract. He/she presents findings to the on-site security supervisor and the customer's designated representative (who may be the CSO and/or property manager). Quality assurance is the principal objective. It often takes the form of a quarterly review and an annual inspection, as well as interventions that are needed to keep security officer performance in line with customer expectations.

ASSURANCE

The signing of a contract for security services is the starting point of a potentially tempestuous journey. Two travelers, the contractor and the customer, make the journey together. The contractor's function is to deliver services; the customer's function is to ensure that services are delivered according to contract specifications. The customer's agent for ensuring security officer performance is the CSO.

Assurance does not involve directly supervising contract security operations; nor does it involve meddling in the administrative affairs of the contractor, such as questioning security officer performance ratings or intervening on behalf of a disciplined officer. These actions could open the door to legal problems; for example, becoming a defendant in a civil suit alleging security officer negligence.

The relationship between customer and contractor has to be robust but kept at arm's length. When the customer gets overly close to the contractor, a co-employer situation is said to exist. Co-employment opens a Pandora's box of legal woes. The interaction between customer and contractor should be at the management level (e.g., the CSO reports his concerns to the contractor's account manager, who decides the corrective actions and reports results back to the CSO).

To be effective at assurance, the CSO has to pay attention to what is happening. This can be done by simply watching security officers at work and talking with people on the receiving end of security officer services. When security officer performance appears unsatisfactory or service receivers complain, the CSO acquires specifics and irons out problems with the contractor's account manager.

The purpose of assurance is not to carp in order to strengthen demands but to enlighten so that improvements can follow. The opportunity to enlighten is through frequent (at least weekly) meetings, the ground rules of which require dialogue in both directions. The CSO avoids an adversarial approach. Topics for discussion can include the contractor's strengths and weaknesses, problem-solving and quality-enhancing ideas, and solutions as opposed to iteration of problems. The CSO should also mention upcoming changes that might impact security officer operations. This can also be an appropriate occasion for the contractor to make the customer aware of new technologies or services [5].

VALUE OF GUARD SERVICES

The value of security officer services is difficult to measure because the output is intangible (i.e., it cannot be held, weighed, or measured). No one knows for certain the amount of loss that was avoided because a security officer was present as a psychological deterrent or because the officer acted in a particular way to prevent a loss.

The marketing and customer relation aspects of service often overlap the operations function. A service delivered with excellence may be perceived as poor if the relationship between the account manager and the customer contact is fractious. Not only is service value difficult to measure, it is often measured by the wrong yardstick.

Although security services are customer centered, the customer is not always present when the service is delivered. Excellent performance provided out of sight may go unrecognized, whereas a minor lapse that occurs when the customer is present attracts attention.

CUSTOMER AND CONTRACTOR RELATIONSHIPS

The relationship between the customer and the contractor is best viewed as a partnership in which both sides strive for open communications. The CSO expresses what is wanted; the contractor listens carefully and follows up with action. If the contractor representative cannot deliver on what is wanted, he/she is obligated to say so. The CSO's expression of wants proceeds from a short list of internalized questions (see Figure 10-7), such as the following.

- Is the contractor delivering services that correspond to the organization's overall goals and the security group's objectives?
- Does the contractor have and deploy resources that meet these goals and objectives?
- Does the security force have the right mix of officers, and do their individual and collective talents match the work they perform?
- Are security officers performing unnecessary tasks?
- Is the security force properly utilizing security aids such as access control and intrusion detection systems?
- Is the contractor meeting contract specifications?
- Are there any operating costs that can be reduced or eliminated?

Mutual Respect

Respect is an essential element for successful partnering. The CSO respects a contractor who asks if the services are on target, pays attention to the answers, tries honestly to deliver, and is not afraid to innovate. The CSO wants his partner to act like a winner, show a positive attitude, and be determined to do what it takes to satisfy.

The contractor's respect for the CSO is based on demonstrated competence. The CSO's image rises when he/she displays an understanding of the processes and technologies that drive the contractor's line of business. Competence is also reflected in the CSO's ability to work with people, to negotiate in good faith, and to give a little when merited. At the back of the contractor's mind is a concern that the CSO's expectations may exceed capabilities. Yes, the contractor wants to deliver high-quality services, but the costs have to be controlled.

Checklist for Assessing Security Officer Operations

Yes	No	
___	___	Do standards exist for recruiting, selecting, training, and supervising the security officer force?
		Are security officers screened prior to employment? If so, does screening include:
___	___	Criminal records check?
___	___	Drug and alcohol abuse?
___	___	Psychological testing?
		Have security officers received pre-assignment training in:
___	___	Criminal law and powers to detain and search?
___	___	Security equipment and procedures?
___	___	Safety and fire regulations?
___	___	Fire-fighting procedures?
___	___	CPR and basic first aid?
___	___	Oxygen and defibrillation assistance?
		Is follow-up training given as to:
___	___	Regulations that apply to the site?
___	___	Specific job duties?
___	___	Layout of the installation, vulnerable points, and hazardous areas?
___	___	The use and maintenance of security equipment?
___	___	Safety and fire regulations?
___	___	Emergency equipment such as generators, UPS systems, and control switches?
___	___	Are security officers licensed or certified as required by law?
___	___	Is the number of security officers adequate for the site?
___	___	Are officer replacements and reinforcements available?
___	___	Do the work shifts have the correct number of officers?
___	___	Are the work shifts too long or too short?
___	___	Is the guard organization structured to facilitate a clear chain of command?
___	___	Are security officers rotated between stationary posts?
___	___	Do the officers know how to respond when alarms are activated?
___	___	Are officer duties specified in emergency plans?
___	___	Do officers understand their emergency duties and are they tested by practical exercises?
___	___	Are officers familiar with the use of basic fire-fighting equipment?
___	___	Are patrol officers equipped with radios?
___	___	Are the officers provided with written instructions that cover their duties?
___	___	Were such instructions drawn up in consultation with all interested parties?
___	___	Is an updated copy of written instructions available to security employees on duty?
		Is there a logbook in which the following are reflected?
___	___	Supervisory visits.
___	___	Shift change.
___	___	Incidents/occurrences.
___	___	Special instructions.
___	___	Does the person responsible for security review the logbook on a regular basis?
___	___	Is there a method for supervising and monitoring patrols?

Figure 10-7 A list of pertinent questions can be helpful when assessing the security force.

Agreement Issues

The contract between a customer and a security services provider requires the provider to perform on behalf of the customer certain services according to specified standards. When a service is not performed as specified, the customer may at first seek to negotiate a satisfactory solution. A contract will often contain a "Failure to Perform" provision requiring the provider to reimburse the customer for costs incurred as a result of the provider's failure to carry out the agreement. For example, the provider might be obligated to pay the customer's cost for finding a substitute security officer when the provider's employee failed to show up. The failure-to-perform concept is sometimes enforced punitively. The contract may require the provider to pay a monetary penalty to the customer, a common practice in the matter of over-billing. If the CSO or other person charged with checking and approving the provider's bills detects an over-billing (or a pattern of over-billing), the customer can deduct from the bill a stipulated amount. Failing a settlement between the two parties, the customer may seek a remedy in civil court for breach of contract.

Liability

Of great concern to the CSO is a fear of a lawsuit arising out of an improper act by an employee of the security services provider. Even though a contract has assigned to the provider clearly stated responsibilities, courts have held that the customer is fully or partly liable. The improper acts of security officers that seem most common are unlawful detention, assault, battery, infliction of emotional distress, defamation, and causing injury to persons or damage to property [6].

A legal principle called *respondeat superior* says that an employer can be held liable for injuries caused by an employee. The injured party, such as a shopper wrongly detained by a department store security officer, will usually sue the officer, the security guard company, and the department store.

Lawsuits are avoidable, mainly through training and supervision. Security officers have to be taught the applicable laws in the jurisdiction where they work, the limitations on their enforcement powers, and the actions that may be taken against them in criminal and civil courts.

LIFE SAFETY PROGRAM

On the menu of services provided by the security group is a life safety program that anticipates a full range of life-threatening emergencies such as fire, serious injury or illness, severe weather, bomb incidents, terrorism, and civil disorder. Because the organization's guard force has roles to play in such emergencies, a supervisor of the security force is often brought into the program.

The security supervisor can be assigned to

- Confer and liaise with local agencies (e.g., fire, municipal police, and ambulance services, civil defense and emergency management services, and organizations that provide specialized services).
- Help prepare an overall Life Safety Plan, as well as an emergency preparedness manual that delineates the specific responses of security officers.
- Designate life safety responsibilities to individuals in the security force and designate backup officers for the key positions.
- Train guards to look for and report fire and other hazardous conditions, operate the public address system, operate fire extinguishers and other emergency response equipment, coordinate evacuation of the premises, and assist emergency response personnel such as firefighters and police officers.
- Conduct periodic tests of emergency response equipment (e.g., fire detection devices, fire extinguishers, public address system, and air-handling system).
- Help educate employees as to how fire is detected and reported, building evacuation procedures, and the evacuation assembly areas. Also explain the tasks performed by security officers.
- Keep a name and phone number list of people involved in life safety, such as floor wardens.
- Keep a daily attendance roster of people who perform essential life safety duties, such as floor wardens and building maintenance workers, and be prepared in an emergency to designate security officers to fill in for life safety responders who are absent from the workplace.
- Maintain in ready condition life safety equipment such as bull horns, flashlights, first aid kits, stretchers, and wheel chairs.

THE SECURITY SYSTEM

A facility's security system has three pillars: people, physical safeguards, and procedures. Security officers are in the people pillar. Without security officers, all three pillars would topple. People cannot fully respond to an emergency if there is no one to inform them of it. A CCTV system has no value if there is no one watching the monitors. Procedures are words on paper when there is no one to bring them into action.

Not only are security officers critical to the operation of the facility's security system, they are more likely to commit errors than the other two pillars. The probability that an intrusion sensor will fail is in the range of one to two percent. Failure of a plan or procedure will happen just once before being corrected.

Managing security officer operations is not easy. Such operations cover a lot of ground and are fraught with opportunities for human error. They require constant management attention because a single failure in a major emergency, such as a terrorist attack, can result in many lives lost and much property damaged or destroyed.

NOTES

1. Bruce L. Berg, *Policing in Modern Society*, pp. 441, Boston: Butterworth-Heinemann, 1999.

2. *Physical Security, Field Manual 19–30*, pp. 160–161, Washington, D.C.: Headquarters, Department of the Army, 1979.

3. Vicki S. Looney and Terry F. Whitley, "Contract Security: Contracting for Guard Services," in *Encyclopedia of Security Management*, John J. Fay (ed.), pp. 179, Boston: Butterworth-Heinemann, 1993.

4. For more than three decades, professional associations have extensively discussed and argued the issue of minimum standards for security officers. Some states have adopted standards; others have not. The standards that do exist are in some respects inconsistent. One point in common agreement among those concerned with standards is the likelihood that the U.S. Congress will step into the picture and establish a set of national standards.

5. John D. Stees, "Monitoring for Peak Performance," *Security Management*, April 2000, p. 26.

6. Philip P. Purpura, "Legal Concerns in Loss Prevention," in *Encyclopedia of Security Management*, John J. Fay (ed.), pp. 464, Boston: Butterworth-Heinemann, 1993.

11. Managing Physical Security

If I had only known, I would have been a locksmith.
—Albert Einstein

BACKGROUND

Buildings are constructed to meet purposes: churches are places where people pray, schools are places of education, and palaces are symbols of power and status. All places for human assembly, regardless of purpose, are arranged with physical security in mind. Indeed, physical security can be the sole purpose of a facility such as a nuclear weapons storage site or a prison.

TYPES OF PROTECTED ASSETS

The term *physical security* refers to a logical set of tangible elements that protect selected assets from damage, compromise, and loss [1]. The tangible elements are integrated and mutually supporting. In an intrusion attempt, for example, a fence slows an intruder down, sensors send alarms, lighting makes the intruder visible, and CCTV cameras track the intruder's direction of travel.

A protected asset can be a site or something within a site. A site is often demarcated by a boundary, which can be a property line, a roadway, or terrain features such as rivers and shorelines. A portion of the surrounding land, although not an actual part of the site, is sometimes included in the umbrella of protection.

When the protected asset is within the site, its location can be small, such as a cabinet or room, or larger such as a wing of a building, a building, or a group of buildings. A group of buildings could be a college campus or a petroleum refinery. Some structures are assets that contain assets such as planes carrying passengers, ships carrying cargo, or freight trains carrying toxic chemicals.

SAFEGUARDS

There are two types of security safeguards: human and physical. One cannot be functional without the other. In the previous chapter we discussed the human safeguard — security officers — and in this chapter we'll look at physical safeguards. Physical safeguards vary widely and for various reasons. One of those reasons is the nature of the target. In security lingo, the target is the thing being protected. A target can be a physical object such as the Hope diamond; a nonphysical object such as the formula for Coca-Cola; human objects both individually (e.g., the President of the United States) and collectively (e.g., tourists visiting Egypt); or a structure such as the Golden Gate Bridge. For purposes of clarity, we will refer to the target as a facility or a site. Both are catch-all terms that can mean anything from a grocery store to an entire city.

FACTORS IN SELECTING SAFEGUARDS

Now that we're on the same sheet of music, let's look at factors that influence the CSO's choice of physical safeguards.

Environment

The area surrounding the facility will greatly influence the choice of safeguards. A petroleum production platform operating in the Gulf of Mexico will require safeguards markedly different from those required for an office building in Manhattan or an ammunition plant in the desert of Nevada. For example, within the set of safeguards for the production platform may be specially secured access ways from the sea, the office building may opt for electronic locks on exterior doors, and the ammunition plant may go with a perimeter fence.

Forces of Nature

Also at play in the selection of safeguards are the environment's climate, weather, and natural forces. Certain detection sensor devices cannot or do not work well in extreme temperatures and are vulnerable to tornadoes, hurricanes, floods, earthquakes, and sinkholes. Other impacts to be considered are the interfering effects on sensors of noise and vibrations from external sources (such as aircraft flying overhead or heavy vehicles traveling on adjacent roadways) and the hazards created by operations at nearby facilities such as ground water contamination from spills and air contamination from smokestack releases. These factors point also to the need to have emergency response services readily available. If the community is lacking in these services, the organization will be forced to provide for itself.

Crime

Crime is a major influencing factor. The assessment of risk that precedes selection of safeguards will reveal the nature, intensity, and repetitiveness of criminal acts that have occurred in or near the facility during the recent past. The apparent crime pattern will dictate the necessary counteracting safeguards.

Terrorism

Terrorism is a very important factor in selecting safeguards. The CSO will want to determine if there is a particular terrorist group that may have an interest in targeting the facility. The nature or the activities of the facility may have the attention of some terrorist groups but not others. Along these lines, the thinking process of a CSO at a government building will be much different than that of a CSO at a biological research lab. Terrorist groups, like other violent criminals, favor certain tactics and weapons. This, too, is a factor for consideration.

Site Characteristics

Selection of safeguards can be influenced by the nature of the site, including the following aspects (see Figure 11-1).

- Size, layout, utilities, and compositional materials
- Internal activities
- Assets in or forming a part of the site
- Security experience of the CSO
- Philosophy of the site's ownership or management
- Culture of the workforce

CONCENTRIC PROTECTION

A CSO in a high-security facility often abides by a concentric protection or defense-in-depth theory; that is, the overall security scheme features several rings of security that in the abstract look like a shooting target. The outermost ring, which is at or on the far edge of the perimeter, might be a clear zone in which the approach of an intruder or intruder force can be seen by human and/or electronic means. The next ring might be a wall or fence, and then another wall or fence. Supplementing the walls or fences might be guard posts, patrols, detection sensors, CCTV cameras, and security lighting. The next ring might be sentry-protected and electronically controlled doors to a building or a complex of buildings. Within the building might be another ring of security consisting of access-controlled exclusion areas, and yet another ring within the exclusion areas might consist of safes, vaults, and

Physical Security Safeguards

	Security Control Center	Building Main Entrance	Secondary Personnel Entrances	Common Areas	Interior Doors	Ship and Receive	Perimeter
Electronic lock	X	X			X		
Access control	X	X	X		X	X	
CCTV monitors	X						
Security panel	X						
Integrated server	X						
Annunciator	X						
Lighting controls	X						
Fire panel	X						
HVAC controls	X						
Comm system	X						
Hi-Sec padlock		X	X		X	X	
CCTV cameras		X	X	X	X	X	X
Intercom		X	X			X	
Door closer		X	X		X	X	
Motion lighting		X	X			X	X
Reinforced doors		X	X		X	X	
X-ray equipment						X	
RFID/Bar code						X	
Barriers							X
Fence sensors							X
Electronic gates							X
Guard house							X
Boundary sensor			X		X	X	X
Motion sensor						X	X
Proximity sensor						X	X
Lighting		X	X			X	X

Figure 11-1 A single building can be protected with numerous physical security safeguards.

similar containers, inside of which might be motion-detection devices. The theory operates on the simple premise that an attempted intrusion will have a lesser chance of success when multiple layers of protection stand in the way (see Figure 11-2).

Perimeter

The usual starting point in assessing risk at a facility is the perimeter. Keeping in mind that the fundamental purposes of perimeter security are to detect, deter, and delay unwanted intrusion, the CSO looks for an attainable balance point between what is desirable and what is acceptable. To illustrate, the desire may be to maintain absolute integrity by erecting a formidable fence or wall on the property line supplemented with a patrol force, intrusion sensors, and a clear zone or *cordon sanitaire* on the outside of the fence. However, when such measures happen to be forbidden by law, social mores, or terrain, the

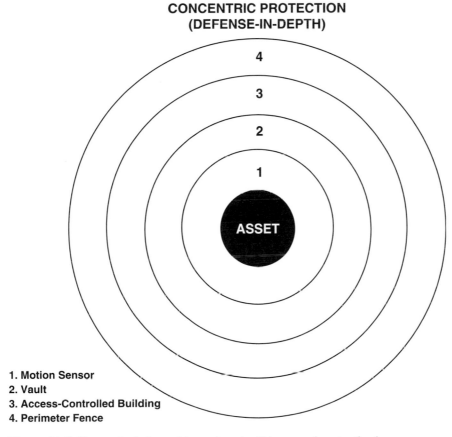

CONCENTRIC PROTECTION
(DEFENSE-IN-DEPTH)

1. Motion Sensor
2. Vault
3. Access-Controlled Building
4. Perimeter Fence

Figure 11-2 The protected asset is enclosed within several protective layers.

CSO may have to lower his or her sights to a different protective scheme, yet one that is attainable and effective at an acceptable level.

Barriers

Within and around a protected facility will be man-made structural barriers; for example, fences, walls, floors, roofs, bars, and grills. Around the facility may also be natural barriers; for example, mountains, ravines, rivers, lakes, and oceans. The facility, primarily through the expertise of the CSO, takes advantage of both forms of barriers because they can discourage or prevent entry and restrict or channel access.

Advantages

Three security advantages can be obtained through the intelligent use of barriers. First is psychological deterrence. A potential intruder is dissuaded when access appears problematic. Second is the actual difficulty in getting through physical barriers. Third are the benefits of reducing the cost of security staffing by substituting barriers for people, and placing security posts in locations that complement barriers.

Barrier Purposes

Barriers vary according to purpose. The following are common purposes.

- Control the movement of people and vehicles into, out of, and within the facility
- Segregate or compartmentalize sensitive areas
- Provide physical protection to objects, materials, and processes of a critical nature

Chain-link Fencing

Chain-link is used almost exclusively for perimeter fencing. The fence is normally 7 feet high, has a galvanized mesh of 9-gauge thickness, and mesh openings not larger than 2 inches. The selvage at the bottom and top of the mesh is twisted and barbed. The mesh is taut and sturdily attached to rigid metal posts set in concrete. The depth of the concrete settings will vary according to soil conditions (e.g., deeper settings will be required in sand and shifting or loose soil).

The integrity of the fence line can be jeopardized by crawl-through openings at the bottom. These openings are usually the result of gullies and similar natural erosions, as well as man-made culverts and ditches. Compensation can be obtained by blocking the openings with additional chain-link or steel mesh and grillwork.

Protection is added when the fence has three strands of barbed wire or razor tape strung equidistantly between supporting arms attached to the top of fence posts. The top guard faces outward and upward, adding at least one foot to the overall height of the fence (see Figure 11-3).

An alternative to a chain-link fence is a masonry wall. It, too, will have a height of 7 feet, a top guard or shards of glass cemented to the top surface, and blocking material at ground-line openings [2].

Lighting Uses

Lighting is very helpful when security officers are tasked to identify entry badges, inspect entering and departing vehicles, detect suspicious activity, and maintain visual surveillance at key points (e.g., clear zone, fence line, building exteriors, loading docks, and storage yards). Lighting can also assist security officers at guard posts and on patrol.

The protective capability of lighting is diminished in the absence of observation by a security officer force. A preventive or reactive response cannot be launched without first having someone in place to confirm an intruder's

Figure 11-3 A fence reduces the need for security manpower. *(Photo courtesy of Burns International Security Services.)*

approach or penetration attempt. A modicum of protection is afforded by the psychological deterrence of lighting, but the greater value by far is lighting supplemented by human intervention [3].

Types of Lighting and Lamps

Protective lighting is often categorized by type or purpose, such as the following.

- Flood lighting is continuous illumination of a protected area during the hours of darkness by means of overlapping cones of light from overhead lamps (e.g., pole- and roof-mounted lamps).
- Glare lighting is lighting directed outward from the protected area so that the intruder is made highly visible and is not allowed to easily see what lies ahead. Glare lighting also adds protection to security officers posted behind the light source.
- Controlled lighting is illumination that does not impede nearby operations such as traffic moving on a roadway, aircraft landing at an airport, and ships traveling in navigable waters.
- Moveable lighting consists of manually operated portable lamps. They often supplement or temporarily replace other forms of lighting.
- Emergency lighting consists of standby lamps that come into operation when a primary lighting source goes out of operation due to power failure or emergency condition. The power source of emergency lighting is usually a backup generator or an arrangement of batteries. Lamps

mounted in a stairwell that automatically light up during a fire fall into the emergency lighting category.

The following are lamps commonly used for security reasons [4].

- *Incandescent lamp:* Operates the same way as the light-bulb type of lamp used at home, and immediately goes on when electric current is applied to a filament. Incandescent lamps are manufactured in a wide variety of wattages and sizes and meet the requirements of many security needs.
- *Fluorescent lamp:* Also common in the home, has an elongated tubular shape and is typically ceiling mounted. It is efficient and economical but casts illumination over a relatively short distance.
- *Gaseous discharge lamp:* Goes on when electric current is applied to a luminous gas. Mercury (blue-white color) and sodium (golden-yellow color) lamps operate on the gaseous discharge principle. These lamps have a relatively long life and produce a high degree of light, but arrive at full illumination slowly.
- *Quartz lamp:* Produces a bright white light that when directed into the eyes (e.g., the eyes of the intruder) is intensely glaring. This lamp reaches full illumination almost as quickly as the incandescent lamp and is often utilized in outdoor and portable applications where brightness facilitates detailed work, such as that performed at the scene of an accident.

Lighting specifications as to purpose (flood, glare, controlled, moveable, and emergency), location of use, efficacy, efficiency, light distribution, coverage, illumination distance, and foot candles are obtainable from manufacturers, publications [5], and industry associations such as the Illumination Engineering Society of North America (IESNA).

SENSORS

Sensors perform three main functions: (1) detect intruders, (2) open a portal, and (3) turn on another device. For example, sensors that react to motion, sound, and body heat meet the function of intrusion detection; a sensor that reacts to the presentation of a card key performs the function of opening a door; and a sensor that reacts to changes in light conditions satisfies the function of turning security lights on or off in a parking lot.

Sensor Reactions

Sensors designed for detecting intrusion react to the following:

- Breaking of a circuit
- Interruption of a light beam
- Movement
- Sound

- Vibration
- Change in an energy field

Sensors variously detect penetration of a boundary, unexplained presence within a zone, and unexplained presence in close proximity to a zone or a protected object. Intrusion detection sensors are calibrated to activate when a monitored norm is altered beyond a predetermined level. The activated sensor causes an alarm to be sounded or a signal to be sent to a monitoring station such as the security control center of a protected facility.

Sensor Groups

Detection sensors, both exterior and interior, are essential components in any serious protective scheme. When properly installed, calibrated, and serviced, sensors are accurate and reliable, not to mention economical compared to the cost of labor. Sensors that operate out of doors are said to be exterior sensors. Sensors that operate within a structure are called interior sensors. Some sensors can be exterior and interior.

The sensor group selected will be influenced by the physical nature of the environment in which it will operate. For the outdoors environment, the factors to be considered include topography, soil composition, weather, and radio or electrical interference. For the indoors environment, the choice can be affected by building structure, tremors, and sound resulting from the facility's operational activities, as well as by unintended interference by persons performing their routine duties. Sensors are also selected on the presumed capabilities and intentions of potential intruders, and the capabilities of the security force to respond to and effectively negate intrusion attempts.

Distinct Characteristics of Sensors

Sensors are grouped according to a distinct characteristic among the following. These categories are discussed in the material that follows.

- Exterior
- Interior
- Passive
- Active
- Volumetric
- Line detection
- Line-of-sight
- Terrain-following
- Covert
- Visible
- Covert or visible

Exterior sensors: These devices are typically installed in open areas, such as in a clear zone; atop, on, or inside a fence or wall; and under the ground.

They can be manufactured to withstand extreme temperatures and operate in severe weather conditions. On the other hand, by comparison with interior sensors they have a reduced probability of detecting intrusion and an increased false alarm rate. This results mainly from uncontrollable factors such as standing water, blowing debris, and stray animals. When uncontrollable factors are present, two or more sensors — each operating on a separate principle of detection — can be set up to cover the same area or asset.

Interior sensors: Unlike their exterior counterparts, these sensors are unaffected by weather and terrain features and are less affected by uncontrollable factors. In addition to detecting intrusion, interior sensors can be used to detect fire, contaminated air, and in-progress attempts at sabotage or theft of critical assets.

These sensors detect intrusion into or within a building or complex of buildings and are largely (though not exclusively) unsuitable for outdoor applications. They fulfill their functions by detecting the following.

- Approach and/or penetration of an intruder
- Movement of an intruder within a protected area
- Touching or moving of a protected object

Interior sensors are not immune to false alarms, but due to the relatively benign environments in which they operate they are reliable to a higher degree than exterior sensors. When an exterior sensor is defeated, the culprit is almost always an outsider trying to get in. When an interior sensor is defeated, the culprit can be an inside employee or an outsider.

Passive sensors: This sensor group does not emit energy. It reacts to energy emitted by the intruder or to a change in a field of energy caused by the intruder. The phenomena reacted to can include heat (e.g., body heat of the intruder), vibration (e.g., opening of a door), sound (e.g., breaking glass), and capacitance (touching an object or being in close proximity to it). The passive infrared sensor, a commonly used sensor, detects thermal energy (body heat) and therefore falls into this group.

Active sensors: These sensors send energy into a defined area, which may be a zone through which an intruder must pass to reach the protected asset. The energy, usually radio frequency (RF) energy, is disturbed when it encounters something that should not be in the zone. The disturbed energy is returned to the sensor device. This requires a transmitter for sending energy and a receiver for receiving returned energy. As opposed to a passive sensor, which emits no energy, the energy of an active sensor is detectable by an adversary outside the protected zone.

Volumetric sensors: This sensor group detects movement in a given volume of space (i.e., a zone). The zone is filled with an energy form such as magnetic, electric, or RF energy. When the "normal" pattern is altered to a degree indicative of movement within the zone, the sensor activates.

An advantage of the volumetric sensor is that it detects movement anywhere within a zone, whereas boundary sensors can only inform the monitoring station that a penetration occurred at some place on the edge of the zone.

Line detection sensors: These sensors react to penetration. They can be placed on fences, gates, doors, and windows to detect vibration; on objects to detect touching; and on buried cables to detect above-ground passage.

Line-of-sight sensors: These sensor devices have a transmitter and receiver. A continuous signal moves between the two. When the signal is interrupted, the sensor reacts. The signal is often a beam of light.

Terrain-following sensors: This sensor group might better be called the non-line-of-sight group because it can be used just about anywhere the line-of-sight sensor can't be used. Also, "terrain-following" is a little misleading because in addition to the sensor being functional on irregular ground surfaces it is functional on fences and walls that are curved or angular. On irregular ground surfaces, the sensor is typically a buried cable that variously reacts to changes in electric and magnetic fields radiating upward, and to seismic sounds and pressure at ground level caused by the weight of a passing person or vehicle. On fences and walls, the terrain-following sensor reacts to magnetic and electric field changes, vibration, and tension.

Covert sensors: As the name suggests, sensors in this category are concealed from the view of an intruder. A rationale for use of covert sensors is apprehension of the intruder.

Visible sensors: These are visible to an intruder. A rationale for use of visible sensors is deterrence.

Covert and visible: These sensors can be used both ways.

Sensor Types

As explained, each of the sensor groups described previously has a distinct characteristic, e.g., exterior or interior. Sensors are also categorized by what they detect: vibration, motion, sound, interruption of an electric field, a magnetic field, or a photoelectric beam, and weight. These are types of sensors, and a sensor type will fall into any or all of the sensor groups. For example, a magnetic field sensor (a type) is used in the exterior environment, it is passive, detects on a line, follows the terrain, and can't be seen. The chart titled "Sensor Configurations" depicts the relationships.

The more common types of sensors are listed below. These types are discussed in the material that follows.

- Vibration
- Taut Wire
- Magnetic Field

- Electric Field
- Fiber-Optic Cable
- Seismic
- Pressure
- Ported Coaxial Cable
- Active Infrared
- Passive Infrared
- Microwave
- Video Motion
- Magnetic Switch
- Capacitance
- Sonic
- Ultrasonic

Vibration.   This type of sensor is attuned to vibrations caused by pulling on or cutting through a fence, breaking glass, and sawing or smashing through a wall. A transducer in the sensor detects low frequency energy associated with brute force intrusion. In the exterior environment, the sensor is often mounted on a fence fabric (metal mesh or chain link) or on the top mount of a fence (barbed wire or razor tape). In the interior environment, the vibration sensor can be installed on or inside walls or on glass surfaces.

Taut wire.   In this application, a strain-sensitive cable is mounted on a fence. When the cable is stretched, such as by climbing or shaking the fence, an electric circuit is broken and a signal is sent to the monitoring station. A variation is a conduit containing a line that transmits and receives electrical energy. Cutting, shorting, or removing the conduit will alter the flow of electrical energy passing along the line.

Magnetic Field.   A magnetic field sensor reacts to the movement of metal in a magnetic field set up by wires buried in the ground. They are useful in detecting weapons and/or vehicles moving into a guarded area.

Electric Field.   This device creates an electrostatic field through an array of wire conductors and an electrical ground. Change or distortion of the field results when an intruder enters an exterior zone or approaches a barrier such as a fence or wall.

Fiber-Optic Cable.   It helps to think of this device as a "pipeline of light." The pipeline is a cable that encases a light-carrying fiber strand. The cable can have any number of curves without affecting the light; however, once the cable has been installed, any bending of it will trigger an alarm. Fiber-optic cables are often arranged in a mesh pattern placed slightly below the surface of the ground. A person or vehicle passing over the ground causes the mesh to bend.

Seismic.   This sensor consists of geophones placed under the soil. Vibration of the soil, such as that caused by a walking person, creates high frequency energy which in turn activates the sensor.

Pressure.   In the exterior environment, this sensor consists of a hose containing a pressurized liquid. Like the seismic sensor, it is placed under the soil. A person walking on the soil changes the pressure. In the interior environment, the sensor is a pressurized mat placed under a carpet or slightly flexible flooring.

Ported Coaxial Cable.   This sensor detects movement of humans and metallic material. Inside the cable is wiring that radiates a signal. The cable's sheathing has holes (i.e., ports) that permit the signal to "leak out." The cable is buried. When the signal comes into contact with a person or metal object, the sensor activates.

Active Infrared.   This sensor can be used outdoors and indoors. Think of it as an electronic trip wire: a transmitter sends an infrared beam to a receiver, and activation occurs when the beam is interrupted. In the outdoors environment, the active infrared sensor is free-standing, i.e., it can be moved from place to place. Indoors, the transmitter and receiver are typically wall-mounted, with the beam passing across entrances (doors and windows) and intruder pathways (hallways and staircases).

Another form of the active infrared sensor broadcasts a curtain-like pattern of infrared energy extending to the boundaries of the protected area. The energy pattern is reflected back to a receiver. The reflected energy pattern is analyzed, and if found to be in an altered state causes an alarm.

Passive Infrared.   The passive infrared sensor does not transmit at all. It is sensitive to thermal energy received from the intruder. Typically, the sensor covers several contiguous zones. Activation occurs when an intruder crosses two adjacent zone boundaries or twice crosses the same boundary within a specified time. Like the active infrared type, it can be used indoors and outdoors.

Microwave.   This motion-detecting device transmits a microwave signal along a perfectly straight line that can extend as far as 1,500 feet. A zone is created on both sides of the line. Movement within the zone sets off an alarm.

A microwave sensor can be supplemented with a passive infrared sensor. An alarm is sent when both sensors react to a change in their different energy fields. These sensors are often installed along a perimeter fence or wall and arranged to detect an approach to the zone, an actual intrusion, or both. In high-security situations where there is an advantage to viewing and recording intruder movement, the microwave alone or the microwave in tandem with passive infrared can be supplemented with closed circuit television cameras.

Microwave sensors can be used indoors as well.

Video Motion.   This sensor is called a video motion detector (VMD) and it can be used outdoors and indoors. A closed circuit television (CCTV) camera views a scene of interest. Movement within the field of view sends an alarm signal. Outdoors, VMDs are usually mounted on towers, light poles, and walls. Indoors, they are mounted on walls and ceilings, with the usual scenes of interest being doors, hallways, and rooms.

Magnetic Switch.   This simple device activates when the magnetic field between two contact points is broken. For example, one contact is mounted on a window with a corresponding contact on the windowsill. When the window slides open, the contact is broken and an alarm signal sent.

Capacitance.   The capacitance sensor is similar to the electric field sensor. Three closely spaced wires produce an electric field around an object. The capacitance of the electrostatic field is changed when an intruder approaches or touches the object. In the outdoors environment, the object can be a handle on a gate or delivery door; in the indoor environment it can be a door knob, lock, combination dial, or the protected asset.

Sonic.   This sensor operates on the principle of sound detection. It is typically mounted on a stable interior surface that serves as a barrier. It reacts to sound waves such as those produced by forced entry. When noise is unpredictable (sonic boom, thunder, engine backfire), it can be supplemented with another sensor operating on a different detection principle.

Ultrasonic.   This motion detection device reacts to high frequencies associated with intrusion attempts. The sounds of metal striking metal, an acetylene torch in operation, and the shattering of concrete or brick are in the high frequency range of the sensor. It is usually wall- or ceiling-mounted and supplemented with another sensor form such as the passive infrared sensor.

DETECTION RELIABILITY

Infallible is not a term associated with sensors, or for that matter any other detection device. The reliability of detection hinges on the following.

- Amount and pattern of energy emitted by the intruder. The more definitive the pattern, the greater the reliability of the sensor.
- Size of the intruder. The larger the intruder, the greater the reliability.
- Distance between the sensor and the intruder. Reliability rises as distance shortens.
- Speed at which the intruder is moving. Very slow and stealthy movement decreases reliability.
- Direction of intruder movement. Lateral movement is more easily detected than straight-on movement.
- Characteristics of the energy waves of the intruder and of the environment in which the sensor operates. The greater the contrast between the energy waves of the intruder and the environment of the zone, the greater the reliability of detection.

Sensor Configurations

Sensor Type	EX	IN	PA	AC	VO	LI	LS	TF	CO	VI	CV
Fence vibration	X		X			X		X		X	
Fence taut wire	X		X			X		X		X	
Magnetic field	X		X		X			X	X		
Electric field	X			X	X			X		X	
Fiber-optic cable	X		X			X		X	X		
Seismic	X		X			X		X	X		
Ported coaxial	X			X	X			X	X		
Active infrared	X			X		X	X			X	
Passive infrared	X		X		X		X			X	
Microwave	X			X	X		X			X	
Video motion	X		X		X		X		X		
Magnetic switch		X	X			X					X
Capacitance		X	X			X			X		
Pressure mat		X	X			X			X		
Ultrasonic		X		X	X					X	
Sonic		X		X	X					X	
Vibration		X	X			X			X		
Passive infrared		X	X		X					X	
Fiber-optic cable		X	X			X					X
Microwave		X		X	X					X	

Legend

EX	**Exterior**	**PA**	**Passive**	**VO**	**Volumetric**
IN	**Interior**	**AC**	**Active**	**LI**	**Line**
CO	**Covert**	**VI**	**Visible**	**CV**	**Covert or Visible**

Figure 11-4 This chart depicts configurations by type of sensor.

INTRUSION DETECTION SYSTEMS

An intrusion detection system (IDS) is an arrangement of one or more sensors, one or more sound alarms (annunciators), alarm processor, alarm monitoring station, circuitry to send and receive signals, a person or persons to monitor and operate the system, and security officers to respond to suspected intrusions. Signals within the IDS move from one device to another along wires or wirelessly.

Assessment

When the IDS detects an intrusion, the operator of the system "reads" an alarm panel and determines the location of the intrusion. The officer assesses the nature of the intrusion, the assessment is given to one or more security officers, and the security officers go to the scene to investigate.

The IDS control panel is almost always located in a security control center or on a console monitored by an officer performing other duties such as checking passes. IDS sensors can be standalone, such as free-standing devices that search for movement ahead and sensors buried in the ground. Most sensors are attached to physical structures such as fences, doors, windows, and locked containers.

Three Characteristics

The CSO charged with selecting intrusion detection sensors would do well to examine the following three characteristics.

- The reliability of sensors, taking into consideration their sensitivity, the nature of the environment, and the assumed behavior of the intruder.
- The false alarm rate; that is, the expected frequency of alarms resulting not from intrusion but from faulty equipment, poor installation, maintenance, and calibration, and a host of uncontrollable factors such as loss of power, earth tremors, high wind, heavy snow, flooding, and the movement of animals.
- Resistance to defeat; that is, the ability of the sensors to detect attempts to thwart or circumvent intrusion detection. Resistance to defeat can be increased by overlapping sensors in contiguous coverage areas, installing more than one sensor per coverage area, and installing multiple sensors that operate on different principles.

The objective of the CSO is to establish an IDS that has high reliability, a low false alarm rate, and high resistance to defeat. After selecting sensors, the CSO selects an alarm processor, a monitoring capability, and a communication mode that connects the components. Fortunately, a wide variety of alarm processors are commercially available in off-the-shelf packages that include computer hardware, software, operating procedures, and training for system operators. The software for most of these systems allows the purchaser to choose options that correspond to specific needs.

Monitoring and Communication

The monitoring function can be performed at a security console operated by the purchaser's own security group or at a central alarm station operated by a vendor. A common feature is both an audible and visible alarm annunciation. The audible signal is usually a buzzer, horn, or other distinctive sound. The visual signal is usually a flashing light and alarm data displayed on a screen such as a CCTV monitor or the screen of a desktop computer. The alarm data can consist of text, icons, maps, floor layouts, and other formats that tell the operator what is happening and where. A highly sophisticated system can also provide a real-time CCTV view of the penetrated area and the path of the intruder. Instructions in text and/or sound prompt the operator to initiate appropriate response actions.

The communication protocols of the system will vary according to purpose and agreeable interfaces. In some cases it will be advantageous, if not necessary, to place a preprocessor between the computer and the rest of the system. The purpose of the preprocessor is to eliminate signal delay by reducing tasks that would otherwise be handled by the computer.

TAMPER DETECTION

Nearly all alarm systems have a tamper detection feature (called line supervision) that indicates if a line has been cut or bypassed. An intruder who knows a system has line supervision may attempt undetected entry by entirely cutting off the system's power supply. A system is vulnerable to this form of attack when it lacks an immediately operating automatic restart capability. For this reason it is critical that an alarm system have an uninterrupted power supply (UPS) and alternative power sources.

LOCK AND KEY SYSTEMS

By any reckoning, the lock is the most widely used physical security device, yet it is hardly foolproof. All locks are vulnerable to physical force, and against a determined and knowledgeable intruder the best a lock can be expected to achieve is delay. The duration of delay is largely a matter of the locking principle and the resistance of the lock to force. Locks are also vulnerable, although to a lesser degree, to non-force techniques. A key-operated lock can be picked and impressions made secretly of keys. A combination lock can be defeated by manipulation of the spindle or compromise of the lock's numeric or symbolic code.

Figure 11-5 Checking locks on trucks is a standard security officer duty. *(Photo courtesy of Burns International Security Services.)*

Types of Locks

Locks operate on various principles and are manufactured in a variety of sizes, shapes, and defeat-resisting abilities (see Figure 11-5). Locks commonly used in business, industries, and the military are usually of three general types: key, combination, and electronic. These types are discussed in the material that follows.

Key lock: This multi-purpose lock opens upon the insertion and turning of a key. In a lock that secures a door, the turning action of the key causes the bolt to retract from the strike (a recess in the door frame); in a padlock, the turning action allows the shackle to be lifted free. Many forms of key locks have an interchangeable core (the component that receives the key) that can be removed and replaced by a core that operates with a different key. Variations of the key lock have names that correspond to their internal movements. For example, the warded lock has ward cuts in the key that correspond to wards (obstructions) in the keyway or lock; the wafer or disc tumbler lock has spring-tensed wafers that retract when the correct key is inserted; the pin tumbler lock opens when pins are moved by a key having cuts in the key blade that line up with the pins; the lever lock has spring-tensed levers that properly align upon insertion of the correct key; and the dead bolt lock has a bolt that retracts when the correct key is turned.

Combination lock: This lock is incorporated in padlocks, safes, vaults, and doors. The operator turns the spindle in a specified order of right and left directions to reference points on a dial. Tumblers inside the lock release the

Figure 11-6 In this electronic lock an internal battery moves the cylinder. The key contains embedded data about the key holder, authorization level, and the times and dates of permitted access. *(Photo courtesy of Videx.)*

locking mechanism. Three is the usual number of tumblers, although four or five tumblers are a feature of so-called high-security locks.

Electronic lock: In this category are digital locks that open when the correct code is entered by pushing buttons, and electromechanical locks that open when an electronic signal is received. The received signals arrive at the lock after the user's identification and right to entry are verified. Verification can be made by an assessment of the distinguishing features of the user such as signature dynamics, fingerprints, and the retina. In some devices, a handheld key contains in electronic format the user's identification and access privileges plus battery power to operate the cylinder (see Figure 11-6).

Key Control

The key-operated lock used in the typical office building will open for anyone who possesses the correct key. This simple fact explains why key control is so vitally necessary when protection is an objective of building management.

Protecting Keys

A variety of physical techniques are available for protecting keys not yet issued. These include strategies such as keeping keys locked inside a wall-mounted box, filing cabinet, floor safe, and so on. The degree of physical protection, of course, can vary widely with the choices of protection determined by building management.

A popular high-security approach is to store keys in a locked and permanently affixed cabinet in continuous view of security personnel or other trusted employees. A less secure approach is to store them in a penetration-resistant container that is not continuously under observation. The container's penetration resistance in this case must be greater than that of any locked door in the protected premises. A two-dollar padlock on a key cabinet makes no sense at all when the keys in the cabinet open doors giving access to assets worth thousands.

Procedural Control

The physical side of key control is relatively simple and problem free, at least in comparison to the procedural side. Why? Because procedures involve people and people are human. They make errors of judgment, something a lock can never do. The human procedure that requires demonstration of a right and need to pass beyond a locked door is likely to be met with: "What do you mean I can't have a key? I supervise that office." Breakdowns in procedures occur not because keys can't be physically protected but because the human element of the key control system can't function properly. Whose fault is this? The fault lies not with the security group but with management.

Key Control Is Difficult

Let's look at the usual reasons for key control being difficult. First is the notion that status in the organization confers a right to possess keys. But does the CEO really need a key to every door in the building? Does the CFO really need a key to the power plant?

Next is the proposition that long and faithful service should be rewarded, such as giving a multiple-entry key to an employee who everyone likes and trusts. Close behind is the idea that convenience should count for something. It is convenient, for example, that a secretary possess a master key so that when an employee in her department wants to get into a locked area she can open the door without having to call a security officer. Pretty soon she is handing the key to anyone who asks for it. After that, the key gets lost. Another is issued, and the cycle repeats itself.

The least supportable rationale for issuing a key is to silence a complainer. Putting grease on the squeaky wheel is often cited as a reason for circumventing good practice. "He just kept bugging me until finally I issued him a key."

What is at issue here? Nothing less than the compromise of an entire system. The compromise operates like a disease eating away portions of a living body. A nibble here, a nibble there. Closet keys lost, desk keys stolen, office keys misplaced, floor keys duplicated. Then come the big bites. Too many submasters issued, the master lost, the grand master unaccounted for. The system is soon dead. No choice but to start over.

Compromise

One of the fastest ways to compromise a key system is to disclose the cut code numbers established by the lock manufacturer. These numbers, which are often cut into the thumb grip, identify all keys in a system of keys. They serve as a convenience to the purchaser in placing later orders with the manufacturer. The code number on a key also tells a locksmith that duplication is forbidden. The purchaser is advised to never issue a marked key, but if issuance becomes necessary, to grind off the numbers after recording and storing them securely.

Unauthorized duplication is made more difficult when the keyway of the locks in the system will accept a single key blank, one that is available only to the registered owner of the system. Still, this is not a foolproof precaution because the number of ways to configure the guide cuts in a blank is finite. A determined person with locksmith skill and knowledge can eventually come up with a key blank that will work.

One more point on key blanks is worth mentioning. When duplication of keys is done in-house, the key blanks should be protectively stored apart from key grinding equipment. A signature receipt form is the usual administrative device for key accounting. The form can also be used to impress upon the recipient the concern of management by including, for example, an acknowledgment that personal responsibilities will be met. These might include protecting the key, not loaning it, not duplicating it, and turning it in when asked to do so.

Accountability

Keys that are in daily use for gaining access to particularly sensitive areas — such as keys held by security officers, cleaning staff, and building maintenance employees — require a protective approach that emphasizes periodic accountability. The frequency of accountability can vary. For example, security officers likely turn in their keys at the end of each shift. Signed receipts, log books, or other records reflect the transfer of keys from officers going off work to those coming on.

For cleaning staff, the frequency of key accountability might be once per day, or not at all if the cleaning routine calls for security officers to unlock doors to the areas to be cleaned. For building engineers, keys might be counted as seldom as once per month, depending on the sensitivity of the areas they service and how the engineers are supervised.

Two-person Rule

When the protected area is so sensitive that unaccompanied entry cannot be permitted, key access can be controlled using a two-person rule (see Figure 11-7). One version of the rule is to place the key in a penetration-resistant container maintained by a key custodian (who may or may not be a security officer). The key custodian issues the key only at the simultaneous request of two predesignated persons. A variation is to have two separate locks in place at the protected area, with the keys to those locks held by the key custodian. In this way, both of the predesignated persons must sign for their

Figure 11-7 The two-person rule is common when the stored asset is money. *(Photo courtesy of Burns International Security Services.)*

keys but must be present with their keys at the entry point before either of them can get in.

Dual Systems

In some situations, it may be preferable to operate two systems of key control: one nonsensitive and one sensitive. Locks to the nonsensitive areas would be of one brand or one model, and locks to the sensitive areas would be of a different brand or model. Two advantages are present in such an arrangement. First is cost. There is no point in purchasing high-security locking hardware for all doors when only some doors require high-security protection. Cost also weighs heavily when a compromise in the security system requires replacing or re-combinating lock cores. The second advantage is eliminating the possibility that a lock core previously used in a low-security area (where keys are less controlled) would be placed in a high-security area. The difference in brand or model would not allow interchanges.

Finally, many fine software programs are being brought to market for companies wanting to improve the management of their key control systems. These programs variously provide graphics that depict the hierarchy of keys in the system; identification of the persons to whom keys have been issued, when, by whom, and upon what authority; tracking and cross-referencing of keys; and computer-generated forms for requesting, assigning, turning in, and destroying keys.

CONCLUSIONS

A facility's physical security posture is but one part of a larger functional program that typically includes security officer services, fire detection and suppression, access control, investigations, personnel screening, employee education, risk assessment, inspections, and audits.

The buzz term of this decade may turn out to be "integrated systems." The idea that economy and efficiency can be achieved by combining two or more independent systems is especially appealing to cost-conscious purchasers. The more-bang-for-the-buck philosophy has naturally led to the development of integrated fire alarm and security systems featuring two-way communications between linked functions. Although called integrated, many of these systems retain aspects of functional independence, especially in regard to fire detection.

The future augurs greater intimacy. The concept of integrated systems points toward a much fuller merging of functions than has been seen to date. Of concern to fire experts are the integrity and reliability of the fire detection and alarm components. Absolute assurance, they say, must be demonstrated; a failure of a non-fire component cannot be allowed to impact fire components. Experts worry, for example, that a security officer who has access to the integrated system will mistakenly change the system's fire-related program or operate the equipment in a manner that could override fire detection and annunciation. The facility's full program of security can be likened to an automobile engine. The parts are interdependent and function synchronously, with the CSO serving as driver and mechanic (see Figure 11-8).

NOTES

1. John J. Fay, *Butterworths Security Dictionary*, pp. 142, Boston: Butterworth-Heinemann, 1987.

2. *Physical Security, Field Manual 19-30*, pp. 66–73, Washington, D.C.: Headquarters, Department of the Army, 1979.

3. The now defunct Law Enforcement Assistance Administration once concluded that street lighting does not deter the criminal but merely displaces the crime to the daytime or an alternative target.

4. Philip S. Purpura, "Physical Security: Lighting," in *Encyclopedia of Security Management*, pp. 552–553, John J. Fay, editor, Boston: Butterworth-Heinemann, 1993.

5. An excellent source for construction standards is Carl Roper, *Physical Security and the Inspection Process*, pp. 85–96, Boston: Butterworth-Heinemann, 1997.

Checklist for Assessing Physical Security

Yes   No

Environmental Factors
___ ___ Prohibitive seismic activity?
___ ___ Poor surface and subsurface stability?
___ ___ Soil Contamination?
___ ___ Severe weather potential?
___ ___ Prohibitive topography?
___ ___ Flooding potential?
___ ___ Poor air quality?
___ ___ Extreme temperature?
___ ___ Fire hazards?
___ ___ Inadequate utility feeds?
___ ___ Inadequate emergency services?
___ ___ High crime rate?

Threats
___ ___ Crime in the facility?
___ ___ Crime in the neighborhood?
___ ___ Traffic accident potential?
___ ___ Terrorist target?
___ ___ Kidnapping potential?
___ ___ Workplace violence potential?
___ ___ Bomb threats?
___ ___ Employee theft?
___ ___ Electronic eavesdropping?
___ ___ Sabotage?
___ ___ Vandalism?
___ ___ Natural disaster potential?
___ ___ Manmade disaster potential?

Countermeasures
___ ___ Control approach to the facility?

___ ___ Fencing and other perimeter barriers?
___ ___ Protective and/or glare lighting?
___ ___ Anti-concealment landscaping?
___ ___ Gates?
___ ___ Turnstiles?
___ ___ Mantrap zones and cubicles?
___ ___ Guard towers and gatehouses?
___ ___ Intrusion detection sensors?
___ ___ Signage?
___ ___ CCTV?
___ ___ Electronic access control?
___ ___ Badges?
___ ___ Duress alarms?
___ ___ Shielding against eavesdropping?
___ ___ Blast and/or bullet resistant shielding?
___ ___ Fire-rated walls/ceilings?
___ ___ Penetration-resistant walls/ceilings?
___ ___ Bar grates?
___ ___ Vaults, safes, and secure containers?
___ ___ Mechanical and cipher locks?
___ ___ Anti-pass back readers?
___ ___ Uninterruptible power systems?
___ ___ PC-assisted security control center?
___ ___ Video archiving equipment?
___ ___ Alternate security control center?

Figure 11-8 A checklist can be helpful when assessing the adequacy of physical security.

12. Managing Access Control

Every exit is an entry to somewhere.
—Tom Stoppard

BUSINESS RATIONALE

The business rationale for access control stems from the belief that a workplace must be safe and secure for everyone. In practice, the belief is carried out by eliminating harm to people, such as by controlling entry to a hazardous work zone or denying entry to persons posing a threat. The rationale extends to preventing hostile acts that disrupt business operations or result in property damage or loss.

A facility that requires even a minor level of protection exercises access controls. Indeed, a strong argument can be made that a facility without access controls is an unprotected facility. An access control system regulates movement into, within, and from a protected area or facility. The controls are placed upon people, forms of transportation, and materials. The people typically affected are employees, visitors, customers, contractors, vendors, repair and sales persons, and deliverers. Transport forms include automobiles, trucks, motorcycles and bicycles, trains, buses, watercraft, and aircraft. Materials that are under control when entering can include raw materials, supplies, and equipment. Inside the protected area, controls can be placed on cash, valuables, and sensitive documents. At exits to a protected area, controls can applied to finished products, scrap, and refuse, as well as to property hand-carried by employees.

EMPLOYEE BADGES AND VISITOR PASSES

A basic and time-honored access control tool is the employee identification card or badge. A workplace with few employees and low security needs may choose to rely on personal recognition as an alternative to the identification badge, but a workplace with more than a few employees will find the identification badge useful.

The control of visitors works differently. Visitor passes issued at an entry control point substitute for identification cards. Visitor passes are typically constructed of paper and may have a feature that causes self-destruction after one or two days. The pass is dated and issued for a set period, usually one day; is applied for at a reception or security desk adjacent to the entry point; and requires the visitor to present a form of photo identification such as a driver's license. A condition of issuance may be approval by an employee. In some situations, only certain employees are allowed to approve visitor access, and the day and time of visit must be prearranged. In medium- to high-security situations, the visitor is escorted while inside the facility.

In a safety-sensitive workplace, a visitor may have to undergo a briefing, view a film, sign a release, and put on protective apparel such as a hard hat, safety glasses, and steel-toed boots. A record of the visit is wise.

TYPES OF IDENTIFICATION CARDS

Control of access at a protected facility is very likely assisted by a card identification system designed to verify each entering person's authority to enter. As one can expect, the efficiency and effectiveness of the system is affected by the reliability of the card identification equipment, number of entry points, size of the workforce, operating hours, and above all else human competence. A well-designed and skillfully managed identification system achieves the basic goal of controlling access without impeding the flow of work.

Many different types of identification cards are available. The type of card purchased will correspond to the system's hardware. A few types carry just the owner's name, affiliation, and signature, whereas most incorporate a head-and-shoulders photograph laminated to the card, a tamper-detecting feature, and a post office box number for mailing found cards back to the issuing organization.

Nearly all access cards are of the same general size and shape, and in overall appearance look somewhat like a credit card. The common types are Hollerith, magnetic stripe, barium ferrite, bar code, Wiegand, proximity, and smart card. These types are discussed in the following material.

Hollerith: This very early form of access card has small holes that can be read by a light source or contact brushes. Today's use of Hollerith cards is pretty much limited to hotel security. The guest slides the card into a slot above the door handle. The lock disengages when a reading of the card matches a guest's registration at the lobby desk. This very simple technology is usually not suitable for higher-level security.

Magnetic stripe: This type of card has a data-encoded stripe on one face. When the card is withdrawn from or swiped through a reader, the stripe passes over a magnetic head not unlike that of a tape player. The code on the stripe is compared to access criteria that were earlier entered into the system. Access criteria reflect the cardholder's identity, the areas the cardholder is authorized to enter, and time frames for entry (normal operating hours, evening hours, weekends, holidays).

Compared to other card types, the magnetic stripe costs less and can hold a large amount of data. However, the magnetic stripe can wear out or become damaged over time, and the vinyl plastic construction of the card can lead to chipping and breaking.

Barium ferrite: This type of card is sometimes called a magnetic spot card or magnetic sandwich card. It is cut from three-layer plastic stock. The middle layer, or core, is barium ferrite that has been magnetized with a pattern of dots arranged in a readable pattern. The pattern is a code fixed by the magnetic polarity of the spots. The barium ferrite card is slightly more expensive than the magnetic stripe card. It is also subject to problems resulting from wear and tear, and is vulnerable to deciphering.

Bar code: This card bears on one side (usually the front) a series of lines forming a code readable by an optical scanner. The pattern of lines (i.e., the bar code) looks very much like the pattern of lines found on the outside of supermarket items.

Because a bar code is easy to duplicate, it is not suitable for good security practice. This card, however, can be used for tracking inventory; for example, a late-shift security guard with a hand-held reader can determine the locations of desktop assets. A processor at the security control center conducts an analysis and prints out findings such as when an asset has been moved, the asset's current location, and assets that are missing.

Wiegand: The Wiegand card is also called an embedded-wire card. The technology is based on the Wiegand effect, a phenomenon observed when specially prepared ferromagnetic wires suddenly reverse themselves upon exposure to an external magnetic field. Wires inside the Wiegand card are formed in a permanently tensioned helic twist. The order and spacing of the wires establish a unique code for each card. The magnetic reversals in the wires are converted into distinct, consistent electrical pulses that are read and processed. The card's thickness and composition of stock make it resistant to pocket damage. It is, however, susceptible to malfunction arising from wear after many passes through reader slots.

Proximity: The proximity card has an embedded microcircuit that emits frequencies detectable by a reader. The reader reacts to the frequencies when the card is placed in close proximity (2 to 4 inches) [1].

Sturdy composition makes the card resistant to tampering and the interfering effects of weather and shock. Two other features of the card make it attractive. The emitted frequencies are sufficiently powerful for the reader to be concealed behind a thin wall or mounted inconspicuously (possibly for aesthetic reasons), and the card can work through clothing or a handbag.

Smart card: Regarded as the card of the future, the smart card contains its own processor, making it capable of running its own internal programs.

Figure 12-1 Door entry is just one of many uses made of access control cards.

The very large amount of data that can be contained in a smart card allows it to serve purposes that go beyond access control. For example, the cardholder's medical history can be stored for quick retrieval in a medical emergency and cashless purchases recorded [2].

The downside to the smart card is cost. On the other hand, it offers several advantages: the card is durable and tamper resistant, counterfeiting and duplication are difficult, encryption presents an obstacle to compromising the code, the card can be programmed to expire on a certain date, and smart card technology is suitable for many applications [3]. Figure 12-1 shows one use of access control cards.

TRAFFIC CONTROL

Control of vehicles can start and end at a property line distant from or in close proximity to the operating portion of the facility. If the property line is immediately adjacent to a crowded public roadway, the CSO may want traffic to be directed. Local police officers can be hired to perform traffic-directing duties. This option has three advantages: safety is enhanced, vehicle flow is smoothed, and the drivers of entering vehicles are reminded that access control is taken seriously.

During the hours of high-traffic movement, it may be advisable to open more entry gates. If manning more gates is not practical, the alternative may be gate arms that lift when a proximity card is passed near a card reader. If the entry is to a parking lot or garage, the gate arms can be locked into the open position to allow faster movement.

Traffic control can be simple, yet problematic. Signage, marked lanes, and a visible security force should be sufficient to regulate vehicle movement, yet some individuals insist on driving and parking in areas where they are not permitted to be.

The growing number of vehicle bomb incidents calls for the use of traffic-slowing devices, such as jersey barriers, installation of crash protectors (such as bollards), and placement of parking areas outside the blast zone.

MATERIALS CONTROL

Materials requiring control of movement (see Figure 12-2) include supplies and raw goods entering the facility, items worked on or produced (sensitive documents, manufactured goods), tools of work (office equipment, desktop

Figure 12-2 The receiving area of a warehouse is often the special target of thieves. *(Photo courtesy of Burns International Security Services.)*

assets, communication devices, plant equipment), and materials leaving the facility (finished products, returned items, scrap, paper trash).

Inspection Entering and Moving Internally

Mail, truck-delivered and courier-delivered packages, containers hand carried by employees and visitors, and small shipments received outside a facility's supply channel can be made subject to routine inspection. Care must be made to inspect, not search. An inspection is an administrative control known to and agreed by persons subject to inspection. A search is a law enforcement action ordered by a court and performed by police officers.

Only specially trained individuals should perform inspections. Examples are security officers inspecting baggage at an airport and mailroom employees looking for the indicators of mail bombs. Metal detectors, X-ray viewing equipment, explosives detectors, bomb barrels and bomb-resistant rooms, and sniffer dogs facilitate the work.

The use of inspections is a policy matter decided at senior management level, with input from the CSO. Typically, a policy will prohibit introduction to the facility of explosives, firearms and ammunition, knives, poisons, drinking alcohol, stolen property, offensively pornographic items, illegal drugs, and drug-administering paraphernalia.

Movement control can also apply to e-mail messages and electronically transmitted materials such as classified documents, business plans and strategy, and trade secrets. Inspection of this type, in addition to being an issue of policy and the personal sensitivities of employees, is often restricted to what the computer hardware and software permit.

Accounting for Property

A reasonable business necessity is prevention of loss and prevention of unauthorized use of organizational assets. The necessity can be satisfied with a system for controlling the movement of property from the facility through pedestrian portals, such as property in the possession of employees and visitors who leave by the front door, and a system for tracking the migration of physical assets within the facility.

A property removal system can require the remover to obtain a removal pass signed by an authorizing supervisor. The pass is attached to or enclosed with the property to be removed. At the exit point, the pass is shown to a security officer. The pass can be taken by the officer and be held on file for reconciliation purposes.

An assets-tracking system keeps track of items such as desktop equipment and valuable tools. The items are tagged, labeled, imprinted, or encoded in some way. To illustrate, a bar code sticker is affixed to an item. The sticker identifies the type of item, its location, and identity of the person responsible for its custody. During the midnight shift, a security officer moves throughout the facility passing an electronic wand across bar code stickers.

A microprocessor or computer in the security control center reads each sticker and matches it against a database. If the match is not perfect, such as the item being in the wrong location, an exception is noted by the computer. At the end of the midnight shift a report is printed. All noted exceptions are highlighted. Copies of the printout are placed in the company's mail room for delivery to supervisors responsible for custody of the items. Items that were not tracked can be assumed missing or stolen.

Inspection of Materials Leaving

Some facilities, for public safety reasons, simply demand inspection of departing vehicles. Examples are nuclear energy plants, weapons storage buildings, and precious metal processing factories. Certain necessary prerequisites apply: ensuring that the inspection program conforms to the Constitution, laws, contracts, and agreements with bargaining units; ensuring that people affected by the inspection program are informed in advance; and ensuring that the security officers or others who perform the inspections have been trained [4].

ACCESS CONTROL AND PHYSICAL SECURITY

An access control system (see Figure 12-3) is necessarily supplemented by perimeter barriers (fences and walls), physical devices (vaults, safes, and locks), lighting, intrusion detection sensors, and human resources (employees generally and security officers particularly). Holding everything together are sets of written directives. The CSO monitors operation of the system and tweaks it when needed.

Figure 12-3 Access control is exercised at shipping and receiving docks. *(Photo courtesy of Burns International Security Services.)*

Layered Protection

Access controls are often layered to decrease the chance that an attempted intrusion will succeed. A layered system could, for example, start with a requirement that an entering employee stop at an unmanned electronically operated gate at the outer perimeter of the property, and through a key pad on a stanchion punch in the correct sequence of an alphanumeric code. As the employee approaches the operating portion of the facility, he/she is again stopped, this time at a sentry gate. After saying good morning and showing the guard an identification badge, the employee passes under a raised gate arm and parks in a fenced area patrolled by or under the observation of a security officer (see Figure 12-4). The next control point is the outer door of the building where the employee works. An electronic lock on the exterior door releases after a valid card key is placed in close proximity to a card reader. The exterior door leads to a central lobby monitored by a security officer.

After displaying an identification badge, the employee enters an elevator that operates when a card reader accepts a valid card key. In the elevator lobby of his/her floor, the employee takes note of the CCTV camera mounted high in one corner. The employee again presents the card key to pass through a door into a suite of offices. The employee next inserts a mechanical key into an office door. Inside the office, the employee uses other mechanical keys to unlock a desk and credenza, and on a filing cabinet the employee turns a combination in the correct sequence. The employee pushes the start button on a Mister Coffee machine, sits down, and pushes the start button on a desktop PC. When the screen lights up, the employee is prompted to enter a log-on

Figure 12-4 Access control is exercised at vehicle entry points. *(Photo courtesy of Burns International Security Services.)*

password and a network password. The workday for the employee at this protected facility is now underway.

Layered protection and concentric protection, which is discussed elsewhere, are similar but different. Layered protection is designed to facilitate entry of authorized persons; concentric protection is designed to deny entry by unauthorized persons.

Uniformity and Diversity

An electronic access control system is uniform because it conforms to internal rules and logic, and in the external domain treats transactions the same way every time. For example, a certain door always opens when a valid card key is presented and never opens when presented with a invalid card key. The parts of the system operate with one another, which is another flavor of uniformity.

On the other hand, diversity is a norm. The devices driven by the software or that activate the software will be diverse in shape, purpose, and operating principle. All doors, locks, lights, and sensors cannot be identical for the simple reason that each has a unique function.

Access control systems also vary from place to place. The CSO at Facility A may decide that entry control is best done with a biometric technology, whereas the CSO at Facility B may decide that entry control can be done with a card key technology. At Facility A, the biometric choice may be fingerprints as opposed to retinal pattern, and at Facility B the card key choice may be Weigand as opposed to magnetic stripe. Security needs and CSO preferences vary widely, making diversity a common theme.

Even within a single technology there are variations in components, logic, options and price. All access control systems, regardless of technologies, have one thing in common: they are dependent on humans. A fatal mistake of the CSO can be to neglect the human side while overemphasizing the technology side. This sometimes happens when the CSO sees an opportunity to reduce costs by replacing security manpower with electronics.

CLOSED-CIRCUIT TELEVISION (CCTV)

A security officer sitting in front of a monitor can be at many places simultaneously. Decisions can be made quickly to allow authorized persons to enter controlled areas far from the nearest security officer. But access control is only one of many tasks that can be harnessed to CCTV. These include deterrence, detection, validation, apprehension, and investigation.

Deterrence occurs when conspicuously mounted cameras persuade a criminal opportunist to try elsewhere. Detection occurs when a security officer sees on a CCTV monitor an intrusion in progress. Validation occurs when CCTV confirms an event reported by an intrusion detection sensor. Apprehension occurs when security officers take into custody an intruder spotted on CCTV.

Figure 12-5 Security officers monitor CCTV screens in a security control center. *(Photo courtesy of Burns International Security Services.)*

The investigation objective is met when a CCTV tape identifies the person involved in the act of interest.

Business owners acquire CCTV systems for any or all of the capabilities just mentioned. A hotel proprietor, for example, can use CCTV to evaluate persons seeking entry to the hotel lobby late at night, deter robbery and auto theft in the hotel parking garage, detect a person attempting to force open a ground floor window, verify that a buzzer went off because someone broke through a back door, give to security officers information they need to locate and take into custody a person committing a crime, and provide clues for police officers conducting a post-incident investigation.

CCTV has quality control and training applications. A security supervisor can use CCTV to evaluate visitor processing and replay tapes that teach officers how to process visitors more effectively (see Figure 12-5).

Comfort Level

Even where CCTV is not justified by prior incidents, business owners favor the method because it gives them a level of comfort. An owner of a public building, such as an office tower, wants assurance that people entering through unlocked doors at street level are under observation. Protection of the public, employees, and property is both a duty and a business necessity.

Pros and Cons

On the positive side of the CCTV ledger are the following advantages.

- Many locations can be watched simultaneously from one central location.
- The approach of intruders and attempts to intrude can be detected early.
- Costs can be lowered by replacing expensive manpower with a less expensive CCTV system.
- Human performance errors can be mitigated.
- An overt, conspicuous system can act as a deterrent.
- A covert system can help catch intruders.
- Overt and covert systems can create a visual record of an incident and aid in a post-incident investigation.

On the negative side, a CCTV system

- Can be expensive to purchase and complex to operate.
- Can require considerable preinstallation time.
- Can suffer from bugs and glitches.
- Requires periodic maintenance and calibration throughout the life of the system.
- Can become dysfunctional in extreme conditions such as tropical heat, arctic cold, wind and sand storms, flooding, and earth tremors.

System Features

A simple system can be a video camera cabled to a monitor. A complex system can have many bells and whistles: multiple digital cameras that pan and tilt, zoom in and out, display of many views simultaneously, sending of digitized images to a computer; and compression of images to facilitate storage. Systems that lie between the simple and complex are usually quite adequate for most security purposes [5].

Using white and infrared light, cameras can capture clear, high-resolution images under poor lighting conditions. Cameras can operate remotely, react to movement in the field of view, track objects, and scan slowly. They can be mounted in weather-resistant housings and send signals via fiber-optic cable.

Monitoring and recording equipment vary in the manner images are captured, displayed, and stored. Real-time and time-lapse recorders are growing in popularity. Some recorders automatically display and record images upon receipt of a signal from an intrusion detection sensor and retain several hundred hours of images on a single medium.

A top-shelf uninterrupted power supply (UPS) is essential. In addition to providing backup power, it overcomes interference caused by electrical spikes and surges, and its instant restoration of power neutralizes an intruder's attempt to avoid detection by shutting down a sensor's electric circuit.

Also essential in choosing an electronic access control system is quality, both in equipment and installation. A bargain can turn out to be false economy when equipment malfunctions and requires repair, recalibration, or retrofitting.

Managing a Purchase

Before purchasing a CCTV system, the CSO would do well to be absolutely clear as to what is needed and what is not. A state-of-the-art system can be sufficiently enthralling to draw the CSO's focus from consideration of the protected facility's most basic requirements.

Requirements, of course, are identified by characterizing the nature of the threat and determining what is needed to counter the threat. These steps are followed by cost/benefit analysis. A common approach is to compare the costs of acquisition and operation against dollars saved by reducing the need for security manpower and preventing losses that would result absent the system.

Operating the System

Before a system can be operated, the operators need to be trained. The purchase agreement often includes provision of training by the manufacturer or supplier. The job description of a system operator, which is prepared by the CSO, can serve as a training reference. A follow-on step is to prepare written procedures supplemented with literature of the manufacturer.

System Performance

Ensuring system performance is a CSO responsibility. Carrying out the responsibility requires attention to detail and exactitude, with the focus on performance of equipment and operators. Performance errors tend to be moderate to great in the period immediately following system start-up, with few errors occurring over the remaining life of the system. As each error is detected, corrections are made to equipment, tasks of the operators, written procedures, and training content. An important yet often unconsidered correction is to make the system operator's job challenging and as interesting as possible.

Maintenance

Keeping the system up and running at an optimum level calls for technical support delivered quickly. The relatively complex and rapidly evolving nature of CCTV requires a level of technical knowledge not often found in a security group. Knowledge includes an understanding of the facility's security needs and the CSO's concept of protection.

As is the case with most major purchases, the CSO looks at or obtains three offers. Generally, the manufacturers of top-shelf systems are able to provide high-quality technical advice and service. The leading manufacturers of CCTV systems advertise in security products catalogues. Figure 12-6 indicates how managing a CCTV system can be a step-by-step process.

CCTV System Guidance

Pre-Acquisition

Conduct a risk analysis to determine the facility's security needs. Examine the site during both day and night conditions, take photos and make video tapes, prepare notes and a layout sketch, and evaluate environmental factors that may impact the operation of a CCTV system. Also evaluate possible interference of nearby facilities such as roadways, airports, and industrial plants.

Identify CCTV applications that correspond to the identified security needs. Develop a scheme for tying the CCTV applications into a single system.

Determine how the CCTV system will interface with other security systems such as intrusion detection and access control.

Draft a technical design and conduct a cost-benefit analysis.

Acquisition

Select a supplier (on a bid basis, if appropriate).

Require the supplier to test the system and/or system components prior to their delivery to the site.

Prepare a schedule for receiving, installing, testing, and accepting the system.

Ensure installation under supervision of the supplier's in-house expert.

Ensure calibration by the supplier. Calibration factors include lens angles, resolution, fields of view, panning, programming, and interfaces with sensors and adjunctive systems.

Develop written procedures to guide every person involved in system operations.

Train system operators.

Test the system.

Correct problems before accepting the system.

Post-Acquisition

Conduct periodic maintenance, calibration, and trouble-shooting.

Conduct refresher training and training of new system operators.

Evaluate the installed and functioning system vis-à-vis what had been planned and expected.

Look for cost-effective revisions and add-ons.

Update written procedures.

Figure 12-6 Managing a CCTV system can be a step-by-step process.

INTRUSION DETECTION

An extremely critical function in controlling access is detection of intruders. In a very real sense, intrusion detection is at the core of the access control rationale. Without it, the integrity of a facility is in question.

An intruder detection system (IDS), as discussed in the chapter on physical security, is an arrangement of electronic devices for detecting the entry or attempted entry of an intruder and sending an alarm. An IDS involves the substitution of electronic surveillance for human surveillance.

An effective, long-life IDS is professionally designed, planned, and installed, and is serviced regularly. Without these minimum standards, an IDS may be vulnerable to circumvention, malfunctioning, and false alarms.

IDS Components

The basic components of an IDS are as follows:

- Sensors
- Circuitry that connect sensors to a control unit and the control unit to an alarm display panel
- A control unit that monitors the sensors, receives signals from them, and transmits an alarm signal
- An alarm display panel with visual and/or audible annunciators that alert monitoring personnel to an intrusion

Sensor Selection

Sensor selection is determined by the intrusion threat, the operating environment (e.g., indoors, outdoors, sub-sea, hostile climate), and power source constraints. Types of sensors are as follows:

- Volumetric and spatial sensors that detect movement within a confined area, such as a room, and are referred to in terms of their scientific principles. These are, for example, ultrasonic (sound waves), microwave (interruption of a linear signal), and passive infrared (detection of body heat).
- Beam sensors that operate on infrared and microwave principles.
- Contact sensors that activate when an electric circuit is broken by the separation of magnets such as those commonly attached to doors and windows.
- Vibration sensors attached to rigid structures. These are, for example, the inertia switch that reacts to physical vibration, the geophone that reacts to sound vibration, and the crystal vibration switch that reacts when a piezoelectric crystal is compressed by physical vibration.
- Closed-circuit sensors that activate when an electrical circuit is broken; for example, by the cutting of a charged wire inside a wall or inside the mesh of a window screen.
- Sensors that activate when weight is applied to a surface such as a pressurized mat concealed under a rug.
- Video motion detectors that activate when movement is picked up by the lens of a video camera.

Minimum Expectations

The CSO should expect an intrusion detection system to

- Operate despite potentially interfering environmental phenomena such as extreme weather and climate, tremors, topographical obstructions, and loud noises.
- Resist and detect tampering.

- Be fail safe (i.e., continue to operate when the primary power source fails and report equipment. malfunctions).
- Have a backup power source.
- Be linked to a monitoring station.
- Have a designated response capability.
- Be designed and planned by an IDS-certified engineer.

THREAT INDIVIDUALS

The nature of a threat confronting a protected facility can be viewed from two perspectives. The first is tradition, or what has happened in the past. Concern is shaped by what has been learned from experience. We ask: What is the chance it will happen again? When, where, how?

The second perspective looks at the type of threat. Is it nature related or human related? In the context of access control, the nature-related threat does not apply. However, it can be useful to compare the two. Logic tells us that there would not be a nature-related threat to even think about unless it had occurred in the past. We know from experience that a hurricane has occurred in the past. Our good judgment tells us that a hurricane will occur again, that it will most likely occur during a certain part of the year, and that it will come from a certain direction. We know that at well-understood velocity levels it will damage property to a certain extent. In short, a nature-related threat has a baseline that permits prediction and preparation. By comparison, a human-related threat has a partial, murky baseline at best.

Our experience and good judgment can tell us only that threats posed by humans exist. We can guess at what they target, how they will go about it, and the loss or damage they will inflict. We can make even more shaky judgments about their capabilities and resolve. The best we can do is label them according to who they are and what they want.

Right off the bat we can say that human-related threats exist within and outside the organization. For example, a disaffected employee is an internal threat, a criminal opportunist is an external threat, and a terrorist is both.

Our greatest concern, although not always our greatest exposure, is with external threats. We tend to not consider the possibility that someone within the tent has evil intentions. We do this because our natural thinking process makes us trust those that are close and distrust those that are not.

The Insider

The inside threat is typically manifested in theft, disruption of operations, destruction and damage of property, and harm to people. An accountant embezzles, a wise-guy hacker erases important files, a disgruntled employee tosses a monkey wrench into machinery, and a terrorist sympathizer sets off a bomb in the lobby.

A combination of physical and procedural safeguards can be valuable in thwarting the inside threat. Access controls, at least those that regulate movement of people entering the facility, will not impede the insider. Barriers and sensors at critical points around critical assets can be effective. The trusted insider, however, can be expected to have access to lock combinations and keys, have a good working knowledge of security equipment and procedures, and enjoy freedom from restraint and suspicion.

The Opportunist

This individual, typically an outsider and a thief or rapist, looks for chinks in the protective shield. He/she believes or thinks that behind the shield are valuables worth taking or prey worth assaulting. If it appears that the shield cannot be penetrated, the opportunist moves on to more promising territory. If it appears that the shield is vulnerable, the opportunist follows a path of least resistance. If detected or challenged, the opportunist flees and does not return. If penetration succeeds, the opportunist checks out the new surroundings and selects one or two routes of escape. The thief begins looking for exposed valuables of a type that can be concealed until he/she is out of the facility and on safe ground. The rapist begins looking for an apparently submissive victim and a secluded place to commit the assault. More often that not, the opportunist is a petty criminal lacking in sophistication, intelligence, and skill.

The best tools for reducing crimes of opportunity are deterrents such as fences, lights, signs on the perimeter, and guards at vehicle gates and pedestrian doors. A less recognized but important deterrent is maintenance. When the facility is shabby, the opportunist tends to connect poor maintenance with uncaring occupants. The thought process is, "Here is a place where I can get inside, move about freely, and get away without getting caught."

Of all deterrents, the human presence is most effective. It is best shown by alert, well-groomed guards and employees that challenge strangers.

The Professional

A third type of external threat is the skilled professional. He/she has a particular target in mind, possesses technical knowledge of security devices and how to defeat them, has security-defeating tools and other resources, and operates from a plan. The professional is likely to be assisted by an accomplice inside the protected facility.

The professional is often patient and willing to abort when he/she confronts an unanticipated risk. When trickery does not succeed in getting past a security guard, the professional makes an attempt to use stealth. If confronted, the professional has a believable cover story and false identification. The professional is thwarted by physical safeguards, sensors in particular, well-trained security officers, and suspicious employees.

The Ideologue

The ideologue frequently operates alone but is almost always supported morally or materially by a group rooted in a cause: religion, nationalism, human rights, animal rights, and environmental protection. The ideologue cleaves to the group's beliefs and agenda, accepts the group's set of targets, and follows its standard attack scenario. The ideologue is not always comfortable committing acts that harm people.

As a general rule, material greed and unmet psychological needs are not motivators for the ideologue. However, the ideological group does have a history of resorting to robbery, extortion by threat, and kidnapping to acquire operating revenue. Individual and group tactics range from terrorist acts, such as bombings and assassination, to purely symbolic acts such as splashing blood on walls or burning a flag in a public place. The ideologue may or may not be skilled, is likely to be intelligent, very likely to be strongly committed and dedicated, willing to take chances, and willing to suffer the consequences of being caught.

Because ideologues make no bones about their enemies and lodge their protests every way they can, the CSO to some degree is able to anticipate an act of some type and prepare to deal with it. The appropriate countermeasures are similar to those that apply to the professional.

The Avenger

This type of individual can be inside or outside the protected facility. Of the two, the inside avenger represents the greater risk. However, when the outside avenger was an insider at one time the risk is highest. This individual has knowledge of how to get inside, and if successful in doing so the chances are great that an adverse act will follow. There can be little motivation to get inside when the resolve to act is weak.

The number of incidents involving violence by an employee or former employee against co-workers and supervisors has increased dramatically in recent years. The number of injuries and deaths at work has also increased. When robbery-related shootings are factored in, workplace killings are a leading cause of on-the-job deaths.

Workplace homicides are often the result of an unstable employee being laid off or terminated. The worker returns with a gun and kills the supervisor and others who get in the way. When layoffs and terminations rise, violence also rises.

An employee that releases frustration through acts of violence is likely to have a history of violence and is likely to demonstrate frustration through temper tantrums, threat making, and bursts of anger. It is too late at this time to apply the best countermeasure: preemployment screening. It is not too late, however, to teach supervisors how to spot the indicators of frustration and how to intervene. The time for teaching is always, with special emphasis during periods of outsourcing and downsizing.

Terminated employees have a right to be decently treated during the termination process. At the same time, however, the organization has a right to take protective steps. One of these is to quickly remove reentry privileges and put into effect corresponding security procedures. More discussion on these issues can be found in the workplace violence chapter.

The Terrorist

By definition, terrorists are persons that use force or violence against others to intimidate or coerce, often for religious or political reasons. In the context of access control, terrorists can be seen to possess some of the characteristics of opportunists, professionals, ideologues, and avengers. But the resemblances are obscured by the magnitude of human casualties and destruction inflicted by terrorists. They have demonstrated the know-how, capability, and resolve to carry out their acts. For these reasons they are at the top of the intruder list and are the first priority for protection.

A terrorist attack through intrusion is likely to be made by numerous terrorists acting simultaneously and employing a combination of trickery, stealth, and direct assault. The resistance capability can be overwhelmed, even at high-security facilities.

A terrorist acting alone can be as destructive as a group of terrorists acting in unison. We have seen that the driver of a van carrying explosives can destroy an entire embassy and kill nearly all people in it, whereas a band of terrorists assaulting an embassy can succeed in destroying little in the way of structure and killing relatively small numbers of people. The epitome of a terrorist acting alone was Timothy McVeigh.

The capacity of a security system to neutralize or resist the single terrorist or band of terrorists can be enhanced when the CSO is plugged into an intelligence-sharing group. One of the oldest is the State Department's Overseas Advisory Council. CSOs send information to and draw from a body of processed data received from U.S. embassies and consulates worldwide. CSOs of major corporations in a single industry have always shared information concerning common adversaries. In the petroleum industry, for example, CSOs of Exxon, Shell, and British Petroleum meet regularly to swap information about criminal and terrorist activities occurring in their separate domains. Similar groups are forming in sectors of the critical national infrastructure. The Environmental Protection Agency serves as a repository and clearinghouse for security-related information pertaining to water and waste water plants. The Department of Transportation does the same for the aviation, rail, trucking, city transit, maritime, and pipelines industries.

CONCLUSIONS

The security domain operates with numerous concepts, such as concentric and layered protection, redundancy, crime prevention through environmental design, and psychological deterrence. All concepts share a common purpose: keep the adversary away from the target. The nature of the target is somewhat beside the point. It can be a person, such as a celebrity; an object, such as a nuclear bomb; information, such as a trade secret; a structure, such as the White House; a city, such as New York City; or a critical national infrastructure, such as the banking and finance sector. Although the techniques and targets vary, the main objective is access control.

NOTES

1. Ed San Luis, Louis A. Tyska, and Lawrence J. Fennelly, *Office and Office Building Security, Second Edition*, pp. 216, Boston: Butterworth-Heinemann, 1994.

2. Lionel Silverman, "End User Demand Spurs Multiple Technology Cards," *Security Technology & Design*, June 1999, pp. 28.

3. Gary Funck, "Smart Card Interfacing," *Security*, June 1999, pp. 51.

4. John J. Fay, "Access Control: People, Vehicles, and Materials," in *Encyclopedia of Security Management*, pp. 8, John J. Fay, editor, Boston: Butterworth-Heinemann.

5. Emily M. Harwood, "Everything Is Coming Up Digital," *Security Technology & Design*, June 1999, pp. 50.

13. Managing Investigations

Truth is more of a stranger than fiction.
　　　　　　　　—Mark Twain

BACKGROUND

The investigative function is part and parcel of the organization's efforts to protect assets. In respect to crime-related losses, the CSO's overall responsibilities are to [1]

- Determine where loss exposures exist and devise controls to eliminate or minimize them.
- Recommend changes and additions to loss prevention controls.
- Enlist the support of employees in discovering and remedying loss exposures.
- Open formal investigations when loss prevention controls break down.

This chapter deals with the last of these four responsibilities.

INTERNAL THEFT

One of the most frequently investigated incidents in the business environment is employee theft. Ending, or least controlling, theft by employees begins with management. Three imperatives are placed on the CEO and the executive team.

- Decide that internal theft is unacceptable.
- Do something about it.
- Involve employees in bringing it to an end.

It is generally accepted by bonding companies and security professionals that a workforce divides into three groups insofar as honesty is concerned. The first group, about 25 percent, is consistently honest no matter what. Another 25 percent are outright thieves; they are consciously looking for ways to steal.

Employee Theft

Some employers choose to do nothing in the face of internal theft. They don't want to upset their workers.

Some employers are simply unaware of theft or make no effort to be aware.

Some employers keep an eye on internal theft and take preventive action only after losses reach a pre-defined level.

Some employers choose to keep dishonest employees on the payroll in order to give them an income that will permit restitution.

Some employers and their employees believe that stealing is in the natural order of things and should therefore be allowed.

Many employees have never been told not to steal or that stealing has consequences, such as being fired.

Low-pay employees tend to feel justified in stealing.

High-pay employees steal but because they are fewer in number than low-pay employees the overall impact of their stealing is usually less.

New employees are more likely to steal than long-time employees.

The opportunity to steal is more often present than the motive to steal. Some employees steal, not because they need or want something, but because they have a chance to steal.

Many honest employees see other employees steal but do not report it, often for stupid reasons.

Figure 13-1 Do any of these observations apply where you work?

The honesty of the remaining 50 percent is up to management. This half of the workforce can fall on either side, depending on opportunity. If opportunity exists, the temptation exists. Given sufficient temptation and the example of theft by co-workers, many employees in the 50-percent category will steal also [2].

Close to a third of businesses that fail do so in large part because of internal theft. On the surface it might appear that a business went down the tube because it could not compete in a highly competitive and evolving marketplace. If you look below the surface, which is the role of investigation, the truth is likely to be employee dishonesty — and not just the dishonesty of the occasional embezzler but of employees collectively.

For it to be said accurately that employee dishonesty is deviant behavior, there must first be rules and controls to deviate from. The lack or poor construction of rules and controls is a management failure — a failure that can lead to a downward spiral of ever-increasing dishonesty, the corollaries of which are loss of productivity and customer dissatisfaction [3].

According to some experts, the cost of crime to American business is in excess of $40 billion per year (see Figure 13-1). Perhaps the biggest problem is that most corporate managers do not even know if they a problem. They do not know how to find out if they have a problem or even if they want to know they have a problem. Some managers seem to prefer to keep things as they are and to regard any suggestion of increased security as criticism of their ability to protect the employer's assets [4].

Although internal theft does not account for all crime inflicted on business, its pervasiveness and heavy impact on the bottom line strongly indicate the need for a security program designed to prevent internal theft, and where prevention fails, to thoroughly investigate. Following investigation is the pursuit of restitution, termination of offenders, and vigorous prosecution in court when appropriate.

Signals of Internal Theft

The signals of theft by employees are not all that subtle and are fairly easy to spot. The main reason they are not spotted is that supervisors and co-workers don't think to look for them, and when spotted they are attributed to other causes. The signals include the following.

- Gambling
- Borrowing
- Living above apparent income level
- Writing bad checks
- Indebtedness
- Drug and alcohol abuse

Things stolen by employees range widely, and include the following.

- Cash such as receipts in a cash register
- Merchandise such as items sold directly to consumers
- Materials in production, storage, or transit
- Desktop equipment such as PCs, fax machines, printers, and scanners
- Furniture
- Supplies
- Sensitive information
- Time, such as cheating on time cards and being away from work without permission

In addition to theft is the misuse of company assets. Many employees wrongfully use company equipment. Violations range from copying personal documents on the office copier to using the mainframe computer to operate a side business.

Fraud

In many circumstances, internal theft is carried out by fraud or deception. But fraud is not entirely an internal offense. It can involve collusion with outsiders or outsiders operating alone.

The ordinary ritual is for crimes to be reported after they have occurred. The investigator goes to the place of the crime, interviews the victim and witnesses, and tries to figure out what happened. This is not always the case with crimes involving fraud. Very often, the crime is discovered while in progress, often after it has been going on for an extended period of time. Because the place of the crime is usually the place where the offender is working, the investigator must collect evidence and interview witnesses cautiously. The investigator does not want to give the offender an opportunity to destroy pertinent records before they can be seized. Neither does the investigator want to allow the fraudulent activity to continue unabated.

The term *fraud* is a short-hand way of describing one or a combination of crimes that have formal names, such as bribery, embezzlement, and theft by deception. Some of the more common forms of fraud involve the following [5].

- Invoicing for goods below set prices and then obtaining cash kickbacks from the purchasers
- Increasing the amounts of suppliers' invoices and keeping the excess or splitting it with the suppliers
- Paying suppliers' invoices twice and keeping the second check
- Destroying delivery records or other evidence that some service was performed so that commission agents or others who collect from customers can pocket the proceeds, part of which goes to the employee who destroyed the records
- Pocketing checks collected from presumably dead accounts
- Forging checks and destroying them when returned with bank statements
- Failing to record returned purchases, allowances, and discounts, and keeping the difference
- Padding payrolls as to rates, times, or amounts produced
- Issuing checks in payment of invoices from fictitious suppliers and cashing them through a dummy company
- Pocketing the proceeds of cash sales and not recording the transactions
- Pocketing small amounts from incoming payments and then applying subsequent remittances on other items to cover the missing amounts
- Charging customers more than the duplicate sales slips show and pocketing the difference
- Misappropriating cash and then charging the amounts taken to fictitious accounts

Fraud is not necessarily crime committed by employees that wear white collars. The criminal can just as well be a shipping dock employee as a senior executive. In fact, the term *white-collar* has nothing to do with apparel and everything to do with the nature of the crime. The common elements are nonviolence, deceit, corruption, and breach of trust. The crime has no boundaries; victims can include individuals, businesses, schools, churches, and governmental units.

Characteristics of Fraud

It is often discovered by accident or reported anonymously.
It is difficult at first to figure out.
It has been going on for some time.
It is likely to span several investigative/prosecutorial jurisdictions.
It usually violates more than one law.
It is the act of a respected and intelligent individual.
It often involves record destruction, such as when the criminal learns
that an investigation has been opened.

Figure 13-2 At the conclusion of a fraud investigation, the investigator is likely to note the presence of these characteristics.

Characteristics of Fraud

Business fraud operates out of view and is difficult to detect. The victim is not aware of the loss, which usually takes the form of repetitive, incremental thefts. When discovery is made, it may be too late to recover even a small portion of the loss or to take strong action against the thief. Also, the mixed-bag nature of fraud techniques rules out the application of a universal test for determining the existence of a fraud in progress. The best a business can do is to make sure that loss control standards are operating properly and investigate when it appears they are not. Business fraud is complicated by a strange willingness of the courts and public to forgive fraudsters, and an inability of police detectives to deal with complex business-related crimes. The general characteristics of fraud are as follows (see Figure 13-2):

- Detection is frequently accidental.
- Offenses are frequently reported anonymously.
- There is usually no complainant.
- The scheme has been in existence over a long period of time.
- The crime tends to cover a large geographical area, often spanning several prosecutorial jurisdictions.
- The scheme tends to involve several violations of law.
- The guilty party is usually well known, respected, intelligent, and in some cases, influential.
- The scheme is sometimes difficult to decipher.
- Evidence tends to "get lost or destroyed" when the guilty party learns that an investigation is in progress.

Common Types of Fraud

As previously discussed, the guilty parties in a fraud can be employees only or employees working in concert with outsiders. The sections that follow discuss examples. Figure 13-3 points out warning signals of fraud.

Indicators of a Fraudulent Business Opportunity Scheme

Claiming affiliation or association with a large, successful company.
Presenting a misleading credit rating such as a false Dunn & Bradstreet report.
Citing false business and personal references (e.g., Better Business Bureau, Chamber of Commerce, and well known individuals).
Inflating marketing experience and national sales.
Misreporting the size of the firm.
Promoting a unique product or service that has a high public demand and need.
Projecting unrealistic sales and profits.
Presenting doctored marketing surveys.
Claiming easy sales during spare time and/or at home such as filling orders for retail stores and selling via direct mail.
Offering exclusive territory with leads and potential customers furnished.
Offering a repurchase or buy-back option.
Providing free training and free servicing and repair of the product to be marketed.
Representing that the manufacturer or sponsor will provide saturated advertising.
Advising that the offer to "get on board" will soon expire.
Changing the contract at the last moment.

Figure 13-3 These warning signals can arouse investigative interest.

Medical Fraud

Employers who provide health benefits are often cheated through double billing, over-billing, and billing for services not performed. Bills are sent to the employee, the employer, and the health insurance carrier for the same medical service or product. The crime can also be committed by billing for services provided by another physician or hospital. This is done by gaining access to the other provider's records and billing for the other's as-yet-unbilled services. Also included in medical fraud is ping-ponging, a practice in which the employee-patient is given unnecessary treatment at the same time needed services are performed (see Figure 13-4).

Bid Rigging

In this scheme, a contract awarded through competitive bidding is corrupted by connivance among the bidders. For example, the bidders collectively decide who will be the low bidder. For the next contract, a different contractor is chosen to deliver the low bid. In addition, the low bid and all of the other bids are greatly inflated. Bid rigging can be difficult to prove when the bidders operate from a tacit understanding, as opposed to a planned and premeditated conspiracy.

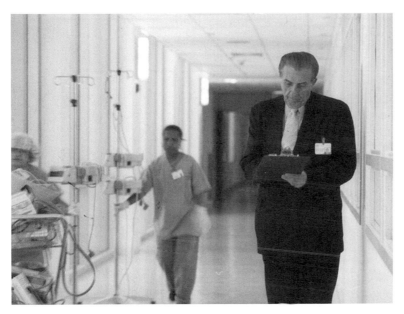

Figure 13-4 Billing for medical services not performed is a national problem.

Computer-assisted Fraud

Computer-assisted frauds can be made to work in just about any way a computer can be made to work. Ingenuity of the criminal plays a large part in making the loot substantial and the fraud undetectable, at least in the short run.

Computers can be used unlawfully to secretly read proprietary data, such as a business plan or a trade secret formula; change data to alter entitlements; obtain personal identification data for making purchases on credit cards issued to others; destroy or manipulate data; transfer funds to accounts accessible by the criminals; make payments where none are due; and order movement or delivery of goods. Computers can also construct a framework for perpetrating a fraud at a future time or wipe out the evidence of past and current fraud.

False Billing

In a false billing scheme, a criminal sends to a company an authentic-looking invoice for products or services never ordered or received. The criminal hopes the company will process and pay the invoice without scrutiny.

Some criminals, using lists of business addresses obtained from open sources (such as The Yellow Pages), mail invoices with the hope that poor accounting procedures will result in payments. In some cases, the criminal will telephone companies and use enticing or high-pressure tactics to obtain orders for exorbitantly priced products. These sales persons falsely represent that the business has already ordered the product, either currently or in the past.

Workers' Compensation Fraud

Be skeptical when these facts are present in a workers' compensation claim.

> The injury was sustained in one week and reported the following week.
> The accident occurred very close in time to a strike, a layoff, or a job termination.
> The accident was not witnessed.
> The claimant has a history of filing workers' compensation claims.
> The claimant's initial description of the injury does not agree with the medical report.
> The claimant is often not at home when called.
> The claimant refuses a diagnostic examination to confirm the injury.
> The claimant has hired a lawyer to pursue the claim.
> The claimant's physician has a history of being involved in suspect claims.
> The claimant switched to another physician after receiving a release from work.

Figure 13-5 The investigation of fraudulent workers' compensation claims is often assigned to the security group.

Workers' Compensation Fraud

A workers' compensation claim is likely to land on the investigator's desk when the circumstances of a workplace accident or injury point to the possibility of fraud (see Figure 13-5). A claim can be judged suspicious when the alleged injury was not witnessed, the injury not reported immediately, and treatment not administered by a physician approved in the company's health benefits plan. Another indication is a difference between the employee's description of injuries and the report of medical treatment. The plot thickens when the employee retains an attorney within days after the alleged injury.

When a questionable claim is indeed false, the claimant fears two outcomes: not getting the fruits of the fraud and getting caught in the attempt. To avoid those outcomes, the claimant will do everything to thwart the inquiry, such as not agreeing to be interviewed and accusing the investigator of unlawful tactics.

Care must be taken by the investigator to operate strictly within the law and ethical standards. For example, taking photographs of the claimant through a window of his/her home may seem like a good idea at the time, but it's an invitation to be charged for trespassing and invasion of privacy.

An example of a privacy violation was a case decided by the Georgia Court of Appeals. The plaintiff testified that the defendant (a private detective) cut a hole in her hedge so that he could peer into her window, eavesdropped on her activities inside her home, followed her when she left home, and behaved in visible ways that caused her neighbors to talk about her. The court found the surveillance unreasonable and awarded considerable damages to the woman.

Surveillance operations carry other types of risks. Stalking laws, which are relatively new, can place the investigator in legal hot water. As a general rule of thumb, an investigator gets into trouble in this area when the person being watched is placed in reasonable fear of bodily injury or is caused substantial emotional distress.

Other risks associated with surveillance involve wire taps, video and audio recordings, and intercepted voice mail and e-mail. An example is a finding by a federal court jury that the American Broadcasting Company committed fraud and trespass against Food Lion in an undercover investigation of Food Lion's alleged doctoring and bleaching of spoiled meat and fish. An ABC employee hid a camera in a head wig and taped a microphone to her chest. A jury held that ABC had gone too far in gathering the evidence.

Bribery

Bribery in the business environment is most often related to contracted services. It occurs when a corrupt employee working in a responsible position accepts a payment of some type in exchange for special consideration. Payment can be cash in advance or at a later time (i.e., a kickback), discounts on personal purchases, gifts, leased automobile, home improvement, or other reward. The special consideration given to the person making the payment can include awarding a contract improperly, overlooking deficiencies in the performance of the contract, certifying payment for unsatisfactory work or work not performed, and purchasing materials at inflated prices.

PROBLEMS IN PROSECUTING

At state and local levels, prosecution of crime against business is generally erratic and inefficient. Jurisdiction is often unclear and there is an across-the-board lack of technical expertise in building strong cases. Prosecutors also place higher priorities on cases that capture the public's attention, such as crimes of uncommon violence (e.g., the Jeffrey Dahmer killings) or crimes committed by uncommon people (e.g., the CEO of Enron).

Fraud offenders frequently avoid trials or face half-hearted prosecution efforts. When convicted, the sentences are usually relatively light. Unlike crimes of violence committed by common felons, offenders are punished economically. The courts tend to view them as decent people who exercised bad judgment. A fine and public exposure are often seen as suitable punishment.

THE FORENSIC INVESTIGATOR

A fairly new job title has entered the lexicon of investigations. The forensic investigator is a specialist in bringing to light and proving a wide variety of white-collar offenses. When not turning over stones, the forensic investigator is conducting due diligence inquiries, tracking hidden assets, making financial evaluations, setting up countermeasures to industrial espionage, and assessing the effectiveness of security in the client's technical areas such as computer and communication operations.

The forensic investigator is sometimes a consultant or independent contractor, and sometimes an in-house employee. The work is often performed on behalf of large business sector organizations (e.g., multinational corporations, upscale law firms, and the Big Six auditing companies). The investigator typically holds one or more degrees in accounting, financial management, business administration, law, and computer science.

Like their counterparts in mainline investigative pursuits, the forensic investigator is inquisitive, resourceful, tenacious, and competitive. He/she has little training in the traditional investigative skills, such as crime scene processing and interrogation, but is highly trained and very capable in risk analysis, statistical sampling, and auditing.

COMPLIANCE INVESTIGATIONS

A compliance investigation is launched when an organization (typically a large corporation) learns that its officers or other senior managers have engaged in misconduct that may expose the organization to criminal or civil liability, or administrative sanction. An order by a CEO that resulted in the dumping of toxic chemicals in violation of an environmental protection law is an example of misconduct that would lead the organization's chairman or board of directors to order an investigation.

The overall goal of the investigation is to gather information for the purpose of reducing the employer's potential exposure to prosecution or litigation arising from the violation. The objectives are to develop firsthand knowledge of facts that may expose the employer to risk, correct the situation as quickly as possible, make the regulatory agency aware of the situation, and in doing so avoid indictment [6].

WHISTLE-BLOWER RULES

A reflection of government and public attitudes against corporate criminals can be seen in the adoption of whistle-blower rules that protect employees when they report the sins of their supervisors. Whistle-blower protection is a specific provision of a law called Federal Sentencing Guidelines. More ominous for corporate criminals are mandatory sentencing provisions. They call for the imposition of stiff jail sentences and strong economic penalties for people whose business decisions or conduct violate a law or impede the resulting investigation.

The origins of the guidelines are interesting. In 1984, Congress created a commission and charged it with developing a guide for federal judges to follow when sentencing offenders. The problem to be corrected by the guidelines concerned sentencing practices that did not reflect the seriousness of the offenses. Wide variances were often occurring in the name of judicial discretion. Congress wanted to make it clear that sentencing had grown excessively lenient and that a stronger stance on crime was needed.

The commission produced a document that worked remarkably well — so well, in fact, that in 1988 Congress expanded the mandate of the commission to add guidelines for the sentencing of corporations. The corporate-related guidelines substantially increased the fines imposed on companies convicted of crime, introduced a concept of corporate probation, and called for self-reporting of crimes.

COUNTERINTELLIGENCE INVESTIGATIONS

It is no secret that some companies spy on other companies to gain a competitive advantage. The practice is called business espionage, which is criminal activity and is distinct from competitive intelligence gathering, which is legal and reasonable. Counterintelligence investigations detect and deflect business espionage and competitive intelligence gathering, which are legal and reasonable. (Further information on business espionage can be found in the chapter on information security.)

INFORMATION OBTAINABLE ON THE INTERNET

Investigators tasked with protecting employers from the actions of opposing interest groups can obtain a surprising amount of useful information by taking a ride on the information highway. Almost every group imaginable has a web page of some type used for various purposes, such as to propagandize in general, castigate their enemies, recruit new members, raise money, attract attendance at their various events, announce intentions, and boast of achievements.

Interest groups found on the Internet go far beyond advocacy of standard issues such as conserving the planet, protecting the ecology, and observing animal rights. They include terrorism, anarchism, religious issues, and patriotism — just about anything that is ardently believed. And because advocacy in one direction is often savagely attacked from another direction, it is in the nature of advocacy groups to protect themselves every way they can.

Many advocacy groups have set up their web sites so that visitors who stop to do more than read (such as download or inquire) are identified by their electronic footprints. The technology allows the web site owner to trace back through the system and learn such details as the visitor's phone number. After that, it's a simple matter of using the phone number to learn the visitor's name or company, and the address. From there, all manner of details can be acquired. If purchases are made on the Internet, such as to order advocacy group publications, the purchaser opens a path of discovery to credit card information.

The paranoia that infests so many advocacy groups opens a real possibility that even an innocent pause by a corporation on an interest group's web site is seen as an act of war, if not proof that the big corporation is spying against little people whose only objective is making the world a better place. A corporation worried about retaliation, yet prudent enough to want to check out the opposition via the Internet, will insist that its investigators cover the electronic footprints.

How is that done? By setting up a drop box for billings and providing cover identification for the address. The idea is to have a trace-back lead to a phone number or credit card not associated with the corporation or the investigators. A drop box that quickly comes to mind would be one in the name of a college student (real or false) using a post office box number. A credit card with a modest line of credit, such as $500, adds an element of credibility.

Web sites maintained by advocacy groups are not the only places to go on the Internet for useful information. Electronic newsletters and bulletin boards are sites where Internet travelers can stop to read articles and notices posted by various groups and individuals. Not all sites, of course, are radical in nature. Many deal with perfectly ordinary topics such as stamp collecting or poetry writing. The investigator's interest is on sites that advance a point of view running counter to the corporate interest.

A third source of Internet information is the people finder, address finder, and map-searching services at search engine sites. These no-cost facilities can be especially helpful in developing information.

THE POLYGRAPH

Employee Polygraph Protection Act (EPPA)

The Employee Polygraph Protection Act (EPPA) of 1988 permits the testing of employees only for the investigation of crimes in which the employer has an interest. An employer may test an employee who falls under a cloud of reasonable suspicion. Reasonable suspicion can be shown when the employee was at the place of the crime at or near the time of the crime, had opportunity (such as access to property that was stolen), and is implicated by a credible witness. A showing of reasonable suspicion is also present if an employee lied when questioned about the crime.

Written Consent Required

Testing can be done only with the written consent of the suspect. Prior to obtaining the consent, the employer and/or the polygraph examiner must disclose to the suspect the specific offense under investigation, time and place of the offense, and why the employee is a suspect. If reasonable suspicion is supported by a witness, the name of the witness can be withheld from the suspect.

Figure 13-6 A polygraph examination can help whittle down the number of persons having the opportunity to commit the crime under investigation.

Polygraph Theory

Lie detection is based on the assumption that when an individual experiences apprehension, fear, or emotional excitement his or her respiration rate, blood pressure, and galvanic skin resistance sharply increase. A polygraph instrument records the changes as the individual is questioned by a trained examiner. The examiner interprets the recordings and renders an opinion as to the truthfulness of the person examined.

The theory behind the polygraph technique (see Figure 13-6) holds that a conscious mental effort to deceive made by a normal, healthy person will cause certain physiological changes detectable by the polygraph instrument. These changes are driven by the autonomic nervous system, which regulates the body's internal environment and is generally involuntary. The parasympathetic nervous system, a division of the autonomic nervous system, dominates in relaxed situations. It performs routine "housekeeping" functions such as digestion and maintenance of body temperature. No matter how hard an examinee might try, he/she will not be able to prevent physiological changes in respiration rate, blood pressure, and galvanic skin resistance.

Polygraph Accuracy

Hundreds of studies conducted over the years to determine the accuracy of the polygraph technique have produced less than conclusive judgments. Still, a preponderance of the data indicates that when properly trained examiners utilize an established testing procedure the accuracy of their decisions is generally in the range of 85 to 95 percent for specific-issue investigations. Few studies have been made to determine the range of accuracy for preemployment testing.

One of the problems in judging overall accuracy is a misunderstanding of the term *inconclusive* as it used in the reporting of test results. An inconclusive result simply means that the examiner was unable to render a definite conclusion. By way of illustration, if 10 polygraph examinations were administered and the examiner was correct in 7 decisions, wrong in 1, and had 2 inconclusive test results, the percentage of accuracy is 87.5 percent (7 out of 8). Others would say the percentage is 70 percent (7 out of 10).

Polygraph Errors

Polygraph errors are nearly always human errors. They tend to center on the examiner's failure to prepare the examinee for the test and correctly read the data on the polygraph charts.

A false positive test report occurs when a truthful examinee is reported as being deceptive. A false negative report occurs when a deceptive examinee is reported as truthful. It is widely believed that negatives occur more frequently than positives, perhaps because examiners would rather let a deceptive individual get by than to declare an innocent individual deceptive.

PHYSICAL EVIDENCE

Evidence is anything that tends to prove or disprove a fact. Within that general definition, physical evidence is any material substance or object, regardless of size or shape. Generally, there are three categories of physical evidence. Movable evidence is an item that can be transported or moved, such as a tool or glass fragment. Fixed or immovable evidence is an item that cannot easily be removed, such as a tree or utility pole. Fragile evidence is an item that is easily lost, destroyed, contaminated, or subject to degradation. Examples include hairs, fibers, snow, ice, dust, and perishable food.

In many cases the success or failure of an investigation depends on the investigator's ability to recognize physical evidence and derive understanding from it. This process of evaluation begins with the initial report of a crime and concludes when the case is adjudicated. Evaluation is usually carried out in concert with laboratory technicians, a prosecuting attorney, other investigators, experts in certain fields, and other persons whose knowledge contributes to a better understanding of physical evidence items and their relationship to the case at hand.

EVIDENCE COLLECTION

Identification markings: Evidence must be marked for identification as soon as it is received, recovered, or discovered. Identification markings help the investigator identify the evidence at a later date. Markings are normally made by placing initials, time, and date on the items. If not practical to mark, the evidence is placed in a container and sealed. The container is then marked for identification.

Evidence tag: Identification markings are supplemented by an evidence tag that is filled out at the time the evidence is acquired. Entries on the tag are made in ink, and the tag accompanies the evidence from the moment it is acquired until it is relinquished. An evidence tag is an administrative convenience for locating evidence while it is in custody; it is not a substitute for marking evidence.

Chain of custody: When an item of evidence is received it is recorded on a document called a chain-of-custody document. Because all persons who handle an item are considered links in the custody chain, the number of persons who handle the item should be kept to a minimum. An investigator in possession of evidence is personally liable for its care and safekeeping.

TESTIFYING

Security group investigators are often important witnesses at legal proceedings. They may be the only persons able to give a complete, coordinated view of what happened. The importance of a good presentation on the witness stand cannot be overemphasized. Day after day of highly competent investigation may be wasted when the investigator's testimony is poorly presented. The trier of fact (judge, jury, hearing officer) enters the proceeding with no prior knowledge of the matter to be decided. The picture the trier gets will depend largely on the ability of the investigator to tell the story. The opposing attorney will do everything legally permitted to distort and twist the investigator's testimony. If the investigator appears confused, hazy, or unsure of important facts, the trier will be similarly confused and hazy. An opposite and positive effect results when the investigator presents facts clearly, calmly, and fairly. A verdict favorable to the investigator will be happily received, but will accomplish little in the long run if inaccurate testimony affords opposing counsel grounds for a new trial or for reversal on appeal.

Three Fundamental Obligations

The investigator has three fundamental obligations. First is to tell the truth, even if the truth hurts. This is an obligation that stands above the outcome of the lawsuit. Second is to be fair. This does not mean that the investigator has to give equal favor to both sides, only that he/she does not overstate or color the facts. Third is to be accurate.

Preparing to Testify

Testimony cannot be effective without solid preparation. Notes, sketches, reports, photographs, and physical evidence are carefully studied. Because the time between the closing of an investigation and the opening of a legal proceeding is normally quite long, the investigator needs to expend considerable effort in memory refreshment.

Memory can be assisted by organizing case details in a chronological order (i.e., as a chain of events). Testimony given in this manner can be interesting and convincing. The investigator may be allowed to refer to notes when memory fails while on the stand. In the doing, however, opposing counsel earns a right to examine the notes and pursue a line of questioning about them. This development can be risky because the investigator cannot anticipate and therefore adequately prepare for the unexpected questions of opposing counsel.

Pre-trial Conference

Preparation includes, of course, one or more meetings between the investigator and representing counsel. Details are examined so that both investigator and counsel have a clear and shared understanding of the case.

Counsel wants to stimulate the investigator to recall highly relevant details and to go over expected testimony. The investigator wants to ensure that the attorney knows all the facts, favorable and unfavorable. A sharp focus is placed on key points to be made by the investigator on the stand. Fuzzy details are examined and reexamined to ensure they will not impede an effective presentation.

As a matter of strategy, the attorney may be very interested in some facts and less interested in others. The attorney may lead the investigator through a practice run of questions he/she will ask and questions likely to be asked by the opposing attorney. Rehearsal of this type is perfectly proper provided that the investigator is not influenced to deviate from the truth.

Courtroom Procedures

The oath: A legal proceeding is carried out in accordance with established rules. Among these are the taking of an oath, direct examination by the attorney who called the witness, and cross-examination by the opposing attorney. Redirect and recross questioning may follow.

Direct examination: Securing information from a witness is by a question-and-answer method. The questioning by an attorney on direct examination guides the witness. After direct examination, the witness may be subject to cross-examination by the opposing counsel.

Cross-examination: Questions on cross-examination have the opposite purpose of those asked on direct. Cross-examination questions may be devious, deceptive, or innocent in appearance, masking the opposing counsel's real objective, which is to discredit or minimize the effect of the witness's testimony.

Giving testimony: Despite peculiarities that may attach to a particular proceeding or to the individual case before it, the investigator-witness is expected to act in ways that conform to courtroom procedures. For example, at a trial with a judge and jury the investigator does the following:

- Listens carefully to each question asked, and if the question is confusing asks to have it repeated
- Does not rush to answer a question and pauses long enough to allow friendly counsel or the judge to intervene if needed
- Answers in a confident and straightforward manner, speaking clearly, loudly, and slowly
- Looks at the attorney asking the question but directs answers to the judge and jury
- Speaks in conversational English, free of slang, jargon, and unnecessary technical terms
- Is respectful and courteous
- Addresses the judge as "Your Honor" and each attorney as "Sir" or "Madam."
- Does not become angry or argumentative
- Displays an attitude of neutrality
- Is truthful, even when truth is favorable to the other side
- Does not distort or exaggerate
- Does not try to cover up personal mistakes
- Asks the judge for an opportunity to fully respond to a yes or no question when it cannot properly be answered in that manner
- Is specific to enhance clarity
- When citing time, distance, size, and similar details, gives approximations
- When referring to a map or sketch, identifies location points clearly
- Immediately corrects his/her wrong or ambiguous answers
- Stops talking instantly if the judge or an attorney interrupts during the answer

Tactics of opposing counsel: The other side will do everything possible to downplay, discredit, or nullify the investigator's testimony. The common tactics are are as follows:

- Attempt to show that the investigator did not have the proper opportunity to obtain true facts
- Suggest the investigator was inattentive, mistaken, is prejudiced, or has a poor memory
- Suggest the investigator is lying or leaving out facts
- Goad the investigator with disparaging words in hope of throwing his or her concentration off track

The Deposition

Purpose: A deposition is an out-of-court proceeding conducted for the purpose of preserving the testimony of a witness for later use in court. In this case, we are talking about the investigator-witness.

Setting: A deposition is usually held in a reasonably comfortable setting, often the conference room of an attorney's office. The persons present are the investigator, a notary public to administer an oath, a court reporter (usually a notary), and lawyers for all parties concerned.

Procedures: The deposition begins with the investigator being placed under oath. The lawyers take turns in asking questions. A lawyer may skip a turn or take more than one turn. The proceeding is relatively informal, although serious to the final outcome of the case. The reporter takes down everything said and the reporter's record is later typed and bound in a document called a deposition or transcript.

Discovery: The deposition is essentially a discovery tool for opposing lawyers. Each side wants to learn what the investigator's testimony will be at trial. In a civil suit, for example, the plaintiff's lawyer in deposing the investigator wants to

- Discover what the investigator knows concerning the facts involved in the matter being litigated.
- Discover if the investigator knows of any facts that may be damaging to the defendant (e.g., that the defendant may have been careless or failed to do something).
- Commit the investigator to the statements made under oath so that at trial his or her testimony cannot be changed, at least not without difficulty.
- Look for ways to discredit the investigator.
- Use the investigator's testimony to discredit other defense witnesses.
- Attempt to learn the basic theory and strategy the defense will rely on at trial.

Although a deposition can embarrass or even damage the reputation of the investigator, this is not a legitimate purpose of the proceeding. When it happens, it is often the result of inadequate preparation.

JURISDICTION

Crimes, wherever they occur, fall into the jurisdiction of law enforcement. Responding to and investigating crimes are tasks performed by law enforcement officers. They work for and are paid by the public.

Incidents that involve wrongdoing, but do not constitute a violation of criminal law, may be investigated by the private parties involved. The CSO of an organization that is party to such an incident is often placed in charge of the investigation. Almost always, the incident results from a violation of a work rule or policy. Examples include a rule against bringing certain prohibited materials into the workplace and a policy that prohibits sexual harassment. In these two examples, law enforcement is not involved, but with employee sabotage and workplace violence the opposite is true because they are crimes.

As already stated, crimes that occur on company premises fall under the jurisdiction of the police. In some cases, the tasks of the investigation can be more easily performed by the CSO; for example, the originals of forged documents may have to be found, descriptions of stolen materials may have to be drafted, or costs estimated for replacement of vandalized equipment. Under these circumstances, the CSO would very likely be asked to assist.

Ongoing criminal activity can also bring the CSO into partnership with the police. Drug sales and trafficking on a company's premises is a good example. The CSO might assign an investigator to work with the police during a stakeout on the premises or place an undercover operative in a job position that might bring the operative into contact with the criminal enterprise.

CONCLUSIONS

Investigation is a complex and sophisticated function. The CSO, who manages investigations, does not need to be an expert in the details. It is sufficient that he/she be able to recognize when intervention is needed to get an investigation back on track or to keep it from straying outside the boundaries of the law. The investigator's focus is on basic tasks that bring a single issue to a satisfactory conclusion. The CSO's focus is on the major goal of aligning the investigative function with other loss-preventing functions performed within the security group.

NOTES

1. In the security environment, a rights advisement (i.e., the Miranda Warning) is not required by law. Some organizations, however, will insist that an advisement similar to the Miranda Warning be given and a record made.

2. Charles F. Hemphill, Jr., *Management's Role in Loss Prevention*, pp. 9, New York: Amacom, 1976.

3. Ed San Luis, Louis A. Tyska, and Lawrence J. Fennelly, *Office and Building Security, Second Edition*, pp. 148, Boston: Butterworth-Heinemann, 1994.

4. Louis A. Tyska and Lawrence J. Fennelly, *150 Things You Should Know About Security*, pp. 97, Boston: Butterworth-Heinemann, 1998.

5. James E. Broder, *Risk Analysis and the Security Survey*, pp. 41, Boston: Butterworth Heinemann, 1984.

6. Jack Bologna and Paul Shaw, *Corporate Crime Investigation*, pp. 19–20, Boston: Butterworth-Heinemann, 1997.

14. Preemployment Screening

We can try to avoid making choices by doing nothing, but even that is a decision.

—Gary Collins

An earlier discussion of preemployment screening guided the CSO in how to staff the security group with competent, honest, and nonviolent individuals. This discussion is directed to the CSO's role in screening job applicants throughout the total organization.

RATIONALE FOR PREEMPLOYMENT SCREENING

Employers conduct preemployment background checks because laws and regulations place a duty on them to maintain a safe and secure working environment, including the duty to protect workers, guests, and the public from the harmful acts of employees.

When harm occurs and the employer cannot show that it acted reasonably to maintain a safe and secure working environment, severe penalties can result from civil lawsuits and sanctions by watchdog agencies.

Harmful acts committed by prospective employees cover a wide number of criminal acts, such as murder, rape, assault, and drug dealing. Harmful acts also include safety violations that injure and kill. Job applicants with a potential to commit harmful acts can be filtered out of the hiring process through preemployment investigations.

Employers also find that background investigations can improve productivity and reduce costs. Job applicants with poor work habits and excessive absences from the job can be screened out, along with persons that drive up medical insurance costs due to injuries to themselves and others.

EMPLOYMENT APPLICATION FORM

The employment application form is the main administrative device for capturing employment and personal references. Quite commonly, dishonest applicants provide some truth in their references. For instance, they might provide the correct name of a former employer and change the location, or provide the proper city and state of their school but change its name. These deceptions can come to light by simply using the services of long-distance information.

The application reviewer should never place great reliance on work references provided by the applicant. Work references given by a criminal are likely to produce excellent recommendations that may be totally false. The reviewer should ask to speak to past and present co-workers other than the persons named on the form [2].

Certain questions cannot be asked on an employment application form, or for that matter in any manner connected with a hiring decision. The prohibited questions relate to the following:

- Religion
- Age
- Marital status
- Number of children and number of times married
- Ethnicity
- Disabilities
- Political leanings
- Sexual orientation

An applicant can be asked about criminal convictions but not about arrests [3].

EMPLOYEE RELEASE

Before the checking process can begin, the applicant must sign a release (see Figure 14-1). The release can be part of the employment application form or a standalone document. A release protects the employer and gives fair warning to the applicant. When asked to sign a release, an undesirable applicant is inclined to withdraw the application and look elsewhere for employment. Following is an example of the wording in a release: "I hereby authorize the ABCD Company, or their agents, to make inquiries of my background and to obtain, examine and/or make copies of any and all records or reports pertaining to my employment, credit and financial status, criminal record, military record, education and training records, driving record, insurance records, business and personal references, and representations made by me in connection with my application for employment."

REFERENCE CHECKS

Keep in mind that it is the applicant who provides employment and personal references, and that the people identified as references can be expected to answer glowingly when queried. Checking references by mail or e-mail is not as effective as checking in person or by phone. People tend to be candid in face-to-face and voice-to-voice situations. Facial expressions, pregnant

AUTHORIZATION TO RELEASE INFORMATION

This release hereby authorizes _____, or his/her agents, to make inquiries of my background and to examine and/or make copies of any and all records or reports pertaining to my employment, credit and financial status, criminal record, military record, education and training records, driving record, insurance records, and business and personal references.

Printed Name of Individual Authorizing Release: _____

Signature of Individual: _____

Date: _____

Figure 14-1 Before starting a preemployment background inquiry, a form of this type must be obtained from the individual seeking employment.

pauses, and voice inflections can reveal a great deal. More can be learned from the manner of response than the content of it. Verbally asking "Would you rehire this employee?" is potentially more revealing than a form letter that comes back with a check mark in a box [1].

RECORDS OF INTEREST

Not every record will be of interest to the CSO. He/she may want to choose from the following.

- Education, training, vocational licenses
- Personal identification, address, and telephone number
- Military history
- Citizenship status
- Criminal history
- Credit history
- Civil complaints filed by or against the applicant
- Driving history
- Social Security registration
- Former and current employment
- Former and current business ownership

FAIR CREDIT REPORTING ACT (FCRA)

The Federal Trade Commission is mandated by the FCRA to ensure the accuracy and privacy of information used in consumer reports. A consumer report is information about a consumer that is sold to creditors, employers, insurers, and other businesses. A consumer report contains details as to where the consumer worked and lived, how bills and debts were paid, bankruptcy filings, criminal history, and civil actions. Companies that gather and sell this information are called consumer reporting agencies (CRAs). The most common type of CRA is the credit bureau.

Credit Information

Where fiscal responsibility is an issue, the employer may want to gather credit information about the following:

- Debt load
- Payment history
- Garnishments
- Liens
- Bankruptcies

Consumer Report

Under the FCRA, a consumer has a right to obtain a copy of his or her consumer report. In addition, anyone who takes action against a consumer in response to a report supplied by a CRA—such as denying an application for credit, insurance, or employment—must give the consumer the name, address, and telephone number of the CRA that provided the report. The CRA also must provide a list of everyone who has requested the report within the past year. For employment related requests, the time period is two years.

An employer or prospective employer cannot obtain or seek information from a CRA without the job applicant's specific consent. The same holds true for medical information requested by an employer, creditor, or insurer.

Investigative Consumer Report

A type of consumer report is an investigative consumer report, a detailed file containing interviews with the consumer's neighbors or acquaintances concerning lifestyle, character, and reputation. The investigative consumer report may be used in connection with insurance and employment applications. The FCRA requires that the consumer be notified in writing when such a report is ordered.

Negative Information

Negative information in a CRA file has to be purged at the end of seven years unless the information pertains to the following:

- A criminal conviction
- A bankruptcy action, in which case the purge is made after 10 years
- An application for a job with a salary of more than $75,000
- An application for more than $150,000 worth of credit or life insurance
- A lawsuit or an unpaid judgment (when a statute of limitation applies, the information can remain on file until the limitation runs out)

Only people with a legitimate business need, as recognized by the FCRA, can obtain a consumer report.

Credit Application

If a consumer's credit application is turned down, the consumer can demand to know why. Another law, the Equal Credit Opportunity Act, requires the creditor to specify the reason the application was denied. In many cases, the reason will be that the consumer had no credit file or had a credit file reflecting delinquent obligations.

A consumer may sue in state or federal court for most violations of the FCRA. If the consumer wins, the defendant has to pay damages and reimburse for attorney fees to the extent ordered by the court. Credit reports can also be used to corroborate information already acquired, such as previous addresses and prior employers cited by the individual.

Local Records

Police stations, city halls, and county courthouses are rich sources of public records (see Figure 14-2). In most cases you need only appear and state the purpose of your visit. You will be shown or given a copy of the record or instructed in how to search for records on your own, such as operating a microfiche machine or computer terminal. Records that are generally available include the following:

- Criminal records
- Lawsuits and judgments
- Doing Business As (DBA) files
- Divorce and marriage records
- Property tax records, deeds, and mortgages
- Uniform Commercial Code (UCC) liens and secured transactions
- Voter registration files
- Estate records and bankruptcy filings
- Permits and inspection files
- Motor vehicle registration files

State Records

Records at state level are fewer in number but can be helpful in making a thorough check. These include the following:

- Corporation filings
- Workers' Compensation claims
- Licensing board files
- Driving license files

REPORT OF CRIMINAL RECORDS CHECK

Name of Person: _____

Aliases: _____

Date of Birth: _____

SSN: _____

Address: _____

                        _____

Records of the _____ County Criminal Court, covering the period _____
were checked and the following findings are reported:

_____ No record was found.

_____ A record was found and the following information noted.

Name As Shown on the Record:_____

Date of Birth: _____

SSN: _____

Addresses: _____

                        _____

                        _____

Docket Number: _____

Date of Arrest: _____

Charges: _____

                        _____

                        _____

Disposition: _____

                        _____

Name of Person Submitting Report: _____

Name of Reporting Agency: _____

Date of Report: _____

Figure 14-2 A report of this type is forwarded to the user, such as an employer contemplating a hiring action.

Federal Records

The Freedom of Information Act (FOIA) was enacted in 1966 to give to any individual or organization access to certain government records. The goal of the FOIA is to make all federal government agency records available to the public, unless those records are protected by one of nine FOIA exemptions.

FREEDOM OF INFORMATION ACT (FOIA)

All federal agencies are required under the FOIA to disclose records requested in writing by any person. However, agencies may withhold information pursuant to nine exemptions and three exclusions contained in the statute. The FOIA applies only to federal agencies and does not create a right of access to records held by Congress, the courts, or by state or local government agencies. Accessible records include the following:

- Defense Locator Service (military records)
- Veterans Administration
- Social Security Administration
- Federal Bureau of Investigation

PRIVACY ACT OF 1974

The Privacy Act of 1974 protects certain federal government records pertaining to individuals. In general, the Privacy Act prohibits the unauthorized disclosure of the records it protects. It also gives individuals the right to review records about themselves, to find out if these records have been disclosed, and to request corrections or amendments of these records unless the records are legally exempt.

The purpose of the FOIA and the Privacy Act is to give the public access to existing government records. These records include consumer complaints, investigations, and administrative records.

DATABASE SEARCHES

Database searches can provide extensive information at low cost and are useful when the applicant has worked or lived in numerous places. A local search, such as one made at a county courthouse, will not reflect an individual's criminal conviction in another county or state. Success with a database service will depend on the quality and quantity of the identifying data provided by the employer. For each name run through a database, there may be hundreds of persons with the same name. Full and accurate information input at the front end can produce good information at the back end.

COST-AVOIDING ADVANTAGES

Cost-avoiding advantages can derive from preemployment screening. For example:

- Applicants that are felons, violence-prone individuals, drug abusers, and that pose safety risks can be filtered out, thus reducing costs associated with theft, injury, accidents, and medical assistance benefits.
- Applicants with skills and knowledge that correspond to vacancies can be filtered in, thus reducing costs associated with training.
- Applicants that demonstrate the potential for long-term commitment can be filtered in, thus reducing costs associated with turnover.

The principal interest of the CSO is in the first advantage, but he or she will not overlook the other advantages when speaking in support of preemployment screening.

TESTING

Drug and Alcohol Tests

Testing for the use of illegal drugs and the abuse of alcohol is widely used to screen job applicants. The most common method of drug testing is the analysis of urine. For alcohol, it is a blood-alcohol concentration (BAC) test. In both cases, the applicant is asked to submit to testing. A signed consent form demonstrates the applicant's permission. If the applicant declines to consent or refuses to take or cooperate in the administration of the test, the application process ends for that job seeker.

Two-step approach: Testing for illegal drugs and alcohol abuse follows a two-step approach. If nothing is found in the first step, the result is declared negative and the applicant has passed the test. If something is found, the specimen is tested a second time using a different technique. If the second test fails to confirm the first test, the specimen is declared negative and the applicant has passed the test. If the second test confirms the first test, the specimen is declared positive, and the applicant has failed to pass the test.

The employer in almost every case will decline to hire an applicant who cannot pass a drug or alcohol test. Some employers will suspend the application for a period of time, usually one month, and allow the applicant to go through the testing process a second time. A drug or alcohol test, unlike a paper-and-pencil test, can be the sole criterion for rejecting an applicant.

Paper-and-Pencil Tests

In a general context, testing methods in organizational settings fall into one of three categories: selection, classification, and intelligence. A selection test simply helps a decision maker accept or reject a job candidate. A classification test, which is much more complex to administer and interpret, helps the organization decide if the candidate fits the criteria of a job. An intelligence test is often constructed for use by one organization specifically. It may measure, for example, an applicant's knowledge of concepts related to the job or the applicant's potential to learn and intellectually grow in the job. Within these general categories are tests of a more specific nature.

Achievement Tests

Achievement tests assess current performance in a knowledge area. Theory holds that achievement is both an indicator of prior learning and of future success. An achievement test typically measures vocabulary, language competency, reading comprehension, arithmetic computation, and problem solving. To the extent that the competencies tested are essential to job performance, the achievement test is suitable.

Aptitude Tests

An aptitude test predicts future performance in an area in which the applicant is not currently trained. Employers often use aptitude tests when filling specific vacancies. A variation of aptitude testing helps clarify an employee's career goals. Another variation examines a broad range of skills pertinent to many different jobs. An example is the General Aptitude Test Battery, which assesses general reasoning ability, perception, motor coordination, finger and manual dexterity, and other attributes.

Intelligence Tests

A variety of intelligence tests measure specific proficiencies and/or the capacity of an individual to cope with life generally. The test scores, known as intelligence quotients or IQs, reflect the individual's position in comparison to a representative group of people of the same age.

Interest Inventories

An interest inventory is a questionnaire in which the applicant chooses personal preferences from among a variety of activities. The questionnaire, for example, may ask the job candidate if he or she would prefer to march at the head of a parade, in the middle, or watch the parade from the sidelines. The applicant's answer, when considered with answers to similar questions, may give the employer a sense of the applicant's capacity for and attitude about leadership. Other attitudes, such as respect for property, are similarly measured. The attitudes reflected on the questionnaire generally reflect the expectations of the employer.

Interest inventories, while not predictive of job performance, can provide general insights. An applicant whose inventory reflects a penchant for dishonesty would not be the best choice for a cash-handling job.

Objective Personality Tests

These tests measure social and emotional adjustment. Items that describe feelings, attitudes, and behaviors are placed into groups, each representing a separate personality or style, such as extroversion or introversion. Taken together, the groups provide a profile of the personality as a whole. One of the most popular tests of this type is the Minnesota Multiphasic Personality Inventory (MMPI).

Test Validity

The overall value of a preemployment test is the assistance it gives for making reasonable predictions about a job applicant's likely behavior in specific situations. When a test proves to be an accurate predictor, it is said to possess validity. For validity to be demonstrated, the test must yield consistent, reliable measurements.

Problems in Design and Interpretation

Challenges to preemployment tests are made for many reasons, some good, some not so good. Challenges sometimes mention complaints such as that the words were too technical, the instructions were unclear, the test administrator did not like me, my pencil broke, and so forth.

Behind the complaints may be genuine problems: poor test design and poor interpretation of test results. Both issues are related to human error, and human error is never easily overcome. Because these testing deficiencies exist and because they impact the lives of the test takers, employers are cautioned to not base their hiring decisions solely on tests. Consider the following anecdote.

CASE STUDY

Barry Coleman, CSO at Lithicol (a large chemical company), had seen his department shrink from 15 to two employees in less than a year. His only consolation was that similar trimming had occurred in other departments. The information technology (IT) department had been hardest hit. Nearly every technical function in the IT department had been turned over to Wong Liu International, an outside contractor.

In addition to seeing many new faces in the workplace, Barry began to see many new reports of theft, particularly of desktop PCs. In every case, one or more Wong Liu employees were among the suspects. A witness told him, "Look, these IT people have free rein of the building. It is in the nature of their jobs to be always moving around, sometimes carrying PCs to offsite repair labs. There's no way to keep track. Another thing: the Wong Liu faces change almost daily. Lithicol doesn't pay enough to Wong Liu to be able to keep good employees around for the long haul. At least half of the Wong Liu employees at any given time are looking for better opportunities elsewhere. Somebody quits without notice on Friday. On Saturday the Wong Liu human services people are on the telephone desperately searching for a replacement. Come Monday, a replacement shows up for work, a warm body with no real talent. I hate to say it but that's how I was hired. They called me, and I was a complete stranger to them. I went to work at Lithicol the next day."

In one particular theft, Barry narrowed the suspect list to a single individual, Richard Johnson, a former Wong Liu employee. Johnson's last day at Lithicol happened to be the day of the theft. Barry called Wong Liu's human services director and learned that Johnson had not been a Wong Liu employee at all, but an independent subcontractor who took odd jobs here and there. The human services director did not know where Johnson was currently working or where he had worked previously. Barry asked for Johnson's home address and telephone number but the human services director refused, saying, "It is against our policy to provide that kind of information."

Knowing that a door had been slammed in his face, Barry obtained a copy of the agreement between Lithicol and Wong Liu. It stated that in assigning employees and subcontractors to the Lithicol workplace Wong Liu was obligated to "exercise a degree of care equal to that exercised in Lithicol's hiring practices."

Barry went to Henry Tisch, a Lithicol executive who managed the Wong Liu contract. Barry cited the rise in theft that accompanied the outsourcing arrangement, Wong Liu's apparently nonexistent background screening practices, and the refusal of Wong Liu's human services director to cooperate. Tisch told Barry he'd check into it.

A week later, Barry was summoned to Tisch's office. "The good news," Tisch said, "is that the Wong Liu human services department is willing to provide the information you wanted about Richard Johnson. The not-so-good news is that they firmly believe they are meeting their contractual obligation to exercise hiring practices at least equal to our own. Equal, they say, does not mean identical. They say that if they were forced to do exactly what Lithicol does they would not be able to meet work deadlines imposed on them, with the imposer being me. On that point, I have to agree. I do, in fact, hold their feet to the fire on getting X amount of work performed in X amount of time." A look on Tisch's face told Barry that the X amount of work was not up to expected standards.

Tisch concluded the meeting by saying, "The biggest and most important task before me is to ensure the success of the Wong Liu outsourcing project. The CEO has committed to making it work. I simply cannot jeopardize the project by coming down hard on this preemployment screening issue. Also, from a purely business standpoint, the cost of the thefts is very minor compared to potential losses in productivity that might result if Wong Liu is pushed too hard."

NOTES

1. Ed San Luis, Louis A. Tyska, and Lawrence J. Fennelly, *Office and Office Building Security, Second Edition*, pp. 156, Boston: Butterworth-Heinemann, 1994.

2. Francis James D'Addario, "Pre-Employment Screening," in *Encyclopedia of Security Management*, pp. 561, John J. Fay, editor, Boston: Butterworth-Heinemann, 1993.

3. Louis A. Tyska and Lawrence J. Fennelly, *150 Things You Should Know About Security*, pp. 132–133, Boston: Butterworth-Heinemann, 1998.

15. Emergency Management

An ounce of prevention is worth a pound of cure.
—Henry de Bracton

EMERGENCY MANAGEMENT PROCESS

Emergency management is the process of preparing for, mitigating, responding to, and recovering from an emergency. The emergency management function requires a plan for each anticipated incident such as fire, explosion, or severe weather, plus an overarching plan that incorporates all of the incident plans. The overarching plan is called the emergency operating plan (EOP). For the most part, this chapter addresses the EOP.

Mitigation

Mitigation is a combination of measures taken in advance to prevent the occurrence of an incident. Mitigation measures vary: fences and lighting, guards and training, weapons and portable radios. Mitigation is important because it prepares the organization to reduce risk by countering threats.

Remediation

Remediation is a combination of measures taken during or in the immediate aftermath of an incident to ease the consequences of an incident. Remediation measures also vary: evacuation and shelter in place, triage and medical treatment, cleanup and repair of essential equipment. Remediation is important because it is directed at helping people caught in a crisis and restoring critical business functions as quickly as possible.

Emergency Management and Risk

Emergency management deals with risks that are identified in a process called vulnerability assessment (VA). A later chapter is dedicated to that process.

Risk is offset when the organization's management

- Prevents death and injury, financial loss, regulatory fines, loss of market share, damage to equipment or products, and interruption of business.
- Reduces exposure to civil or criminal liability that may arise as the result of an incident.
- Facilitates compliance with regulatory requirements.

EMERGENCY OPERATING PLAN (EOP)

A number of serious incidents fall under the meaning of emergency and are addressed by the EOP. They include the following:

- Fire
- Hazardous materials spills
- Major accident
- Severe weather
- Earthquake
- Civil disturbance
- Radiological release
- Explosion
- Workplace violence

Although each incident has its own plan, all emergencies come under the EOP. For the sake of clarity, we will use the term *incident plan* when the plan addresses a single incident such as fire, and we will use *EOP* when referring to the larger plan that covers all incidents.

Most, if not all, incidents require involvement of security, and certain of them require of the CSO a very high degree of participation. These include emergencies resulting from fire, injury and illness, natural disaster, criminal acts, civil disorder, and terrorist acts [1]. The involvement of the CSO can run the full gamut of managing a security-related incident. That is, the CSO anticipates the possibility of an incident, makes preparations to mitigate and remediate its effects, sets up prevention measures, and ensures an effective response by members of the security group.

Anticipation

Judging the likelihood of an incident and assessing its probable impact reside at the center of risk management, a collaborative process that taps into the collective expertise of the organization. Risk identification and risk control are elements of the SVA process mentioned previously.

Accurate prediction of specific scenarios is never possible. The CSO might anticipate that a bomb incident is a possibility but cannot accurately predict the time, date, place, method of detonation, and type of bomb.

The best that can be done is to abstract the anticipated incident in a general scenario that leaves room for a flexible response.

The anticipatory process is ongoing and often intuitive. In keeping abreast of bombing incidents around the world, the CSO may notice trends such as remote detonation of explosives packed in a parked vehicle or anthrax sent in the mail. A thoughtful evaluation can prompt the CSO to modify the organization's defense tactics; for example, train security officers to keep vehicles away from people-congested areas and train mailroom employees to look for suspicious envelopes and packages.

Anticipation is also putting two and two together. The CSO in a lumber harvesting company should expect that the company's announcement of planned harvesting in a previously untouched forest will provoke reactions from militant environmental groups, and the CSO should expect fallout from Arab groups when the company acts in a way that appears to be pro-Jewish. The possibilities can be numerous and subtle.

Preparation

The first step in preparing for an emergency is planning, and the primary focus of planning is prevention of the undesirable incident. The secondary focus of planning is to reduce undesirable consequences when prevention does not succeed. These twin objectives cannot be achieved through the efforts of the CSO alone. Key contributions will come from many persons in and outside the organization. Who those persons will be corresponds to the nature of the event; for example, the organization's property manager will be a key player in responding to a fire but not to a kidnapping.

By its very existence, an EOP expresses management's concern for its employees and property. The depth of that concern is demonstrated by management's commitment of resources (i.e., funds, expertise, and materials). Think of the EOP as an umbrella. Beneath it are a number of plans, each of which:

- Addresses a particular threat.
- Dedicates a particular combination of people and resources.
- Operates according to a particular arrangement of procedures.

No two plans can be alike because no adverse incident is alike. In a few plans, the response team is the same; in others, it varies. Different incidents call for different skills, tools, and materials. The one common denominator is command and control, which is the core element of the EOP. The command-and-control group is often called the Emergency Management Group (EMG).

The CSO is the principal author of some plans (e.g., kidnap, civil disorder, workplace violence, and bomb threat) and a contributing author to others (e.g., fire and explosion, severe weather, hazardous materials release, and medical emergencies).

Procedures

An incident plan is often supplemented with one or more sets of procedures that spell out in greater detail the specific tasks of the responders. An incident plan that calls for the CSO to "deploy security officers to protect employees during an incident of workplace violence" has to be supplemented with implementing procedures that guide the CSO and the security officers. Every incident plan that calls for action by the security group should be supplemented with detailed procedures, reinforced by training and practical exercises. The CSO is responsible for developing the procedures and ensuring that training and practical exercises are conducted. The CSO is also responsible for coordinating security actions with actions of other response groups.

The common practice is to append security group procedures to the incident plan and emergency operating plan. The procedures of other groups are appended as well. For example, an incident plan for dealing with fire is likely to be appended with procedures that integrate responses of the security group, floor wardens, and building maintenance employees. Supplementing the procedures are report forms, logs, progress reports, decision trees, organizational charts, maps, photographs, diagrams, equipment operating instructions, contact lists, and the like.

The incident plan package is held and kept current by a designated administrator, usually a responsible person working in the company's emergency management office. Each incident plan has a senior coordinator who during plan execution reports to the EMG. For some incidents, the senior coordinator is the CSO; in others it can be the company's safety officer, property manager, or superintendent of operations. In some organizations the practice is to place the EOP and all of the incident plan packages in an emergency response center.

An incident plan package is the full script for preventing the incident to the extent that prevention is possible. For example, a workplace violence plan can have many preventive elements: a training program for teaching supervisors how to spot and respond to potential violence, an education program for encouraging employees to report co-workers who commit violent acts, and a self-referral program that gives confidential diagnosis and counseling to troubled employees.

Training

Training for responders is another matter specified in the plan. The training program's curriculum and practical exercises correspond to tasks assigned to plan responders. Developing and delivering incident plan training is not as large a project as one might suppose. The responders, after all, are assumed to be professionals in their fields and not in need of training in the fundamentals. A counselor in a workplace violence plan does not need to be taught counseling; a negotiator in a kidnap plan does not need to be taught negotiating;

a CSO does not need to be taught the law on deadly force. The major focus of responder training is to ensure that the various response groups are all on the same sheet of music.

Response

Response to an incident can take place all at once or in stages. Response to a fire is always immediate, whereas response to a hurricane may be done in stages. Fire does not arrive with advance warning and does not tolerate delay. A hurricane can be predicted, spotted, and tracked in terms of strength and direction of movement. A triggering mechanism of a fire plan is smoke or visible flame. Many response actions are undertaken simultaneously: the fire department is called, employees are instructed to evacuate, and an in-house fire brigade initiates a holding action until arrival of the fire department. A hurricane plan can have several triggering mechanisms linked to warning levels such as those issued by the U.S. Weather Service. At a low warning level the premises and valuable equipment may be physically strengthened, at a moderate level the employees may be sent home, and at a high level the premises and property may be abandoned.

A response is conditioned by the perceptions of senior managers and business owners. The cost of a response can exceed the value of the assets at risk, or in circumstances influenced by religious beliefs, politics, and war the perceived consequences of a response can rule out making a response. Insurance plays a part as well. When the at-risk asset is people, the only acceptable option is a full and dedicated response.

No company can consider itself immune to emergencies and no management is free of the responsibility of being prepared. Preparation provides for the protection of life and property and the containment of loss or damage [2].

DEVELOPMENT OF THE EOP

The methods for developing an incident plan and an emergency operating plan are essentially the same. Where differences exist, they relate to size and complexity. The EOP is much larger and more complex than any one of the incident plans it incorporates. If a planning team can develop an EOP, it can certainly develop an incident plan. With that little bit of wisdom in mind, let's go through the process of developing an EOP.

Planning Team

We begin by forming a planning team that corresponds to the organization's operations, requirements, and resources. A planning team composed of persons knowledgeable in the various sciences that underlie the organization's processes can increase the chances that obscure yet vitally important issues are addressed in the plan. In addition to scientific disciplines, the team can include representatives from a variety of functional areas, such as the following.

- Senior management (the EMG)
- Human resources
- Engineering and maintenance
- Safety, health, and environmental affairs
- Public information
- Security
- Community relations
- Sales and marketing
- Legal
- Finance
- Purchasing

Ideally, the leader of the EOP planning team will be the senior executive serving on the team. He/she may choose to designate an alternate when circumstances do not allow the team leader to attend. The team leader has the authority to "command the presence" of a team member if that becomes necessary, authorize the expenditure of funds and use of materials, and by personal example demonstrate a commitment to emergency management.

External Support Agencies

External support organizations such as the following also need to be represented on the planning team.

- Law enforcement
- Firefighting
- Emergency medical agencies
- Local hospitals
- Local government agencies
- American Red Cross

Experience tells us, however, that representatives of external organizations are not able to attend every planning session. Special invitations should be extended when warranted. For example, the law enforcement representative should be urged to attend when a law enforcement issue is on the planning agenda.

The following entities also play various parts in responding to major emergencies. Members of these agencies may or may not be asked to join the planning team, but they are definitely coordinating points.

- Community emergency management office
- Mayor or Community Administrator's office
- Local Emergency Planning Committee
- American Red Cross
- National Weather Service

- Public Works Department
- Planning Commission
- Telephone companies
- Power companies
- Water plants

Involving a large number of people and agencies can result in the following:

- Develop "buy-in" across the board and up and down the organization and within the local community
- By apportioning tasks, increase the amount of time and energy each participant is able to give
- Enhance the visibility and stature of the planning effort
- Provide to the planning team a broad perspective

Input to Planning

The work of the team has to follow a schedule and meet deadlines for the production of input to the planning process. Timelines can be modified as priorities become more clearly defined. A member of the team, such as the purchasing representative, can be assigned to develop a budget to cover the costs of clerical support and supplies, research materials, duplicating, printing, consulting services, and other costs incurred during plan development. The team leader should issue a mission statement that in addition to being supportive of the plan is supportive of the overall goal (i.e., management of emergencies). The elements of a mission statement can include the following.

- Purpose of emergency management
- Necessity of an overall plan for responding to emergencies
- Composition of the planning team
- Authority and mandate of the team

The planning team needs to have at its disposal a number of documents, many of which are readily attainable. These include the following:

- All of the subordinate incident plans (each of which contains response procedures for various departments such as security, safety, and maintenance)
- Engineering drawings and similar materials that describe the site, structures on the site, utilities, roadways, and so on
- Maps and similar materials that describe the site's position relative to other matters of interest such as nearby facilities, population centers, lakes, waterways, topography, seismic characteristics, and so on
- Weather maps and similar materials that describe wind currents, temperature extremes, and so on
- Mutual aid agreements with external agencies

- Policies dealing with security, safety, human resources, organizational health, and the environment
- Rules of regulatory agencies such as OSHA and the EPA
- Fire codes
- Transportation and motor vehicle regulations
- Zoning codes
- Insurance policies
- Union agreements
- Land use restrictions

Operational Activities

Matters for the planning team to consider include the organization's operational activities, its dependence on technological systems, the physical environment surrounding the organization's site, the possibilities of human error, and the organization's history of adverse events. The team identifies and characterizes the following.

- Nature of goods and services produced by the organization
- Facilities, equipment, and people involved in the production of goods and services
- Hazardous materials on site such as chemicals, biological agents, explosives, and nuclear or radiological materials
- Production processes, including work performed by people
- Dependencies on utilities such as communications, power, water, and sewage
- Dependencies on vendors, especially sole-source vendors
- Culture of the organization
- External constraints imposed by government, politics, religion, and cultural mores

Technological Systems

The planning team has to consider possible failure of business-essential utilities that provide power, water, and conditioned air; process data and provide for telecommunications within and outside the organization; detect fire and unauthorized intrusion; and control access to the site and sensitive locations within the site.

Physical Environment

An issue of concern to the planning team is the proximity of the organization to the following:

- Flood plains
- Dams

- Rivers, lakes, and oceans
- Roadways, bridges, and railroad lines
- Airports, seaports, and ground transportation terminals
- Seismic faults
- Terrain
- Nearby facilities of concern such as a nuclear plant or an ammunition storage warehouse

Human Error

Questions to be asked by the planning team are the following:

- What human errors are possible?
- What would be the likely consequence of a human error?
- What would be the likely magnitude of consequence?
- What is in place to reduce human error?
- Are employees trained to work safely?
- What is the organization's safety record?
- Does the organization directly combat factors that lead to human error such as substance abuse, fatigue, carelessness, poor maintenance, and misconduct?

History

History repeats itself. Incidents that occurred in the past are indicators of incidents that may occur in the future. The planning team should look at safety violation reports, injury and illness reports, security incident reports, accident reports, workers' compensation claims [3], liability claims, and reports of loss or damage resulting from acts of nature, such as hurricanes and earthquakes, and acts of humans such as theft and assault.

Plan Structure

The EOP is many things: a working tool, a job aid, a constantly evolving manual, an official document, and a formal expression of the management's philosophy concerning the control of risk. The following is an example of a plan's basic structure.

- Title
- Implementing date
- Identification of the authorizing person or agency
- Purpose
- Rationale
- Scope
- Definitions of terms
- Identification by name or job positions of the plan's team leader and team members

- Identification of the EMG
- Mitigation measures
- Communications
- Notifications
- Assignment of group or department responsibilities
- Assignment of individual responsibilities
- Response actions
- Remediation measures
- Support services
- Post-response actions
- Public relations
- Appendices

PLAN ORGANIZATION

The organizing function brings all of the plan's actions into a logical and cohesive whole. Said another way, organizing is the accomplishment of a goal by an orderly arrangement of people working together. First in this endeavor is to assign the work of the plan so that the right people are assigned the right work and that no one person is assigned to perform too much work. Second is to make sure that everyone understands what is expected of them and who is in charge. Third is to make sure that persons in charge are not overburdened by having too many persons to supervise. Next is to align the plan participants in a chain of command that allows everyone to know his or her place in plan execution, know the persons authorized to issue them instructions, and know the persons to contact for reporting information. Last, everyone must know and agree with the objectives of the plan. Consider the following scenario.

CASE STUDY

Anita Fowler was the CSO of Hallen Air Tools, a company that manufactures avionic components for a new generation of Army helicopters. When the company decided to update the emergency operating plan, Anita was assigned a key role on the planning team. She pointed out to the team that the Army, which commissioned production of the avionic components, would certainly evaluate Hallen's emergency operating plan. During deliberations of the planning team Anita noted that Harvey Schlicht, the company's CFO and member of the Emergency Management Group, was vetoing for reasons of economy certain critical security measures that required expenditures of funds. When Anita lodged opposing views, a consensus of the planning team agreed that Schlick was right and that she should use existing in-house resources to establish the critical measures. Anita tried but was unable to do so.

   The planning team went on to construct an emergency operating plan that did not incorporate Anita's recommendations. An Army inspection team subsequently tested the plan with a tabletop exercise, an actual drill, and a review of the organization's vulnerability assessment. Plan execution demonstrated the flaws Anita had warned against. Without saying so, some members of the team, including a few that served on the emergency management group, faulted Anita because the flaws were security related.

Equipping Plan Responders

At this point the writing of the plan has ended, at least for the moment. Now it is time to equip and train the responders. Not all equipment needs to be issued in advance of the incident. Items of this nature are usually not essential to day-to-day operations. They are placed in locations that make them readily accessible to the users. Weapons, personal protection gear, sensors that "sniff" the air in search of chemical and biological agents, vehicles, portable lights, bolt cutters, special communications gear, and bull horns immediately come to mind. Keeping these items in storage also rules out loss or damage and facilitates periodic inspection such as lubricating weapons, checking the charge of fire extinguishers, and calibrating sensors. Equipment placed at the disposal of the CSO for issue or storage can include the following:

- Pistols, shotguns, ammunition, tasers, and stun guns
- Flak vests, body shields, and Mace
- Helmets, clear face masks, and batons
- Personal protective equipment and foul-weather gear
- First aid supplies, defibrillator, and oxygen resuscitator
- Bull horns, stretchers, stanchions, and yellow tape
- Mobile communications center, handheld radios, communication codes, and radio-equipped vehicles
- Portable lighting, flashlights, and small tools
- Water and food

Training the Plan Responders

Plan responders need to be trained in the tasks they are designated to perform and to properly utilize the equipment provided to them for this purpose. The responsibility to ensure that training is given to all responders for all incidents belongs to the EMG. In most cases, this responsibility is delegated downward to the senior coordinator of each incident plan.

Preassignment Training

The senior coordinator for incident plans that involve the security group may be the CSO or a direct report to the CSO. The training administered by this person is generally given in stages that begins with core tasks and ends with specialized tasks. Preassignment training (i.e., training administered before a security officer goes on the job) typically includes first aid treatment techniques, cardiac pulmonary resuscitation, operation of an oxygen resuscitator and defibrillator, and how to protect against blood-borne pathogens.

Firearms Training

If the officer is to carry a gun in the performance of duties, firearms safety and qualification firing are mandatory. In many states, a gun-carrying officer is said to be certified or registered and must obtain a permit to carry a firearm, and the permit is not valid outside the scope of the officer's employment.

On-the-Job Training

During a probationary period the officer might be taught how to patrol, identify safety hazards, operate fire extinguishers, and summon the fire department when fire breaks out. This might be followed by instructions on what to do upon receipt of a telephonic bomb threat, how to search for a bomb, and how to assist employees evacuate the premises. Next could be familiarization with access control, intrusion detection, and operation of the security console. All or nearly all training administered in the probationary period is delivered on the job by a supervisor or an experienced, skilled officer.

Refresher Training

Following the probationary period the officer receives training that refreshes what has already been taught. Refresher training is often conducted in a classroom. At a later time the officer returns to the classroom as a seasoned professional and undergoes advanced training that is more cerebral than hands-on. The topics might be the nature of terrorism, terrorist tactics, and the early signals of terrorism.

Task Performance Training

Throughout all phases of the training, the officer is additionally taught how to respond to incidents that call for security assistance — which happens to be a requirement in nearly all incidents. Periodically, under the supervision of the security supervisor the officers practice tasks delineated in an incident plan. Performance of some tasks is simulated; others are done actually. Tasks can be making announcements on the public address system, making calls to supervisors, turning equipment on or off, opening or closing air intakes, directing traffic, walking stairwells, rendering first aid, and keeping a log of actions taken.

Practice

The final and most decisive stage of preparing for emergencies is practice, and there are two types: the tabletop exercise and the practical exercise.

Tabletop

In the tabletop, a day is set aside for the exercise. The EMG knows the time and date but others may not. An outside consultant in emergency management or a member of the in-house emergency management office triggers a hypothetical incident with a single telephone call. The EMG goes to the emergency control center, which is often a dual-purpose conference room preequipped with communications gear, maps, easels, chalkboard, log books, and so on.

Each EMG member is guided by predetermined procedures outlined in the EOP. The team begins issuing instructions by telephone and radio to the senior coordinator and other managerial/supervisory persons that perform tasks in support of the response. These persons can be a property manager, public information officer, human resources specialist, and so on. Notification can also be made to external agencies such as the local police and fire departments, emergency medical agencies, hospitals, and government emergency management offices. All of the notifications contain a clearly expressed statement that the incident is simulated.

Plan responders, except for EMG members, are at their workstations but act as though they are "in the field" performing the tasks they learned in prior training. For the sake of discussion, we will say that the hypothesized incident is a bomb explosion at a manufacturing plant some distance from the organization's home office, and that the senior coordinator for bomb incidents is the CSO. Adhering to the EOP, the CSO performs (through simulation) his or her assigned tasks such as ordering evacuation of the plant pending a search for secondary explosive devices, briefing subordinates, ordering the call up and deployment of off-duty security officers, giving instructions to the security supervisor at the plant, and notifying law enforcement. Other responders perform their assigned tasks such as supervising the evacuation, setting up a triage area, and arranging for the movement of stored equipment and supplies to the site. Meanwhile, the CSO travels to the scene, where a tactical operations office has been set up in a nearby building. From there, the CSO directs the security group's response, all of which is simulated.

The emergency management consultant observes the EMG and from time to time alters the scenario. Modification of the response is ordered. Instructions flowing down from the EMG and status reports going up the chain of command keep the exercise moving.

Practical Exercise

A practical exercise works the same way as the tabletop, except that it is played in the field, not at workstations. For example, the CSO actually goes to the scene and works from a tactical operations center, reserve security officers are called out and assigned to temporary posts, and so on.

Evaluation

When the incident has been brought under control and the exercise concluded, the consultant chairs an after-action session designed to examine flaws in the plan and in the execution of it. In later days, the consultant provides a written report. Identified shortcomings in the plan are corrected by the EMG, with input from the senior coordinator and the EOP planning team. Problems in execution, which may or may not have resulted from plan flaws, are corrected by follow-up training.

DEALING WITH THE MEDIA

Sugar is to flies as a major emergency is to news agencies. Reporters from television, radio, and newspapers begin instantly to buzz around, asking questions, photographing, videotaping, and generally getting in the way of response efforts. The key responders, whose full attention is focused on the emergency, cannot allow themselves to be distracted. Two characters come to the fore: the public information officer (PIO) — who dishes out information — and the CSO, who maintains the integrity of the incident scene. The PIO dispenses the sugar while the CSO keeps the insistent flies in a tight formation.

Priorities

The first priority is to deal with the crisis; the second is to communicate the facts; and both are addressed simultaneously. The public wants to know what happened and what is being done about it. This is not to suggest that the public's demand for information is limited to emergency events. Every newsworthy topic, be it tomorrow's merger or today's explosion, is within the knowledge domain of the public. Business leaders are very aware of the public's interest and, when it is possible to do so, look ahead before making statements. They understandably wish to avoid the impression of placing profit above community interests, especially where public health and safety are concerned. When liability is a possible outcome, as would be the case when a worker is killed on the job, management tends to be overly circumspect. In addition to charges that may be brought in a criminal or civil court, the business may suffer public relations losses, fall out of favor politically, and face restrictions imposed by regulators and legislators responsive to the public mood.

Security Problems

Problems of a security nature can be anticipated in the post-incident period. They include attempts by the curious to approach the scene of the incident prior to making the scene safe, disruption of cleanup and repair operations by the media in their attempts to acquire information, and unauthorized release of information from sources within the organization.

The CSO, who is a central person in managing emergencies, may be asked by the media to provide information, often by interview. The usual business procedure, however, is to channel media requests and inquiries to the PIO who, by policy and procedure, may be designated to speak for the organization, to meet with news representatives, and to arrange and be present at interviews of company employees. The PIO is trained to be sensitive to the needs of the media, particularly with respect to meeting news deadlines. Whereas reporters are racing to capture the news, the PIO is concerned about releasing details that are both accurate and considerate of the organization's view.

Demands of the Media

Incidents involving death, serious injury, substantial property loss, damage to the environment, and risk to the public constitute significant news. The PIO serves as a control valve for preventing the release of distorted versions and protecting against disclosures that may be harmful to the organization or its individual employees. Whether business likes it or not, the media present news in a manner intended to attract attention, and in the process make news reporting more important than the incident itself.

When an incident of any magnitude arises, the media wants, indeed demands, the facts. Often they ask for information even before management is aware of the incident. Through arrangements with governmental response agencies, such as police and fire departments, media employees learn of incidents on a real-time basis and proceed to the scene immediately. Television, radio, and press reporters can arrive before the first responders.

When the organization's headquarters is located a considerable distance from the site of the incident, which is frequently the case, senior management may authorize an on-scene manager to act as the organization's initial spokesperson or may instruct the on-scene manager to refer all inquiries to the PIO. The objective is to provide available details as quickly and as intelligently as possible. The media demands to know what happened, how, when, where, and why; the number of persons involved and their names; the number and nature of deaths and injuries; and the extent of property damage, particularly damage to the environment.

From the media's point of view, an on-scene manager is preferred over the PIO. Authenticity and credibility are enhanced when the spokesperson has a direct connection to the scene. When the connection involves security, the CSO may be the designated spokesperson. The central task in that eventuality is to provide the pertinent facts and include important details. Being quoted out of context is a risk that can be avoided by speaking in short sentences and repeating key phrases that convey the correct point of view. This technique is particularly helpful in television interviews where reporters are obliged to select only the briefest, most salient comments from an interview that may have taken an hour or more to tape.

Rumor and Exaggeration

Rumor and exaggeration are the organization's nemeses in a time of crisis. Accuracy, although difficult to maintain in the very early stages of an incident, is extremely important. Information flowing from the scene has to be carefully weighed, particularly as to the extent of casualties and cause. A golden rule is to not release the names of persons killed or injured until the next of kin have been notified and to not speculate as to the cause of the incident. Another rule is to avoid saying "no comment." Legal counsel may like this response because it closes off a line of questioning that could be troublesome, but use of the phrase suggests to the media and the public that the organization has something to hide.

The organization and the media each have a right to be wary of deception. The organization may feel it has an overriding and legitimate reason to be reserved in its response, and the media know from prior experience that businesses have engaged in denials and half-truths. Good reporters usually can see through a lie and have it in their power to make the organization look the worst for it. Reporters hungry for a headline story may be more attuned to negatives than positives, and some may have an anti-business bias or be ignorant of business needs. Fortunately, most reporters genuinely want to present a responsible view and will work with an organization that deals squarely with them.

If saying the wrong thing can hurt the organization, why not impose a no-comment policy? The problem with this approach is that speculation, conjecture, and rumor substitute for facts. Fiction and fantasy rapidly fill the vacuum of official silence. By saying nothing, the organization makes itself vulnerable to unfounded perceptions. Perception takes on a reality all its own in a world strongly influenced by mass communications.

The principal cause of tension between business and the media is their differing perspectives. Business operates in accord with policies it believes are proper. In defending policies in the face of criticism, a business can be unyielding and resolute. Executives tend to be resentful when taken to task by reporters who do not understand the organization's policies and the reasons for them. Reporters tend to get angry when denied information. They believe their responsibility is to inform the public, especially when it appears that executives are at fault and trying to conceal the truth.

The PIO, like the CSO, operates from a plan and procedures that customarily call for him/her to go to the scene of a major emergency, and once there serve as a single point of contact with the media. When the emergency is significantly destructive, such as an oil spill or toxic discharge, the PIO is likely to be accompanied by one or more top executives, possibly including the CEO. Virtually no crisis incident is too small or unimportant to warrant senior management attention.

Functions of the Public Information Officer

Some of the media-related functions that require prompt attention at the scene are the following:

- Verifying key details, such as casualties and damages
- Meeting and escorting reporters
- Setting up and making announcements at press conferences

- Updating and reporting developments as they evolve
- Clearing the statements and comments of management

To the extent that circumstances permit, the PIO sets up a press center at or close to the scene. The center could be on the organization's premises, at a hotel nearby, or at any safe and reasonably convenient place having telecommunication facilities. It is not necessary or even appropriate for the PIO to provide food or refreshments at press center meetings, but it is a given that news personnel are entitled to receive honest answers with least possible delay. The answers are delivered courteously and in a manner ensuring that all news reporters receive information the same way at the same time.

Verbal announcements are often supplemented with a written handout designed to facilitate accurate reporting. Working from the handout, the PIO is able to focus on facts that are fully known. Dangerous conjecture, which sometimes arises in the face of insistent questioning, can be avoided by commenting only on what has been put into writing. Also, in the case of releasing the names of persons injured or killed the chances of word-of-mouth name errors are reduced by providing a written list.

As an incident winds down, the PIO may hold one or more follow-up meetings with the media. By then, the causes of the incident and the extent of damage may be known and open to discussion. Positive messages would include assurances to the community with respect to safety and the restoration of jobs destabilized by the incident, progress reports on assistance given to families and repairs made to property and the environment, the effectiveness of the organization's preventive and responsive actions, and credit to local response agencies that assisted in bringing the emergency under control.

Functions of the Chief Security Officer

As touched upon earlier, the CSO has a full plate during a major incident. Depending on the nature of the incident, there can be requirements to provide first-responder medical assistance, establish access control at the incident scene, and protect people and assets exposed to continuing risk. Meeting these requirements involves coordination with many persons inside and out of the organization.

The services performed by a CSO that relate narrowly to the media fall generally under access control. The following three services stand out.

- Preventing entrance to an unsafe incident scene by unauthorized personnel. After an incident has been declared safe, the CSO may be involved in escorting media representatives interested in taking pictures, making notes, and in some controlled situations, interviewing employees at the scene.
- Preventing close-in access to PIO representatives and senior managers at meetings with the press. Distraught relatives of victims and

issue-oriented persons antagonistic to the organization may use a press meeting to physically attack the organization's spokespersons.

- Preventing access to travel conveyances utilized by senior executives. A person, deranged or motivated by revenge and/or the desire to gain attention to a cause, may attempt to place a bomb aboard or otherwise sabotage the plane or automobile used to transport the organization's top management.

Security support to the PIO cannot be properly executed if it is based on a misunderstanding of the PIO's role, or if the CSO's planning and preparation have been inadequate. The CSO simply can't wait until an emergency occurs and then ask the PIO: "Oh, by the way, what is it exactly that you do?" and "How am I supposed to help?" At that point it is too late for the CSO to assist substantively.

The quality of security support is examined, to the CSO's credit or discredit, at the conclusion of an emergency. In some form or fashion, the organization will assess the full situation from beginning to end and summarize the lessons learned. A CSO who prepares by putting effort into learning PIO needs and in developing a support capability ensures a quality response and a creditable rating personally.

BUSINESS CONTINUITY

Restoration of normal operations is a main focus of management following an event that produced significant damage. A business continuity plan (BCP) is designed to facilitate return to essential operations as quickly as possible. A BCP complements incident plans for events of considerable magnitude such as fire, explosion, earthquake, flooding, hurricane, and terrorist attack.

Assumptions

A BCP takes into account the contingencies that face the organization and the organization's inherent vulnerabilities. Certain assumptions are necessary. For example, the plan may assume that some catastrophic events are more likely than others. A company located near the edge of a tectonic plate has to recognize the possibility of earthquake; on a subtropical coastline, the assumption may be hurricane; on a flood plain, flooding; near an airport, air crashes; in a Third World country, civil unrest, terrorism, and war. The plan may also assume that a hugely catastrophic event, such as a nuclear explosion, will fall outside the scope of the BCP.

The plan rests on other assumptions or best estimates concerning human resources, working space, equipment, supplies, and business-critical data that are available in the immediate aftermath of the event. Estimates are made as to the time required to bring the company's operations back on line partially and fully.

Objectives

Business continuity objectives are typically few in number and highly focused. They might include helping employees stabilize their personal and family lives in order to speed their return to work, cleaning up the physical mess caused by the event, restoring operations on site or moving to a temporary or new site, and setting a schedule for resuming operations with priorities assigned to the most critical of the critical functions. Consider the following anecdote.

CASE STUDY

The management of a company located in a high-rise office building on the San Andreas Fault believes that a moderate to strong earthquake occurring in close proximity to the building most likely will kill and injure employees and severely damage the structure and its content. A planning group is tasked to develop a business continuity plan that will project a worst-case scenario and provide guidance for timely restoration of critical business functions.

The chief information officer (CIO) is named head of the planning group. Members include leaders from finance, telecommunications, procurement, real estate, human resources, external affairs, health, safety, and security. The security leader's contribution is to build into the BCP a set of safeguards for protecting the human and physical assets that will be marshaled for restoration of critical business functions.

Because the company's critical business functions heavily depend on computer and telecommunication equipment, the planning group reasonably assumes that an earthquake will fully disrupt normal operations. The planners turn to finding a solution. "What do we do?" is the big question. Moving company operations to a nearby office building with comparable computer and telecommunications equipment would be a convenient solution, and ideal because it would allow the nonaffected employees to continue to commute to work from home. Although convenient and ideal, the solution rests on a couple of false assumptions: that nearby office buildings would not be damaged and that other companies will not compete for what little office space and equipment might be available.

The planners shift their attention to cities away from the earthquake zone. They determine (with executive team guidance) that a "hot" site is preferred over a "cold" site and that outsourcing will be the primary source of labor. The planners believe, and build into the BCP, an expectation that 50 percent of critical functions can be restored within one week and that full restoration can be achieved in six months.

Senior management approval of the BCP places a requirement on each manager of a critical function to develop a set of procedures and implement them through training and rehearsal. Although procedures will vary from function to function, the BCP prescribes common elements such as a purpose statement, scope, designation of responsibilities for making decisions and initiating actions, assignment of key tasks, resources to be readied, communication channels, persons to be informed, recovery priorities, working interrelationships, flow diagrams, and decision trees (see Figure 15-1).

The security leader calls in his direct reports and hands each of them a copy of the newly approved BCP. He tells them, "Study this and be prepared to meet with me in three days to begin drafting a set of procedures for carrying out security expectations."

CONCLUSIONS

The art and science of emergency management is undergoing revolutionary change resulting in the main from the terrorist threat. The security literature

CHIEF EXECUTIVE OFFICER'S STATEMENT ON BUSINESS CONTINUITY

Purpose

A Business Continuity Plan (BCP) will be created for the purpose of facilitating a quick and coordinated return to the essential business operations of the Company during the immediate aftermath of a disaster or catastrophic event impacting corporate headquarters. The BCP will complement and serve as a follow-on plan to contingency plans already in place, e.g., Fire Protection Plan, Bomb Threat Plan, and Severe Weather Plan. The BCP will pick up where those plans end.

The BCP will take into account the Company's heavy dependence on information, e.g., leading edge software, computer technology, and telecommunications. A disaster or catastrophic event will have a severe impact on computer programs and telecommunications services, which in turn will severely impact critical business functions. For this reason, the Chief Information Officer (CIO) will be in charge of developing the BCP and ensuring that plan objectives are carried out. The managers of critical business functions will be responsible for developing procedures within their units that

Assess the degree of loss of critical functioning.

Notify key people.

Deploy resources needed to restore critical functioning.

Key points in such procedures will vary from manager to manager, but may include a mission statement, scope, decision-making responsibilities, assignment of key tasks, resources required, a process for communicating with employees immediately following a disaster or catastrophic event, a list of persons to be notified, the composition of recovery teams, recovery priorities, working interrelationships, work flow diagrams, decision trees, and training. Each set of procedures will be attached to the BCP, which managers will keep ready for use as needed.

Assumptions

Some catastrophic events, such as a nuclear explosion, will be so severe as to fall outside the scope of the BCP.

The catastrophic event impacting corporate headquarters is likely to be a wind storm, such as a hurricane or tornado, more so than other business-disrupting events, such as major fire, earthquake, bomb, civil unrest, or labor strike.

The time required to bring corporate headquarters back to normal operating routines will take not less than two days and not more than thirty days.

Temporary working space, equipment, data, supplies, and vendor services needed to carry out critical functions will be available within forty-eight hours following the event. This assumption recognizes that when other companies are impacted by the same event (e.g., a hurricane), extraordinary demands will be placed upon the community's business services infrastructure, thereby placing the Company into competition with other companies for needed facilities, equipment, supplies, and services. Advanced planning and preparation by service groups, such as IT and building management, will be essential.

Key employees will be available to implement the BCP. Recognition is given, however, to delay that might result from the need of all employees to first attend to the needs of their families should the catastrophic event extend into the community at large.

Objectives

Restore the most critical of all critical functions within two days.

Restore all or most all of the critical functions within seven days.

Restore all business functions within thirty days.

Business Continuity Team

Information Technology (Team Leader)

Real Estate

Procurement

Human Resources

External Affairs

Security

Figure 15-1 In this statement the CEO has established the framework of the organization's business continuity plan.

prior to September 11, 2001, contained very little concerning emergency management. Nor was there much discussion of the relationship between security and emergency management. That omission is being corrected rapidly.

Change is also occurring in the technology of emergency management. State-of-the-art equipment coming off the production line can warn organizations of potential threats, thwart attacks, and increase protection of people and property. In the services sector, education and training programs are teaching emergency management principles to security professionals, first-responders, and a host of other practitioners now firmly connected to the emergency management function.

An emergency of a destructive nature has to be brought under control before business recovery can begin. Agencies such as those appearing in the following list (Figure 15-2) can be helpful.

NOTES

1. John J. Fay, *Security Dictionary*, pp. 94, Arlington, VA: American Society for Industrial Security, 2000.

2. Randy Uzzell, "Emergency Management Planning," in *Encyclopedia of Security Management*, pp. 280, John J. Fay, editor, Boston: Butterworth-Heinemann, 1993.

3. John J. Fay, *Model Security Policies, Plans, and Procedures,* pp. 150, Boston: Butterworth-Heinemann, 1999.

State Emergency Management Agencies

Alabama. Alabama Emergency Management Agency 5898 S. County Rd.41 Drawer 2160 Clanton, AL 35045-5160 (205) 280-2201

Alaska. Department of Military & Veteran Affairs P.O. Box 5750 Camp Denali, AK 99595-5750 (907) 428-7000

Arizona. Arizona Division of Emergency Services National Guard Bldg. 5636 E. McDowell Rd. Phoenix, AZ 85008 (602) 231-6245

Arkansas. Office of Emergency Services P.O. Box 758 Conway, AR 72032 (501) 321-5601

California. Office of Emergency Services 2800 Meadowview Rd. Sacramento, CA 95823 (916) 262-1816

Colorado. Colorado Office of Emergency Management Camp George West Golden, CO 80401 (303) 273-1622

Connecticut. Connecticut Office of Emergency Management 360 Broad St. Hartford, CT 06105 (203) 566-3180

Delaware. Division of Emergency Planning and Operations P.O. Box 527 Delaware City, DE 19706 (302) 326-6000

District of Columbia. Office of Emergency Preparedness 200 14th St., NW, 8th Floor Washington, DC 20009 (202) 727-3159

Florida. Division of Emergency Management 2555 Shumar Oak Blvd. Tallahassee, FL 32399-2100 (904) 413-9969

Georgia. Georgia Emergency Management Agency P.O. Box 18055 Atlanta, GA 30316-0055 (404) 635-7001

Hawaii. State Civil Defense 3949 Diamond Head Rd. Honolulu, HI 96816-4495 (808) 733-4300

Idaho. Bureau of Disaster Services 650 W. State St. Boise, ID 83720 (208) 334-2336

Illinois. Illinois Emergency Management Agency 110 E. Adams St. Springfield, IL 62706 (217) 782-2700

Indiana. Indiana Emergency Management Agency State Office Bldg., Room E-208 302 W. Washington St. Indianapolis, IN 46204 (317) 232-3980

Iowa. Iowa Emergency Management Division Hoover State Office Bldg. Level A, Room 29 Des Moines, IA 50319 (515) 281-3231

Kansas. Division of Emergency Preparedness 2800 S.W. Topeka Blvd Topeka, KS 66611 -1401(913) 274-1401

Kentucky. Kentucky Disaster and Emergency Services 100 Minutemen Pkwy Frankfort, KY 40601-6168 (502) 564-8682

Louisiana. Office of Emergency Preparedness Department of Public Safety LAMilitary Dept. P.O. Box 44217 Capitol Station Baton Rouge, LA 70804 (504) 342-5470

Maine. Maine Emergency Management Agency 72 State House Station Augusta, ME 04333-0072 (207) 287-4080

Maryland. Maryland Emergency Management and Civil Defense Agency Two Sudbrook Ln., East Pikesville, MD 21208 (410) 486-4422

Massachusetts. Massachusetts Emergency Management Agency P.O. Box 1496 Framingham, MA 01701-0317 (508) 820-2000

Michigan. Emergency Management Division Michigan State Police 300 S. Washington Sq. Suite 300 Lansing, MI 48913 (517) 366-6198

Minnesota. Division of Emergency Services Department of Public Safety State Capitol, B-5 St. Paul, MN 55155 (612) 296-0450

Mississippi. Mississippi Emergency Management Agency P.O. Box 4501, Fondren Station Jackson, MS 39296 (601) 352-9100

Missouri. State Emergency Management Agency P.O. Box 116 Jefferson City, MO 65102 (573) 526-9101

Figure 15-2 A state's emergency management office can be a helpful partner in planning and responding to major emergencies.

Montana. Emergency Management Specialist Disaster and Emergency Services P.O. Box 4789 Helena, MT 59604-4789 (406) 444-6911

Nebraska Nebraska Civil Defense Agency National Guard Center 1300 Military Road Lincoln, NE 68508-1090 (402) 471-7410

Nevada. Nevada Division of Emergency Services 2525 S. Carson St. Carson City, NV 89710 (702) 687-4240

New Hampshire. Governor's Office of Emergency Management State Office Park South 107 Pleasant St. Concord, NH 03301-3809 (603) 271-2231

New Jersey. Office of Emergency Management P.O. Box 7068 W. Trenton, NJ 08628-0068 (609) 538-6050

New Mexico. Emergency Planning and Coordination Department of Public Safety 4491 Cerrillos Rd. P.O. Box 1628 Santa Fe, NM 87504-1628 (505) 827-9222

New York. State Emergency Management Office Bldg. #22, Suite 101 Albany, NY 12226-2251 (518) 457-2222

North Carolina Division of Emergency Management 116 West Jones St. Raleigh, NC 27603-1335 (919) 733-5406

North Dakota. North Dakota Division of Emergency Management P.O. Box 5511 Bismarck, ND 58502-5511 (701) 328-3300

Ohio. Ohio Emergency Management Agency 2825 W. Dublin Granville Rd. Columbus, OH 43235-2206 (614) 889-7150

Oklahoma. Oklahoma Civil Defense P.O. Box 53365 Oklahoma City, OK 73152-3365 (405) 521-2481

Oregon. Emergency Management Division Oregon State Executive Department 595 Cottage St., NE Salem, OR 97310 (503) 378-2911

Pennsylvania. Pennsylvania Emergency Management Agency P.O. Box 3321 Harrisburg, PA 17105-3321 (717) 651-2007

Puerto Rico. State Civil Defense Commonwealth of Puerto Rico P.O. Box 5127 San Juan, PR 00906 (809) 724-0124

Rhode Island. Rhode Island Emergency Management Agency 675 New London Avenue Cranston, RI 02920 (401) 946-9996

South Carolina. South Carolina Emergency Management Division 1429 Senate St., Rutledge Bldg. Columbia, SC 29201-3782 (803) 734-8020

South Dakota. Division of Emergency and Disaster Services State Capitol, 500 East Capitol Pierre, SD 57501 (605) 773-3231

Tennessee. Tennessee Emergency Management Agency 3041 Sidco Dr. P.O. 41502 Nashville, TN 37204-1502 (615) 741-6528

Texas. Division of Emergency Management P.O. Box 4087 Austin, TX 78773-0001 (512) 424-2000

Utah. Division of Comprehensive Emergency Management Sate Office Bldg., Room 1110 Salt Lake City, UT 84114 (801) 538-3400

Vermont. Vermont Emergency Management Agency Dept. of Public Safety Waterbury State Complex 103 S. Main St. Waterbury, VT 05671-2101 (802) 244-8271

Virgin Islands. Territorial Emergency Management Agency A & Q Building # 2c Estate Content St Thomas, VI 00820 (809) 773-2244

Virginia. Department of Emergency Services P.O. Box 40955 Richmond, VA 23225-6491 (804) 674-2497

Washington. Division of Emergency Management 4220 E. Martin Way, MS-PT 11 Olympia, WA 98504-0955 (360) 923-4505

West Virginia. West Virginia Office of Emergency Services State Capitol Complex Room EB80 Charleston, WV 25305-0360 (304) 558-5380

Wisconsin. Division of Emergency Government 2400 Wright St. P.O. Box 7865 Madison, WI 53707 (608) 242-3232

Wyoming. Wyoming Emergency Management Agency P.O. Box 1709 Cheyenne, WY 82003 (307) 777-7566

Figure 15-2 *continued*

16. Incident Management

In every operation there is an above the line and a below the line. Above the line is what you do by the book. Below the line is how you do the job.
—John Le Carré

INCIDENT MANAGEMENT AND THE CSO

The proposition is well accepted that the organization's CSO is a player in the management of serious incidents. When a serious incident has security implications, such as workplace violence, the CSO is more than just a player. He/she is the main player. Even in the absence of indications that a serious incident is likely, now or later down the road, the CSO must anticipate the possibility, plan for it, and have the security group ready to respond.

Every emergency situation calling for a security officer response is thoroughly explained in a standard operating procedure (SOP). SOPs provide specific and detailed instructions in several general areas:

- Communications procedures among security officers and with other responders
- Whom to notify of the emergency and when and how to do it
- Special duties such as moving valuable equipment to protected areas, boarding windows before the arrival of severe winds, piling sandbags, operating emergency pumps, directing traffic, closing valves or dampers, and turning off power
- Evacuation procedures, escape routes, and assembly areas
- Attention that must be given to the protection of valuable files, documents, photographs, equipment, and so on
- Medical assistance to injured persons
- Coordination with outside agencies such as the police and fire departments, ambulance services, trauma hospitals, civil defense, and FEMA
- Deployment of emergency equipment and supplies such as portable lights, handheld loud speakers, foul-weather gear, barricades, warning signs, first aid kits, and stretchers

BOMB INCIDENTS

Terrorism has brought bomb incidents to the forefront of security concerns (see Figure 16-1). The belief that bombing incidents might occur in the United States and its territories has been replaced by a belief they will occur. Questions are raised by the certainty: When, where, and how will they happen? Will the targets be physical assets or human assets? What tactics will be used and what terrorist groups will be involved?

Proactive Measures

An organization's program for managing bomb incidents includes proactive steps such as the following.

- Coordinate with law enforcement agencies to learn the methods and operating locales of groups known to use bombs. Determine if the organization is a potential target.
- Stay current with new developments in bomb construction and concealment.
- Confer with security counterparts to learn the bomb incident experiences of other organizations. Set up information-sharing agreements.
- Liaise with bomb disposal experts who can be helpful in conducting training programs for employees whose duties would bring them into contact with bombs such as package or mail bombs.
- Control suspect packages entering the workplace. Control can include examining packages in a separate building adjacent to the main workplace or at an offsite location.

Figure 16-1 The bombing of a federal building in Oklahoma City delivered a tragic reminder to Americans of the cruelty of terrorists, homegrown or otherwise.

- Identify strangers who enter the workplace, keep an eye on them, and prevent them from gaining uncontrolled movement within the workplace.
- Educate employees to look for and report strangers in the workplace, and educate employees and visitors to not leave personal items, such as briefcases and gym bags, unattended in the public areas.
- Identify areas where a bomb could be planted with little chance of detection and where detonation would cause personal injury and interruption of operations. The areas to think about concerning personal injury are lobby, cafeteria, work areas with high concentrations of people, and executive offices. Regarding interruption of operations, the places of concern are telephone switching center, computer room, electrical power plant, and places where critical physical assets are located.
- Educate employees generally, and security and maintenance personnel specifically, to be alert for suspicious persons and activities.
- Require security officers during each tour of duty to make random checks of public areas to look for unauthorized persons who may be hiding in or reconnoitering the facility.
- Ensure physical protection of key assets against bomb damage. Fire-resistant safes and vaults can protect sensitive documents, cash, small valuables, magnetic media, and similar materials.
- Educate fire wardens and other bomb incident responders to look for and report unusual activities that might signal the early stage of a bombing attempt.

Program

A program to manage bomb incidents is not unlike any other incident management program. It moves through three stages: develop a plan, prepare procedures that implement the plan, and train/equip persons who perform the procedures. The CSO, who is logically the principal developer of the program, identifies the following:

- Purpose and objectives
- Major preventive, anticipatory, and response functions
- Responsibilities assigned to particular positions
- Interfaces with outside response agencies, such as police and fire departments
- Equipment required
- An approach for bringing various elements of the plan together to form a synchronous whole

Flexibility and Coordination

The bomb incident plan should be sufficiently flexible to allow more than one response option at the outset and during the course of the incident. Because the plan commits to action a number of units and persons not employed by the security group, development of the plan will require the CSO to coordinate the plan with all interested parties — not least of which is the organization's emergency management office.

The interested parties inside the organization are likely to be the security officer force, building maintenance workers, and fire wardens. If the organization is a tenant, the landlord or building management office will be involved in plan development and execution. Outside parties could include an explosives detection team, a bomb disposal team, fire control units, ambulance services, and post-incident investigative agencies.

Planning

Developing a plan is more than just putting pen to paper. The plan itself will be the product of a systematic and logical process. The following is a simple process outline.

- Decide a general strategy
- Prepare a plan that incorporates actions consistent with strategy
- Implement the plan
- Test the plan
- Evaluate results
- Adjust the plan as needed

Decide a general strategy: A strategy takes into account the organization's exposure and vulnerability to a bomb attack. The CSO must obtain answers to the following questions.

- Is the organization a target of a militant adversary?
- Is the organization partnered in any way with an organization or government that is targeted? Partnering can include working with or providing products, materials, and assistance to another organization.
- Has the organization or its leaders contributed money to, provided support for, or been politically affiliated with any charity, aid program, cultural exchange, or educational program that could be construed as affiliated with a target of terrorism?
- Does the organization support political or social causes that would make it a likely target for radical hate groups?
- Has the organization refused to do business with, withdrawn from, or failed to successfully negotiate business contracts with companies, organizations, or governments that are affiliated with terrorist groups?
- Does the organization manufacture or produce military arms or equipment?
- Have any of the organization's leaders made public statements, been quoted or interviewed, or authored papers critical of terrorist groups?

Answers to the preceding questions can lead to further questions.

- Is the organization a target?
- What is the probability of an attack?
- Who are the likely attackers?
- What are the motives and capabilities of the attackers?
- What will be the form and delivery method of the attack?
- Is the organization vulnerable to an attack?
- What are the organization's specific areas of vulnerability?

Now coming into play is the experience of the CSO and his/her ability to tap into valuable information sources: reports of government intelligence and law enforcement agencies, the expertise of consultants, the experiences of security peers, and the research capabilities of professional associations serving the security industry. Also helpful can be the findings of intraorganizational security inspections and surveys and the application of plain old common sense. News media stories, such as those that followed the Pan Am 103 bombing (see Figure 16-2), can serve as information sources.

A given in the determination of a strategy is the recognition that perfect security is impossible, no matter how much money and effort the organization may be willing to expend. The strategy will reflect a balance between cost and effectiveness. When the homework has been done, the CSO is able to calculate the increases and decreases of risk associated with proposed increases and decreases in security. For example, the installation of an electronic access control system has dollar costs that can be readily determined and placed into contrast with the reasonably estimated dollar costs of injury, death, property destruction, and loss of business opportunity that would result from a bomb explosion.

Figure 16-2 The Pan Am 103 bombing was a worldwide wakeup call to the threat of terrorism.

Prepare the plan: Although bomb incident plans vary widely among organizations, they typically contain

- A statement reflecting management's concern about bomb incidents, support of the plan, and authority to expend resources needed for plan execution.
- The objectives of the plan. At least three objectives apply: provide for the safety of people, protect property against damage or destruction, and restore the organization to normal operations.
- A description of the threat and an assessment of risk.
- Definitions of terms important to understanding the plan and assigning accountability.
- A delineation of job positions and units, including external agencies, which have plan responsibilities. The delineation reflects lines of communication and formal authority.
- A description of the facility in terms of geography and demography, access routes, physical construction, entry points, utility interfaces, hours of operation, types of work activities, and numbers and types of persons within the facility.
- A description of the dedicated resources such as a security control center and public address system. This description could also mention evacuation routes and assembly areas.
- An identification of procedures that carry out the plan; for example, procedures used by
  - Maintenance personnel in shutting down utility systems.
  - Fire wardens in evacuating the facility.
  - Security officers in conducting bomb searches.

Implement the plan: Procedures that flow from the plan provide detailed guidance to the responders. Procedures vary for the simple reason that responders vary. The CSO, for example, develops procedures for security group responders and the property manager develops procedures for maintenance employees.

Written procedures might be found smack dab in the middle of a plan or as an appendix at the end of the plan. Where they are located in the plan is beside the point; the important thing is that they make sense and are understandable to the people who carry them out. More than anything else, procedures are directives that leave no room for interpretation. This is so because the potential for severe consequences requires absolute clarity.

Test the plan: A plan can be tested partially or fully. A partial test might be a simulating exercise (e.g., an unidentified caller has stated that a bomb has been concealed on the premises). The CSO orders that a search be made. Security officers conduct the search in accordance with the plan's procedures. Other security officer actions (also simulated) include making notifications and communicating search findings. Practice of this type is a form of hands-on training. Essential knowledge and skills are applied, and response equipment — such as the public address system and radio communications system — are put into use. Briefings and orientations for familiarizing the responders with the established procedures precede the exercise, and immediately following is a critique designed to improve future performance. Learning acquired in this manner is powerful and lasting.

Evaluate results: The exercise is assessed objectively and an after-action report prepared. The response procedures, as well as the plan itself, are modified in light of lessons learned. But evaluation by the CSO does not end there. It takes place everyday in the observation of security officers doing their jobs and of equipment operating in support of security. It is present when terrorist groups refine or alter their tactics and when bomb technology advances.

A CSO understands that a determined adversary will find a chink in even the finest defensive armor. The point has been proven many times: the bombing of the Marine barracks in Lebanon, the Air Force barracks in Saudi Arabia, two U.S. embassies in Africa, the Murrah Building in Oklahoma City, and the World Trade Center bombing of 1993.

Responding to Bomb Threats [1]

An elementary observation about bomb threats is that they are rarely made in person, sometimes conveyed in a written format, and almost always made over the telephone. The bomber prefers the telephone, believing that it presents the lowest risk of identification.

If the format of threat message has been written or typed, the document is handled carefully, touched by as few persons as possible, and the envelope or any other accompanying materials preserved as evidence. Observing these simple precautions is extremely helpful to a post-incident investigation.

The hoax call: If one is to assume that a bomb threat is real, it logically follows that the person communicating the threat has knowledge about the bomb. Our immediate interest is in learning from the caller what the bomb is made of, where it has been placed, and when it will go off. Knowing these facts can save lives.

We can also assume that the call is a hoax but we dare not do so. Any bomb threat, regardless of delivery method or format, has to be treated seriously and with great caution. In the American workplace a very high percentage of bomb threats are hoaxes, but the other side of that reality tells us there is no way to be absolutely sure. Any bomb threat decision has to be heavily biased toward protection of life.

Details of a call: The opportunity of the CSO or other management person to make a close examination of a bomb threat received by telephone can be lost or severely diminished when the person receiving the call fails to capture relevant details. When a caller says "There's a bomb in your building," panic can be a natural reaction. A good way to keep that from happening is to teach employees how to respond and provide them with a checklist that can be kept handy for use. Those employees most likely to receive bomb threat calls should be a specially trained. In this group are switchboard operators, security officers, receptionists, and executive secretaries. The key points are

- Keep the caller talking for as long as possible.
- Ask the caller to repeat the message.
- Take notes. Write down exact words.
- Ask the caller to specifically state where the bomb is located and when it is set to detonate.
- Ask what part of the facility should be evacuated first.
- Ask for a description of the bomb. What does it look like? How is it packaged? What is it made of and how does it work?
- Ask why the bomb was placed and what group is responsible. Ask the caller if he/she was the person who placed the bomb. Ask where the caller is now.
- Tell the caller that the facility is occupied and that a detonation could result in death and serious injury to many innocent people.
- Listen closely to the caller's voice. Is the caller male or female? Calm or excited? Accent? Speech impediment?
- Pay attention to background noises that may give a clue as to the caller's location. Traffic sounds, music, and voices heard in the background may be important.
- Keep the line open after the call has ended. It may be possible to trace the call.
- Notify the security control center immediately after the caller hangs up. Be ready to be interviewed and to hand over notes made during the call.

Evaluating a call: The very first task of the CSO who has been informed of a bomb threat call is to evaluate it. Interviewing the person who received the call and examining notes taken during the call are the preliminaries to a judgment. The evaluation takes into account the details and characteristics of the call itself, prior bomb threat calls, and similar threats that have been made in the community or against other organizations. Evaluation is essentially a process of judging the credibility of the threat; in other words, is the call a hoax or is it the real thing?

The CSO has to recognize that absolutes are never possible and that if an error in judgment is to be made it has to be made on the side of caution. For example, in considering the details of a call the CSO may note that the caller was described as a giggling young girl; hard rock music was heard in the background; and the girl's answer to the question as to motive was that "you people are so, so uncool." In this case, the CSO may conclude that the call is probably a hoax. Another case can have entirely different indicators, such as an adult male who expresses anger against the organization, reveals knowledge of the workplace, and knowledge of bomb construction. This threat could be genuine. In still another case, the indicators may be few and unrevealing, a circumstance that requires the CSO to treat the threat as if it were real.

The CSO's evaluation is not always the only evaluation. The property manager of the facility may be tasked by policy or plan to share in making a joint evaluation or making the evaluation independent of another's judgment. The same can apply as well to the operations manager, the CEO, or the senior executive in the facility at the time the threat is received. Like too many cooks spoiling the broth, too many evaluators can spoil the evaluation and waste time that could be better spent evacuating the premises.

Response options: Evaluation of a bomb threat call falls into one of three categories: we think it is a hoax, we think it might be real, and we don't know. Other factors may apply as well. For example, a regulatory standard of a safety-sensitive industry may require immediate and full evacuation irrespective of how management views the threat, or a collective bargaining agreement could require that employees be informed of the receipt of a bomb threat and those who wish to leave may do so. Another influence may be management's worry about liability arising from injuries sustained by employees as they evacuate the facility.

Time is the enemy when deciding what to do when a bomb threat is received. Decision time is reduced when the decision maker has participated in drills and practical exercises that tested the bomb incident plan. Three options are available.

Search without evacuating: This option is appropriate when the threat is very, very likely to be a hoax. This option allows upgrading to evacuation when, for example, a suspected bomb is found or when a subsequent determinative threat call is received.

Evacuate partially or fully and then search: This option is appropriate when the threat might be real. The caller may have said the bomb is located in a particular area, in which case that area and its surrounding areas would be evacuated and then searched. Alternatively, the caller may have described multiple bomb locations or a bomb that is devastating, in which case the entire facility would be evacuated and then searched.

Fully evacuate and do not search: This option is appropriate when the threat appears to be very, very real. The caller may have revealed knowledge of bomb construction, mentioned revenge, or said that he/she is a member of a militant group known to be in opposition to the organization. Events that occurred prior to the call may be relevant, such as recent attempts at arson or sabotage. This option reflects the management's belief that the best course of action is to get out of the facility right away. If detonation does not occur within the next 12 hours or so, a conclusion can be made that a detonation will not occur.

How to search: Bomb searching is in most cases conducted by persons familiar with the workplace and almost never by police officers. Public safety policy often discourages the participation of police officers in bomb searches on private property, unless probable cause exists to believe that a bomb is

Figure 16-3 Security and police organizations often use trained dogs to search for bombs.

in fact present. Probable cause can be established by the details of the bomb threat call or by the discovery of a suspect bomb. With a belief established, the police are more likely to want to be actively involved in making or directing the search. Although employees at the workplace have a greater familiarity with the possible places of bomb concealment, officers trained in bomb disposal know how to avoid booby traps and mistakes that can lead to detonation (see Figure 16-3).

Thoroughness: Searching has to be thorough. The searchers are people familiar with the physical environment (e.g., security officers, maintenance workers, and other employees who know the nooks and crannies).

Thoroughness is affected by the size and configuration of the workplace. It is fair to say that making a thorough search is not easy in any working environment. Even small environments uncomplicated by multiple workstations, equipment, and labor-intensive activities present problems. Large and complex environments, such as manufacturing plants and high-rise office buildings, are searchable on a genuinely thorough basis only with substantial expenditure of effort and time. A 20-story office building, for example, might require 48 hours of uninterrupted looking with a 20-person team before it can be said with assurance that a bomb is not in the building.

It is seldom possible in a large and complex environment to conduct a comprehensive search because time does not allow looking into false ceilings, examining every file cabinet, and removing panels from equipment. Neither is it acceptable to disrupt or shut down work operations for two full working days while a search is in progress. A practical solution might be to prioritize, as part of the planning process, those places that should and can be thoroughly searched within the time available for searching. What this means is that searching with thoroughness remains firm, but that selectivity is introduced with respect to what should be searched.

Care: Searchers have to be careful. To exercise care, searchers must know what a bomb looks like, or more accurately spot and be wary of innocuous-appearing containers that can be used to conceal bombs. The searchers need to be watchful for booby traps.

Caution: Anything of a suspicious nature has to be approached with great caution. A searcher who discovers what may be a bomb withdraws to a safe distance, warns others to leave, and reports the circumstances immediately. At the other end of the line is a security officer prepared to act according to procedure, which may be to make a public address announcement, notify the fire department, summon emergency medical assistance, inform the police, and ask for the services of a bomb disposal team.

Probability and Criticality

In deciding what to search, two factors are pertinent: probability and criticality. How probable is it that a bomber would be able to penetrate the organization's security defenses? If the probability is high, how probable is it that a bomb or bombs would be placed in some areas as opposed to others? An evaluation of probability might lead to a search priority that concentrates on areas that are outside the umbrella of high-security control, such as lobbies, garages, and other areas easily accessible to the public. Criticality takes into account a priority for searching areas where the greatest damage can be done.

Probability and criticality need to be balanced. For example, it may not be sensible to set a high priority on searching the computer center when the probability is low that a bomb could be brought into the computer center without detection. On the other hand, the computer center may demand a search because of its criticality to business operations.

Prioritizing

Prioritizing a search can be assisted by the use of a card system. Each area to be searched is represented by a card that names and describes the location. The cards are coded according to priority and are handed out to search team members at the quickly convened briefing that precedes the start of a search. At the end of the search, check marks or signatures on the cards provide a quick reference for ensuring that no areas were overlooked.

Nonevacuation Search

As the name suggests, this search method is utilized when a decision has been made not to evacuate. It is performed in a walkthrough, but not cursory, manner. The searchers are usually security officers and maintenance workers and they work alone. They move in a steady, unhurried pace looking for objects that seem out of place. Employees engaged in normal work activity can be a source of information in judging if an object is really suspicious. In areas where few or no employees are present, the searcher should give close attention to containers, closets, and places that offer concealment.

Post-evacuation Search

This method is utilized when employees are absent, such as following an evacuation or during non working hours. The searchers examine workstations, offices, conference rooms, shelves, wastebaskets, storage bins, and the like. Even though searchers can move faster when employees are not in the way, any time gained is expended by searching with greater intensity. Also, if the search is conducted after hours the search team is not at full force because the day workers who would normally assist in the search are off duty.

Discovery of a Suspicious Object

The size and location of a suspect bomb has an influence on the extent of evacuation. For example, a suspect bomb about the size of a cigarette pack that is found in a storage room on an empty floor might not merit evacuation, partial or otherwise. As a general rule, 300 feet of lateral area around a suspect bomb should be cleared of all nonessential response personnel. The vertical areas above and below a suspect bomb should also be cleared. For example, if a suspect bomb is found on a floor of a multistory building the floor involved plus the floors immediately above and below should be cleared.

Total evacuation is mandatory when a suspect bomb is judged to be genuine and capable of inflicting injury. In the absence of that judgment, certain employees (such as security officers and maintenance employees) may remain to perform essential life-protecting and shutdown tasks.

The rule about not touching a suspicious object is a rule that cannot be ignored. The rule, however, cannot apply until an object is seen, evaluated, and determined to be suspicious — all of which can be done in the blink of an eye. Because a bomb is likely to be concealed in places such as cabinets, drawers, and trash receptacles, the searchers have to probe and touch. But at the instant a suspicious object is detected all touching must stop. Actions that follow can include:

- Questioning employees who may be able to account for the presence of the suspicious object
- Ordering a partial or full evacuation
- Notifying the bomb disposal team
- Notifying the fire department
- Readying first aid supplies and calling for standby medical personnel and equipment
- Asking the police to assume command of the situation

The bomb disposal team leader or the fire officer in charge may ask for further information about the location of the suspect device relative to stored fuels, chemicals, flammables, power plant, and fire exits. Because of the possibility that more than one bomb has been planted, orders may be made for the search team to continue examining areas that have not yet been searched.

BOMB TYPES

Bombs can be constructed in many different ways and easily disguised. Small to medium-size bombs can be placed in purses, briefcases, paper and plastic bags, backpacks, and tote bags. Large bombs can be carried inside motor vehicles and carts of many types.

Bombs are often given names that correspond to a dominant characteristic (e.g., low-explosive, high-explosive, vehicle, postal, incendiary, improvised, propelled, timed, remote detonated, barometric, pressure, pressure release, chemical, biological, radiological, and nuclear). The sections that follow describe bomb types.

High-explosive Bombs

These bombs kill, injure, and damage by blast effect, shrapnel, and flying debris (particularly glass shards). A bomb small enough to be hidden in a hand-carried bag can create an enormously powerful blast. Bombs of this type are typically made with commercial or military explosives in blocks or sticks. Some will include an electric detonator, timer, or power source and will be incorporated in some way with the explosive material.

The best protection against a high-explosive bomb is to prevent it from being brought on or close to the property. The preventive measures include stringent access control, inspection of packages, and the use of explosives-detecting devices, supplemented with rules that prohibit parking immediately adjacent to the property and leaving packages, parcels, and bags unattended. Hiding places in areas accessible to the public should also be eliminated, and maximum use made of technical surveillance equipment such as CCTV and intrusion detection sensors. An excellent preventive measure is the collective watchfulness of employees.

Vehicle Bombs

A motor vehicle of any type can be the means for delivering a bomb to the target. The protective measures include controlling access to parking areas, searching vehicles at entry points, and patrolling the parking areas. An excellent deterrent is the appearance (and fact) of high security in adjacent parking areas.

Figure 16-4 The Molotov cocktail is a favorite of street rioters.

Incendiary Bombs

The purpose of these bombs is to cause fire. They can be small, difficult to spot, and innocuous in appearance. They can be brought piecemeal into the targeted premises, assembled, and detonated. Detonation is possible with something as simple as a burning book of matches.

Another form of the incendiary bomb is the Molotov cocktail, a glass bottle filled with a flammable liquid and a flaming rag attached to the mouth of the bottle. (See Figure 16.4.) This bomb is thrown. Upon impact with a hard surface, the glass breaks and the flammable liquid ignites.

Letter and Parcel Bombs

These bombs, which are intended to kill or injure, are usually designed to detonate upon opening. They are often delivered by the postal service or a commercial delivery service. The following are indicators of this type of bomb.

- Foreign mail, airmail, or special-delivery markings
- Restrictive markings such as "Confidential" and "Personal"
- Nonmetered postage
- Too many stamps
- Handwritten or poorly typed address
- Incorrect title
- Title but no name
- Misspellings
- Oily stains or discoloration

- A smell like marzipan or machine oil
- No return address
- Excessive weight
- Heavier in some places than others
- Rigid envelope
- Lopsided or uneven envelope
- Soft outer wrapping over rigid content
- Protruding wires or tinfoil
- Excessive wrapping materials such as masking tape and string.

Upon receiving notification of a suspect parcel bomb, the CSO's options are as follows:

- Interview the individual who discovered the item
- Isolate the item if it is safe to do so
- Inquire of the addressee:
  - Do you know the sender?
  - Are you expecting correspondence from the sender?
  - Are you expecting correspondence from the place where the item was mailed?
  - Are you aware of any friends, relatives, or acquaintances in or near the place where the item was mailed?
  - Did you purchase or order anything from anybody in or near the place where the item was mailed?
- Call the local bomb squad if suspicion cannot be removed.
- Notify senior management.
- Stand by to offer assistance to the bomb squad.

AFTERMATH OF AN EXPLOSION

The response actions that immediately follow an explosion are spelled out in various procedures dealing with building evacuation, emergency medical services, and rescue operations. All of these actions involve the CSO, plus one other important action: protection of the scene. The objective is to not disturb evidence, and the way to do that is to demarcate the scene, establish a temporary perimeter, and control access.

Debris Search

A bomb scene, in spite of massive destruction, can yield valuable clues to the identity of the person or persons responsible. A search begins with the premise that everything at the scene at the instant of explosion is still there unless vaporized. **Even with considerable vaporization, as demonstrated in Figure 16.4, much can be learned through searches conducted by trained persons.**

Figure 16-4 A terrorist attack on a peacekeeping force in Dhahran, Saudi Arabia, left 19 dead and hundreds injured.

The search is carried out by trained specialists operating from a single plan and will have intertwining objectives: find everything that can be found and identify everything that has been found. The first occurs at the scene; the second occurs for the most part in a forensic laboratory. When the two objectives are achieved, conclusions are possible as to what happened and who made it happen.

Jurisdiction

A bomb incident is managed from a single point and conducted in two dimensions. One is the examination of the scene, and the other is a general investigation that seeks to identify and take custody of the responsible parties. In major incidents, overall management is by the Federal Bureau of Investigation. The search is conducted by agents of the Bureau of Alcohol, Tobacco and Firearms and the FBI, and general investigative work is handled by the FBI.

Command Post

A command post and an evidence collection center are often set up nearby. Many tasks are performed simultaneously: taking photographs, collecting fingerprints, sifting debris, and protecting and tagging physical evidence. Supervisors at the command post oversee the search and coordinate the efforts of the many specialists involved.

Safety is a concern. Searchers recognize the possibility of a secondary bomb, a "jammed" bomb, or live explosives in the debris. They also are aware that walls, ceilings, and floors can collapse upon them as they work.

Forensic Examination

Bomb remains are examined to identify bomb components such as switches, batteries, blasting caps, tape, wire, timing mechanisms, fabrication techniques, unconsumed explosives, and overall construction of the bomb. Instrumental examination is made of explosives and explosive residues, and bomb components are examined microscopically for tool marks. Timing mechanisms can sometimes be identified as to type, manufacturer, and model, and determinations are sometimes possible as to the time displayed by the mechanism when the explosive detonated and as to the relative length of time the mechanism was functioning prior to the explosion.

FIRE EMERGENCIES

Collaboration

Dealing with fire emergencies is a collaborative process that involves the manager of the protected property, a fire marshal or inspector, and the CSO. Collaboration can also include professionals representing the safety and risk management disciplines.

Criminal and civil liabilities that can arise from a fire emergency place a grave responsibility on the property manager — a responsibility that dictates a prominent role in developing the fire response capability and in leading the fire response effort pending arrival of the fire department. The fire marshal or inspector ensures that response procedures meet fire code requirements. In some communities, the fire department provides instruction in how to identify and correct fire hazards, operate extinguishing equipment, and evacuate a building.

The CSO represents the interests of his/her employer. The employer can own or rent. If the employer is the building owner, the property manager and the CSO are on the same payroll (except when the owner has outsourced the property management function, in which case the property manager is a contract employee). Regardless of the arrangement, the property manager and the CSO, each operating from separate disciplines, are attentive to ensuring the integrity of the premises and the safety of the occupants (see Figure 16-5).

Fire Control System

Preparing for a fire emergency takes into account the property's fire detection and suppression system. If the property is a modern office building the system will feature a combination of manual pull stations, ionization detectors,

---

Inspections to Prevent Electrical Fires

This guide can be used as a checklist for conducting inspections to prevent electrical fires. The inspecting officer should ensure that

A certification label is attached to each electrical product or its packaging. Certification labels are issued by independent testing companies such as UL (Underwriters Laboratories) or ETL (Electrical Testing Laboratories). Products with these certification labels meet current industry safety standards. For extension cords, look for a permanently attached certification label on the cord near the plug. For power strips and surge protectors, look on the underside of the casing.

Electrical cords, power strips, and surge protectors have polarized plugs with one blade slightly wider than the other, or grounded three-pronged plugs.

Air conditioners, portable electric heaters, and freezers have special, heavy-duty extension cords.

Extension cords used outdoors are specifically designed for such use.

Electrical plugs are fully inserted.

Extension cords are not placed under rugs or other smothering materials.

Extension cords are not overloaded.

Extension cords are not dangling in such a way that an appliance can be tipped over.

Extension cords that feel hot to the touch are replaced.

Extension cords that are cracked or worn are replaced.

Extension cords are used only when necessary and only on a temporary basis.

Figure 16-5 Inspecting electrical connections to prevent fire is a fundamental duty of security officers.

overhead sprinklers, fire extinguishers, alarm horns, voice speakers, pressurization fans, firefighter telephones, and an emergency generator for backup power.

Floor Wardens

A chief responsibility within the purview of the property manager is a floor warden (or fire warden) program. A program of this type usually designates one or more floor wardens per floor, depending on floor size and configuration. The wardens are trained initially and periodically. Initial training provides skill development in using handheld fire extinguishers, administering CPR and first aid, operating defibrillation and oxygen resuscitation equipment, and avoiding the risks of blood-borne pathogens. Periodic training refreshes these skills and provides complementary knowledge in subjects of current concern. Fire drills, which are often monitored by a fire department representative, provide an opportunity for practice and improvement.

Tasks: A floor warden is almost always a volunteer and rarely rewarded monetarily. Acceptance into the program is predicated on physical agility, stamina, and a work schedule that provides reasonably high assurance that the warden will be present for duty when fire occurs. Cooperation of the floor warden's supervisor to permit attendance at training and practice sessions is a must. A floor warden's tasks include the following.

- Educating co-workers concerning their individual responsibilities for fire prevention, reduction of safety hazards, how to report a fire, how to evacuate, and where to assemble following evacuation
- Preventing, reporting, and correcting fire and safety hazards inspecting the floor daily
- Exercising leadership during an evacuation by directing co-workers down stairwells and ensuring that no one has been left behind
- Providing first-responder medical assistance to persons who are in need of first-responder medical aid
- Knowing the locations of the fire stairwells, pull stations, and escape routes
- Posting an escape route diagram and related information on bulletin boards and other conspicuous places
- Enlisting the services of helpers to direct employees away from the elevators and down the fire stairwells in fire emergencies
- Briefing every new person on the floor concerning what to do in case of an emergency
- Keeping a list of persons on the floor for head counting purposes immediately following an evacuation
- Identifying persons with medical conditions, such as asthma or pregnancy, who may need help during an evacuation and arranging to provide the needed help
- Being alert for fire hazards (e.g., overloaded electrical circuits, unattended cooking appliances, and materials blocking stairwell doors)

Operation of Equipment

A fire alarm sounds when an electronic sensor detects heat or smoke or when a human manually activates a pull station or similar device. Typically in a high-rise building, an alarm will sound on the floor where the sensor or pull station activated, plus the floor above and the floor below. This procedure avoids evacuating the entire building when a fire condition is minor or not actually a fire at all.

In addition to automatically sounding an alarm, the fire control system opens and closes louvers and activates fans. The effect is to force smoke out of the building and bring fresh air into stairwells.

Fire Condition

A fire condition is not necessarily a fire. It may be the result of a malfunctioning fire detector, smoke indicative of a minor short circuit, a smell suggestive of fire, or heat that should not be there. On the other hand, a fire condition can be the result of an actual fire such as moderate smoke, smoke with flame, flame, or intense heat.

When a Fire Alarm Sounds

When an alarm sounds, floor wardens begin immediately to look for a fire condition, starting with coffee and copying rooms, in that these are the places where fire is most likely to occur. If a search reveals moderate smoke, flame, or intense heat, the warden pulls a manual pull station, the effect of which is to confirm the electronic detection made seconds earlier. This dual reporting, one by a scientific instrument and the other by a human action, is registered by sound and sight on a panel of fire control equipment that is most often located within a security control center or the property manager's office. (In our present discussion, we will assume that the building has a security control center.)

The fire control system automatically signals the fire department. Also, the security officer monitoring the panel telephones the fire department to ensure the message has been received.

Simultaneously, an announcement is made over the fire control system's public address component. The announcement can be made by a taped voice message or a message spoken live. If live, the property manager or designee orders the message to be sent. Message content can inform employees that a fire condition has been detected in the building and that employees are to take one of the following three actions.

- Stand by for further instructions.
- Proceed to the nearest fire exit and stand by for further instructions.
- Immediately evacuate.

Meanwhile, the floor warden who verified the fire condition and activated a manual pull station is also calling the security control center and fire department. (A cherished preference of fire departments is to receive multiple calls.)

The telephonic report to the fire department dispatcher is done quickly but clearly. The person making the call reports the pertinent details: name of the company, street address, where the fire is located specifically, and whether or not people are trapped or have been injured or killed. The caller should expect the dispatcher to ask for the caller's name and return phone number, and to keep the line open.

When a Fire Condition Is Serious

When a fire condition is smoke with flame and heat, the floor warden instructs employees to exit the floor (even when the public address message may have told employees to stand by or await further instructions). When the floor is apparently empty of people, the floor warden makes one last check to see if this is so. If so, the floor warden notifies the security control center by telephone, by handheld radio issued to the floor warden for use in fire emergencies, or

EXAMPLE OF SEQUENCES WHEN A FIRE ALARM IS PULLED

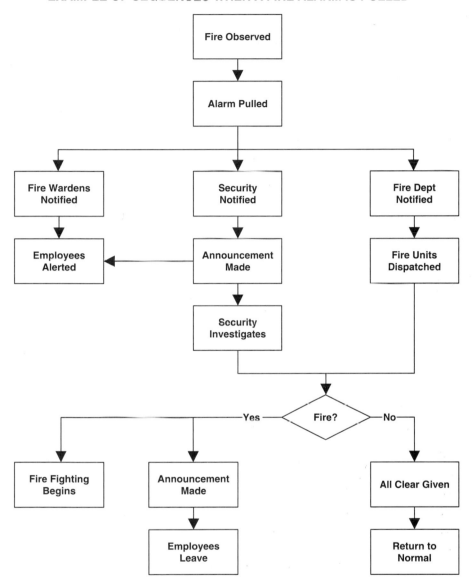

Figure 16-6 A fire alarm signal initiates a planned process.

in person. A security officer or security supervisor inside the security control center keeps track of which floors have been fully evacuated.

By this time, the property manager and CSO are in the security control center. The property manager is making on-the-spot decisions and the CSO is ensuring correct performance of security officers. The above diagram (Figure 16-6) depicts a logical process that begins when fire conditions are first reported.

When a Fire Condition Is Minor

When the fire condition involves small to moderate smoke only, the floor warden awaits arrival of a member of the company's fire control team (typically a building maintenance engineer) and/or a firefighter.

For a flame not larger than the size of a waste paper receptacle, the floor warden can attempt to put it out with a handheld extinguisher. If the attempt fails, the fire condition is no longer minor; it has escalated to serious. Alternatively, the floor warden can elect not to attempt putting out the fire, in which case the condition goes from minor to serious.

When a Fire Condition Does Not Exist

When the floor warden's search does not reveal fire conditions, he/she reports that fact to the security control center and waits for the arrival of the fire control team. The fire control team makes a second search of the floor. In some jurisdictions, fire code or fire department policy requires that any reported fire condition be evaluated by a firefighter. If this procedure applies, the floor is triple checked. After all checks have been made, the security control center is notified and the property manager makes an all-clear announcement.

Fire Control Team

The property manager also organizes and supervises what can be called a fire control team. Team members consist mainly of building engineer staff, with possible augmentation by security officers. Duties of the team include going without delay to the scene of the reported fire condition to determine the presence or absence of fire, and if fire is present attempt to contain, suppress, or extinguish it.

If the fire spreads or increases in size, the extinguishing attempt is aborted. Heat generated by a moderate to large fire will activate a sprinkler system, assuming that a sprinkler system is installed.

If fire is not verified, the team determines the reason for the false alarm. A malfunctioning or overly sensitive fire or smoke detector is often the culprit. A smoke detector that is perfectly functional may confuse dust with smoke.

The fire control team makes a report of findings to the property manager. Depending on the fire control team's report of findings the property manager uses the public address system to communicate one of the following three messages.

- Evacuate (a serious fire is in progress).
- Stand by for further instructions (the fire control team is unable to make a definitive judgment or the fire is minor and being extinguished).
- Return to normal work activities (there is no fire).

If evacuation is ordered, the fire control team's next task is protection of human life by fighting or containing the fire and/or directing employees to leave or helping incapacitated occupants out of the building.

Security Officers

The efforts of floor wardens and members of the fire control team are supplemented by security officers. And this is where the CSO has a prominent role. The CSO develops, and ensures through training and practice, procedures that guide security officers in the following:

- Detecting and correcting fire hazards
- Reporting fire conditions
- Monitoring and responding to annunciations of the electronic fire detection equipment
- Assisting or filling in for floor wardens and fire control team members
- Directing traffic to allow unhampered access of firefighting vehicles and equipment
- Operating radio and telephone equipment for command and control purposes

An effective fire response capability relies on a 24-hour-per-day human presence augmented with reliable sensing and communicating equipment. The human presence ideally consists of security officers trained to perform fire response duties. In the scheme presented here, the sounding of a fire alarm after hours sends a security officer to the affected area to look for a fire condition. In essence, the after-hours security officers assume floor warden response tasks.

Occupants

A fire response plan includes provisions for educating occupants as to their individual responsibilities with respect to reporting fire hazards, preventing fire, and following instructions during a fire emergency. Fire drills, which normally occur at six-month intervals, are part of the education process.

An excellent method of educating employees is one-on-one and small group briefings by floor wardens. Every occupant should be thoroughly briefed at least once, preferably on the first day of employment. Briefing points include the location of detectors and pull stations, escape routes, and stairwells; the procedural steps of an alarm and the order to evacuate; the rule against using or trying to use an elevator to evacuate; the rule against running during an evacuation; and the location of the evacuation assembly area (see Figure 16-7).

Building Evacuation Checklist

Y	N		Y	N	
		On the Floors	☐	☐	Do the security officers test the equipment once a month?
☐	☐	Are there at least two primary means of escape from each floor?	☐	☐	Do the security officers make monthly checks of fire extinguishers?
☐	☐	Are same-floor escape exits separate from each other?	☐	☐	Does the SCC have on hand emergency medical supplies?
☐	☐	Do escape routes avoid dead ends?	☐	☐	Are security officers trained in evacuation procedures?
☐	☐	Are escape routes posted?			
☐	☐	Are escape routes highlighted with strobe lights or other markers?	☐	☐	Are evacuation procedures in writing and current?
☐	☐	Are escape exits marked and lighted?	☐	☐	Do security officers enforce fire zone parking rules?
☐	☐	Are escape stairwells equipped with emergency lighting?	☐	☐	Do security officers direct traffic to assist arriving emergency vehicles?
☐	☐	Are escape stairwells free of obstructions?			**In the Property Management Venue**
☐	☐	Are escape stairwell floors covered with a non-skid surface?	☐	☐	Does the Property Manager prepare and keep current an emergency
☐	☐	Are arrangements in place to help handicapped persons escape?			response plan that incorporates the activities of floor wardens, security officers, maintenance employees, and
☐	☐	Are life-saving equipment and supplies (e.g., stretcher and first aid kit) on hand?			others?
☐	☐	Are escape stairwells fire resistant?	☐	☐	Has the emergency response plan been approved by the fire department
☐	☐	Are escape stairwells equipped with blowers to keep out smoke?			and coordinated with the police department?
☐	☐	Is there a procedure for crossing from one stairwell to another?	☐	☐	Does the Property Manager manage ongoing programs of safety
☐	☐	Does each floor have an adequate number of floor wardens?			awareness for building occupants and specific training for response
☐	☐	Are floor wardens trained in evacuation procedures?			employees?
☐	☐	Are floor wardens equipped, e.g., with a flashlight and bull horn?	☐	☐	Does the specific training program include fire prevention, evacuation procedures, and first-responder
☐	☐	Are building occupants educated as to evacuation procedures?			medical assistance such as CPR and First Aid?
☐	☐	Are evacuation drills conducted at least every 6 months?	☐	☐	Does the Property Manager assume overall control of a building
☐	☐	Are fire alarm pull stations operational and conspicuous?			emergency pending arrival of fire or police departments?
☐	☐	Are smoke/heat detectors operational and placed appropriately?	☐	☐	Are maintenance employees trained to operate fire suppression systems
☐	☐	Can the public address system be heard everywhere on a floor?			and to activate/shutdown ventilation and other systems as needed?
		In the Security Control Center	☐	☐	Do maintenance employees periodically inspect heat/smoke
☐	☐	Does the SCC have a dependable back-up power source?			detectors, water sprinkler systems, stand-pipe equipment, and back-up
☐	☐	Is the fire detection panel in the SCC?			power systems?
☐	☐	Is the public address system in the SCC?	☐	☐	Are maintenance employees equipped with radios and do the
☐	☐	Are the security officers trained to operate SCC equipment?			radios interface with the SCC?

Figure 16-7 Many tasks are performed simultaneously when evacuating a building.

MEDICAL EMERGENCIES

Security Officer Responsibilities

A chief reason for employing security officers is to have readily available a capability to respond when an employee or visitor is injured or becomes seriously ill. Just having security officers at hand is not enough. They need to be trained to deliver assistance in situations involving asphyxiation, cardiac arrest, severe bleeding, unconsciousness, poisoning and drug overdoses, burn, electric shock, heat exhaustion, and bone fractures.

In these situations, the victim is cared for until the arrival of skilled medical professionals whose assistance is focused on saving a life or improving pulse, temperature, and breathing (vital signs). In minor emergencies, security officer actions may prevent a victim's condition from worsening and provide relief from pain.

The nature of the assistance corresponds to the victim's needs. Delivery of the assistance depends on the responder's knowledge and skill. Knowing what not to do in an emergency is as important as knowing what to do (see Figure 16-8). Moving a person with a neck injury, for example, can lead to permanent spinal injury and paralysis.

The Fundamentals

Several fundamentals apply to all medical emergencies. The CSO is responsible for delineating these fundamentals in standard operating procedures for

Figure 16-8 Security officers are key to an effective response in a medical emergency. *(Photo courtesy of Burns International Security Services.)*

security officers and ensuring competent performance through training and practice. The fundamentals are as follows:

- Call for professional medical help without delay.
- Determine that the scene is safe before attempting to provide first aid.
- Move the victim only as necessary to prevent further injury.
- Inform the victim, if conscious, that medical aid has been requested.
- Assess the scene, asking bystanders or co-workers about details of the injury or illness, any care that may have already been given, and pre-existing conditions such as diabetes or heart trouble.
- Look for a medical bracelet or card that describes the victim's special medical conditions.
- Assess the victim to determine if life-threatening conditions exist, for example:
  ◦ Examine the airway to see if it is open and unobstructed.
  ◦ Look, listen, and feel for breathing.
  ◦ Feel for a pulse.
  ◦ Look for external bleeding.
  ◦ Check skin color and temperature for indications of circulation problems.
- Place the injured person's head in line with the body.
- If no evidence exists to suggest potential skull or spinal injury, place the injured person in a comfortable position.
- If nausea is a condition, position the victim on one side so that vomit does not obstruct the airway.
- Look for the indications of shock: anxiety or restlessness; pale, cool, clammy skin; a weak but rapid pulse; shallow breathing; bluish lips; and nausea.
- Treat shock by covering the victim with blankets or warm clothes and elevating the feet.

Untrained or poorly trained first responders can make serious mistakes when confronted with medical emergencies. Mistakes can be avoided or mitigated by referring to written guidance such as that shown in Figure 16-9.

Cardiopulmonary Resuscitation (CPR)

CPR is a life-saving technique that combines the application of artificial respiration (rescue breathing) and artificial circulation (external cardiac compression). The technique complements defibrillation. Three phases constitute CPR: clearing the victim's airway, breathing into the victim's mouth, and compressing the victim's chest.

Airway: In this first phase, the rescuer

1. Places the victim flat on his/her back on a hard surface.
2. Shakes the victim at the shoulders and shouts, "Are you okay?"

Guidance to First-Responders

Asphyxiation. Cessation of breathing can cause brain death within 4 to 6 minutes unless relief is administered. The most common technique for preventing asphyxiation is artificial respiration. In a case of drowning, artificial respiration should be attempted even if the victim appears dead. People submerged in cold water for more than 30 minutes have responded to artificial respiration and recovered.

Cardiac Arrest. Position the victim face up on a firm surface and clear the airway. Tilt the victim's head back and lift the chin forward. Give the victim two breaths by mouth. If no pulse is detected at the carotid artery (located in a groove beside the windpipe in the neck), kneel next to the victim and place the heel of one hand on top of the other over the lower half of the sternum. Depress the chest about 2 inches, which forces blood from the heart into the victim's arteries. When the pressure is released, blood flows back into the heart. Apply pressure in short, rhythmic thrusts about 15 times every 10 seconds. Continue until the victim revives.

Severe Bleeding. Welling or spurting blood is a clear sign of severe bleeding. If a major artery ruptures, a person may bleed to death within a minute. Shock usually follows loss of blood, and must be prevented as soon as the bleeding has been stopped. Bleeding is stopped by applying pressure directly over the wound and, when possible, elevating the bleeding body part. Hold a sterile dressing or clean cloth firmly over the wound. If the bleeding is from an arm or leg, reduce blood loss by applying pressure at a point adjacent to the bleeding. Arteries pass close to the skin at these points and can be compressed against underlying bone to reduce bleeding.

Loss of Consciousness. This condition occurs when the brain does not receive enough blood. Elevate the unconscious person's feet or lower the head below the height of the heart. Make the victim warm to prevent shock. Loss of consciousness may result from a variety of causes, including head injury and epilepsy. If the victim is breathing, provide comfort until medical help arrives. If the victim is not breathing, administer artificial respiration.

Poisoning. A poisonous substance introduced into the body causes symptoms such as nausea, cramps, and vomiting. First off, prevent further poisoning, such as by removing the victim from a toxic environment. Next, identify the poison, for example, by asking the victim to name it or look for suspicious containers or call the nearest poison control center. Knowing the poison determines the appropriate treatment. Unless instructed to do so by the poison control center or medical professional, emergency treatment does not include giving the victim anything to eat or drink, nor inducing the victim to vomit.

Drug Overdose. Drug overdose is difficult to diagnose because the symptoms vary widely and often appear connected to an illness or injury. Symptoms include dilated or contracted pupils, vomiting, difficulty in breathing, hallucinations, and in severe cases unconsciousness and slow, deep breathing.

Burn. First-response actions are: remove the source of the burn as quickly as possible; immediately cool the burn with cold water; on less serious burns apply a clean, cold wet towel or dressing to ease pain and protect against contamination; treat a chemical burn by continuously bathing it with running water for at least 20 minutes; do not use wet dressings and ointments; apply dry, sterile dressings held in place by bandages; and obtain prompt medical attention.

Electric Shock. Contact with electrical current is often fatal. Do not touch the victim's body before the source of the shock is turned off. If the victim has stopped breathing and has no pulse, administer CPR.

Figure 16-9 Information of this nature can be used as a training aid or job tool.

Heat Exhaustion. Exposure to excessive heat depletes body fluids and body salts. Symptoms include pale and clammy skin, heavy perspiration, weak pulse, shallow breathing, headache, and vomiting. A victim should rest in a cool area with feet elevated. Further cooling can be achieved with cool water compresses and a fan. Fever-reducing medication should not be used. A victim may feel nauseous at first, but after resting for a period, may be able to sip minimally salty water or an electrolyte solution to replenish lost salt.

Bone Fracture. Great pain, an inability to move the affected part, a deformed appearance, and pain or tenderness at a specific point indicate a fracture. Do not straighten or move a broken limb until medical help arrives. If a person is found with the head or body in an unnatural position, a fracture of the spinal column is a possibility. Do not attempt to straighten or move the injured person's body because of the chance of permanent paralysis or death.

Figure 16-9 *continued*

3. Summons emergency medical assistance if the victim does not respond.
4. Tilts the victim's head back, lifts the chin up, and looks into the victim's mouth to see if the airway is blocked.
5. If blockage is present, removes it by hand or use of the Heimlich Maneuver (abdominal thrusts).
6. Goes back to the second step if the victim does not revive.

Breathing: In the second phase, the rescuer

1. Places a pocket mask on his/her face to protect against exposure to infectious agents.
2. Positions his/her cheek close to the victim's nose and mouth and faces the victim's chest.
3. Looks, listens, and feels for breathing (5 to 10 seconds).
4. If the victim is not breathing, pinches the victim's nose closed and gives two full breaths into the victim's mouth.
5. If the breaths won't go in, repositions the victim's head and gives two more breaths.
6. If the airway appears to be blocked, performs the Heimlich Maneuver.

Circulation: In the third phase, the rescuer

1. Checks for carotid pulse by feeling the carotid artery at the side of the victim's neck for 5 to 10 seconds.
2. If a pulse is detected but the victim is not breathing, breathes into the victim's mouth at a rate of one breath every five seconds.
3. Checks again for carotid pulse and if a pulse is not detected begins chest compressions.
4. Gives chest compressions by placing the heel of one hand on the lower part of the victim's sternum and with the other hand directly on top of first hand pressing the sternum to a depth of 1.5 to 2 inches and immediately releasing.
5. Performs 15 compressions at a rate of 80 to 100 per minute.

6. At the end of each minute, checks the victim's pulse.
7. Continues the compressions until a pulse is restored or emergency medical assistance has arrived.

If it appears that the victim has suffered cardiac arrest, defibrillation is administered.

Defibrillation

Defibrillation is a process by which an electronic device delivers an electric shock to the heart. This helps reestablish normal contraction rhythms in a heart having dangerous arrhythmia or in cardiac arrest. The automated external defibrillator (AED) is a portable device for administering the electric shock [2].

An AED is put into action when CPR used alone fails to revive an unconscious or nonresponsive person. During the AED process, CPR is given when the AED is attached to the victim.

The AED Protocol

The AED protocol has seven steps.

- *Step 1:* If the victim has no pulse and is not breathing or is breathing abnormally, the rescuer goes to Step 2.
- *Step 2:* The rescuer summons emergency medical assistance or makes sure that it has been done, and then gets the AED to the scene.
- *Step 3:* The rescuer opens the victim's airway and checks for breathing. If there is no breathing or breathing appears abnormal, the rescuer gives the victim two slow breaths.
- *Step 4:* The rescuer checks for pulse. If there is no pulse, the rescuer turns on the AED. A second rescuer administers CPR until the AED is attached.
- *Step 5:* The AED is attached by placing one electrode pad on the upper right chest and the other pad on the lower left chest.
- *Step 6:* The rescuer makes sure no one is touching the victim. He/she presses the "Analyze" button on the AED.
  - If the AED indicates that the victim does not need to be shocked, the rescuer checks for pulse again. If there is no pulse, CPR is resumed (ventilations and chest compressions) for one minute and the pulse is checked again. If pulse is still not restored, the rescuer makes sure no one is touching the victim and presses the "Analyze" button.
  - This sequence of CPR and analysis continues until medical help arrives or until the AED indicates "Shock Advised." When shock is advised, the rescuer goes to Step 7.

- *Step 7:* The rescuer makes sure no one is touching the victim and presses the "Shock" button.
  - If the victim's pulse is restored, the process ends.
  - If the victim does not revive, the rescuer analyzes and administers a second shock.
  - If the victim does not revive, the rescuer analyzes and administers a third shock.
  - If the victim still has no pulse after three shocks, the rescuer performs CPR (ventilations and chest compressions) for one minute.
  - If there still is no pulse, the rescuer continues to give sets of three quick shocks, interspersed with one minute of CPR. This is done until the AED prompts that no shock is advised.

The AED process is not as complicated as it sounds. The AED coaches the rescuer with visual and/or audio prompts.

Exposure to AIDS and Hepatitis B

The acquired immune deficiency syndrome (AIDS) and hepatitis B diseases merit serious worry to providers of first aid, CPR, and defibrillation. The chief concerns are infection through contact with blood and other body fluids. Persons at a high-risk level are security officers with first-response duties.

Because AIDS and hepatitis B infections occur in the workplace the Occupational Safety and Health Administration (OSHA) has developed recommended practices to protect against exposure. The practices include precautions for mouth-to-mouth contact and contact with blood and other body fluids.

AIDS is a blood-borne and sexually transmitted disease that invades the body, damages the immune system, and allows other infectious agents to invade the body. AIDS is spread primarily by blood and semen.

Symptoms: The usual symptoms of acute hepatitis B infections are flu-like and include fatigue, mild fever, muscle and joint aches, nausea, vomiting, abdominal pain, diarrhea, and jaundice. A severe hepatitis B virus (HBV) infection may be fatal. It is also preventable by the administration of a vaccine. The vaccine is recommended for persons at risk of infection, including security officers and other first responders.

Protective equipment: Protective equipment and devices must be on hand for immediate use. They consist of the following:

- Gloves when blood, blood products, or body fluids may be touched
- Gowns, masks, and eye protectors when there is a potential for splashing of blood or body fluids
- Pocket masks, resuscitation bags, or other ventilation devices when CPR is administered

Practices: Prudent practices for security officer protection include the following.

- Wearing protective gear such as pocket mask and gloves
- Cleaning up blood spills immediately with detergent, water, and household bleach diluted at 1 to 10 parts of water.
- Washing hands thoroughly after removing protective gear and immediately after contact with blood or body fluids.
- Informing co-workers and others concerning modes of transmission and prevention of infection. The key points are
  - Get a vaccination.
  - Treat all blood and body fluids as potentially infectious.
  - Obtain medical evaluation following an exposure incident.

Exposure incident: The CSO or other responsible manager prepares a post-exposure report documenting details of the incident (i.e., how the incident occurred, persons exposed, and the name of the source individual). An exposure incident is one that results from the performance of a job duty such as a security officer giving first aid or administering CPR to an injured or ill person. Exposure means contact between the infectious agent (blood or body fluid) and an eye, mouth, or other mucous membrane and non-intact skin.

The source individual's blood should be tested for infection as soon as possible and after consent is obtained. If consent is not obtained, that fact should be documented. When the source individual is already known to be infected, testing need not be repeated. Results of the source individual's testing should be made available to the exposed employee, and the employee informed of applicable laws and regulations concerning the identity of the source individual.

The General Duty Clause of the OSHA Act requires employers to provide employment and a place of employment free from recognized hazards. Employers must comply with OSHA standards or state standards. States with occupational safety and health programs embrace comparable standards.

NATURAL DISASTERS

A natural disaster, in the context used here, is an event that causes death, injury, and significant property damage. The common natural disasters most dreaded by business organizations, and therefore anticipated by their planners, are floods, earthquakes, hurricanes, and tornadoes.

Act of God

A natural disaster is sometimes called an Act of God because it is an occurrence not caused by human intervention or negligence. As a point of law, it is ordinarily held that a person or entity cannot be charged with responsibility

---

Key Points in Disaster Preparation

Contact the local offices of the Federal Emergency Management Agency and Civil Defense to assure that your organization's disaster emergency plans are in harmony with the local government's comprehensive disaster plans. A key point is the emergency communications network.

Confirm that insurance coverage is adequate and in effect, that current photographs of insured property are on file, and that any specifications required by your insurance policy have been met and are confirmed in writing.

Confirm that response-related supplies and materials are on hand or will be available when needed.

Communicate response procedures with employees, contractors, customers, and other interested parties.

Conduct drills and practice scenarios.

Concentrate on disasters that are likely.

If located in a multiple-occupancy facility, communicate plans and procedures to co-tenants.

Prepare detailed maps depicting key items such as utility equipment, power shutoff points, sources of auxiliary power, potential hazard areas, emergency equipment and supplies, communication equipment, first aid stations, and escape routes. Prepare process diagrams and decision trees.

Designate and equip a command and control center at the facility and a back-up location.

If computer operations are critical to the business, set up an alternate site and make arrangements for the transfer and storage of back-up data.

Ensure that responders understand the operational processes, physical layout, and equipment.

Assign to employees specific responsibilities for areas and operations of the facility. Designate teams and make them responsible to key people.

Conduct and record frequent inspections, correct problems immediately, and involve your insurance agent.

Prepare and maintain disaster preparedness gear. Items can consist of radios, walkie-talkies, batteries, first aid supplies and equipment, flashlights, bullhorns, lumber, portable generators, special clothing, oxygen tanks, defibrillators, rope, hand tools, and repair supplies.

Develop a method for cascading information to employees.

Figure 16-10 The CSO can compare these points against the organization's disaster plans and procedures.

for the injuries or losses resulting from an Act of God. For example, a failure to complete a construction schedule on the date agreed because a lightning bolt knocked out a key piece of construction equipment does not create a liability. With or without liability, a company's management has to be prepared. Figure 16-10 contains points worth considering.

Natural Disaster Planning

The CSO is one of several persons charged by management to plan and prepare for natural disaster. The organization's planning group, in which the CSO is expected to play a key role, will invariably network with external agencies among which is the Federal Emergency Management Agency (FEMA). An independent agency of the U.S. government, FEMA is concerned with earthquake hazard reduction, dam safety, natural and nuclear disaster warning systems, and the consequences of terrorist incidents. FEMA's main functions are to anticipate, prepare for, and respond to major civil emergencies by deploying civil defense systems and other available resources.

Partner agencies of FEMA at the local level are civil defense and emergency management offices. The main goal of FEMA and local agencies is to protect lives, property, and the means of economic production threatened by large-scale emergencies. Civil defense includes the organization and training of volunteers, maintaining warning systems, providing shelters, stockpiling food and medicine, firefighting, performing rescue operations, removing wreckage, and restoring order. The main responsibility for peacetime civil defense lies with each state government. A civil defense organization that is part of a local branch of government can be a business organization's most important partner in preparing for and responding to large-scale disasters.

A local emergency management office typically operates a command and control center, tracks impending disasters (e.g., hurricanes and rising floodwaters), and communicates conditions to first-responder agencies.

Severe Windstorm

The most common form of natural disaster is the severe windstorm, and four in this category stand out. First is the tornado, a violent storm (often local) with whirling winds of speed that can reach 200 to 400 miles per hour. It appears as a rotating, funnel-shaped cloud extending toward the ground from the base of a thundercloud. Next is the severe thunderstorm, which frequently appears with lightning, damaging winds of greater than 50 miles per hour, hail three quarters of an inch or more in diameter, and heavy rain. A tropical storm has winds near the center greater than 38 miles per hour (33 knots) but less than 74 miles per hour (64 knots). A hurricane is a violent storm originating over tropical waters with winds near its center reaching 74 miles per hour (64 knots) and higher.

In preparing for a severe weather incident it can help to get everyone working from the "same sheet of music." Being familiar with the terms shown in Figure 16-11 can be helpful.

Severe windstorm plan: Preparedness for a severe windstorm starts with a plan that assigns to specific persons and groups specific responsibilities. The essence of the plan is to ensure the safety of employees and prevent loss and damage to physical assets. Plan preparation is a collaborative effort, usually involving representatives from external affairs, human resources, information technology, legal, safety, telecommunications, property management, and security.

Severe Weather Terms of Reference

Hurricane Advisory. Information about where the tropical storm or hurricane is located, how intense it is, where it is moving, and what precautions should be taken.

Hurricane Watch. Information issued when a tropical storm or hurricane becomes a threat to the coastal area. It indicates that the storm is near enough that everyone in the affected area should listen for advisories and be ready to take precautionary action.

Tornado Watch. An announcement that conditions are favorable to the possibility of tornadoes.

Tornado Warning. An announcement indicating that a tornado has actually been sighted in the area, or is indicated by radar.

Flash Flood Watch. An announcement that conditions are favorable for flash floods and rapidly rising waters.

Flash Flood Warning. A warning that conditions exist or are imminent for flash floods.

Severe Thunderstorm Watch. An announcement indicating the possibility of tornadoes, thunderstorms, frequent lightning, hail, and winds of greater than 75 mph.

Figure 16-11 Defining terms facilitates understanding of the plan.

A severe windstorm plan addresses a number of preparation and response actions. Persons designated in the plan

- Identify, obtain, and keep in readiness the equipment, supplies, and materials required for response. Perishable supplies can be procured when an approaching storm is detected.
- Establish trigger points for initiating response actions, such as shutting down computers, installing window shields, moving valuable equipment to interior space, and sending employees home.
- Establish communication methods for persons who are assigned response duties.
- Form and train an emergency response team (ERT).
- Inform employees concerning response procedures and their individual responsibilities.

Storm phases: With the exception of a tornado, severe windstorms are amenable to timely detection and tracking. In the case of a hurricane, the development of which is largely predictable, alert levels can be applied. The following four levels are common.

- Phase I goes into effect when a developing hurricane has the potential to strike company premises. The plan at this point may direct the ERT to begin monitoring storm reports provided the U.S. Weather Service or a commercial severe weather reporting service. The reports project the potential impact of the hurricane and its magnitude and direction.
- Phase II becomes effective when the hurricane develops in or enters a 200-mile radius of company premises. The ERT may begin to forward storm reports to the company's executive team at a frequency of about every two hours.

- Phase III begins when winds ahead of the hurricane are within 48 hours of premises. The ERT may start forwarding storm reports to the executive team every hour. At this juncture, the executive team may elect to initiate a shutdown of company operations, partially or fully.
- Phase IV starts when winds ahead of the storm are within 24 hours of the premises. When this phase is reached, the plan obliges the executive team to be ready to give a shutdown order.

Emergency response team (ERT):   The members of the severe windstorm planning group often do double duty (i.e., develop the plan and serve on the ERT). The CSO's role typically includes serving as a point of contact with emergency responders external to the organization (e.g., representatives of police, fire, ambulance, and medical services) and directing or monitoring security officers in the performance of their response tasks. An organization not having an emergency response center from which to operate may choose to use the security control center for that purpose. If so, the security officers receive and disseminate storm reports, keep key responders informed, make general announcements to employees, and maintain an event log. At a minimum, security officers would be required to help in "storm-proofing" the building exteriors, moving valuable equipment to predesignated safe havens, and administering emergency medical assistance if needed.

Security control center: A security control center that doubles as a command and control facility in severe windstorms can serve also as a facility for monitoring local weather conditions 24 hours per day, year round. Monitoring can be done by a weather alert scanner locked onto the National Weather Service (NWS) broadcast frequency. A weather alert scanner receives and announces NWS alerts automatically, without the need for human intervention. Alerts received at the security control center are forwarded to designated persons such as the leader of the ERT and the senior executive present.

Command and control: The ERT leader initiates actions commensurate to phases described in the severe windstorm plan. These can include the following.

- Removing loose items from the tops of desks, credenzas, cabinets, shelves, and window ledges
- Putting the blinds down and turning slats to shut position
- Securing company records and locking file cabinets
- Covering open shelves with plastic
- Moving artwork and personal items to interior space
- Disconnecting electrical office equipment
- Moving computer hardware away from windows to interior spaces

The alerts sent from the security control center to the senior executive present can serve as prompts to a decision to shut down operations and send employees home. If the storm moves so quickly that a release of employees places

---

Preparing for a Severe Windstorm

Review your severe windstorm plan and update it appropriately. Ensure that
    Critical assets are covered by the plan.
    Shutdown procedures are correct and understood.
    Back-up equipment is in place.
    Notification lists are current.
    Safe-haven areas are ready to accommodate employees.
    Protected storage space is ready to receive valuable assets and critical business records.
    An alternate operating location, such as a data processing hot site, is ready.
    Agreements are in place with external emergency response agencies, such as an ambulance service, and with contractors on retainer for services such as boarding up doors and windows and making repairs during and after a windstorm.
    Emergency supplies, materials, and tools are on hand.
Ensure that plan responders understand their roles and are ready.
Verify that the designated weather watcher is on alert and prepared to issue alerts and advisories.
Remind senior management of pre-determined checkpoints that require decisions such as sending employees home and boarding up windows.
Remind operational managers of their responsibilities under the severe windstorm plan.

Figure 16-12 A checklist of this type can be a valuable readiness aid.

them in danger, the employees are informed through the public address system as follows

- Close all doors to exterior offices.
- Move quickly to the core of the building for shelter (i.e., the centermost corridors and rooms).
- Sit down and put heads between knees, if conditions warrant.
- Remain in a safe area until directed otherwise.

If the decision to shut down is made during non-business hours (as would be the case if the storm arrived during the night), an announcement might be aired on local radio and television stations or given by a tape-recorded message on a company phone line. Well before making a shut-down decision, management has to at least make preparations. A checklist, such as that shown in Figure 16-12, can be useful.

Anticipating and preparing to respond to Acts of God start early and they consider potential effects such as high winds on roofs, flood waters at ground level, and earthquake tremors on support beams. A rapid response working from a carefully prepared plan can greatly limit loss.

NOTES

1. John J. Fay, *Model Security Policies, Plans, and Procedures*, pp. 163–166, Boston: Butterworth-Heinemann, 1999.

2. More on this topic can be found in "Sudden Cardiac Arrest," National Center for Early Defibrillation, 2004, at *www.early-defib.org*.

17. Information Security

My sources are unreliable but their information is fascinating.
—Ashleigh Brilliant

INFORMATION IS EXPANSIVE

Unlike other business resources, information is expansive, with limits imposable only by time and the thinking capabilities of humans. Information may age, but it tends not to diminish. Rather, it tends to accumulate. Information is compressible and transportable at very high speeds, and can impart advantages to the holder. Many work endeavors—such as research and development, education, publishing, and marketing—are very highly dependent on information.

INFORMATION REQUIRES BARRIERS

In ancient times the walled city was a human's way of protecting self and property. Walls were a key defense against armies, they kept roving bands of robbers at bay, and at night (when the gate was closed) they blocked the escape of criminals. After the sack of Rome, walls became a way of life. During the next thousand years, which we call the Middle Ages, people and their property found refuge behind walls. It was not until the Renaissance brought a period of renewed interest in art, science, and commerce that people began to venture out from their walled cities.

The ancient walled city is analogous to the modern business corporation. Starting in the middle of the last century, when computers began to play a commanding role in processing and storing information, a businessperson could feel safe because information assets were behind electronic barriers inside centrally controlled equipment located within the protected confines of a computer room—sort of like a city with three walls. Then came the "computer Renaissance." Many companies moved from a centrally based approach to a system of widely dispersed personal computers, which we call a LAN (local-area network).

In a typical LAN, nearly every employee has a PC at his or her workstation, many have company-owned PCs at home, and some employees carry portables everywhere they go. Instead of holding information at one central location, in the custody of a handful of trusted technicians, information is made available to nearly every employee. In companies where this is the case, information assets have moved out from behind protective barriers.

INFORMATION IS COSTLY AND IMPORTANT

Information is deserving of protection for at least two reasons: (1) it is costly to acquire and maintain and (2) it is important to the success of the business enterprise. Information fuels a business and has value in much the same sense that people, physical property, and financial assets have value. Information an enterprise assembles for making a major business decision or for developing a new product may cost many millions of dollars and be absolutely essential to viability. For example, an oil exploration company can easily spend in excess of a hundred million dollars just to get to a point that allows a sensible decision to be made about where to place the drill bit. If the decision proves correct, oil-producing operations are assured and the company stands a good chance of recouping its investment many times over.

INFORMATION IS COVETED

And, like anything of value, information is coveted. When something has value, count on the certainty that someone will be looking for an opportunity to take it away. The bad guys are not thugs and common sneak thieves; they are intelligent, clever, and ruthless people such as the professional spy who steals information without the owner ever knowing it, the executive who defects to a competitor carrying a briefcase full of proprietary secrets, or the disaffected scientist who sells R&D data.

INFORMATION HAS A LIMITED LIFE

Efforts to safeguard information assets in an open environment are made difficult by a host of realities. Chief among these is a recognition that a piece of information has a limited life (i.e., that at some point in time, which is usually sooner than later, the information will lose all or most of its value). Within the time frame of value, the owner of the information will want to extract from it the maximum worth possible. This means making the information available to users whose special talents can exploit it. Often the users of the information are numerous and are spread across a global landscape. In these circumstances, the information has been duplicated repeatedly and transmitted widely by a variety of communications media. During the time information is in a state of flux, the opportunities for compromise are many and diverse. Worse still, when compromise occurs it is difficult, if not impossible, to detect.

INFORMATION IS DIFFICULT TO PROTECT

Problems in protection are compounded when a company finds it necessary to share its information with outsiders, such as joint venture partners and contractors. As an example, a joint venture's operational information, which is routinely available to all partners, may be of a nature that if released to the public would affect stock prices, a result that might be good for some partners but not for other partners. When sharing information with contractors, two examples of exposures stand out. First is the risk that sensitive information entrusted to the contractor will leak out, a likelihood that increases when the contractor works for competitors. The second type of exposure is present when an outsourcing arrangement puts the contractor in control of a company's critical business data or of the systems that massage the data. In a like sense, the arrangement called partnering, which brings a company and a vendor into a mutually rewarding relationship, can result in both organizations sharing each other's sensitive business data.

INFORMATION IS VOLUMINOUS

Another reality is that companies are dealing in larger volumes of information than ever before. Great amounts of raw data are needed to make fully developed analyses, and the judgments that flow from them produce not just a favored recommendation but a range of options, each with its own set of variables and predicted outcomes. Of even greater moment is the reality that the criticality of information is increasingly on the rise. Not only is there more information but it is high-impact information.

Factor in the reality that the means of communication are changing. The fax machine, cellular telephone, electronic mail, modem, and voice answering device are examples of changes in the way companies communicate. All of these have serious security vulnerabilities. The task of protecting information is daunting to say the least.

OPERATIONS SECURITY (OPSEC)

Operations Security (OPSEC) is the name of a program initiated and used for the most part by the Department of Defense (DoD). Due mainly to the terrorist threat, the program moved into high gear and is now generating a high degree of interest on the part of security professionals in the private sector. An OPSEC program differs from an information security program.

Its focus is on the concealment of sensitive activities as opposed to the protection of sensitive information. OPSEC is the process of

- Denying to potential adversaries information about DoD capabilities and/or intentions by identifying, controlling, and protecting evidence of plans and practices related to sensitive activities.
- Analyzing unfriendly attempts to penetrate the protective shield surrounding sensitive information.
- Concealing in-house activities that if known to an adversary would have a detrimental effect on national defense.
- Identifying seemingly innocuous information exposures that if collected by an adversary over time would have a detrimental effect on national defense.
- Finding and eliminating vulnerabilities [1].

The attractiveness of OPSEC to CSOs is a "get tough" approach. For the business organization it means having strict information security rules, enforcing the rules and meting out punishment for violations, and making referrals to the criminal justice system for egregious offenses. The OPSEC approach can be harnessed to three business-survival imperatives:

- Prevent loss or compromise of privately owned technology.
- Prevent business competitors from learning the intentions of the organization.
- Prevent terrorist groups from characterizing the organization's most critical assets and assessing weaknesses in the protection of them.

SENSITIVE INFORMATION

Security professionals use the term *sensitive* when referring to information that has value and is protected. The main forms of sensitive information are

- Proprietary business and technical information.
- Personal data concerning applicants, employees, and former employees.
- Proprietary information owned by partners and obtained through an agreement.

Access to or knowledge of sensitive information is based on a need-to-know connection to job tasks. An employee whose job is to invoice vendors does not need to know the CEOs plan to spin off a subsidiary. Jobs and groups of jobs are compartmental by nature. Confining sensitive information to compartments helps prevent information leaks.

Information protection is also afforded by avoiding careless talk outside the compartment, being careful on the telephone and in sending e-mail messages, placing sensitive information in secure containers when not in use, and ensuring that sensitive documents are turned over or distributed to authorized persons only.

Classification

Organizations assign classifications to their sensitive information. The usual classification model is a three-tiered hierarchy. The names assigned to the tiers vary from organization to organization and include SECRET, RESTRICTED, CONFIDENTIAL, PRIVATE, and PERSONAL. The names are sometimes emphasized with preceding terms so that they appear, for example, as TOP SECRET or HIGHLY CONFIDENTIAL. For the purpose of discussion here, the three tiers from top to bottom are SECRET, RESTRICTED, and PRIVATE.

SECRET: This is information the unauthorized disclosure of which could cause serious damage to the organization's business. Its use and access to it are strictly limited. Examples include the following:

- Trade secrets
- Plans to merge, divest, acquire, sell, or reorganize
- Information that could affect the price of shares
- Information with high political or legal sensitivity
- Information prejudicial to the interests or reputation of the organization

RESTRICTED: This is information of such value or sensitivity that its unauthorized disclosure could have a substantially detrimental effect on the organization's business. Examples include the following:

- Marketing strategies
- Customer files
- Agreements and contracts
- Contentious or litigable matters

PRIVATE: This is information relating to employees. Examples include the following:

- Salaries, bonuses, and wages
- Health and medical matters
- Disciplinary actions
- Job performance

For convenience, sensitive information can be referred to in a project context (e.g., a project to construct a new building might be called Project Phoenix, and information related to that endeavor might be called Project Phoenix information). In this example, only certain types of information, such as financial data, are classified. Another project might be so hush-hush that all information relating to it is classified.

Sensitive information can also be regarded as falling under the "ownership" of a particular employee such as the originator, the person who assigned a classification to it, or the person who holds primary responsibility for putting the information to work. Ownership carries with it a responsibility to change or remove the classification as needed. (Ownership does not mean that an employee has rights to the information.)

An important task of the CSO is to learn which information is sensitive and which is not. The CSO has to know which is which because classification is assigned to sensitive information only. The classification program will collapse of its own weight if overburdened. If all of an organization's information was declared sensitive there would be no need for classification, and to the extent that nonsensitive information is given a classification the effectiveness of the classification program is diminished.

The CSO's task of separating the sensitive from nonsensitive cannot be done without input from managers and supervisors. This is the case because the CSO, like all other employees, has access to sensitive information on a need-to-know basis. The CSO does not need to know where a drill bit is to be placed, only that a body of information exists concerning drilling. Using the three-tiered matrix discussed earlier, the manager or supervisor has decided if classification is merited, and if so has selected the appropriate classification level. The CSO merely verifies that the process was followed and that the body of information still merits protection.

A CSO will think what would happen if particular information was to fall into unfriendly hands. A number of possible scenarios can lead the thinking process to an identification of what should be protected, the adversaries, the probable nature of attempts by adversaries to acquire the information, the exposures of the information to the hypothesized attempts, and an estimate in dollars of the value of the information [3].

Marking

Classified information (regardless of form) is marked, distributed, copied, mailed, transported, stored, and destroyed in accordance with established procedures. The procedure for marking a document might require every page to bear in the top right-hand corner the word *RESTRICTED*, stamped in uppercase letters, red in color, and not smaller in height than one-half inch and not taller than one inch.

Awareness

The operation of an awareness program is within the purview of the CSO. The program is continuous, uses many forums, reaches out to employees at all levels, and emphasizes the duty of everyone to protect the organization's sensitive information. An awareness program sometimes includes an orientation session before an employee is granted access to classified information, one or more refresher sessions throughout the duration of the employee's access, and a debriefing at the time the employee's access is removed. These sessions, which are ordinarily conducted by the employee's supervisor, can include the signed acknowledgments by the employee and warnings as to personal consequences of violations.

The awareness program is also directed at preventing careless talk and release of details about plans, strategies, and other sensitive matters. Prior approval may be required when an organizational matter is to be discussed by an employee in a speech, article, or presentation.

Clean Desk Policy

A clean desk policy is the name given to a work rule that requires employees to

- Place classified materials under lock and key when not in use. Materials of chief concern are classified correspondence, maps, photos, diskettes, and compact disks.
- Not leave keys unattended or hidden.
- Destroy unneeded classified materials.
- Switch off, disconnect, or lock PCs when not in use.

Confidentiality Agreement

This safeguard is intended to prevent unauthorized disclosure of classified information by employees, consultants, contractors, and other outside parties that have business ties to the organization. Confidentiality agreements can be crafted to apply to sensitive information generally or to certain forms of information specifically.

Noncompetition Agreement

A noncompetition agreement (see Figure 17-1) grants protection to an employer from the unauthorized use of the employer's intellectual property by a current or former employee. It typically incorporates one or more of the following three basic conditions.

- Restrictions on competition by departing employees
- Definitions of what constitutes property that the employer can legally protect from use by others
- Requirements that employees are obligated to cooperate with the employer in efforts to protect its intellectual property

Proprietary Information

Proprietary information is information owned by a company or entrusted to it that has not been disclosed publicly and has value. Information is considered

NON-DISCLOSURE AGREEMENT

Effective Date: _____

Participant: _____

In order to protect certain confidential information that may be disclosed by Discloser ("DISCLOSER") to the "Participant" above, they agree that:

1. The confidential information disclosed under this Agreement is described as:_____
   _____
   _____

2. The Participant shall use the confidential information received under this Agreement for the purpose of: ____
   _____

3. The Participant shall protect the disclosed confidential information by using the same degree of care, but no less than a reasonable degree of care, to prevent the unauthorized use, dissemination, or publication of the confidential information as the Participant uses to protect its own confidential information of a like nature.

4. The Participant shall have a duty to protect only that confidential information which is (a) disclosed by DISCLOSER in writing and marked as confidential at the time of disclosure, or which is (b) disclosed by DISCLOSER in any other manner and is identified as confidential at the time of the disclosure and is also summarized and designated as confidential in a written memorandum delivered to the Participant within 30 days of the disclosure.

5. This Agreement imposes no obligation upon the Participant with respect to confidential information that becomes a matter of public knowledge through no fault of the Participant.

6. The Participant does not acquire intellectual property rights under this Agreement except the limited right of use set out in paragraph 2 above.

7. DISCLOSER makes no representation or warranty that any product or business plans disclosed to the Participant will be marketed or carried out as disclosed, or at all. Any actions taken by the Participant in response to the disclosure of confidential information by DISCLOSER shall be solely at its risk.

8. The Participant acknowledges and agrees that the confidential information is provided on an AS IS basis.

   DISCLOSER MAKES NO WARRANTIES, EXPRESS OR IMPLIED, WITH RESPECT TO THE CONFIDENTIAL INFORMATION AND HEREBY EXPRESSLY DISCLAIMS ANY AND ALL IMPLIED WARRANTIES OF MERCHANTABILITY AND FITNESS FOR A PARTICULAR PURPOSE. IN NO EVENT SHALL DISCLOSER BE LIABLE FOR ANY DIRECT, INDIRECT, SPECIAL, OR CONSEQUENTIAL DAMAGES IN CONNECTION WITH OR ARISING OUT OF THE PERFORMANCE OR USE OF ANY PORTION OF THE CONFIDENTIAL INFORMATION.

9. Upon DISCLOSER's written request, the Participant shall return to DISCLOSER or destroy all written material or electronic media and the Participant shall deliver to DISCLOSER a written statement signed by the Participant certifying same within 5 days.

10. The parties do not intend that any agency or partnership relationship be created between them by this Agreement.

11. All additions or modifications to this Agreement must be made in writing and must be signed by both parties.

12. This Agreement is made under and shall be construed according to the laws of the State of Massachusetts.

DISCLOSER

_____

Authorized Signature

_____

Name

_____

Title

PARTICIPANT

_____

Authorized Signature

_____

Name

_____

Title

_____

Address

Figure 17-1 This is an example of an agreement between a "discloser" (the owner of confidential information) and a "participant" (such as a partner, contractor, or vendor).

proprietary when

- It is not readily accessible to others.
- It was created by the owner through the expenditure of considerable resources.
- The owner actively protects the information from disclosure [2].

Very critical forms of proprietary information are intellectual properties. Most countries recognize and grant varying degrees of protection to four intellectual property rights: patents, trademarks, copyrights, and trade secrets.

Patents

These are grants issued by a national government conferring the right to exclude others from making, using, or selling the invention within that country. Patents may be given for new products or processes. Violations of patent rights are known as infringement or piracy.

Trademarks

These are words, names, symbols, devices, or combinations thereof used by manufacturers or merchants to differentiate their goods and distinguish them from products that are manufactured or sold by others. Counterfeiting and infringement constitute violations of trademark rights.

Copyrights

These are protections given by a national government to creators of original literary, dramatic, musical, and certain other intellectual works. The owner of a copyright has the exclusive right to reproduce the copyrighted work, prepare derivative works based on it, distribute copies, and perform or display it publicly. Copyright violations are also known as infringement and piracy.

Trade Secrets

These can be formulas, patterns, compilations, programs, devices, methods, techniques, and processes that derive economic value from not being generally known and not ascertainable except by illegal means. A trade secret violation in the vocabulary of the law is a misappropriation resulting from improper acquisition or disclosure. The key elements in a trade secret are the owner's maintenance of confidentiality, limited distribution, and the absence of a patent.

The Paris Convention is the primary treaty for the protection of trademarks, patents, trade names, utility models, and industrial designs. Established in 1883, the convention is the oldest of the international bodies concerned with the protection of intellectual properties. It is based on reciprocity; that is, it grants the same protections to member states as those granted to its own nationals, and provides equal access for foreigners to local courts to pursue infringement remedies [4].

DATA PROTECTION

Data are a valuable corporate asset. Consider the following examples.

- In the minerals extraction industry, finding ores depends on data. It is no exaggeration to say that before a single shovel is placed into the ground, hundreds of millions of dollars will have been spent collecting and interpreting seismic and other scientific data.
- Hotels routinely build patron-oriented information databases that enable them to provide personalized service.
- Retailers collect data to help their managers monitor the flow of products moving from manufacturing plants to warehouses, stores, and ultimately purchasers. The process makes sure that sellable items are on the shelves in the right stores, at the right time, and in the right quantities.
- Transportation firms routinely track movement of packages, even to the extent of allowing customers to access the information.
- Manufacturers have refined data-dependent "just in time" techniques to ensure that source materials reach the beginning of the production line not a day sooner or later than required and that the final products leave the plant already sold.

Today's successful organizations are very competent at collecting and making good use of data. Only a few, however, are fully competent in protecting their data assets.

Data and Dollars

Data assets are growing in value and volume. In some circles information moves from owner to owner, not unlike the way money moves in financial markets. Three dynamics seem to be at play: knowledge has become an economic resource, information technology is expanding, and the number of people familiar with information technology is growing by leaps and bounds.

Emergence of knowledge as an economic resource: Production in the United States is moving away from a dependence on capital, natural resources, and blue-collar labor. One hundred years ago, the Nation's wealth derived from oil, coal, minerals, ores, and farmlands. Today's wealth derives from the creation and use of knowledge, and the raw materials that create knowledge are in the form of data.

Expansion of information technology: A second dynamic is information technology. New computer hardware and software come on line every day in dazzling arrays. All functions and subfunctions of business are addressed

E-Mail Tips

Be suspicious of unexpected messages, especially those with a teasing subject header.
Be leery of attachments. If in doubt, don't open.
Don't answer SPAM or forward chain letter messages.
Don't use vacation messages that can tip off criminal opportunists.
Close your e-mail application when it is not in use.
Save sensitive messages in a secure folder.
Choose a hard-to-guess e-mail password.

Figure 17-2 In e-mail use, even a small dose of prevention can have a large impact.

in the information technology marketplace. The Internet, company intranets, and multicompany extranets open doors wide for the collection and dissemination of huge volumes of information. Critical data, such as client lists and strategic plans, are moved around the globe in the blink of an eye by e-mail, fax, and cellular phone (see Figure 17-2) .

Emergence of an information worker class: A third dynamic is the increasing ability of the average employee to work competently and comfortably with data. Add to this a very large and rapidly growing new employee class called information workers. In some companies, the entire workforce consists of people who work only with data.

Data Use and Protection

Data protection is a challenge not easily met. For example, how does an organization balance the need to use data and the need to protect it from harmful disclosure? The clash between use and protection is problematic. An operations manager will consider data an essential resource to be fully exploited, therefore requiring it to be accessible at all times. He/she will say, "If data can't be used, our bottom line suffers." The manager is right; the value of the data is directly related to its use.

The CSO may agree with the operations manager but feel compelled to point out: "If our data are damaged, lost or compromised, the company may fail." The CSO's concern appears valid in light of at least one study. An insurance company found that 40 percent of companies that experienced major data loss as the result of disaster (e.g., fire, flood, hurricane, and terrorist action) never resumed business operations and a third of the companies that initially recovered went out of business within two years.

Steps in protection: The CSO can enhance data protection by employing to following commonsense suggestions.

- Stay on top of the issue.
- Keep pace with data-related technology, not necessarily at the detail level but certainly at a level that permits a clear understanding of the risks.

- Look for countermeasures that take advantage of new techniques and leading edge technology.
- Maintain a frank and ongoing dialogue with data managers about risk avoidance, and don't be preachy or harp on a shortcoming unless you have a solution in mind.
- Spread the word among supervisory employees that data protection is their responsibility.

RISK ASSESSMENT

Organizations are increasingly reliant on automated and interconnected systems to perform key information-processing functions. The benefits of such systems are enormous yet they carry with them risks of data loss and damage, fraud, and disruption of productivity. Information systems have long been at risk from malicious actions, inadvertent user errors, and natural disasters. The risk rises relative to complexity, interconnectivity, and the accessibility of the systems to a larger number of individuals. Fueling the risk are the increased number and skills of hackers and the motivations that spur them.

Breakdowns

With grinding repetition, the news media report breakdowns in the security of automated systems. A recurring theme is the failure of the system's management to take a risk-based approach in determining what needs to be protected and how to go about it. The intelligent use of resources requires management to consider factors such as the value of the system at risk, the threats to it, its vulnerabilities, and the protective safeguards in place (see Figure 17-3).

Risk Assessment Process

Assessing risk is one step in a broad stairway of risk management activities. Other elements include establishing a central management focal point, implementing policies and procedures, promoting awareness, and monitoring and evaluating the effectiveness of controls. A risk assessment, whether pertaining to information or other type of asset, can provide decision makers with

- An understanding of events and circumstances that can negatively influence operations.
- Options for preventing and mitigating risks.

The risk management function is performed widely: mortgage bankers manage the risk of loan defaults, nuclear power plant engineers manage the risk of nuclear emissions, and pharmaceutical officials manage the risk of product contamination. As reliance on computer systems and electronic data has grown, loss of information has joined the list of business risks that merit

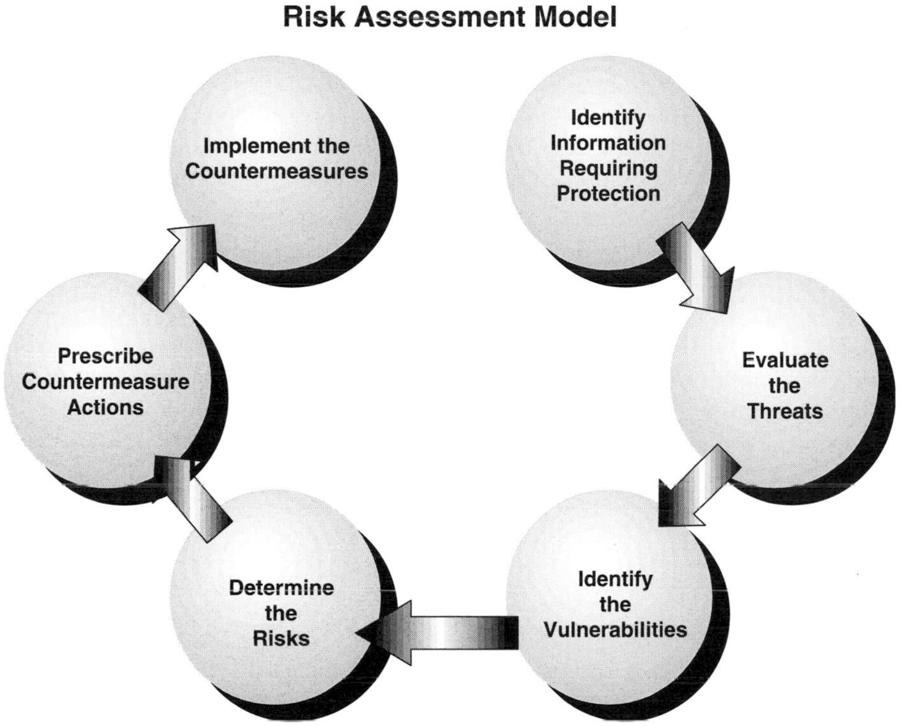

Risk Assessment Model

Figure 17-3 As is the case with other key assets, risk assessment applies to information.

careful management. Several key actions go into making an effective risk assessment.

- Obtain support from the top.
- Designate focal points.
- Build a consensus.
- Communicate.

Obtain support from the top: Senior management support helps ensure that

- Resources are made available to conduct risk assessment.
- Assessment activities and findings are taken seriously at lower levels.
- Resources are made available to implement changes recommended in the assessment.

Top-level support is evident when senior managers assist in determining the scope of the assessment and handpicking the key participants. Next is agreement with the assessment's findings and approval of an action plan. Finally, and most importantly, support is shown when senior management funds the action plan.

Designate focal points: A focal point is a person, a team, or a group of individuals charged with assessment tasks. A focal point will often possess expertise: the CSO is an expert in security, a planning group has expertise in planning, and the head of the information technology department understands the complexities of the information system. A focal point will sometimes be an employee who has been a champion of the very change that is needed to reduce risk. Very importantly, one or more focal points will be "big picture" people who can ensure that organization-wide issues are addressed.

Build a consensus: A risk assessment is a mechanism for reaching consensus on which risks are the greatest and what steps are appropriate for mitigating them. Consensus building involves encouraging discussions of the issues, resolving dissonance, and obtaining agreement on controls necessary to carry out the action plan.

Communicate: Communication from beginning to end is essential. The matters to be communicated include the following.

- Rationale or business necessity for the risk assessment
- Goals and objectives of the assessment
- Identification of participants
- How employees can help
- Milestones and progress
- Findings
- Schedule of actions planned
- Actions completed

A summary of the risk assessment report can be a helpful communication tool. A caveat, one to be made by the CSO, is to be silent on vulnerabilities. There's nothing to be gained by letting adversaries know the system's weak points.

Assessment Policy

The organization's information security policy provides the framework and tone of the risk assessment. A policy lays out requirements. Generally, the requirements specify the frequency of assessments, a plan and procedures for conducting an assessment, disruption categories, unacceptable risks, distribution of the risk assessment report, and responsibilities for corrective actions.

Frequency: An assessment of the security scheme that protects information assets is appropriate

- Prior to or immediately following a significant change to the scheme.
- After a serious security incident.
- Whenever a new significant risk factor is introduced.
- At least once every two or three years.

Plan and procedures: An information security policy will typically

- Name the objectives and methodology of the assessment.
- Assign assessment responsibilities to positions, teams, groups, and departments.
- Identify assessment team size and composition.
- Identify modes for ensuring compliance and administering punishment for noncompliance.

Disruption categories: The policy will set parameters of loss, damage, or business disruption; for example:

- *Category I:* Loss of or severe damage to critical proprietary information or serious disruption to the system
- *Category II:* Loss of or serious damage to noncritical proprietary information or disruption of the system
- *Category III:* Loss of or serious damage to noncritical, nonproprietary information or minor disruption of the system

Unacceptable risks: Some risks are acceptable and some are not. Determinations are made by senior management and take into account many variables (e.g., threats and their probability, history of loss, financial strength of the organization, and others). Also considered will be the extent to which the organization will go to remove unacceptable risks.

Report distribution: The policy may specify the job positions that are to receive the report. These are positions that have been assigned responsibilities for the protection of information.

Corrective actions: The policy cannot predict weaknesses identified by risk assessment, but it can set requirements for correcting them when they are identified. Corrective actions can include acquiring needed equipment or material, improving knowledge and skills, and making changes to plans, procedures, and practices. Consider the following anecdote.

CASE STUDY

Chuck Short, CSO for an engineering company, read the last sentence of the memo carefully. "The new firewall will add an extra dimension of security." The memo bore the signature of Ted Armbruster, head of the information technology department.

Chuck punched in four numbers and Armbruster picked up on the second ring. "Just got your memo," Chuck said. "Looks good to me. One recommendation, though."

There was no mistaking the ice in Armbruster's voice as he asked, "What do you have in mind?" "An IT security policy." Chuck didn't remind Armbruster, which would have been about the hundredth time, that the absence of an information technology (IT) security policy was undermining Chuck's attempts to establish and enforce compliance with simple procedures such as selecting good passwords and logging off at the end of the workday. Chuck believed that if the top IT man does not think it important enough to state the security rules the employees won't think it important enough to follow them. It wouldn't help either for Chuck to mention to Armbruster the ongoing investigation into the disappearance of 10 laptops from an unlocked storage room in the IT department.

"Put your recommendation in writing," Armbruster said before clunking the receiver down. An hour later a wry smile tugged at the corners of Chuck's mouth as he signed the recommendation. Extra-large bulleted points highlighted the key actions.

- State a business necessity for the policy. Explain how IT contributes to the company's mission and how violations of IT security detract from the mission.
- Identify job positions subject to the policy (e.g., regular, temporary, contract, and subcontract employees). My view is that anyone with access privileges should be subject to the policy.
- Assign responsibilities. A responsibility not assigned is a responsibility not performed.
- Name activities prohibited by the policy (e.g., prohibitions against not protecting passwords, using IT equipment for other than company business, and e-mailing sensitive company information in nonencrypted modes).
- Name the enforcement actions. Describe the controls in place to detect policy violations (e.g., mention that supervisors will look for unattended PCs that have not been shut down, and that during non business hours security guards will look for hidden notes showing employee passwords).
- Identify the penalties for violations. Specify the range of disciplinary actions. You'll need to confer with HR on this issue.

A month went by without a reply, so at lunchtime one day Chuck managed to join Armbruster at a table in the company cafeteria. After a curt greeting from the head of IT, Chuck asked, "So what did you think of my recommendation?"

Armbruster ran a paper napkin across thin lips. "A policy may be in order, but your outline is much too detailed for what I want."

"Hmm," Chuck answered using his top-of-the-line professorial demeanor. "No reason why the policy has to be detailed. Let the details be spelled out in procedures that implement the policy. Supervisors would write the step-by-step instructions that support the duties assigned to them by the policy. Supervisors would also oversee compliance with the instructions. The nitty-gritty stuff would be spelled out in the trenches, not at your level. You'd provide the direction, not the detail."

That mollified Armbruster. "Might work," he conceded. Chuck couldn't resist a postscript. "But the policy can't be so short as to be vague. People have to know what they are expected to do in the way of security." "Standards?" Armbruster loved standards.

"Exactly. Standards remove confusion. They tell people what is expected of them." It was Armbruster's turn to offer a professorial "Hmm," and he did. He took a bite of a veggie sandwich and chewed at length. "A task force," he said at last. "That's what's needed. The task force can write the policy. Under my direction, of course." "Yes," Chuck agreed. "And I'm your first volunteer."

Armbruster did not appear overjoyed at the prospect but knew he could not shut out the company's CSO. While he pondered the implications, Chuck made another comment: "Rope in key people who have a stake in the policy. You know, HR and operations, and your own people, of course."

"Of course," he said, as if he had thought of it himself. That's when Chuck knew he had him. The company was finally going to get an IT security policy.

Cyber Offenses

A cyber offense is a premeditated criminal attack against information, computer systems, computer programs, and data. (See Figure 17.4 for preventing cyber offenses.) When the criminal act is minor, such as an attack that uses a nuisance virus or results in a denial of service, the commonly accepted (and

---

The Don'ts of Internet Use

Don't connect to the Internet except on connections provided by the employer.

Don't download software from an Internet source of questionable reliability.

Don't download from an Internet source without scanning for viruses.

Don't ignore licensing and export restrictions on software and shareware obtained through the Internet.

Don't change the security settings on your PC or web browser.

Don't use for the Internet the same passwords you use for other services.

Don't open electronic mail attachments that appear suspicious.

Don't mix internal and external e-mail addresses in a single distribution list.

Don't include embarrassing information in e-mail messages.

Don't auto-forward the organization's e-mail address to an external e-mail service.

Don't send sensitive information on the Internet without first encrypting.

Don't send or forward chain letters.

Don't unnecessarily send or download large files.

Don't browse inappropriate web sites.

Don't import inappropriate material.

Figure 17-4 This list can be used as a job aid for employees whose duties take them onto the Internet.

frequently misused) term is hacking. When the act is greater than minor, such as a malicious attack that results in damage or destruction, the term cybervandalism seems appropriate, and when the purpose of the act is to steal, such as acquire identification data that results in the taking of another's property, the usual term is cybercrime. When a cybercrime is politically motivated and results in violence against non-combatant targets, the appropriate term is cyberterrorism. All of these crimes involve information technology and the Internet.

The Internet

The Internet is a massive collection of computers located around the world, all of which are linked together and accessible from anywhere. The Internet is often called the Information Superhighway because it works like a path leading to the information desired. It is therefore very useful as a source of business information, a means of communication, and a facilitator of electronic commerce. Significant benefits accrue from having access to the Internet, but a companion of access is risk.

CSOs understand that attacks launched from the Internet can have devastating effects. It is fortunate that a majority of computer system penetrations have been carried out by noncriminal hackers. It is also fortunate that antivirus software programs are effective at deflecting many hacker attacks. (see Figure 17-5).

Anti-Hacker Tips

Determine the risks and choose measures to control them.

Place your web site on a server different than your internal network servers.

Enforce the rules on passwords.

Control access to hardware.

Stay abreast of hacker methods and viruses.

For a critical system, use more than one security method, e.g., passwords, separate servers, and firewalls.

Check regularly for vulnerabilities; use penetration tests.

Encrypt sensitive information before sending it over the Internet.

Require your online partners to take the same precautions you do.

Take advantage of up-to-date expertise and technology.

(Sources: Helmut Epp, Dean of DePaul University's CTI School, and the staff of Fortune Small Business Magazine.)

Figure 17-5 Common sense actions work against hackers.

On the unfortunate side of the ledger is the short shrift given to computer security by companies in a hurry to get their e-commerce applications up and running. Because hacker damage in the historical perspective has been relatively benign, some companies are choosing to assume the risk of hacking rather than install costly protections. Another reason to expect more frequent and more spectacular hacker events is the growth of computer literacy in the population as a whole. Computer-savvy criminals, terrorists, and others with an inclination to damage are learning the mechanics and use of a powerful weapon. Especially at risk are companies and consumers who meet on the Internet for commercial purposes.

Attacks on major commercial web sites reveal collaboration among hackers of varying types (e.g., virus writers, Trojan Horse bombers, and e-mail spammers). A collaborative or mixed attack occurs when a hacker places an undetectable program on a network. The program monitors important information passing along the network, and copies small chunks of data over an extended period of time. The chunks, which might be Social Security numbers or bank account numbers, accumulate. The hacking activity has now moved from a minor crime to a major crime. The final step is to download the stolen data and use it for a criminal purpose such as identify theft or theft of funds from bank accounts.

Hackers have been depicted in the media as fun-loving teenagers and technical whiz kids acting out a "boys-will-be-boys" scenario. Their only crime, apologists will say, is an intellectual fulfillment attained from entering the protected portals of the electronic world. A more accurate depiction might be to think of several madmen swinging baseball bats inside a china shop. The damage they do is done quickly, easily, and with stunning results, but putting the broken pieces back together is nearly impossible. With hackers of various stripes working together, a difficult challenge is presented to CSOs.

Restrictions on Internet Use

The CSO shares responsibility with information technology leaders for controlling unacceptable employee behaviors when they are on the Internet. Ways to control Internet behavior can include the following.

- Limit use to official business.
- Monitor Internet use and admonish/punish those who use the company's time and equipment for personal purposes.
- Prohibit viewing, downloading, or distributing obscene or abusive material.
- Prohibit employees from advertising on or participating in illegal or unethical Internet activities.
- Require respect of copyright laws.
- Prohibit communication of sensitive information via the Internet.

Intranet

An intranet is a collection of web sites owned and operated by the organization. Although an intranet operates on the Internet with standard browser software, it is open only to designated persons such as employees, partners, and contractors. Passwords, firewalls, and other protective methods help keep an intranet secure from outsiders (see Figure 17-6).

The chief purpose of an intranet is information sharing. Large amounts of useful information (although not necessarily sensitive) can be stored in the intranet's servers. Many different types of information are typically

---

Intranet Guidelines

Information that is classified at the highest level (e.g., SECRET information) must not be placed on the Intranet.

Information that is classified at the next lower level (e.g., RESTRICTED information) may be placed on the Intranet but only with access restrictions.

Information that is personal employee information (e.g., PRIVATE information) should not be placed on the Intranet.

Other information, although not classified but of a sensitive nature, should not be placed on the Intranet.

Information displayed on the Intranet should be accompanied by a notice of viewing privileges.

Partners and contractors must be informed of their Intranet viewing and publishing responsibilities.

Figure 17-6 Following these few guides can help maintain the integrity of a company's intranet.

available: policies, plans, procedures, rules and regulations, standards, phone and address lists, maps, technical drawings, travel advisories, and so on. The CSO, for example, might access the intranet to determine the engineering department's standards for perimeter fence construction; an employee planning to travel to Bogotá might use the intranet to identify hotels and restaurants that provide good security; and a clerk preparing to type a classified document might go on the intranet to be refreshed on procedures for marking and distributing a classified document.

An intranet is a means of sharing information and facilitating business processes. It can be helpful to companies large and small, and is particularly beneficial to organizations that are highly dependent on information. However, like other information facilities an intranet is accompanied by risk.

The need to protect information riding the intranet can be quite high in some situations. For example, information moving between the executive team and a joint venture partner may be so important as to require extra protection. However, the extra protection is meaningless when the joint partner's receiving portal is unprotected.

A large responsibility for intranet security lies with the provider of the information. Authors, owners, and custodians of information are charged with assessing the sensitivity of the information and determining the appropriate readership. It is not excusable to ignore security precautions for the sake of information flow. The correct approach is to make the information available, yet secure.

Passwords

A password is a sequence of characters that gives an authorized user access to a computer system. A password should not be easy to guess. A good password contains a combination of characters, numbers, and symbols that do not form a word. Computer systems usually limit the number of attempts to enter a correct password.

An auxiliary feature is a handheld device called a password authenticator. During log-on, the computer displays a challenge number, the user enters the challenge number into the password authenticator, and the authenticator replies directly to the computer. If the reply is correct, log-on is granted.

Another access-control device is the token, a tamper-resistant plastic card embedded with a microprocessor chip containing a stored password that automatically and frequently changes. When a computer is accessed using a token, the computer reads the token's password, as well as a password entered by the user. Access is granted when the computer finds a correct match of the passwords.

State-of-the art log-on systems combine passwords and biometric readings of fingerprints and retinal patterns. DNA profiles are on the horizon.

Firewalls

Firewalls are to a computer network what castle walls are to a king's home: they keep invaders out and keep insiders a safe distance from the king. Friends can get through the outer wall when they present proper identification at entrance points, and the king's attendants can move past inner walls depending on trust given them by the king. The analogy makes an important point: firewalls protect against intrusion from both external and internal sources. Damage caused by outside hackers is costly and well understood; damage caused by employees is even more costly and not widely acknowledged.

A firewall can be constructed within hardware, by software, or through a combination of both. The so-called network firewall will block incoming messages that are infected by viruses, sent from unwelcome sources, or fail to meet certain entry criteria. An application firewall prevents messages from moving directly between networks.

Firewalls are often complemented with equipment that looks for predefined "attack signatures" and then sends out an alert to the security network administrator. The equipment can be set up to automatically cut off a connection that appears suspicious [5].

Security Servers

A security server provides secure connections between networked computers and outside systems such as database storage and printing facilities. These security systems use encryption in what is called the handshaking process (i.e., an electronic exchange in which two systems confirm each other's authority to connect).

Encryption

Encryption is the process of converting messages, information, or data into a form unreadable by anyone except the intended recipient. Encrypted messages must be deciphered, or decrypted, before they can be read. The coding and decoding functions are performed using mathematical formulas (algorithms) and secret public keys [6].

Some of the newer encrypting techniques are nearly unbreakable. They are highly complex, guarded very carefully by their owners, and resistant to most code-breaking techniques. They use public-key encryption in which the authorized user gets two keys: a public key for encrypting and a private key for decrypting. It is virtually impossible to determine the private key, even when the public key is known.

INDUSTRIAL ESPIONAGE

Industrial espionage is the secret collection of proprietary business information. The owner or possessor attaches a value to the information and takes steps to protect it. The term *espionage* most commonly relates to government security and generally has a national security connotation. Industrial or business espionage is associated with economic and marketplace advantages. Although the venues and motives differ markedly, the methods of espionage are fairly standard.

Espionage has been romanticized by the mass media, but in truth is a dirty game played out of sight. Spying involves recruitment of operatives, encouragement of disloyalty, wiretapping, bugging, electronic and photographic surveillance, bribery, coercion, intimidation, fraud, and plain old stealing.

Industrial Espionage is Not New

Industrial espionage has flourished in America since the birth of the Industrial Revolution. The founding in 1789 of Slater's Mill in Pawtucket, Rhode Island, is the earliest known example. Samuel Slater had memorized the plans of the layout of an English textile mill where he had worked as an apprentice. Under the prevailing English law, the export of factory plans was forbidden, as was the emigration of textile workers. Slater nevertheless managed to slip out of the country and find passage to the New World, where he established a textile mill from the plans he had committed to memory [7].

Espionage has always been a vital tool of politics, diplomacy, and war, and in recent years a tool of business. Today, nearly every large corporation engages in strategic planning, a function heavily reliant on information about the marketplace and competition. Corporate leaders are undeniably interested in the plans and objectives of their competitors. Despite laws against and public disapproval of industrial espionage, spying practices are routinely carried out. Because industrial espionage is difficult to detect and prove, the law against it is infrequently enforced.

Industrial Espionage and Technology

Operating a business in today's highly competitive environment places demands on businesses to collect and use large amounts of information, which in turn spawns new technological tools. These same information-handling tools are vulnerable to compromise. Not surprisingly, businesses turn to their CSOs for protection. The duty cannot be taken lightly since survival of the business may be at stake.

Government-sponsored Industrial Espionage

The clandestine nature of industrial espionage rules out making a reliable identification of those engaged in it. However, it can be said with some degree of accuracy that in certain countries industrial espionage is government sponsored. The FBI estimates that loss due to theft by foreign governments of U.S. technology and sensitive economic information is in the range of one hundred billion dollars annually.

Industrial espionage is acknowledged as a serious threat to the viability of a business and in a much larger sense to entire industries and national economies. As companies, industries, and nations move to dependence on technologically intense products and services, business spying will continue to expand and intensify.

Industrial Espionage Targets

Information targeted by industrial spying is usually proprietary in nature (i.e., it is information owned by a company or entrusted to it that has not been disclosed publicly and has value). Trade secrets, patents, business plans, R&D discoveries, and the like are examples. Proprietary information is generally under the owner's protective shield, except when it is also classified government data entitled to protections afforded by the government.

Mechanics of Industrial Espionage

Industrial espionage moves through five stages: decide the information to be collected, collect the targeted information, refine it, and distribute it to the end user (where a decision is made to use or not use the information).

Decide the information to be collected: The focus of interest may be long-term and broad, such as to learn and track a competitor's overall research and design capability, or short-term and narrow such as to learn the details of a new product launch.

Collect the targeted information: In this stage, the espionage apparatus learns where the information is located, how it is protected, and how best to obtain it. The information may be collectable overtly — such as paying attention to newspapers, books, articles, and speeches — or it may be collectable through covert means such as planting a mole, subverting an employee, or installing electronic listening devices.

Refine the collected information: This step is like working a jigsaw puzzle. Information is organized and evaluated to arrive at an answer to the question initially asked (e.g., Is the competitor about to introduce a new product?).

Distribute the refined information: The processed information is given to the decision maker and/or the people who can make use of it. To be useful, the information must be timely, accurate, and understandable.

Ignore or act on the information: The users have two choices: ignore the information or act on it. Undesirable consequences may follow when the information happens to be accurate and is ignored, or happens to be faulty and is acted upon.

Industrial Espionage Spies

Professional: The most effective among espionage spies are professional agents. They operate from various motives:

- Greed
- Financial need
- Revenge
- Ambition
- Political, religious, or cultural ideology
- Belief in a cause

Professional agents (often self-promoted as legitimate consultants) earn hefty fees and are inclined to dismiss greed as a primary motive. Many are former government or military intelligence officers, private investigators, or security consultants. Other types of paid collectors are persons who have been carefully recruited and enticed into cooperation by the promise of reward.

Professionals (see Figure 17-7) sometimes pose as head hunters to engage in conversation with key employees of the targeted organization. Bogus job interviews can be a rich source of inside information. The more odious tasks performed by hired hands are searching trash, breaking and entering, and blackmailing the vulnerable.

Informant: The use of informants, paid or unpaid and witting or unwitting, is a standard technique of the professional spy. Informants are often a rival's regular, temporary, or contractor employees, suppliers, vendors, or clients, as well as wives, children, and friends. Also under the broad heading of informant

---

Questions in the Mind of the Industrial Spy

How can I get access to the targeted company's paper trash?

Who are the targeted company's contractors, vendors, suppliers, and lenders? Can I obtain those details from watching the loading dock and reading license plates in the visitor parking area?

Who in the targeted company possesses or has easy access to the information I'm after?

Can I get access to these key employees by e-mail, telephone, and mail? What will be my cover story?

Have any of the key employees submitted papers to or are scheduled to speak at industry symposia? How do I get the papers? How best to make personal contact? What will be my cover?

Will a bogus job offer get me in contact with key employees? What questions can I ask that will not raise suspicions, yet lead to an inadvertent leakage of sensitive information?

Should I make contact as a job applicant, a bidder, or a prospective vendor or repairperson?

Where does the executive team meet when making major decisions? Is the meeting place vulnerable to electronic surveillance?

Figure 17-7 The industrial spy follows a unique thought process.

Figure 17-8 Aldrich Ames spied for the Soviet government.

are infiltrators and undercover operatives who penetrate the rival organization. Their activities can consist of recruiting and directing unsuspecting helpers, copying sensitive documents, intercepting communications, photographing, videotaping, and placing covert listening devices.

Volunteer: Volunteers motivated by an ideology or cause tend to be erratic, which requires careful treatment by their handlers.

Mole: A highly prized collector is the "mole" or operative-in-place. This individual is typically in a position of trust with access to highly sensitive information.

One of the best examples of a mole is Aldrich Ames (see Figure 17-8), head of the CIA's counterintelligence branch, who in 1983 began calling for the files on every important CIA operation involving Soviet spies. He sold the files to the Soviets in order to fund tastes not affordable by his salary. Dozens of U.S. operatives were exposed and many killed. Until his arrest and conviction for espionage in 1994, Ames received nearly $3 million for his treason [8].

Spies operate in a variety of ways. The following are examples [9].

Setup agent: This smooth-talking con artist assumes many guises to entrap the innocent or ignorant insider. One is the pretext telephone call: the agent calls an unsuspecting employee and pretends to be a vendor, such as for a company that prints architectural drawings, and elicits sensitive information by asking questions about a nonexistent work order. Another is the pretext letter: the letterhead bears the logo of a respected professional association. The letter invites the addressee, often a researcher, to submit a professional paper for publication.

Trespasser: This person gains access to the facility by breaking and entering or by ruse. In the former, the trespasser enters by stealth and either steals or copies files, documents, computer tapes, and so on. In the latter, the trespasser presents false credentials that permit access to the facility and/or to restricted areas within.

Listener: This eavesdropper uses sophisticated wiretap and bugging devices to capture conversations or simply overhears conversations at employee hangouts.

Lookout: This spy maintains physical surveillance of personnel of interest, looking always for the hook—a personal indiscretion, a contact of questionable character, or any shortcoming that may be exploited to extort information.

Pollster: Using phony questionnaires that ask apparently innocuous questions, the pollster obtains information useful in itself or useful in confirming an organization's activities such as developing a new product or moving into a new market.

Financial wizard: This spy gains access to a company executive by outlining an enticing proposition. In a one-on-one situation and subsequent telephone calls, the wizard spews attractive numbers that lead the executive to reveal sensitive proprietary information. Once the information is obtained, the wizard calls off the deal. The executive may not even discover he/she had been hoodwinked.

Blind advertiser: This spy advertises an employment opportunity. Interested persons are encouraged to mail their resumes to a post office box. If a resume indicates that the applicant is employed by a company of interest, the spy makes a follow-up telephone call or meets the applicant over lunch or cocktails. During discussion of the job, the spy says that a hiring decision cannot be made in the absence of specific (and sensitive) information about the applicant's job duties.

Reverse engineer: This person may be the spy or a person employed by the spy. Proprietary information that has been obtained about a product or process is broken down into examinable components. The engineer creates or synthesizes a clone of the product or process.

Solicitor: This spy recruits a person by deception or by rewarding a desire or satisfying a need. The recruited person is connected in some way to the targeted organization: employee, vendor, delivery or repair person, customer, contractor, and so on. The solicitor asks for certain types of information and to the extent the information is delivered the solicitor satisfies the person's desire or need.

SPY TECHNOLOGY

Equipment

The techniques of industrial espionage are assisted by an array of technological equipment, such as the following:

- Miniaturized cameras and microphones that can be installed almost anywhere, such as inside telephones, furniture, walls, ceilings, and floors
- Microphones that can hear conversations from great distances
- Wireless devices for tapping into telephone lines
- Devices that can record and translate into useful information the naturally occurring electronic emissions of computers and communication equipment
- Photographic devices operated from aircraft and satellites

The same technological principles, if not the devices themselves, are applicable to countermeasures. The advantage, however, rests with the spy. Only after a spying technique has been detected can a countermeasure be put into effect. The spy, then, is always one step ahead of the counter spy.

Technical Security Countermeasures (TSCM)

TSCM is an inspection and monitoring technique that uses sophisticated electronic devices to detect the presence of covertly planted listening devices that vary widely in type and sophistication. The traditional devices are the telephone bug, line tap, hidden microphone, and parabolic microphone (such as that used on the sidelines of a televised football game to capture bumps and grunts).

Companies that use TSCM regard their proprietary information as a key asset, if not the very lifeblood of their business. These companies usually operate in a highly competitive industry and know that information leakage can adversely affect their market positions. The really large companies usually retain TSCM specialists on staff; others contract for the services.

Inspect: The first step in TSCM is the inspection. If an objective is to "sneak up" on a covert listener, the inspection will feature non-alerting techniques such as monitoring the radio frequency (RF) spectrum and scanning electric power and telephone lines. If done carefully, a physical inspection can be done in a non-alerting manner. Examples include standing on a stepladder and looking above the lift-out tiles in a false ceiling, looking behind air conditioning vents and electrical wall plates, and checking the mouthpieces of telephones.

Sweep: After the non-alerting techniques have been applied, the TSCM specialist transitions to a sweep using electronic tools. The term *sweep* derives from a tool resembling a vacuum sweeper. The specialist examines everything in the area (typically an office suite or a conference room) and everything entering the area such as power lines for telephones, fax machines, desktop computers, and modems.

Monitor: The next step is monitoring. It involves some of the same tools used in inspecting. Think of monitoring in two forms. One has the TSCM specialist remaining at the site for one or two days listening and watching. This approach is often used when the sweep is intended to sterilize a room where sensitive conversations are planned to be held such as at a strategy meeting of senior executives. The monitoring can precede and continue throughout the duration of the meeting. A second form of monitoring has the TSCM specialist returning to the site periodically, say once per month on a random basis.

COMPETITIVE INTELLIGENCE

Purpose

The aim of competitive strategy is not to kill or cripple the competition but to build a position of sustainable competitive advantage. Indeed, it is possible to argue that every organization needs competitors, as without them there would be less incentive for creative thinking, and a tendency for the organization to become sleepy and less sensitive to user needs [10].

Competitive intelligence is the gathering of information from overt sources. It is legal to do and is not the same as spying. Collecting information without skullduggery is both necessary and proper. Competitive intelligence becomes industrial espionage when it crosses the line between right and wrong.

Sources

Perhaps the most "legitimate" source from which confidential information can be obtained is the federal government, which for regulatory and contractual purposes requires public corporations—and even many private companies—to make extensive disclosures regarding their products, finances, and operations. Hence, various agencies of the government are repositories of considerable confidential information, knowledge of which can be useful to business competitors [10].

Legality

There is nothing in law that prohibits studying a rival's products or services; analyzing advertisements, annual reports, published articles, and public records; or conversing with knowledgeable consultants, customers, and suppliers. Some companies that regularly collect information about the competition assign the task to an in-house team committed to the purpose exclusively. Often, the team is a committee or task force made up of specialists in marketing, sales, product development, product management, and one or two members in the executive lineup.

Practitioners

Other companies hire outside vendors with expertise in competitive intelligence. A tacitly understood rationale for using a third party is the defense that a company can put up if the third party crosses the line separating legitimate information gathering from illicit economic spying. More and more security firms and private investigative agencies are moving into twin fields: collecting competitive intelligence for clients and preventing or detecting competitive intelligence and industrial espionage.

Reasonable Steps

The rules of the game require the owner of the information to take reasonable steps to protect the information (e.g., by limiting its distribution and keeping it locked up when not in use). The information also has to be not known generally, not readily ascertainable, and of a nature to confer a competitive advantage upon its owner. A crime is committed when such information is obtained by improper means, such as theft or misrepresentation, and when the obtained information has been used to the disadvantage of the owner.

In the United States, competitive intelligence has been practiced by claim jumpers, cattle rustlers, and oil scouts. The modern-era practitioner is the respected businessperson. The importance and value of competitive intelligence has led some business leaders to mobilize their entire workforces to actively seek information from industry peers; for example, with peers over lunch, on the phone, and at trade shows, professional conferences, and seminars.

Use of Technology

The biggest of new twists is the constantly expanding variety of technological tools. Many information technology devices can be automatically programmed to constantly surf the Internet in search of significant keywords and to download industry-specific news of mergers, personnel movements, and product research and development — all of which is legal to do. The line is crossed when such tools are used to open gateways to protected domains such as a competitor's intranet or e-mail system or a confidential database of the industry's regulatory agency.

Product and Process

Competitive intelligence is both a product and a process. As a product, it is information with use and value that can be applied by decision makers to the organization's particular purposes or goals. As a process, it is the ethical and legitimate collection of information.

Industrial espionage, which is often viewed as the dark underbelly of competitive intelligence, is the collection of information in a manner and for purposes not entirely legitimate or which involve the use of a legitimately developed intelligence product to achieve an illegal end.

Open Information

Many sources of business information are open and publicly available. They include information presented by the news media, public records, government reports, and reports issued by business competitors such as annual reports and stock offerings. On the gray fringe are the competitors' internal newsletters, proposals to prospective clients, and similar documents that are usually not confidential and which would be impossible for the authoring organizations to control in any meaningful way.

For the user of open information, the caveat is extreme caution because the data are often a potpourri of fact, half-truths, and wishful thinking. The challenge to the collector of publicly available information is to ferret out the factual portions and combine them with data obtained from other sources.

Some spokespersons in the field of corporate investigations oddly reject the claim that the Internet has made the quest for competitive intelligence any easier. They boast that the real meat is in the analysis and can only be achieved through exhaustive quantitative analysis of "the numbers." But nothing could be further from the truth. The fact is, the business world is filled with quantitative analysts who can run "the numbers," but there are many fewer professionals who can make reasoned judgments by bringing together a combination of investigative know-how and business experience.

CONCLUSIONS

In recent years, information has come to be valued on a par with equipment, materials, and capital. This utilitarian view emerges from evidence that the possession and use of information can increase profits and improve the ways in which people work and think.

NOTES

1. Carl A. Roper, *Risk Management for Professionals*, pp. 181, Boston: Butterworth-Heinemann, 1999.

2. John J. Fay, *Security Dictionary*, pp. 199, Arlington, VA: American Society for Industrial Security, 2000.

3. Lonnie R. Buckels and Robert B. Iannone, "Proprietary Information: A Primer for Protection," in *Encyclopedia of Security Management*, pp. 582, John J. Fay, editor, Boston: Butterworth-Heinemann, 1993.

4. John J. Fay, "Intellectual Property Rights," in *Encyclopedia of Security Management*, pp. 400–401, John J. Fay, editor, Boston: Butterworth-Heinemann, 1993.

5. Heather Malec, "Firewalls Guard Perimeter," *SECURITY*, June 1999, p. 81.

6. James A. Schweitzer, "Information Security: Levels of Protection for Electronic Information," in *Encyclopedia of Security Management*, pp. 396, John J. Fay, editor, Boston: Butterworth-Heinemann, 1993.

7. Richard Eels and Peter Nehemkis, *Corporate Intelligence and Espionage*, pp. 120, New York: MacMillan Publishing Company, 1984.

8. Tim Weiner, David Johnston, and Neil A. Lewis, *Betrayal: The Story of Aldrich Ames, an American Spy*, New York: Wheeler Publishing, 1996.

9. Norman R. Bottom and Robert R. J. Gallati, *Industrial Espionage: Intelligence Techniques and Countermeasures*, pp. 35, Boston: Butterworth-Heinemann, 1984.

10. David Hussey and Per Jenster, *Competitor Intelligence: New York: John Wiley & Sons, Ltd, 1999.*

18. Substance Abuse Prevention

It is very important to be sober when you apply for a job. Many careers in street cleaning and subway-guitar-playing have been founded on a lack of understanding of this simple fact.
—Author unknown

Let's agree at the outset that substance abuse means the abuse of both drugs and alcohol. Let's also agree that drug abuse means the use of illicit drugs; that is, drugs that are prohibited by law to use, such as heroin and marijuana, and the use of legal drugs in a manner not prescribed by a physician or recommended by the drug manufacturer. And for the purpose of this discussion we'll agree that alcohol, which is legal to use, is abused when it is consumed in violation of the employer's work rule such as use immediately prior to reporting to work and use on the job.

RATIONALE FOR PREVENTION [1]

Why is substance abuse a concern of the employer, and by extension, to the chief security officer? The reasons are many and simple. Substance abuse causes the following:

- Absenteeism, which lowers productivity and shifts the burden of work to nonabusing employees
- Mental and physical lapses that result in poor decisions, wastage of materials, and accidents that injure and kill
- Damage to the health of abusing employees and drives up the employer's medical benefit costs
- Damage to the morale of the nonabusing employees and friction between the abusers and nonabusers
- Problems in supervision that divert the attention and time of managers
- Loss related to employees who steal to support their habits
- Damage to the public image and reputation of the organization

An interesting point is that the typical substance abuser is not an addict, homeless person, or criminal. A majority of substance abusers are gainfully employed. According to the Occupational Safety and Health Administration (OSHA), drug abusers are responsible for 35 percent of all absences, are absent 10 times more often than nonabusers, and the average abuser performs at 67 percent of productivity potential. The Research Triangle Institute announced a similar conclusion: drug-abusing employees are one-third less productive than other employees. General Motors (GM) determined that 70 percent of employee absences were due to abuse. The average abuser, in the year prior to undergoing treatment, was absent 100 days in a 240-days-per-year work schedule. Drug-using employees averaged 40 days sick leave each year compared to 4.5 days for nonabusers. GM determined that abuse among its 472,000 workers and their dependents cost $600 million in one year alone.

Once drug abusers have exhausted their discretionary income, they buy their drugs on credit. Once credit is exhausted, they typically deal or steal. The abuser who deals is likely to sell drugs at work. The abuser who steals is likely to steal from the employer or the employer's customers and vendors [2].

THE CHIEF SECURITY OFFICER'S ROLE

What does all this have to do with the CSO? The connection is the role of the CSO in carrying out the employer's substance abuse policy, which typically prohibits the use, possession, and transfer of abused substances on company premises or while conducting the company's business. Enforcement of this prohibition largely falls into the security purview. Also specified in a typical policy is a requirement to investigate violations of company policy and cooperate with police and prosecutorial authorities in the investigation of drug law violations. Translated into tasks or duties, the CSO ensures that

- Workplace inspections are conducted.
- Abuse substances and paraphernalia prohibited by the policy are confiscated, stored, marked as potential evidence, and disposed of in the manner required by law.
- Violations are investigated and recommendations made for preventing the same or similar violations.

In addition, the CSO may be tasked to evaluate compliance to policy in the matter of the company's drug and alcohol testing program. The questions that management may want the CSO to answer include the following.

- Are fairness and nondiscrimination present in the practice of selecting the employees to be tested? If random selection is specified, is the selection process truly random and free of suggestions to the contrary?
- Are the test specimens (e.g., urine for drugs and breath for alcohol) collected in a manner that provides a reasonable degree of personal privacy yet prevents contamination, switching, or mislabeling?
- Are test specimens transported tamper-free and with attention to chain of custody?

- Are test results distributed on a need-to-know basis and are they given the same or higher level of protection given to medical information?

Even small deviations from the standards of a testing program can cause large problems, and if the CSO is charged with discovering deviations he or she must have a grasp of testing program fundamentals.

TESTING FOR ILLEGAL DRUGS [3]

Drug testing (see Figure 18-1) seeks to identify in a person's body the evidence of illegal drug use. The most common method of drug testing is the analysis of urine. The individual to be tested is asked (not compelled) to provide a urine specimen. A consent form signed by the individual demonstrates willingness.

The specimen is collected in a manner that prevents cheating and error. The integrity of the specimen has to be unquestionably reliable. Any indication of contamination, switching, or mislabeling will render a test result invalid. To assure reliability, a chain-of-custody form is signed by every person who handles the specimen from collection until final destruction.

A specimen is carefully packaged and quickly transported to a testing lab, where it is analyzed for the presence of drugs. Federal drug testing programs currently test for five drugs: cocaine, marijuana, opiates, amphetamines, and phencyclidine (PCP). Nonfederal testing programs usually test for these same five drugs and others as well, usually barbiturates, benzodiazepines, and methaqualone.

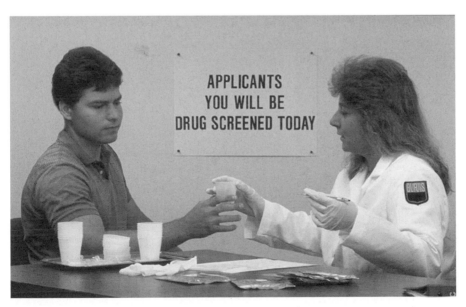

Figure 18-1 Drug testing of job applicants is a common business practice. *(Photo courtesy of Burns International Security Services.)*

Drugs and alcohol are tested in certified laboratories. The testing methodology for drugs is analysis of urine specimens. The methodology usually follows a two-test approach. If no drugs are found in the first test, the specimen is not further tested and is declared negative. If a drug is found in the first test, the specimen is tested a second time using a different technique. If the second test fails to confirm the first test, the specimen is declared negative; if the second test confirms the first test, the specimen is declared positive.

In some programs a positive report is forwarded to a physician who evaluates the report in light of information about the individual. The information may come from what the individual says and what a medical examination reveals. If there is any reliable indication that the positive test resulted from something other than illegal drug use, such as the proper use of a prescription drug, the test is declared negative.

Almost all testing programs provide opportunities for challenging positive test reports, including the right to obtain a retest by the same or equally competent laboratory. Some programs have treatment and return-to-duty provisions, and almost all organizations that conduct drug testing assist employees by identifying treatment resources in the local community.

Sensitivity and Cutoff

The ability of a screening test to detect a drug in a urine sample is called sensitivity. Manufacturers of commercial urine screening systems set cutoff limits well above the sensitivity limits. They do so to minimize the possibility of a sample that is truly negative giving a positive result. For example, although screening tests that detect marijuana are sufficiently sensitive at levels below 20 nanograms per milliliter, the screens take effect at cutoff levels of 50 or 100 nanograms. This not only decreases the possibility of a false positive resulting from operating the test too close to its level of sensitivity, but also significantly decreases the possibility of a positive test resulting from an outside influence (e.g., from passive inhalation of marijuana).

Impairment and Time of Previous Drug Use

Although urine testing is very effective in determining fairly recent drug use, the positive results of a test cannot be used to prove intoxication or impaired performance. Inert properties of a drug may appear in urine for several days or weeks without any accompanying loss of faculties. A positive urine test, however, is good evidence of prior drug use.

Urine specimens that show positive for marijuana signify that an individual has consumed the drug from within one hour to as many as three weeks or more immediately preceding specimen collection. A single smoking session by a casual user of marijuana can produce positive specimens for two to five days. Detection time increases greatly following a period of chronic use.

Detection Times	
Alcohol	2 to 10 hours
Amphetamine	24 to 48 hours
Phenobarbital	2 to 6 weeks
Secobarbital	24 hours
Benzodiazapines (e.g., Valium)	3 days to 6 weeks
Cocaine	1 hour to 4 days
Opiates (e.g., morphine)	1 to 2 days
Methadone	2 to 3 days
Methaqualone	8 days
Phencyclidine (PCP)	1 to 8 days
Propoxyphene	6 to 48 hours
Marijuana	2 days to 11 weeks

Figure 18-2 The detection times for substances range widely.

An individual who has smoked several times a day for several weeks will have to give up the drug entirely for as long as 30 days in order to clear the body system of detectable marijuana metabolites (see Figure 18-2).

False Positive

A false positive occurs when a drug is reported present in a drug-free specimen. False positives happen three ways.

- Another substance in the specimen induces a chemical anomaly that registers positive on the test instrument.
- Human error causes the wrong specimen to be tested.
- A mistake on the part of a laboratory technician produces an inaccurate test result.

A false negative occurs when a test fails to identify a drug in a specimen. False negatives are common when the cutoff level is set so high that low concentrations of drugs are not detected.

Passive Inhalation

Unintentional exposure to marijuana is frequently offered as a reason for a positive test result. Passive inhalation of marijuana smoke does occur and can result in a positive finding. Studies have shown, however, that it is highly unlikely that a person could inhale enough smoke by passive inhalation to produce a positive specimen. The level of marijuana in a passive-inhalation specimen would be far below the detection cutoff level (see Figure 18-3).

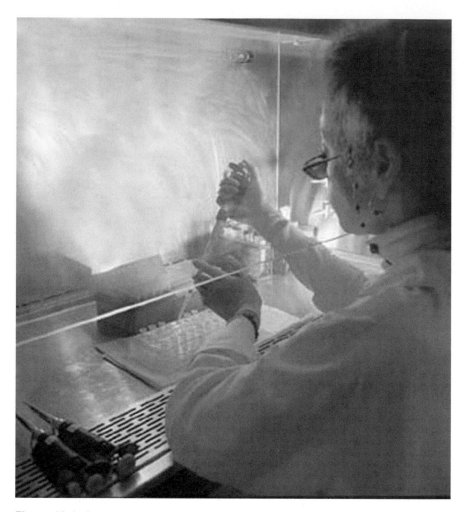

Figure 18-3 Drug testing is performed with highly reliable and accurate scientific methods. *(Photo courtesy of Burns International Security Services.)*

Testing for Alcohol

A test for alcohol measures the concentration of alcohol in the blood. Blood-alcohol concentration (BAC) is the relative proportion of ethyl alcohol within the blood, based on the number of grams of alcohol per millimeter of blood, expressed as a percentage. In a BAC test, blood alcohol zones are the measures of intoxication. Three zones are commonly used.

- Zone 1 includes blood alcohol values from 0.00 to 0.05 percent and is considered fairly good evidence that the person is sober.
- Zone 2 ranges from 0.05 to 0.15 percent and is inconclusive as to whether or not the person is under the influence.

CONSENT FOR DRUG AND ALCOHOL TESTING

Employee Name: _____   Test Date: _____

Social Security Number: _____   Department: _____

Employee Start Date: _____   Supervisor: _____

I understand that I am not obligated in any way to take a drug and/or alcohol test administered by my employer.

I hereby freely and voluntarily agree to take a drug and/or alcohol test administered by my employer.

I also understand that the results of the drug and/or alcohol tests taken by me will me made available to my employer and others having the right by law or regulation to have access to such test results.

Signature: _____   Date: _____

Figure 18-4 Testing requires consent.

- Zone 3 relates to findings above 0.15 percent. At this level a person is considered to be intoxicated. Its equivalent is to drink 8 ounces of whiskey or eight 12-ounce bottles of beer.

The testing specimen can be breath, blood, or urine. In the breath testing technique, a sample of deep lung breath is collected from the subject's air output and held captive in a device that measures hydrocarbons. Hydrocarbons will be present in the deep lung breath of a person who has recently consumed an alcoholic beverage. An exaggerated reading, however, can occur if in the 15-minute period immediately preceding the test the subject consumed or regurgitated alcohol. Thus, a 15-minute waiting period prior to testing is recommended to guard against an exaggerated reading.

A breath alcohol test is often regarded as a screening test (see Figure 18-4), which if positive is immediately followed by a confirmation test using a more sensitive analytical technique such as the analysis of blood or urine.

SUBSTANCE ABUSE AWARENESS

To a very large degree, the CSO meets management's expectations by raising substance abuse awareness within the organization's general employee population and supervisory staff. A primary objective of a substance abuse awareness program is to convince employees that substance abuse in the workplace detracts from everybody's personal interest. The program is essentially one of education: making employees aware of the negative consequences of abuse, influencing them to steer away from it, and obtaining their assistance in helping fellow employees escape the trap of abuse.

Responsibility for administering a substance abuse awareness program is often shared by the human resources, safety, and security groups. The focal points for HR include the disciplinary consequences of violations, employee assistance, rehabilitation, and return to work. The safety group has an interest in accident prevention, and the security group is concerned with keeping prohibited substances out of the workplace, detecting violations, conducting investigations, and coordinating security group efforts with local law enforcement. An effective program will be

- A centerpiece of the organization's overall substance abuse policy. The program will be formal, rationalized, and administered by knowledgeable substance abuse professionals with skills in vocational education and training, and will be subject to normal business processes, such as planning, budgeting, and evaluation.
- An ongoing effort. Although the education program may be initiated with great fanfare and periodically reinvigorated, it will be a continuously operating enterprise.
- Oriented to the particular (and often changing) needs of the business. The effort will be principally dedicated to making the employees aware of their individual responsibilities for maintaining a workplace free of drug and alcohol abuse.
- Innovative in awareness methods and approaches.

The CSO's standing in the program, as well as the larger organization, is enhanced when security-related presentations reflect thoughtful preparation. For example, when selecting topics for presentation the CSO differentiates between the essential and the nice-to-know. The essential topics will be those that are stated in the substance abuse policy; nice-to-know topics are not essential and can be wasters of time. When topics are long or complex, they are broken down into comprehensible parts and arranged with each part building on others. Knowledge retention is enhanced when information is imparted in discrete, digestible portions. The forums for presentation by the CSO go beyond the formal training setting. The following are examples.

- Brown-bag luncheon meetings at which employees view films, slides, and other audiovisuals. Having a subject matter expert on hand to supplement the presentation and answer questions adds credibility. A law enforcement officer, for example, can display paraphernalia used to administer commonly abused drugs, and a medical practitioner can explain the health consequences of abuse.
- Company-sponsored publications such as newsletters and bulletins. Each newsletter issue, for example, can include a drug-related article. Hard-copy materials that reach the home may help promote family involvement in preventing or resolving substance abuse problems.

- Tutorials that meet special needs; for example, teaching supervisors how to look for prohibited items.
- Awareness materials on static and electronic bulletin boards, on the security web site of the organization's intranet, on placards in public hallways, and on signage at safety-sensitive locations. Other materials might be a company-prepared handbook, posters in hallways, and fliers placed inside paycheck envelopes.
- Awareness events such as a security fair that features display booths, literature handouts, video presentations, and talks by local celebrities.

Consider the following scenario.

CASE STUDY

Danny Abbott works the early evening shift as warehouse forklift operator. A few hours before he is due on the job, Danny is at a friend's home. His friend lights up a marijuana cigarette and offers to share it. Danny, who is no stranger to marijuana, hesitates for a moment.

Danny recently attended a company meeting on the subject of drug abuse. The main speaker was the company's CSO, who said that company work rules prohibited employees from being at work while under the influence or with a detectable amount of an illegal drug in the body system. The reason for the rule had to do with accident prevention and, as Danny knew, his own job as forklift operator required strict attention to safety. Danny was particularly impressed when told that effective immediately the company was instituting unannounced and random drug testing of employees in safety-sensitive jobs. Danny's friend takes a long drag from the marijuana cigarette and extends it to Danny.

Employee awareness is an essential component of the organization's substance abuse prevention program. Other program components — such as supervisory intervention, drug testing, and employee assistance — rely on an informed workforce. Supervisors cannot step in to correct abuse situations if they have no understanding of abuse, drug testing will not be fully accepted by the workforce if the why and how of drug testing are not thoroughly explained, and employees will shy away from seeking or accepting employee assistance benefits if they are unsure of implications.

Supervisory Support

Support of the employer's substance abuse policy from supervisors is essential. Support is garnered along two major routes: awareness and involvement. Along the first route the CSO is a presenter in supervisory training programs, a source for awareness materials, and an influencer of the understandings and attitudes of supervisors. The second route has the CSO directly involved with supervisors in showing them how to spot impairment, how to look for prohibited materials, and what to do when impairment is present or prohibited materials found. The awareness route is a path for helping supervisors

- Understand and make a commitment to the company's substance abuse policy and program.

- Obtain a familiarity with the substances of abuse, the methods of administration, and the associated paraphernalia.
- Recognize the human performance indicators of substance abuse.
- Discharge their responsibilities under the policy and to the program (e.g., intervene in situations where substance abuse is apparent, confiscate prohibited materials, and document substance abuse incidents).

Success at intervention requires supervisors to grasp concepts familiar to the CSO. They include reasonable cause, consent to test, search with implied consent, contraband, and chain of custody.

Reasonable Cause

The terms *reasonable belief*, *just cause*, *proper cause*, and *for cause* generally mean the same thing. The term *probable cause* is similar to *reasonable cause* but much more precise and demanding in its application. The term *reasonable* is often used in the context of searching. A search is said to be reasonable when it is based on a good-faith belief that evidence of a certain violation can be found on a particular person or at a particular place.

The term *unreasonable* is often used to describe a search conducted when there are no facts that would lead a prudent person to believe that evidence of a violation will be found somewhere. An example would be a search of an employee's locker for the purpose of finding anything that could be used against the employee. This type of search is unreasonable because it is a type of fishing expedition.

In the context of alcohol and drug testing, a reasonable cause situation involves observed actions. The observed actions are subjected to a decision-making model that helps the intervening supervisor make the correct decision. The decision-making model takes the supervisor through a process of analysis that poses critical questions such as the following.

- Are the observed actions capable of explanation and substantiation?
- Are they specific, contemporaneous, and tangible?
- Are they associated with probable alcohol or drug use?

Two-supervisors rule: Confidence can be greatly increased by application of the two-supervisors rule. The rule calls for a judgment to be made by two supervisors who have knowledge of the facts. They jointly make the determination (see Figure 18-5) to refer the employee for testing, but only after certain critical questions (such as the following) have been asked and answered.

- Is impairment present? Testing cannot be authorized unless facts clearly point to impairment resulting from the use of alcohol or drugs.
- Are the facts reliable? The supervisors can consider the facts of a situation to be wholly reliable when they personally have witnessed the situation.

REPORT OF REASONABLE CAUSE INCIDENT

Name of Individual: _____

Time and Date of Incident: _____

Place of Incident: _____

Brief Description of the Incident

_____

_____

_____

_____

_____

The Individual's Appearance Was:

[ ] Normal	[ ] Sleepy	[ ] Hyperactive	[ ] Tremors
[ ] Bloodshot Eyes	[ ] Runny Nose	[ ] Pale	[ ] Flushed
[ ] Staggering	[ ] Uncoordinated	[ ] Glazed Eyes	[ ] Dreamy
[ ] Nervous	[ ] Confused	[ ] Sweating	[ ] Unkempt

[ ] Other specific details of appearance, including odors:

_____

_____

The Individual's Conduct Was:

[ ] Normal	[ ] Loud	[ ] Abusive	[ ] Disruptive
[ ] Erratic	[ ] Violent	[ ] Giggling	[ ] Rapid Talking
[ ] Mood Swing	[ ] Wandering	[ ] Argumentative	[ ] Sleeping
[ ] Destructive	[ ] Belligerent	[ ] Irritable	[ ] Passive

[ ] Other specific details of conduct:

_____

_____

What the Individual Said or Did

_____

_____

_____

_____

Figure 18-5 Documentation of a reasonable cause determination is essential.

Overall, the Individual Seemed:

[ ] Normal   [ ] Impaired   [ ] Not Usual Self
[ ] Unable To Function   [ ] Unsafe To Be Around   [ ] Under the Influence

Comments

_____

_____

_____

_____

_____

_____

Specimen Collection

After being informed that providing a specimen for laboratory analysis to determine the presence of alcohol or drugs was a voluntary act, the Individual:

   [ ] Voluntarily Provided a Specimen   [ ] Refused to Provide a Specimen

Name of Person/Agency That Collected the Specimen: _____

Time and Date of Specimen Collection: _____

Time and Date Specimen Was Forwarded to Lab: _____

"We, the supervisors or managers whose signatures appear below, have determined that reasonable cause exists to believe that the Individual named in this incident was impaired by or under the influence of alcohol or a drug or drugs at the time, date and place indicated, and that testing for the presence of alcohol or drugs is justified by the circumstances."

Signature_____Time and Date_____

Signature_____Time and Date_____

Figure 18-5 *continued*

Reliability is also established when the facts are reported directly to the supervisors from other persons considered believable and who claim to be direct witnesses.
- Are the facts explainable? A decision to conduct reasonable cause testing must be supported by specific details that can be explained. For example,

it would not be sufficient to say only that an employee appeared to be under the influence. An explanation would need to include details of the observed impairment such as "the employee was staggering and his speech was slurred."

- Is the impairment present now? The supervisor has to be sure that the suspected impairment exists at the moment the decision is being made. There are two good reasons for this: first, the test will most likely be negative if there is no impairment, and second, it would be unreasonable to require a person to take a test based on suspected past impairment.

Consent to Test

Under this concept, which carries the force of law, no person may be compelled to provide specimens. An employer, however, has the right to terminate an employee who refuses to provide a specimen when requested to do so. The employer's right must be supported by prior notice to the employee that consent to test is a condition of employment.

Search with Implied Consent

A search with implied consent is a search conducted as a condition of employment or as part of an employment contract. Conditions of employment and employment contracts frequently express or imply consent to search employees and their belongings.

The rationale for implied consent searching is based on preventing an injurious outcome that can be reasonably expected to occur in the absence of a regularly conducted search program. An injurious outcome could be an explosion or fire in the workplace. The search program would be justified because of the need to ensure that ignition devices are excluded from the workplace. The same can be said for excluding impaired workers whose judgment or lack of motor skills might contribute to an explosion or fire or might detract from the proper emergency response.

An implied consent search (see Figure 18-6) is more like an inspection than anything else. It does not rely on reasonable belief; there need not be an accident, an incident, or a set of suspicious facts for the implied consent search.

Contraband

In the strict legal context, contraband is any item that by itself is a crime to possess. Illegal drugs, untaxed whiskey, stolen property, military explosives, and counterfeit money are contraband. All of these may be prohibited from the workplace because possession of them places the possessor in violation of the law. An employer will sometimes include in its definition of contraband other prohibited items such as firearms and knives.

Figure 18-6 Sniffer dogs are often used in general searches of open premises, such as a company-owned parking lot.

Chain of Custody

This concept relates to procedures for documenting access to a specimen (e.g., a blood or urine sample) as it was taken, transported, processed, and stored. A failure to properly monitor the collection of a urine specimen can result in actions by the donor to substitute a false specimen, contaminate his or her fresh specimen, or switch specimens with another donor.

Looking for Indicators

The best example of a CSO getting involved with and influencing supervisors is hands-on teaching of how to look for prohibited materials. Just observing is a natural supervisory activity and an excellent method for keeping alcohol and drugs off the job. Although the act of observing is natural, so is the common human tendency to not always understand what is seen. In familiar surroundings, such as where we work, we tend to overlook the obvious. The indicators of abuse will not be found when a supervisor does not consciously look for them. And even when there is a conscious intent, the discovery is difficult because the indicators are often carefully masked and easily mistaken for other things.

Observation works best when planned and deliberately carried out. Preparation for observing includes determining where and when to look, knowing what to look for, and making a record of the findings. The process is enhanced when the supervisor predetermines the area to be looked at and considers the operations performed in the area selected for inspection.

Knowing where to look has to complemented with knowing what to look for (i.e., the evidences of use). Planning a walkthrough would involve an itinerary for inspecting rest rooms, employee break and changing rooms, trash receptacles, and parking lots. These are the places where a supervisor may find discarded items such as glassine envelopes that once contained marijuana or cocaine, plastic vials that contained crack, empty adhesive tubes and paper bags that were used for glue sniffing, butt tips from marijuana cigarettes, and soiled paper towels that were used to clean residues from marijuana, hashish, and crack pipes.

Indicators of Abuse

The CSO also helps supervisors look for the indicators of abuse. They fall into three categories: performance, behavior, and general.

Performance indicators: These include

- Frequent no-shows and lateness. Examples include not showing up for work on Fridays and Mondays, and repeated lateness in arriving at work.
- Unexplained absences from the assigned workstation.
- Frequent and long visits to the rest room or locker room.
- Visits to the employee by strangers or other employees for matters unrelated to the job.

Behavior indicators: In this group are

- An unexplained change in disposition in a short period of time. The employee may go from being uncooperative to cooperative, from quiet to talkative, from sad to happy. The reason may be that between the "down" mood and the "up" mood the employee took a drug. If the mood swings in the opposite direction, it may indicate that a drug is wearing off.
- Weight loss and loss of appetite.
- Nervousness that might appear in the form of starting to smoke or increasing a smoking habit.
- Reluctance to show the arms or legs. If an employee is taking drugs intravenously, he or she will try to hide the injection marks by wearing long-sleeve garments and wearing slacks in place of skirts and dresses. Blood spots on pant legs and sleeves may appear.
- Withdrawal symptoms. The employee may show the physiological effects of a drug as it is wearing off. The common symptoms are runny nose, sniffling, red eyes, trembling of hands or mouth, unsteady gait, and a general tiredness.
- Active symptoms. The employee may show signs of being under the influence. Generally, a drug will either relax or excite. A person who has

taken a relaxant (depressant) tends to be "mellowed out," slow moving, dreamily happy, and likely to talk with slurring of words. The person who has taken a stimulant tends to be energetic, twitchy, fast moving, and likely to talk in a rapid and nonstop manner.

General indicators: These indicators are general in nature and may include indicators characteristic of one or both of the other two groups.

- An admission. A drug-abusing employee may admit to use, possibly to seek help or to explain unacceptable performance.
- Possession of a drug without medical reason. Drugs can be in the form of prescription drugs or illegally manufactured drugs. They might appear as pills, tablets, capsules, powders, pastes, leafy materials, gum-like substances, and liquids.
- Concealment. An employee may hide a drug on the body or in some place that is accessible to the user. A user will sometimes favor concealment in an area also used by other employees. If the concealed drug is found, the user can avoid being singled out.
- Paraphernalia. An employee may possess or conceal drug paraphernalia, such as a syringe, needle, cooker spoon, roach clip, or glass pipe.
- Injection marks. An employee may show needle marks, boil-like abscesses, or scabs and scars, especially on the arms, legs, and backs of the hands.
- Drowsiness. An employee may show unusual sleepiness or general lethargy. This can be indicative of a slight overdose of an opiate, especially when it is accompanied by scratching of the body.
- Changes in the size of eye pupils. The pupils will greatly constrict immediately after taking an opiate. The pupils of an amphetamine user will dilate after use.
- Erratic conduct. The opiate user may vacantly stare and be generally unaware of surroundings; the stimulant user may be excited, euphoric and talkative; the user of marijuana, inhalants, and depressants may be sleepy or appear to be drunk; and the user of hallucinogens, such as PCP and LSD, may engage in bizarre and possibly violent conduct.
- Change in eating habits. The abuser of stimulants will go for long periods of time without eating. The narcotics user may have a loss of appetite or consume candy, cookies, soda pop, and sweet-tasting food items.
- Illness symptoms. Users will display a variety of illness symptoms. For example, the opiate user in withdrawal may have the sniffles, flushed skin, muscular twitching, and nausea; the user of hallucinogens may experience an increase in blood pressure, heart rate, and blood sugar, irregular breathing, sweating, trembling, dizziness, and nausea; the cocaine user may have inflamed nasal membranes.
- Drug jargon. The use of drug jargon, awareness of how drugs are administered and their effects, and an attitude that excuses or defends drug use. The possession of magazines or literature marketed for persons interested in drug abuse is another indicator.

- Drug refuse. Trash receptacles in rest rooms and public areas may contain items that suggest drug use. Discarded paper and plastic bags and acrosol cans are the refuse of sniffers. The small vial that contained crack or the glassine envelope that contained heroin might be discarded, as well as metal bottle caps, eye droppers, syringes, and burnt matches that are used for cooking heroin preparatory to injection.
- Frequent absences. Absence from the job for 15 to 30 minutes every four or five hours, especially in cases where the individual isolates himself in absolute privacy, is a telltale sign. This is the time when an addict "shoots up" or "snorts."
- Nothing to show for money. An addict will experience a discrepancy between income and expenditures for necessities, spending on alcohol or drugs most of what is earned, borrowed, or stolen.
- Borrowing. A constant need for money that may appear as borrowing from fellow workers, stealing, writing bad checks, and working as a prostitute.

Consider the following scenario.

CASE STUDY

"None of my people are into drugs," said Kurt Walling, supervisor of an oil field drilling crew. "We work hard and long, but we work safe. Our accident record proves it." The CSO, Hal Anson, listened but was not convinced. As he had explained to Kurt, information developed by a law enforcement agency indicated a sharp rise in local street sales of amphetamine. Hal did not believe the oil field was immune to uppers or any other type of drug. "Just the same, it's good to be on the lookout," Hal said before leaving.

A week later one of the laborers on Kurt's crew lost three fingers when a clamp on a drill bit crushed his hand. A blood test made at the hospital revealed a large concentration of amphetamine in the worker's body system. Hal called Kurt and asked if there was anything he could do to help. "Yes," Kurt replied, "I need you to come out and show me again how to look for that amphetamine stuff."

A very valuable alliance is formed when the CSO reaches out to interact with supervisors in the administration of the organization's alcohol- and drug-free program. Because supervisors are positioned to evaluate human behavior and performance in the operational venues, they gain perspectives and insights that can be of enormous help. Detection is the principle function of the CSO in respect to keeping prohibited substances out of the workplace, and every supervisor represents an extra pair of eyes.

SUBSTANCE ABUSE INVESTIGATIONS

The CSO is a fact finder in violations of substance abuse policy, and is a liaison with law enforcement when policy violations also happen to be violations of law. Violations related to alcohol, which is legal to possess and use, are normally handled in-house, with the CSO providing investigative assistance to the human relations group. The assistance is usually in the form of taking statements from witnesses. The CSO takes on a larger and more active role in violations related to illegal drugs. In these cases, intensive investigation is required. Witnesses are interviewed, suspects are interrogated, and physical evidence is collected and forensically examined. When the violation goes beyond personal use, such as selling or distributing illegal drugs, the applicable law may require involvement of a law enforcement agency [4].

An illegal drug incident rises in seriousness when it involves the use of the company's resources. Many examples exist of employees transporting drugs on company aircraft and vehicles, sending and receiving drugs through the company's mail and package delivery systems, storing drugs on company premises, and laundering drug money through the company's financial systems. When a violation has crossed state or national boundaries, the CSO's notification to law enforcement is often made to the Drug Enforcement Administration or the Federal Bureau of Investigation.

In a drug investigation coordinated with law enforcement, the usual practice is to split the investigative tasks. The CSO handles matters internal to the organization, whereas law enforcement personnel handle everything outside the organization. When an investigation moves to the courtroom, the CSO is teamed with the principal police investigators and a prosecutor.

NOTES

1. Many of the ideas presented in this chapter were drawn from *The Drug-Free Workplace: How To Get There and Stay There*, by John J. Fay, Boston: Butterworth-Heinemann, 2000.

2. Eugene F. Ferraro, *Employer's Guide To a Drug-Free Workplace*, pp. 8, Cincinnati: The Employers Group Service Corporation, 1995.

3. Having a detectable amount of an illegal drug in the body system may be a violation of the employer's policy but is not a violation of law. A positive result on a drug test conducted by the employer is not in and of itself a reason for making a report to a law enforcement agency. When an illegal drug has been confiscated, whether in the workplace or any other setting (and regardless of amount), the law is consistent in requiring that the drug be turned over to law enforcement.

4. John J. Fay, *Drug Testing*, pp. 267–276, Boston: Butterworth-Heinemann, 1991.

19. Executive Protection

The best laid schemes o' mice and men/Gang aft a-gley
—Robert Burns

BACKGROUND

An executive protection program is a security component in many venues: business, government, entertainment, sports, and wealth. Our principal perspective in this book is business and for that reason we will use the term *chief executive officer* (*CEO*) when referring to the protected person. We will also use the term *program* when referring to the executive protection program. Not all CEOs are protected. This is because in some organizations

- The board of directors sees no need for it.
- The CEO sees no need for it or refuses to accept it.
- The threat is believed to not exist or is perceived to be at such a low level that a program is not merited.
- The cost of a program is not affordable.

A program can be small and simple, comprehensive and complex, or somewhere in between. The nature of the threat will determine the nature of program. As the threat level rises, so must the capability of the program.

The protection elements in a small program can consist of guards at the office building and an alarm system in the home. The program enlarges as duress alarms are installed in the executive suite, a security officer is the receptionist at the suite entrance, and secretaries are trained to look for and react to danger. At the home, exterior lighting is added and a security patrol passes by several times during hours of darkness. A comprehensive program can have all of the previous plus a driver and an automobile for local commuting. The driver will be skilled in bodyguard tactics, escape driving, use of a firearm, and administration of CPR and first aid. The vehicle will be resistant to bullets and explosives and have capabilities for quick acceleration, high speed, and tight cornering. The CEO's home will have a controlled entrance gate and one or a few security officers stationed outside. A communications system will allow the driver and other security personnel to communicate among themselves and with a security control center.

Whatever the size and complexity of the program, the CSO is the person in charge. When the program is large, the CSO will be assisted by a person that might hold a position titled executive protection manager (EPM). This individual supervises routine protective activities at the CEO's office and home, and accompanies the CEO when he/she is traveling in high-risk areas and appearing at or attending public events.

PROTECTION AT THE OFFICE AND AT HOME

At the office or the home, the protective shield is a combination of physical safeguards and people. The safeguards and people have three main functions: keep threats away, give warning when a potential threat is near, and summon help. Many physical safeguards serve purposes in addition to executive protection. For example, fences, lights, sensors, alarms, and CCTV at the office are there to protect everyone. Other safeguards serve the CEO only (e.g., duress alarms, bullet- and explosive-resistant walls, concealed room, and specially equipped vehicle).

People who protect the CEO at the office consist mainly of security officers, and they too serve a general population. At the CEO's home the people component is slightly different: nonuniformed security officers and a household staff such as cook, maid, and gardener.

THE THREAT

U.S. businesspersons, both at home and overseas, are targets for kidnapping, assassination, and other acts of violence at the hands of criminals and terrorists. The criminals' usual objective is to acquire money in exchange for their captives. When the criminals are also followers of an ideology, their objective may be to force changes to government policy or business practices or to obtain release from incarceration of their fellow criminals.

Terrorists can also use kidnapping as a means of acquiring money, but their usual objectives are to shape public opinion, overthrow a government, elevate a religion or cult, or simply annihilate people. Experience tells us that CEOs often become the targets of deranged individuals with motives as strange as the acts they commit. For example, a CEO whose decision caused an employee to be disciplined, laid off, or terminated may become the center of the employee's frustrations. The employee may believe he or she was discriminated against, and as a result seeks revenge.

A group intending to kidnap or harm the CEO may attempt to gain entry to the residence or office through pretext. Examples are posing as a cable repairman, slipping past a guard during shift change, and pretending to be a FedEx courier.

The group's target can be the CEO's child. If kidnapping is the objective, the method may be trickery in effecting release of the child from the custody of a babysitter, child-care center, or school. The target can be the CEO's spouse, and the capture may be attempted when he/she is away from the home such as when shopping, jogging, or socializing.

The best guidance for the protectors and the protected is to anticipate possible scenarios, take preemptive steps, look for the early warning signals, and react quickly. The CSO must evaluate the vulnerabilities of the organization with respect to the threat, the current capacity of the organization to resist, and the range of countermeasures necessary. A program has credibility when it is anchored in the authority of an unambiguous company policy, takes into account specific risks, and calls for reasonable countermeasures to lower risk to an acceptable threshold.

KIDNAP

A first step in a company's defense against executive kidnapping is to develop a policy and obtain approval of an anti-kidnap plan. Approval in most cases will be made at the board of directors level and will involve consideration of kidnap insurance, ransom payments, and a crisis management team (CMT). The policy provides direction and authority for the anti-kidnap plan.

Kidnap Insurance

If kidnap insurance is purchased, the carrier will require absolute secrecy with respect to that fact and to any premeditation concerning intent to pay ransom. The carrier may also dictate who is to do the negotiating of ransom payments, require that the organization's response be conducted in accordance with applicable laws of the United States and other nations, and that prompt and full notification be given to law enforcement. A failure by the organization to meet the carrier's requirements can render the coverage null and void or reduce the carrier's obligations to pay.

Anti-kidnap Plan

Although the organization's plan for dealing with kidnapping is a highly sensitive matter, it cannot be developed with such great secrecy that it will reflect the thinking of one or a few individuals who may not have all the right answers. An initial planning group consisting of in-house and outside experts can be helpful in touching all the bases. In addition to the CSO, who has a key role to play within the group, other members can include the following:

- Agents of the Federal Bureau of Investigation (FBI)
- A counterterrorism expert

- A person familiar with the national government of the place where the kidnapping might occur
- A kidnap insurance specialist
- A professional hostage negotiator
- A public affairs specialist
- An electronics communication expert
- A human resources specialist

Kidnap Survey

A survey of the CEO's home can uncover weaknesses correctible with simple safeguards such as trimming the shrubs, adding outside lights, and installing an alarm system inside the home. In high-risk circumstances it may become necessary to add watch dogs and security officers and an alarm system that begins at the perimeter of the property.

Thought in the survey is given to the time needed to execute an appropriate response. When an effective or timely response is uncertain, protection can be supplemented by creating in the home a concealed room. A concealed room typically features a highly resistive door, a panic button, and a telephone. A weapon inside the room is an option.

A survey might call for screening and equipping protective staff. Screening can go beyond routine background checking. Equipping can include defensive items such as bullet-resistant vests, firearms, cell phones, and walkie-talkies.

EXECUTIVE PROTECTION FILE

An important step is to set up a file on the CSO. The file contains details about persons close to the CSO, places the CEO visits, the CEO's unique personal characteristics, and proof-of-life information.

People

In the people category are the CEO's family, relatives, household help, neighborhood friends, close friends, key working associates, physicians, dentists, and others who play a part in the CEO's life.

Places

In the places category are restaurants, lounges, homes of friends and relatives, jogging paths, workout centers, theaters, and other places frequented by the CEO.

Unique Characteristics

The unique characteristics category relates exclusively to the CEO. It includes descriptions of distinguishing characteristics such as blood type, dental records, eye glasses and contact lenses, hairpiece, prosthetic devices, scars, birth marks, tattoos, and jewelry worn. Also included are hobbies, special interests, and medications. Especially important are handwriting and hand printing samples, fingerprints, and palm prints.

Proof of Life

The proof of life category includes one or a few bits of information that would be known only to the CEO. Examples include the name of the CEO's first grade teacher, the name of the CEO's first dog, or the family nickname of an eccentric aunt. In discussions with kidnappers, proof of life information can be used to verify that the CEO is alive.

As much as possible, the executive file is augmented with photographs, maps, sketches, and the like. In a kidnap situation, information of this type can be extremely helpful in determining where the taking occurred.

Training

The CSO, his/her immediate family, and protective staff are at the top of the list for training. Below them are house servants and office workers with frequent access to the CEO. The training topics address the tactics of kidnappers, the early warning signals of a kidnapping attempt, how to respond, and, if abducted, how to survive.

Avoid Attracting Attention

The CEO needs to learn how to avoid attracting attention. Kidnappers are assisted when they possess details of appearance, social activities, local movement, and out-of-town travel. Care has to be taken when talking on the telephone, in restaurants, and in other places where conversations can be overheard. Written information personal to the CEO deserves protection and should be shredded when no longer needed.

Avoid Predictable Patterns

Routes to and from work and the vehicles used need to be frequently and randomly changed; the times, dates, and places of out-of-office business meetings should not follow a discernible pattern; and family and social routines should be varied. (See Figure 19-1.) Consider the Reso case, described in the following.

CASE STUDY

On April 29, 1992, law enforcement authorities were asked to investigate the disappearance of Exxon executive Sidney J. Reso from his home in Morris Township, New Jersey. On the morning of that day, Reso's wife discovered her husband's car at the end of the driveway,

Figure 19-1 Avoiding traffic congestion and varying the route to and from work are common anti-kidnap techniques.

empty but with the engine running. After calling his office and finding he had not arrived, she called the police.

At first, the Morris County authorities handled it as a missing person case. The next day, however, a caller to the Exxon switchboard claimed to have information about Reso and said that a letter could be found at a nearby shopping mall. Convinced then that a kidnapping had occurred, the Morris County Prosecutor's Office (MCPO) called the FBI.

Within four hours, the Reso home became an FBI command post complete with trap, trace, and recording devices on phone lines. The neighborhood and surrounding wooded areas were thoroughly searched and 24-hour surveillance and security was set up at the Reso home and at the homes of four children in Texas, Missouri, California, and Washington, D.C.

A ransom demand letter was picked up at the mall. The kidnappers instructed that a cell phone be obtained for future calls and that the phone number published in a classified ad in the Newark Star Ledger. The letter also contained a demand for $18.5 million in hundred-dollar bills.

Exxon provided the ransom money and the FBI packaged it. A cell phone was obtained and the waiting for a call began. Specialist teams were gathered and made ready to move on an instant's notice. As they waited, the teams practiced skills that ranged from communication intercepts to sniper firing to SWAT exercises.

The kidnappers made eight calls and sent 14 letters before attempting to collect the ransom. The attempt occurred on May 3 but went awry when the kidnappers made a mistake in following their own instructions. More calls, letters, and advertisements followed.

On June 16 the kidnappers seemed ready once again to act. They instructed Reso's wife, daughter, and an Exxon executive to deliver the ransom and to take the cell phone with them so they could receive instructions along the way. Two FBI agents posing as Reso's wife and daughter accompanied the Exxon executive. The kidnappers' instructions took them on a rambling journey. Meanwhile, FBI agents in many separate locations watched out of sight. A break came when an agent observed a heavy-set white man with blonde hair wearing gloves making a phone call at a shopping mall. The agent also observed this same man remove the gloves when he got into a red Cutlass Ciera, which was traced to a rental car company. Shortly after that, one of the kidnappers' calls was traced to a pay phone in an area where a surveillance team was in place. The team observed a woman calling from a pay phone, and the time of the call matched the time of one of the kidnappers' calls.

Agents went to the rental car company and waited. Arthur Seale returned the Ciera. His wife Jackie arrived to pick him up. Jackie Seale turned out to be the same woman who had been seen earlier making a call from a pay phone. The Seales were arrested.

Arthur Seale had previously worked as a police officer and a security official at Exxon. He and his wife decided to kidnap and ransom Sidney Reso in order to get out of serious financial difficulty. They began by watching the Reso house and learning Mr. Reso's morning routine. When they felt prepared to act, they went to the house and moved the morning newspaper from one side of the driveway to the other. They knew that he always picked up the newspaper and took it to work with him. To pick up the newspaper where Seale had placed it, Reso would have to get out of his car and walk around the car. When Reso did exactly that, Arthur Seale approached him quickly and at gunpoint forced him into a rental van driven by Jackie Seale. The gun went off and Reso was shot in the arm. The Seales drove him to a storage facility where, after treating his gunshot wound, they blindfolded him, handcuffed him, gagged him, and placed him in a coffin-like wooden box.

One week after the Seales were arrested, Jackie began cooperating. She said that Reso had died on May 3, just five days after his kidnapping. She and Arthur Seale removed the body from the box at the storage facility and buried it at another location.

The Seales were charged with multiple federal and state offenses. He pled guilty to seven federal counts, including extortion, use of a weapon in the commission of a crime, and a state charge of murder. He was sentenced to 95 years in federal prison to be followed by 70 years' state imprisonment. She was sentenced to 20 years in federal prison for the two counts of extortion.

ABDUCTION

The value of planning and preparation is immediately evident in the aftermath of abduction. Preparation has been made to receive contact from the kidnappers and to respond in a manner that will not place the CEO's life at greater risk. (See Figures 19-2 and 19.3.)

Contact

The kidnappers will likely make contact by telephone, although it could be made by letter or through another party such as a newspaper or radio station. If contact is by telephone, certain protocols are in order.

- Express a willingness to cooperate.
- Ask to speak to the CEO.
- Ask for the proof-of-life code.
- Record the call.

If contact is in writing, the document and its envelope or outside container are carefully protected in order to not adversely affect forensic analyses such as examinations for fingerprints and saliva on the envelope flap. Contact by the kidnappers is reported to the FBI immediately. Notifications to law enforcement agencies of other countries that have jurisdiction are also made. An attempt to handle the situation without recourse to government authorities is likely to fail.

Kidnap Prevention Tips

Instruct family and business associates not to provide information concerning you or your family to strangers.

Avoid giving unnecessary personal details in response to inquiries from information collectors that would be used in such publications as business directories, social registers, or community directories.

Review your organization's security plans to determine their effectiveness. Make certain employees are aware of these plans.

Establish simple, effective signal systems which, when activated, will alert your business associates or family members that you are in danger.

Be alert to strangers who are on business property for no apparent reason.

Vary your daily routines to avoid the habitual patterns that kidnappers look for. Fluctuate your travel as to times and routes to and from the office.

Refuse to meet with strangers at secluded or unknown locations.

Inform a business associate or family member of your destination when leaving the office or home and what time you intend to return.

Lock all doors and roll up windows of your automobile while traveling to and from work.

Figure 19-2 A tip sheet like this one can be given to executives who are exposed to the risk of kidnapping.

If Kidnapping Occurs...

Call the Federal Bureau of Investigation. The telephone number of the nearest FBI office is listed in the front of the telephone directory. The reporting person should be prepared to furnish in an orderly fashion all facts relating to the disappearance of the victim.

Maintain absolute secrecy and do not permit any of the facts regarding the kidnapping or demands for ransom to be known outside the immediate family and the investigating officers.

Do not handle letters or communications demanding the payment of ransom. Turn these over to the investigating officers as soon as possible.

Do not touch or disturb anything at the scene of the crime. Minute particles of evidence not visible to the naked eye may be destroyed.

Be calm and try to maintain a normal routine.

Place full confidence in the investigating officers. Help the investigators by providing photographs, a full description of the victim, and all facts relating to the personal habits, characteristics, and peculiarities of the victim.

Figure 19-3 A tip sheet similar to this one can be provided to the protected executive and his or her business associates and family members.

By the time the kidnappers have made contact, the crisis management team will have been activated. The CMT leader, to whom considerable decision-making authority has been delegated, is the key person in coordinating major issues with law enforcement and other parties of interest. The CMT members perform their preplanned tasks (e.g., notifying next of kin, dealing with the news media, setting up a command center, establishing a rumor control function, coordinating with the kidnap insurance carrier, and obtaining the services of a professional negotiator).

Ransom

Kidnappers often demand an immediate and large payment but do not expect the demand to be met quickly and entirely. They realize that even if an immediate payment can be effected it is not likely to be as large as a payment arranged with deliberate speed. Kidnappers focus on "making a big score" and want to believe that the ransom payer has not contacted law enforcement authorities. An expectation of success suppresses their fear of getting caught.

EVENT PROTECTION

Kidnapping is but one of several threats confronting a CSO. Other threats include assassination, assault, robbery, and non-kidnap threats such as heart attack, sudden illness, or injurious accident. Of these other threats, assassination presents the greatest risk by far.

The CEO is most vulnerable when in close proximity to the public. Potential assassins understand this. They know that the protective capability is much reduced and that with little sophistication and a simple weapon the target can be brought down. We know this from experience. Nearly all assassinations of prominent leaders have occurred in public places, the assassins were able to get close enough to act, and the weapon was easily obtainable such as a knife, firearm, or homemade bomb.

CEOs are in the public, and thereby exposed, when they appear at an event. Events vary but all of them have one thing in common: the CEO is exposed to danger to some degree. Event protection is an activity separate from security provided to the CEO in the office, at home, during commuting, and routine out-of-town travel. Routine security requires a lesser number of people; event security can require numerous people, some of whom may of necessity be outside contractors.

Team Leader

The person in overall charge of event-related protection can have a number of titles (e.g., mission leader or person-in-charge). We will use *team leader* and *mission* when referring to event-related protection activities. The team leader will be the CSO or the executive protection manager. The big-picture functions of the team leader are preparing an operational plan and supervising the mission team. The mission team for an event has four groups: advance party, residence party, baggage party, and protective party.

Advance party: This group travels in advance to the locale of the upcoming mission and performs the following.

- Conducts on-site inspections to evaluate probable risks to the CEO and proactively sets up countermeasures. Inspections take place at arrival and departure terminals, offices to be visited, conference rooms, restaurants, event venues, and other places on the CEO's travel agenda.
- Meets with and initiates working relationships with officials of participating agencies.
- Conducts reconnaissance of local travel routes and makes recommendations to local traffic control officials. Recommendations might include speed, composition, and order of a motorcade.
- Coordinates local ground transportation and arranges for the security of baggage.
- Inspects vehicles to be used for local ground transportation and briefs drivers concerning what to do if a vehicle is involved in an accident or breaks down or if the CSO is injured or becomes ill.
- Prepares sketches, maps, photographs, and written reports to fully inform the team leader and team supervisor.

Residence party: This group provides around-the-clock protection at the CEO's places of stay during travel. Duties can include keeping a log of occurrences, screening incoming telephone calls, checking packages, controlling the access and movements of visitors, and driving the CEO from place to place.

Baggage party: The baggage party provides oversight protection to the CEO's baggage. The function begins at the starting point and continues during travel to the visit location. Oversight is discontinued during the time the baggage is in use by the CEO. The baggage party resumes oversight at the outset of and during the return trip and concludes when the CEO reaches home base. This group does not actually handle baggage but supervises the movement and custody of it.

Protective party: This group conducts surveillance and provides close-in protection prior to, during, and following the event. The protective party consists entirely of or is complemented by persons from the advance, residence, and baggage parties.

The nuts and bolts of the mission, which are covered in the operational plan, determine the tasks of the protective party (see Figure 19.4). Details of the operational plan are known only by the team leader and members of the protective party. Details can be revealed to outsiders only when knowledge of them is necessary for plan execution. For example, if the team is to be armed, this fact is made known to local law enforcement authorities.

Figure 19-4 Protective officers form a shield around the protected executive.

Operational Plan

Information acquired by the advance team is dropped into the planning pot along with information obtained from the CEO's staff. Details can include the type and theme of the event, event agenda, names of event speakers, special guests, characteristics of the audience, travel itinerary, persons traveling with the CEO, modes of travel to and from the event city, social activities, shopping and sightseeing trips, and so on. Also placed into the pot is information about potential threats, especially any threat in the form of a terrorist group. These pot ingredients are a terrorist group's proximity to the event site, its stated intentions, capabilities, resolve, preferred targets, weapons, and tactics. The team leader, along with the CSO, stirs the pot to see what type of stew has been cooked.

Based on what has been learned, the team leader begins to put together a plan. The plan will take into consideration the following:

- The attitude of the CSO regarding the protective shield
- Political, religious, and cultural beliefs that pervade or surround the event
- Duration of risk exposure (i.e., the length of time the CEO will be exposed to a potential threat)
- Coordination with other agencies, particularly law enforcement
- Ability of the protective force to deflect an attack and react effectively
- Laws that apply such as laws dealing with possession of weapons and the application of deadly force
- Means of communication
- Terrain and geography
- Modes of transportation, both routine and emergency

- Availability of emergency medical treatment
- Selection and training of security personnel
- News media

Murphy's Law applies. Even when a plan addresses every possible glitch the unexpected will happen. It is for this reason that planning has to include a strong flavoring of flexibility.

Overseas Event

The situation changes when the event is to occur overseas. For one thing, the organization sponsoring the event may have to perform administrative tasks normally done by the advance team such as acquire maps and photographs and identify routes of travel, emergency care facilities, and private security firms. The sponsor can also introduce the advance team to local agencies involved in the event. When the CEO's organization has an office near the event site, staff from it can help as well.

Events held overseas present out-of-the-ordinary circumstances, some of which can be impediments. Impediments decrease the protective capability, which in turn increases risk to the CEO. Problems are created when assisting persons at the overseas site prove to be unreliable. Small details, such as traffic conditions and ground transportation, are certain to be different and therefore problematic. What may work nicely close to home base may not work nicely overseas. The essential tasks include:

- Book travel and hotel accommodations in the name of the sponsoring organization. Work through a vetted point of contact (POC). Preferably, the POC will be a senior person in a governmental police or intelligence service.
- Maintain confidentiality of details associated with the CSO's travel, accommodations, and attendance. Communicate with the POC and others on a confidential and need-to-know basis.
- Evaluate arrangements made at the location site pertaining to side trips.
- Anticipate potential disruptions, most particularly public demonstrations and actions of unfriendly news media.
- Acquire pertinent maps, sketches, diagrams, photographs, and so on. These will depict the layout of the event site, areas surrounding the event site, travel routes to and from the event site, and places where the CSO will be stationary. Rest rooms are included.
- When the sponsoring organization is company owned or company managed, the POC will be an employee of the sponsoring organization. Make clear to the POC that overall security is the responsibility of the sponsoring organization, subject to approval of the team leader. (Note: bodyguard protection during the event will be provided by the team.)

- Confer with and obtain advice of local law enforcement authorities concerning potential security threats, obtain recommendations, and invite participation and use of local resources in carrying out the mission.
- Consult with other agencies of interest such as an embassy or consular office. Obtain intelligence estimates as to possible security threats.
- Avoid advance publicity.
- Schedule local ground transportation as tightly as possible. Local ground travel will be in a primary vehicle operated or occupied by a team member or a local person vetted, trained in CPR and first aid, and having knowledge of the roadways and of available emergency medical treatment facilities. The primary vehicle and backup vehicle will be equipped with a telephone and cell phone. A primary and an alternate route will be selected and tested in advance.
- Confer with the security professionals at hotels to be used. Evaluate security normally provided to CSOs, and where necessary augment to ensure an adequate level of protection. (See Figure 19.5)
- Escort the CSO throughout the event and give to him/her a contact telephone number to use in case of an emergency, an unanticipated incident, or a change in schedule.

Figure 19-5 Coordination of the functions of law enforcement is a critical element of the plan.

- Employ local security officers only in exceptional circumstances. Hiring should be through a reputable security company recommended by the police. The police must be informed of any decision to use armed persons.
- Obtain the services of an anti-eavesdropping specialist if information security will be an issue at a closed venue.
- Advise the CSO to cancel or reschedule the event if the risk is high or local security capabilities inadequate.

In-depth Defense

This operational concept is used in almost every mission. It consists of one or more layers of protection that an attacker has to penetrate in order to reach the target. For a high-risk mission, the number of layers may be numerous. For example, in a situation where the CEO moves through a dense crowd a tight ring of one to four persons move in unison with him/her, a loose ring of trouble spotters operate 15–25 meters away, and spotters at an elevated location communicate with those down below. In a low-risk situation, the CEO may be accompanied by one or two persons and no spotters.

In-depth defense can be likened to an onion. As each layer of the onion is peeled back, another layer is beneath it, and each layer is increasingly difficult to peel.

The whole onion is mobile. As it moves, the CEO remains at the center and moves with it. The objective of defense-in-depth is delay an attacker long enough to allow the CEO to escape under escort to a safe haven.

After-action Report

A written report is made for the record at the conclusion of a mission. It is written in narrative style, with emphasis on problems encountered and steps taken to resolve them. The report contains recommendations for improvement of performance in future missions.

Problems described in the after-action report give proof of a fact: it is not possible to give absolute personal protection. (See Figure 19.6.) The best that can be expected is to reduce the risks as much as possible. Persons assigned to CEO protection duties have to understand this basic premise. They also have to know and accept the legal and sociological constraints that are present in every mission.

Buy-in

There can no protective program without the CEO's buy-in. A CEO understands risk as a management concept but may not be ready to acknowledge risk in personal terms. CSOs have been known to respond with denial, not unlike alcoholics refusing to look at the evidence of addiction. A program will not work until risk is acknowledged.

Figure 19-6 Every safeguard possible may be taken, but none can guarantee perfect protection.

Buy-in is demonstrated by a commitment to and active involvement in protective arrangements. Involvement has three dimensions: training, interest in the program, and cooperation with the program. The first of the three is problematic. CEOs are often busy and do not assign a high priority to training. The CSO has to find a way to get past the reluctance. In this case, patience is a virtue; persuasion is a must. Horror stories and cajolery, while not recommended, may help.

Fortunately, the key points of training are knowledge based (i.e., they can be learned without actually getting up from a desk). The exceptions would be firearms and self-defense training. For many companies and many CEOs, the use of firearms is not seen as helpful, and for some CEOs self-defense is not practical for reasons of age or inclination.

Training of the CEO has two learning objectives: know how to keep from being kidnapped or assassinated and how to respond if taken hostage. As to the first objective, the CEO learns to closely control information that an adversary needs to be successful, avoid predictable behavior, and stay within the shell maintained by the protective party at public events. As to response, the CEO learns the early warning signals and how to recognize them, actions to take and not take, and most importantly how to survive if taken hostage.

Training is a serious and difficult endeavor. It is serious because death or injury can result if the CEO makes an incorrect response. It is difficult because the typical CEO has little or no familiarity with violence and without training stands little chance of surviving. Can such things be learned easily? The answer is no. Is this something that has to be learned? The answer is yes.

20. Workplace Violence

Guns don't kill people, postal workers do.
      —Bumper sticker

BACKGROUND

Violence in the workplace has always been a top concern for the CSO. Although on-the-job violence is not new under the sun, the most extreme form of it, homicide, has in recent years occurred with increased frequency and major negative effect. Studies made of workplace violence reveal that

- It appears in a variety of shapes and forms.
- There is no absolute, sure-fire method for preventing it in every situation.
- A small amount of preparation can go a long way in reducing injuries and saving lives.
- Prevention and mitigation cannot be achieved through the efforts of the CSO alone. Effective management of workplace violence depends on joint efforts of the CSO and specialists in several disciplines.

VIOLENCE RESPONSE TEAM (VRT)

Companies that have developed a team approach say that supervisors and managers supported by knowledgeable and skilled specialists have a greater willingness to intervene in situations involving disruptive and intimidating employee behavior. A team approach enhances greater odds of success because it promotes confidence and offers the promise of creative solutions that might otherwise not be considered.

Ignoring a problem employee worsens the situation and escalates the risk. Unresolved conflict reduces the morale and productivity of good workers, often causing them to look for employment elsewhere. On the other hand, dealing effectively with hostile and intimidating situations creates a significantly safer and more productive environment. Prompt and decisive intervention has a deterrent effect on employees contemplating violence. The incidence of physical violence can be reduced when violence-prone employees clearly understand that such behavior will not be tolerated and that unpleasant consequences will be applied in every case.

VRT Members

In addition to the CSO, the members of the VRT typically include representatives from human resources, organizational health, safety, public affairs, building management, legal affairs, and unions when applicable. Although many disciplines may be represented on the team and are essential to success, only a few members will be involved in directly responding to violent incidents. The primary responders to incidents come from the security, human resources, and building management disciplines. The nonresponding members of the team can assist in some situations; for example, in dealing with the media and negotiating if hostages are taken.

A unionized company can involve union leadership from the very beginning. The representatives of bargaining unit employees are legally entitled to shape many conditions of employment. Some of the substantive issues relating to workplace violence, especially issues concerning security, may be outside the company's obligation to bargain. However, this does not rule out consultation and discussion with union leadership. It is sensible and practical to involve a union right from the start, before decisions are made. A union can be particularly helpful in training employees in workplace violence prevention and securing employee support of the ongoing program.

VRT Capabilities

The multidisciplined composition of the VRT helps it

- Identify the resources needed to capably prevent and respond to violent situations.
- Carefully and honestly evaluate the organization's current prevention and response capabilities.
- Identify the weak or missing skills and knowledge.
- Develop an ad hoc plan for filling capability gaps.
- Develop an operational plan that formalizes prevention and response actions.
- Develop procedures that supplement the operational plan (e.g., how to report the indicators of potential violence and what to do when a violent situation unfolds).

ASSESSING READINESS

A way to start in determining the company's ability to prevent and respond to violence is to examine previous incidents. Questions that can be asked when looking into the past are: Why did the incident happen? Could it have been prevented? Did any signals precede the incident? How effective was the company's response? Have steps been taken to prevent recurrence and respond more capably? What can be learned from the past and put to good use in the future?

Of particular interest when examining the company's history of workplace violence is to identify patterns of risk and possible prevention strategies. The records may reflect, for example, that a particular work group has had a greater number of violence-related incidents than other groups or that one group appears prone to high violence such as committing acts with a knife or a gun. Consider the following anecdote.

CASE STUDY

The walls of Frank's cubicle were covered with photos and military citations going back to days when he served in the U.S. Army. Frank, an outgoing person, often spoke to co-workers about his fine collection of guns and his membership in the National Rifle Association. A bumper sticker on Frank's automobile bore the words "... when they pry my cold dead fingers..." Frank displayed no emotion when informed by his boss that he was one of several hundred employees to be let go in a restructuring of the company. He politely declined the company's offer of counseling to help him find work elsewhere and was uncharacteristically silent while being out-processed by a human resources specialist.

A week later, Frank returned to the job site. The lobby receptionist called Frank's former boss to obtain authority to issue Frank a visitor's pass. After shaking hands with his former boss, Frank calmly removed a .45-caliber pistol from a shoulder holster under his jacket. He shot his former boss in the chest, killing him instantly. Frank put the pistol back in the holster and sat down in a chair to wait for the arrival of the police.

VIOLENCE VARIES

The nature of workplace violence varies from company to company, as does a company's ability to deal with violence. The factors at play include the following:

- The nature and stressfulness of the work
- The financial ability of the organization to employ in-house specialists such as skilled practitioners in employee assistance, counseling, mediation, conflict resolution, health, safety, and threat assessment
- The availability of specialists in the community such as psychologists, psychiatrists, therapists, and law enforcement officers
- The orientation or culture of the organization
  - Are employees treated as assets or tools?
  - Is organizational profit the only key driver?
  - Is there an "us versus them" attitude affecting on-the-job relationships?
- The perspective of management and the priority placed on an anti-violence program

CASE STUDY

A convenience store clerk was shot and killed in a daytime robbery. The deceased clerk's wife sued the convenience store, alleging inadequate security. The defendant argued that it owed no duty to the clerk because there had been no prior similar crimes on the premises, therefore making the robbery and murder unforeseeable.

After hearing the testimony of an expert witness, the court disagreed with the defendant. The expert witness had described the "inherent risk of robbery and violent crime in the convenience store business" and also pointed out several security inadequacies at the store such as poor visibility from the outside, poor lighting, no security alarm, no video cameras, and no training of employees on security measures. The court ordered the convenience store owner to pay the dead clerk's wife $1.8 million, an award later upheld on appeal.

CONDUCTING AN ASSESSMENT AUDIT

An assessment audit is a mechanism to pinpoint both strengths and weaknesses of the organization's workplace violence program. An audit by a third party is a good choice because it can eliminate the bias and blindness that tend to creep into self-performed audits.

Audit Objectives

The objectives of the audit are to identify the following:

- The key tasks of preventing and responding to violent incidents
- The equipment, supplies, and other resources that must be on hand to properly perform the key tasks
- The positions or groups inside and outside the organization that perform the tasks in partnership
- The interactions between the partners
- Training that is needed to ensure effective performance
- Jurisdictional issues such as police authority and medical emergency responsibility

A matter addressed in an audit can be security force interactions such as the working relationships between guards and console operators and between supervisors and subordinates (see Figure 20-1).

Although the focus of the audit is on the security group, much light is cast upon the readiness of other groups. The team formed to develop an antiviolence program has members in positions of authority or influence to correct or ameliorate noted weaknesses. For this reason alone, it is very valuable when the team's membership includes representatives from community resources (see Figure 20-2) such as the police and fire departments, mental health office, and emergency medical treatment agency.

The assessment phase ends when all the facts have been gathered and studied. The facts should be able to answer a few basic questions: What types of violent acts can be expected? What can be done to prevent or reduce the negative effects of the violence that has been forecast? What does the organization have and not have in the way of pertinent expertise and related resources? What can be done to close gaps in the ability to prevent and respond?

Figure 20-1 Workplace violence is often avoided by maintaining a professional security presence at the point of entry. *(Photo Courtesy of Burns International Security Services.)*

Figure 20-2 Persons arrested for violent behavior are held and turned over to law enforcement.

Developing Plans and Procedures

Two plans come into play at this point. First is an ad hoc plan for correcting weaknesses such as not having access to expertise (such as a crisis counselor), not having equipment or materials (such as an alarm horn, a stretcher, and first aid supplies), and not having a training capability. This plan, which contains cost figures and time lines, is put to bed when the missing pieces have been acquired.

Operational Plan

The second plan is operational and has twin goals: prevention and response. It assigns to particular positions and groups specific functions and responsibilities. Persons in human resources, for example, might be tasked to look for and eliminate job stressors, offer to managers and supervisors guidance in how to construct work activities that reduce the potential for violence, and educate employees in techniques for managing personal conflicts and spotting indicators of brewing violence. The responders might be tasked to intervene using calmative approaches, for which initial and refresher training would be mandatory. Certain responders might be tasked to evaluate emerging or full-blown situations and to activate one or more predefined response options.

A checklist, such as that shown in Figure 20-3, can be helpful in sifting through response options.

Incident reporting: Primary among the objectives of an operational plan is to develop a simple system for ensuring that all incidents of violence, whether large or small, are reported, acted upon, and documented. The reporting channels can include hotlines, supervisors, human resource specialists, and a conspicuously posted phone number that connects to the security desk.

Credibility: The credibility of the reporting system rests on the record; that is, employees will make reports when they believe that reports will be handled quickly and effectively. The reporting system breaks down when reports have no follow-through, are handled improperly, and when the promise of confidentiality is breached. Also important to the success of any reporting system is management's encouragement to report incidents. Consider the following case.

CASE STUDY

Jake, a machinist in an aircraft manufacturing plant, angrily confronted a quality control specialist named Anna. He accused her of unfairly rejecting his work output. When she tried to explain that all work output had to meet precise technical specifications, he told her she was like all women who tried to do a man's job. "You can't handle the stress so you take it out on the men." Before storming away, Jake called Anna a whore and told her he would "punch out her lights" if she didn't stop picking on him.

Anna reported the incident to her supervisor, Harkins. "I don't want to get him in trouble," she said. "But I do want him to stay away from me." Harkins took no notes and

---

Checklist for Dealing With Violence (Late-Night Retail Business)

If Your Business

Requires employees to exchange money with the public, or

Is open during the evening or late hours, or

Is in a high-crime area, or

Has experienced a robbery, a violent incident, threats, harassment or other abusive conduct in the past 3 years:

Do These Things

Keep more than one employee at the business site during operating hours.

Provide employees with an emergency signaling system, e.g., a robbery or duress alarm, and at a minimum, an outside telephone line.

Post emergency telephone numbers adjacent to the phone.

Ensure that the entrance to the business is easily seen from the street.

Ensure bright lighting around the entrance, adjacent areas and parking lot.

Ensure that indoor lights work properly and are on.

Ensure that views from the outside are clear of obstructions.

Place the cash register in plain view.

Install a drop safe or time-access safe.

Enforce strict cash control rules, e.g., when and how to store cash in the safe.

Install security cameras.

Install a bullet-resistant enclosure for employees if the business has a history of robberies and assaults.

Develop proactive and reactive procedures, e.g., how to spot the early indicators of a robbery attempt and how to report a serious incident. Keep the procedures on hand and train employees to follow them.

Train employees in conflict resolution and how to respond to violent behavior.

Post anti-crime signage, e.g., signs declaring that only a small amount of cash is kept in the register and that security cameras are operating.

Enforce strict procedures for opening and closing the business.

Figure 20-3 Retail businesses operating late at night have a higher-than-average rate of violent incidents such as robbery and assault.

concluded by telling Anna that co-worker complaints came with the job of quality control. As far as Anna could tell, Harkins did nothing in response to her report.

A week later, Jake once again confronted Anna. This time he called her a bitch and said he would "punch her silly if she didn't get off his ass." Anna did not report this second incident with Jake. She did, however, continue to reject his unacceptable output, as she did the unacceptable output of other machinists.

In the middle of a workday, shortly after the machine shop had completed a rush project, Jake went to Anna's workstation and pointed a finger in her face. He told her she was "dead meat." Again, Anna did not make a report.

At 5 P.M., as Anna walked to her car in the company's parking lot, Jake stepped from behind a van and blocked her path. "I told you you were dead meat," he said. He punched her in the face, knocking her to the ground. Other employees on their way to their cars rushed to Anna's aid but were too late to prevent Jake from kicking her twice in the head and once in the abdomen. Jake fled.

A plant security officer drove Anna to a local hospital where she received 16 stitches to close a facial laceration. A nurse called the police and Anna filed a complaint.

Jake was fired. He pled no contest to a criminal charge of aggravated assault and was placed on probation. Anna left the aircraft plant for a quality control job elsewhere. Within six months, she filed a civil suit alleging negligence by her former employer and Harkins.

Broad scenarios: The wide variation in violent behaviors does not allow definitive predictions of likely incident scenarios. The best that can be done in an operational plan is to identify broad scenarios; for example, incidents involving actual death or injury, incidents involving lethal weapons, arguments, threats, intimidation, verbal assaults, and bullying (see Figure 20-4).

Checklist for Dealing with Violence (The General Workplace)

Develop A Policy That Will

Prohibit threats, intimidation, harassment, unwanted physical conduct and any form of violent behavior at work.

Prohibit the possession, distribution or use of alcohol and illegal drug use at work.

Prohibit lethal weapons at work.

Apply to all employees at all levels.

Educate employees concerning the unacceptability of violence and the consequences of policy violations.

Train supervisors to recognize the early warning signs of violent behavior and to intervene to prevent violence before it can occur.

Assign clear responsibility for compliance and enforcement.

Screen Job Applicants For

Any history of violent behavior.

Current abuse of violence-inducing substances such as alcohol and illegal drugs.

Investigate

Every threat or suspected threat of violence.

Every complaint of violence.

With investigators specifically trained in the dynamics of violent behavior.

Take Immediate Corrective Action To

Terminate any employee who seriously violates the policy, e.g., commits a physical assault upon another.

Suspend any employee who commits a minor policy violation.

Refer to an approved rehabilitation program any employee who commits a minor policy violation and who shows promise of rehabilitation.

Assist through an employee assistance program any employee who has been subjected to violence.

Follow-Up To

Ensure that every incident has been thoroughly investigated and documented.

Ensure that employees who have returned to work following rehabilitation are not at risk of relapse.

Ensure that victims of violence have been properly assisted.

Ensure that any needed changes to security measures, such as access control, have been made.

Figure 20-4 Measures such as these can be effective in reducing violence in the workplace generally.

In each broad scenario general assignments can be made, and they become in due course the bulleted points in procedures. For example, in a scenario involving lethal weapons the operational plan will almost certainly call for a response by the security group. The security group will necessarily develop a detailed procedure as to the how of the response. The procedure will clearly specify action steps such as summon the police and emergency medical treatment agencies, warn employees of danger, and order an evacuation of the premises. The operational plan document, perhaps consisting of less than 10 pages, can be supplemented with hundreds of pages representing the separate procedures developed within groups that hold responsibilities in prevention and response. The operational plan is broad and flexible, whereas procedures, which execute the plan, are detailed and specific.

Unpredictability: Plans and procedures acknowledge in their content the reality that violence is often unpredictable in timing and intensity but that the injurious consequences of violence can be lessened through planning and being prepared to act swiftly and decisively. Plans and procedures will also provide for primary and alternate responders and for training of responders, with rehearsal an essential element.

Triggering circumstances: An operational plan identifies the circumstances in which the VRT will be called into action. The CSO, or a key player in the security group, will be a member if not the leader. When the circumstances of a violent situation reach a critical juncture, such as the appearance or use of a lethal weapon, the VRT surrenders command and control to law enforcement.

Law enforcement will choose a response option appropriate to the nature of violence and use of lethal weapons (see Figure 20-5).

Figure 20-5 A final step in the resolution of a workplace violence incident can be the introduction of special weapons and tactics (SWAT).

Whether or not an organization has prepared itself to handle an act of violence, it will be forced to do so when one occurs. Violence in any venue is unwanted but must be expected and addressed.

WORKPLACE VIOLENCE POLICY

A policy on workplace violence comes from senior management. It gives broad direction to persons that develop the plan for making the policy come to life. A workplace violence policy will usually

- State the organization's right and obligation to ensure a workplace free of violent behavior.
- Use examples to show what is meant by violent behavior.
- Define terms used in the policy by avoiding misinterpretation and escape holes that could defeat the intent of the policy or precipitate litigation.
- Demonstrate an organizational commitment to deny employment to applicants with a history of violence and to weed out employees who engage in violent behavior. The policy can, for example, require background inquiries of job applicants and automatic dismissal of employees who commit egregious acts of violence.
- Require and encourage policy compliance by all employees.
- Describe how the organization will monitor and enforce compliance. An important element here is to ban lethal weapons at work and to express management's right to look for weapons at entry points and within the premises.
- Assign responsibilities such as requiring employees to report indicators or incidents of violent behavior.
- Name the consequences for noncompliance (e.g., suspension or termination). Avoid a zero-tolerance position because every case will have its own unique set of circumstances. Zero tolerance can also discourage employees from reporting violent behavior. An employee's desire may be to get a co-worker's behavior stopped, not get the co-worker fired.
- Identify training that will be given in support of the policy.
- Name employee assistance benefits (e.g., services available to victims of violence and counseling of violators).

Violence Not Tolerated

A policy places everyone on notice that violence will not be tolerated. This simple message is conveyed well when the policy is stated briefly (but not vaguely) and communicated (not once but continually) to all employees in a variety of formats such as memoranda, bulletin board and electronic messages, employee handbooks, and as an agenda item at employee meetings. Consider the following scenario.

CASE STUDY

Muriel, 62-years old and a 15-year employee with a convenience store chain, knew by name all of the regular customers at her corner store. She was attentive to her job and took pride in holding shoplifting losses to a minimum and maintaining an accurate till. During an audit by a security department investigator she boasted that she had only once been short in the till, and that to keep her good record intact she had made up the shortage out of her own pocket.

A man Muriel did not know entered her store just before closing time. After ensuring that he was the only customer, the man produced a gun and forced Muriel to give him the content of the till, amounting to slightly more than $50. Later, when talking to the company's security investigator, Muriel said she was going to buy a gun and keep it under the counter. "Ain't nobody gonna rob me no more," she said. The security investigator informed her that company policy prohibited guns on store premises and that the proper response to a robber's demand was to cooperate and surrender whatever money was in the till. Muriel replied that she understood the policy but "damn sure didn't like it."

A week later, right at closing time, the same robber returned and demanded she hand over the money. Muriel reached into the till, removed a handful of bills, and threw them in the robber's face. When the robber bent down to pick up the money, Muriel lifted a heavy bottle of dill pickles from the counter in front of her. She crashed the bottle on the back of the robber's head. He stood up, shot her in the neck, and cleaned out the rest of the till before fleeing.

Muriel recovered but the company did not allow her to return as a store employee. After two months as a file clerk in the company's accounts payable department, Muriel quit and went on Social Security.

Warning Signs

Workplace violence does not "just happen." In fact, it can be anticipated. A workplace heavy with stress and marked by antipathy between management and labor is like a powder keg waiting for a spark. Employee grievances are symptoms of trouble on the horizon. Some forms of stress at low levels are natural, even healthy, but all forms of stress at high levels can be counterproductive and conducive to violence. High stress, combined with a heavy-handed management and a workforce culture unable to assuage bitterness and resentment, are the ingredients of volatility [1].

Prior Incidents

The CSO may very well ask, "Who are the potentially violent employees?" One answer source can be the security group's own records. On file may be log entries and incident reports that document an employee (see Figure 20-6).

- Bullying, intimidating, threatening, harassing, and engaging in other forms of aggressive behavior
- Bringing to or brandishing at work a lethal weapon
- Arguing out of the norm with co-workers and supervisors
- Striking another
- Making direct or veiled threats of harm

A strong sense of always being right; others being wrong or inferior. This trait often hides an inner feeling of powerlessness.

A negative attitude. Nothing is pleasing; everything is a downer. People are jerks.

Paranoia. Enemies lurk everywhere.

A pattern of filing grievances.

Small issues become huge crises.

Anxiety; depression; irritability; weight change; crying.

Figure 20-6 Violence brewing inside an employee can sometimes be spotted and acted upon.

- Making statements that:
  - Approve the use of violence to resolve interpersonal problems
  - Indicate identification with perpetrators of workplace homicides
  - Suggest desperation over family, financial, and other personal problems
  - Mention suicide
- Abusing drugs or alcohol
- Exhibiting extreme changes in mood and behaviors

Other Signals

Not likely to be apparent in security group records are other indicators of trouble ahead, such as obsessing over another individual, blaming others for personal shortcomings, vocalizing or rehearsing violent intentions, and exhibiting behavior that is strange to the extent it discomforts co-workers [2].

AVOIDING LIABILITY

If an employee is discharged because of accusations of violent tendencies, the employee may sue for wrongful discharge. Therefore, actual incidents or threats of misconduct must be fully documented [3]. Consider the following anecdote.

CASE STUDY

Several warehouse workers have complained to their boss Robert that a co-worker, Karl, has a bad temper. Among other disruptive acts, Karl has cursed loudly, made threats, and shook his fist at co-workers. After he shoved a female co-worker and told her he would kill her, Karl was called into Robert's office. While Robert was explaining the unacceptability of Karl's behavior, Karl ran his hand across his throat to symbolize decapitation. Robert sent Karl home and suspended him for three days. A memo from Robert to the Human Resources Department documented the current and prior offenses and the disciplinary action taken.

A month later, Karl got into a dispute with Luke, a fellow warehouseman, and slashed his throat with a razor-like tool used to open cartons. Luke died at the scene. Luke's wife had a friend in the Human Resources Department. The friend gave her a copy of Robert's memo concerning Karl's repeated offenses. Shortly following Karl's conviction in criminal court, Luke's wife filed a civil suit against the company and Robert.

Taking Action

A person's past behavior can be a predictor of future behavior, and none can be ignored. Dealing with the indicators is much better than dealing with the outcomes. The avenue for responding to indicators varies according to seriousness. Three general avenues are available.

- Intervention by security and/or the police in situations of violence
- Discipline for actionable misconduct
- Referral to an employee assistance program for nonactionable misconduct

Standard Profiles

The use of standard profiles to identify potentially violent employees is not recommended. Many tend to oversimplify and stereotype. The same can be said of generalizations that automatically connect an employee's personal problems with the potential for violence. Problems such as divorce, bereavement, and job loss are not in and of themselves valid predictors. (Note: A standard profile is a general template. It is not the same thing as a psychological profile, which is specific to an individual and prepared by a person trained in profiling.)

Stalking

Women (or men) who are being stalked and who find little in the way of practical support from the criminal justice system may seek help from the security groups. Although stalking is an individualized problem, it has an impact on the workplace. Murder is now a leading cause of death for women at work. Statistics tell us that one in six violent crimes will occur on the job and common sense tells us that many of these incidents will be preceded by stalking. In a very pragmatic way, employers are recognizing that stalking is more than just an employee's personal problem, but a company problem that affects bottom-line numbers.

Preincident Defensive Actions

For reasons not fully understood, stalking crimes are growing in frequency and seriousness. At the same time, public law enforcement is increasingly unable to provide the type of help that stalking victims require (see Figure 20-7).

Male Stalker Characteristics

A male stalker is likely to be someone who:
Has difficulty developing a meaningful relationship with a woman.
Has a history of unsuccessful attempts at standing out, at being "somebody."
Needs recognition, attention.
Very possessive of women.
Follows the woman of his interest and tries to isolate her.
Is jealous of the woman's male friends.
Is pre-occupied with thoughts of violence.
Is cruel without a sense of remorse.
Is impulsive, insecure, and mistrustful of the woman.
Makes threats.
Has access to weapons.
Has a history of assault.
Has perhaps attempted suicide.
Makes frequent calls and leaves obscene or harassing messages.
Persists in sending letters, e-mail messages, and gifts.
Frequently drives past the woman's house; watches from a distance.
Shows up unexpectedly; arranges "coincidental" encounters.
Contacts the woman's friends, families, and coworkers to inquire of her.

Figure 20-7 A list of this type can be matched against the behavior of a suspect.

A woman who is being stalked can take a number of defensive actions prior to an actual incident. For example, she can change her telephone number, e-mail address, and the automobile she drives. Two other actions are not easily done: changing residence and changing employment. Changing a job inside the same company location can help. Even when the victim's employer arranges a job change to a completely different location, the stalker knows that the places where the victim can hide are finite.

What can a CSO can do in a stalking situation? Three actions come to mind: assessing the threat, developing an intervention strategy, and gathering evidence of the stalking crime.

Assessing the Stalker

Threat assessment begins with sizing up the stalker; determining type, intentions, and ability to carry out intentions. Stalkers come in all sizes and shapes, but three types seem to stand out. First is the "simple obsessive" type, that has had a prior relationship with the victim, and cannot (for whatever reason) accept the reality that the relationship has permanently ended. Next is the "love obsessive" type, who worships the victim even when there has been no prior relationship. Then there is the "erotomanic" type, who believes he/she is being romantically pursued by the victim, even when there is absolutely no evidence of it. Often, the victim is a well-known person such as a political figure or movie star.

The stalker's intentions can be inferred from personality type, announced intentions, and prior acts. When a stalker says he/she will never allow the victim to be loved by another or when a police record shows that the stalker has a history of violence, the threat must be taken seriously. Similarly, a stalker who is known to own or carry a firearm cannot be dismissed as a crank.

Intervention Strategy

An intervention strategy considers support actions: (1) what the victim can do, (2) what the victim's friends and relatives can do, (3) what the CSO can do, and (4) what the police and courts can do. The victim and the CSO work out between them a plan that taps into support resources. Experience has shown that preventing and/or countering the likely actions of a stalker involves the victim being educated as to the dynamics of the situation. For example, a victim may have to be dissuaded from believing that a sit-down, heart-to-heart talk with the stalker is a solution to the problem.

Detach and watch: A technique sometimes used in an intervention strategy is "detach and watch." It seems to work best with the simple obsessive type (e.g., former lover or spouse) and is sometimes called the "engage and enrage" technique because of the effect it can have. The victim makes an explicit no-compromise rejection, cuts off all contact with the stalker, and waits to see what happens. The stalker's reaction then provides a guide to follow-on steps in the overall strategy.

Temporary restraining order (TRO): A TRO is sometimes used as a tool in the strategy, both to ferret out the stalker's intentions and to build a legal case. A TRO, of course, is only a piece of paper. It provides absolutely no protection, and with some stalkers can produce an unwanted reaction. When the victim (or even the CSO) sees the TRO as a potential deterrent, caution must prevail. Any communication from victim to stalker takes into account the probability and nature of the stalker's response.

Documentation

The evidence-gathering function is aimed at creating a well-documented case for presentation in court. Examples of documentation include threatening letters, telephone answering machine messages, voice mail messages, e-mail messages, photos of injuries or damaged property, hospital treatment reports, police incident reports, telephone records (including a log of calls made to the victim by the stalker or people acting on behalf of the stalker), and statements of witnesses. Figure 20-8 shows strategies available to potential stalking victims.

Tips for Stalker Victims

Ignore the individual. Cut off all contact.

Be clear and unambiguous that the relationship is over.

Do not give your reasons why. Do not let the stalker see your concern.

Do not have someone else intervene for you.

Have your answering machine message simply state your telephone number, and use a voice other than your own.

Use caller ID to screen your calls. Obtain an unlisted phone number.

Mark your house number so that police and rescue personnel can find you easily in a response situation. Get a dog.

Do not allow strangers in your home. Keep your address and schedule secret.

Inquire about laws concerning your situation. Join a support group.

Notify authorities every time the stalker bothers you; keep copies of the reports.

Treat all threats as legitimate, and call police every time the stalker shows up.

Press charges every time you can; ask that a condition of a bond forbid any and all contact.

Ask for periodic police drive-bys at your home. Obtain a restraining order.

If the police tell you they have no authority to arrest the stalker, do not ask them to intervene because an intervention without arrest sends a message that your best defense is useless.

Go public. Have an attorney send a registered letter informing the stalker to stop.

Record the stalking with a video camera. Keep a log of stalking activities.

Ask witnesses to testify as to the stalking. Keep all written materials received from the stalker.

Document all medical reports of physical abuse. Take photos of wounds, bruises and acts of vandalism.

Vary your routine. Limit time spent walking alone or along the same route.

Notify neighbors and coworkers about the situation and give them a photo of the stalker; ask them to notify you if he is seen.

Get an unlisted phone number for day-to-day business; use an answering machine.

Have mail screened by someone you can trust. Have coworkers screen calls and visitors.

Have a coworker check with other coworkers to see if the stalker is calling them as well.

Alert security personnel at work. Stay in public areas and travel with friends.

Get a car telephone. Arrange to have your children accompanied to the school bus or school.

Do not park in garages that require surrendering the keys to your car.

Lock your car door when traveling, and be aware of other cars.

Rent a mailbox from a private service.

Lock your outside fuse box, car, garage, and trim hedges near windows.

Put a lock on your car's gas tank.

Install deadbolts at home, and change the keys.

Install outside lighting, and consider installing motion detectors.

If you move, make it difficult for anyone to learn your new address.

Change your job, if necessary. Hire a private security guard.

Have a contingency plan that includes quick access to important phone numbers, a packed suitcase, and "escape" money.

Alert a responsible person to your situation and your plan.

Take legal action, in addition to a restraining order.

Figure 20-8 This list may be helpful to employees concerned with stalking.

PSYCHOLOGICAL PROFILING

The term *psychological profiling* tends to conjure up in the imagination a massive police hunt for a diabolical killer too clever to be caught by standard techniques. In a sense it's unfortunate that profiling is so widely misunderstood. First, the technique is not restricted to serial murders and is not practiced solely by FBI agents trained at the FBI Academy's behavioral science unit. Next, it is not a scientific procedure in the same way that fingerprints and DNA tests conclusively identify individuals. Both an art and a science, psychological profiling is performed by highly trained and educated behavioral scientists with long experience in the field.

Profiling in the Business Setting

Psychological profiling can be used in the business setting. The uses may be to link a particular employee suspect to a particular written communication, to evaluate the possibility that an employee will harm herself or others, or to determine if an employee's demonstrated behavior suggests a link to an unacceptable activity. Profiling has proven itself in a wide variety of corporate-related crimes, such as product tampering, sabotage, extortion, and kidnapping.

A single written communication, such as a threatening letter to a CEO, can provide clues to the author: age, sex, marital status, intelligence level, life style, work habits, motive, and emotional stability. These characterizing details can be applied to a population of suspects for the purpose of ruling some in and some out.

Predicting from a Profile

When an individual's identity is known, profiling can be used as a predictor of behavior. If a corporation, for example, has an employee who has engaged in borderline behavior, a profile can be helpful in assessing future behavior so that an intelligent decision can be made as to whether or not the employee should be terminated or retained.

TRAINING

Instruction in how to respond to workplace violence is needed more by the security group than by any other organizational entity. The knowledge and skills imparted to security group members through training are mirrored in the actions or tasks specified in the operational plan and the plan's implementing procedures. If the plan and procedures call for security officers to use calmative techniques when confronting a violent employee and to apply deadly force in limited circumstances, the officers must be taught the calmative techniques and the limited circumstances of deadly force. Not all tasks or parts of tasks need to be taught. In performing the task of telephoning the police, the security console operator does not need to be taught how to use a telephone but does need to know how to quickly access the police department emergency telephone number.

Ranking tasks by criticality is central to effective training. Tasks with life safety implications deserve highest training emphasis. A distinction needs to be made among tasks that are critical, less critical, and noncritical. The noncritical is never taught because to do so is a waste of time and resources; the critical is always taught and must be learned.

The length of the training program is the sum of hours required at a minimum to teach all of the critical tasks. Training length is never determined by the time that is available or affordable. The training curriculum is task oriented, instructors are required to conform to a curriculum, and attainment of the intended training outcomes is validated and documented.

Training can be helped with visual aids such as photos depicting real-life incidents.

The CSO, in addition to ensuring competence through training of security employees, is often called upon to help train employees outside the security group. Three employee categories stand out: the general employee population, the managers and supervisors, and members of the violence response team. It may be interesting to note that the CSO can be a trainee and a trainer in all three categories.

Figure 20-9 Workplace violence prevention requires employee support. Training employees builds needed support. *(Photo Courtesy of Burns International Security Services.)*

Security Officers and Violence

According to a National Crime Victimization Survey, security officers rank number 4 on the list of professions exposed to violence while on the job. In first place were police officers, followed by corrections officers and taxi drivers.

Figure 20-10 Security officers are exposed to violence on the job.

Training Employees

The training module for employees explains the company's policy and the rationale behind it. One of the key objectives is to develop top-to-bottom employee understanding of and support for the policy — a policy that in essence is a set of rules for maintaining a safe and secure workplace. Topics can include the nature and consequences of workplace violence, policy enforcement, and the responsibility assigned to every employee to report violations.

Training for employees can also revolve around the functions of the violence response team. An objective is to facilitate VRT actions by enlisting the cooperation of employees. For example, during deployment of the VRT the employees may be required to leave the premises. This requirement and the manner of its execution are details covered in the training. A valuable by-product can be confidence in the overall violence prevention program.

Security officers can be the intended or unintended victims of workplace violence (see Figure 20-10).

Because the security group is the organization's natural focal point for receiving reports of violence, the CSO has a role to play in delivering the training module for employees. The CSO's presentation would include when and how to make a report and what to expect after a report is made. Teaching this important information also inspires confidence because it demonstrates management's commitment to deal with violence decisively and with consequences attached.

Training Managers and Supervisors

Here again the CSO can be both a trainee and a trainer. The intended outcomes of a training program for managers and supervisors include understanding how to do the following:

- Meet obligations assigned by the organization's workplace violence policy
- Look for warning signals and how to report and intervene
- Diffuse volatile situations and resolve conflicts
- Refer workers to company-sponsored programs that provide employee assistance, an ombudsman, and mediation
- Follow up to ensure that interventions and referrals are having the intended effect

Training the Violence Response Team

The members of the VRT are expected to be competent in their own professions prior to being trained to carry out the specifics of the violence prevention operational plan. Persons on the team who are designated to mediate in crises are expected to possess mediation skills by virtue of their prior education and experience, and the same expectation applies to other members of the team. The team members arrive at the training door with professional credentials; the training adds to their credentials by supplying the specific knowledge and skills needed to carry out the VRT duties prescribed in the operational plan and procedures. Supplemental benefits that can be derived include team members getting to know fellow team members and getting to see the positive effect of merging separate disciplines in the accomplishment of a common goal.

In this module, more so than other modules, the instructional approach is learning by doing. Practical exercises based on scenarios that have been considered in the plan can be very effective.

PREVENTIVE TECHNIQUES

Among the cultural norms of the American workplace is an admiration for competitive individuals and a belief that interpersonal conflict concludes with one winner and one loser. Research and experience, however, reveal that interpersonal conflict is often resolved through win-win techniques [4].

Ombudsman

An ombudsman is skilled in counseling, mediating, conciliating, and fact-finding. He/she receives complaints; interviews the interested parties; reviews the relevant policies, rules, and remedies; and offers options to the disputants. Typically, an ombudsman does not impose solutions. A disputant can decline an option offered by the ombudsman and is free to pursue a remedy in another dispute-resolving forum.

Facilitator

A facilitator improves the flow of information in a meeting between parties to a dispute. The facilitator does not typically become as involved in the substantive issues as does a mediator. The facilitator focuses more on the process of resolving a matter. Facilitation is most appropriate when the parties are not extremely polarized and have a sufficient degree of trust in each other that they can work together to develop a mutually acceptable solution.

Mediator

A mediator is an impartial and neutral third party having no decision-making authority in the matter in dispute. The mediator helps the disputants voluntarily reach an acceptable resolution. Mediation is useful in highly polarized disputes in which the parties have either been unable to initiate a productive dialogue or the dialogue has stalled in the face of a seemingly insurmountable impasse.

A mediator, like a facilitator, makes procedural suggestions as to how parties can reach agreement. Occasionally, a mediator may suggest a substantive option as a means of encouraging the parties to expand the range of possible resolutions. A mediator often works with the parties individually to develop proposals that might move the parties closer to agreement.

Peer Review

The peer review is a problem-solving technique in which an employee in a dispute with the employer takes the dispute to a panel of fellow employees and managers for a decision that may be binding or nonbinding. If not binding on the employee, and if the panel's decision is unacceptable to the employee, he/she can seek relief in another forum. The peer review technique can be helpful in resolving disputes before they become formal complaints or grievances.

A working familiarity by the CSO with dispute-resolution techniques is helpful, not only for preventing violence but for facilitating day-to-day interpersonal transactions within the security group. Even a small amount of skill at collaboration and compromise can give to the CSO a large amount of confidence.

NONDISCLOSURE OF POTENTIAL VIOLENCE

Employers face potential liability for nondisclosure of problematic employee performance, for example, when they misrepresent that a former employee's performance was favorable. A foreseeable risk of harm to others is created when a violence-prone individual is hired by another company that relies on a former employer's statement.

AMERICANS WITH DISABILITIES ACT (ADA)

The ADA imposes a duty on employers to provide reasonable accommodations to employees who suffer from mental disabilities, including disabilities that might lead to risky behavior. Reasonable accommodations can include opportunities for stress reduction, flexible workloads, and professional counseling. In extreme cases, as when an employee poses a direct threat to the health or safety of other individuals, the only choice may be to remove the employee from the workplace. Employers can defend resulting discrimination claims on the grounds that the employee was not qualified under the ADA because he/she could not perform the essential functions of the job.

Employers have successfully argued in such situations that the essential functions of any job include the ability to deal with criticism from supervisors and co-workers in a civil manner, and to refrain from violent behavior.

NOTES

1. Sandra L. Heskett, *Workplace Violence: Before, During, and After*, pp. 59, Boston: Butterworth-Heinemann, 1996.

2. Michael D. Kelleher, *Profiling the Lethal Employee*, pp. 14, 17, and 21–22, Westport, CT: Praeger, 1997.

3. Thomas Capozzoli and R. Steve McVey, *Managing Violence in the Workplace*, pp. 122, Delray Beach, FL: St. Lucie Press, 1996.

4. Stanley B. Malos, "Current Legal Issues in Performance Appraisal," in *Performance Appraisal*, James W. Smither (ed.), pp. 91–92, San Francisco: Jossey-Bass, 1998.

21. Security Awareness

The secret of business is to know something that nobody else knows.
—Aristotle Onassis

BACKGROUND

The security of an organization rests squarely on the practices of employees. The CSO can design the finest protective programs, obtain the full support of the management team, secure generous funding, form a competent security group, and acquire a complete assortment of equipment. None of these essential components will matter, however, if employees fail to meet their individual security responsibilities. A security agenda, no matter how perfectly conceived and generously supported, is incapable of rising above poor security practices by employees. Like the analogy of the weak link in the chain, an organization's security cannot be stronger than the weakest day-to-day behaviors of employees.

DIMENSIONS [1]

The subject of employee behaviors leads to a question: How does the CSO influence employee behaviors? The answer is by making employees aware of security. In this sense, awareness has three goals: help employees understand their individual security responsibilities, help them meet those responsibilities, and help them engage the first two goals willingly. The first two goals require the employee to gain knowledge. The third goal is distinctly different and almost always difficult to attain because it calls for an attitudinal shift. To illustrate the point, imagine that Bill Smith, a clerk in the accounts payable office, is ready to go home. He knows the rule that requires him to lock away check stock and he knows how to operate the combination dial on the check stock safe.

But Bill is tired, quitting time has come and gone, and Bill is eager to leave. Will he take the time needed to lock the check stock in the safe? His willingness, or attitude, will be the determining factor. Bill knows the rule and has locked and unlocked the safe hundreds of times, but will he do so now?

Much depends on Bill's attitude, and the reality is that Bill's attitude, and that of every other employee, is difficult to shape. The CSO can teach the why and the how of the rule but cannot easily teach the attitude that influences compliance. Yes, the CSO may be positioned to trigger punishment of Bill if he fails to lock the safe, thereby administering to Bill a valuable lesson, or so we would hope. However, the far better scenario, of course, would be to influence Bill's attitude in such a way that he would in every case lock the safe. Alas, however, influencing attitude is easily said but never easily done.

AN ONGOING PROCESS

A security awareness program is routine and ongoing. It is not a one-time effort or an effort that clicks on in response to loss events and clicks off again when things settle down. Although a program may be initiated with great fanfare and periodically reinvigorated, it must operate continuously.

AWARENESS IS LOCAL

Security awareness is a local affair that serves the unique needs of the business unit. Although security topics may be suggested from outside of the business unit, the program is principally dedicated to raising awareness of internal security issues.

When the content of the awareness program aligns with the experiences of employees, a psychological agreement is reached. The content of an awareness program conducted elsewhere will seem alien to the local audience. This principle applies as well to the content of awareness programs purchased off the shelf [2].

MODES FOR PROMOTING AWARENESS

Every forum that can possibly influence the security behaviors of employees is up for grabs in an energetic awareness program. Security fairs, slogan contests, posters, awards, and all things imaginable are considered. Message style and mode of delivery can vary according to the audience. Although a message might remain constant, such as "Take a Bite Out of Crime," style and delivery will likely vary at different levels of the organization.

AVOIDING APATHY

Apathy arises when the awareness program suffers from vagueness and imprecision. Employees are like moviegoers: if bad writing and bad acting make a movie a clunker, some of the audience will fall asleep, others will get up and leave, and some will inwardly curse for having wasted the price of a ticket.

Apathy can arise quickly and exert a devastating effect. The worst thing that the CSO can do is to surrender to it. Although it is true that some individuals may be apathetic on principle to the whole notion of security awareness, it is also true that employee apathy is often offered up as an excuse for program ineffectiveness [3].

THE MESSAGE

When selecting a topic, it is helpful to ask: Is the topic important enough to address? If the answer is yes, then ask: Is the content of the topic doctrinally correct? Is content consistent with company policies and practices?

A topic that is long or complicated can be broken down into comprehensible parts. The parts can be arranged in a logical series with each part building on the other. Packaging the topic imaginatively is also important. Going outside the envelope of traditional techniques grabs attention. Even a small dose of innovation can turn ho-hums into a buzz of excitement, and there is nothing wrong in emulating the techniques of professional idea marketers or borrowing from the successes of security awareness programs in other organizations.

The avenues for raising security awareness include presentations (see Figure 21-1) at employee meetings and bringing in outside experts to

---

Tips on Developing a Presentation

Research the topic. Gather all the information you can.
Organize the gathered information.
Prepare to write.
    Know your purposes.
    Identify main ideas.
    Prepare an outline.
Write a draft.
    Avoid big words and jargon.
    Use active (as opposed to passive) verbs.
    Avoid adjectives that suggest opinion. A presentation should be factual.
    Avoid crutch terms and deadheads, such as "in light of" and "in compliance with."
    Keep sentences short and punchy.
    Support the main ideas with examples, facts, and reasons.
Read your draft and revise it twice.
Have your draft critiqued by one or two persons whose judgment you trust.
Revise one last time.
Choose the appropriate methods for supplementing lecture, e.g., slides, transparencies, films, videos, handouts, chalkboard, and block paper on easel.

Figure 21-1 Preparing the presentation is as important as delivering it.

address topics of concern such as having a bomb threat specialist teach mail-room employees how to spot parcel bombs. Conducting tutorials that meet special needs can be effective, such as showing secretaries how to mark envelopes that contain sensitive documents about to be mailed, and teaching new hires the fundamentals of the fire alarm system.

Awareness messages can be placed on static and electronic bulletin boards, on the security web site of the company's intranet, on placards in public hallways, and on signage at high-risk locations. Helping employees protect themselves from crime can be a facet of the security awareness program. Activities along this line can include directing employees to community operated anticrime programs that deal with burglary, assault, and auto theft programs. Employees can be assisted with advice about the installation of home and automobile alarm systems and the procurement of cellular phones for security purposes.

THE SPOTLIGHT

The CSO can be writer, director, producer, and actor. He/she can ideate the story line (program objectives), write the dialogue and action scenes (program content), select the actors (program presenters), direct the program, obtain the funding, and bring all of the parts together into a meaningful production.

NOTES

1. The concepts of knowledge, skills, and attitudes were borrowed from *Approaches to Criminal Justice Training*, by John J. Fay, Athens, GA: Institute of Government, University of Georgia, 1979.

2. Robert Squarebriggs, " 'Coach' Is Better Than 'Security Supervisor,'" in *Issues in Security Management: Thinking Critically About Security*, pp. 25, Robert R. Robertson, editor, Boston: Butterworth-Heinemann, 1999.

3. *Understanding Crime Prevention*, pp. 7–13, Louisville, KY: National Crime Prevention Institute Press, 1978.

22. Vulnerability Assessment

Knowledge must come through action; you can have no test which is not fanciful, save by trial.

—Sophocles

BACKGROUND

Vulnerability assessment is a methodology for determining the vulnerability of an asset vis-à-vis a particular threat, and is thereby a tool for controlling risk. In this chapter, threats are terrorist threats and vulnerabilities are exposures to terrorist threats.

For the sake of simplicity, we will use the term *facility* or *site* when referring to a terrorist target. The target can be one or more assets at a site, a site plus the surrounding community, or a combination of the two. The facility can be a private or government structure, a single building or a complex of buildings, or other physical entities such as electrical transmission lines or the conveyances of a transportation system.

We will use the term *vulnerability assessment* when referring to a methodology or to the final report produced from application of the methodological process. We leave it up to the reader to make the differentiation.

VULNERABILITY ASSESSMENT PROCESS

The VA process advances step-by-step. The steps are actions:

- Determine authority, scope, and leadership
- Form a multidisciplinary team
- Characterize the target site
- Identify meaningful assets
- From meaningful assets, identify critical assets
- Characterize the potential terrorist group (i.e., the threat)
- Identify the site's current capabilities to counter the threat
- Identify the missing capabilities (i.e., the vulnerabilities)

- Identify and recommend measures to eliminate or reduce the vulnerabilities
- Implement the measures
- Test and revise as needed

Note that these steps, except for the last two, require acquisition and analysis of information. The last two steps are technically not part of VA; they are tangible actions taken by site management on the basis of the VA's findings.

Actions taken by management to correct deficiencies identified in a VA will not likely correspond perfectly to the measures recommended by the VA team. Before deciding on what actions to take, management will pose a number of questions:

- Can we afford the costs of implementing the recommended measures?
- Are the recommended measures cost effective?
- Would implementation of the measures interfere with site operations?
- Are we willing to accept some of the risk by not fully implementing the recommended measures?

VA is essentially Act 1 in a three-act play. In Act 1 the supporting actors (VA team members) reveal details. In Act 2 the protagonists (senior-level executives) make momentous decisions. In Act 3 the supporting actors and protagonists transform a looming tragedy into a happy ending.

Determine Authority, Scope, and Leadership

Sanctioning of a VA is done at an executive level in organizations such as departments in the executive branch of the federal government, state regulatory agencies, and boards of directors. Senior persons in the sanctioning organization decide what is to be evaluated. It may be an entire site, part of a site, all of the assets and processes on the site, assets only, or processes only.

Because a VA is performed by a team, the sanctioning authority will most likely select the team leader, and perhaps the entire team. Tasks of the team leader throughout the course of the VA can include the following.

- Assembling a team
- Collecting the documents that characterize the site
- Distributing the collected documents to team members for study
- Briefing the site's management at the beginning, midpoint, and conclusion of assessment activities done on site
- Determining and assigning to team members tasks they are to perform on site, and facilitating this process with team meetings, small group conferences, and so on
- Authoring and/or directing preparation of the final VA report

Form a Multidisciplinary Team

The VA is done by a team formed for that purpose. The team consists of experts in disciplines that correspond to the facility's core functions and processes. The team disciplines can be emergency management, security, safety, hazardous materials, engineering, law enforcement and fire services, investigations, communications, emergency medical treatment, public health, government administration, civil engineering, toxicology, chemistry, biology, radiology, and bomb construction/disposal. Among these is the CSO, the team's expert in the security discipline.

It is valuable to have on the team people who are familiar with the site. These can be engineers, operations managers, information technology specialists, safety coordinators, and so on. The remaining team members are likely to be consultants, scientists, subject matter experts, and persons "borrowed" from an affiliated organization.

Characterize the Target Site

VA begins before the team steps onto the site. The beginning point may be as long as six months prior. The purpose is to learn as much as possible beforehand so that the team will have a grasp of the layout, know what to focus on, and ask good questions. Much time can be saved if the team arrives at the site with some understanding of its workings. An understanding can be aided by obtaining answers to these questions:

- What are the facility's primary services or outputs?
- What critical activities take place at the facility?
- Who occupies the facility?
- What inputs from external organizations are required for the facility's operations?

The answers to these preliminary questions help describe the facility's infrastructure:

- The probable effect of a terrorist attack on
  - Physical and human assets inside the facility
  - The facility's basic functions and services
  - Sensitive information processed or stored at the facility
- Critical support systems
  - Utilities such as power, water, and air conditioning
  - Communications
  - Information technology
  - Transportation modalities for the movement of people and material
  - Life safety programs for providing "safe haven," evacuating the facility, and treating the injured

- Backups, both physical and human, that are available for continuing the facility's core functions and services and maintaining critical support systems
- The number of people likely to be injured or killed
- Resources essential to reducing injury and death

A great deal of information has to be obtained to answer these types of questions. The team leader contacts site management to ask that one of its members be designated to act as a point of contact (POC). The POC has two primary duties: (1) in advance of the team visit, collect and forward to the team leader a package of documents that describe the facility in detail and (2) during the visit, orient the team to the physical layout of the facility, introduce team members to facility employees that will need to be interviewed, and in general remove obstacles and solve problems. The package of documents collected by the POC and forwarded to the team leader can include the following:

- Regulatory laws, regulations, rules, standards, etc.
- Aerial views and graphical representations, as-built plans, floor layouts, and composition details (e.g., steel, wood, glass, or concrete)
- Applicable plans and procedures
- History of security incidents
- Descriptions of physical security safeguards in place such as access control system, barriers, intrusion detection system, security control center, locks, safes, vaults, CCTV system, and security lighting
- Guard force details such as number of on-site supervisors and security officers, security post locations and hours of operation, personal protection equipment and supplies, vehicles, weapons, communications system, and training
- Hazardous materials (HazMat) details: storage and protection, disposal, containment, spills, and cleanup
- Descriptions of the environment: neighboring businesses and residential areas, surrounding roadways, terrain, flora, fauna, weather and temperature extremes, natural disaster history and potential, incidence of crime, and proximity to sensitive facilities such as air and sea ports, railway terminals, chemical and petroleum plants, military installations, and government buildings

The team leader distributes the documents to team members according to disciplines; for example, guard orders are given to the CSO, HazMat documents go to the team's safety expert, and as-built plans are given to architects and engineers. The entire set of documents is studied prior to arriving at the site.

On the day of arrival at the site or on the day before, the team leader meets with all of the team members (see Figure 22-1). The meeting is in the nature of an icebreaker: introductions are made, disciplines identified, networking initiated. A large part of the meeting is the assignment and agreement of tasks,

Figure 22-1 The VA team leader meets with members of the team.

both specific and general. Specific tasks are technical and relate to specific disciplines. General tasks are nontechnical and include the following:

- Interviewing persons knowledgeable of site operations: employees, contractors, vendors, and people working in external support agencies such as police, fire, and EMT
- Acquiring needed documents that were not included in the package sent by the POC to the team leader
- Making notes and sketches
- Taking photographs
- Visiting the site during normal and non working hours, at night and early in the morning, and on one or more weekends
- Meeting in groups and in whole to discuss, compare, and analyze collected information

The team leader explains that his or her major tasks are to provide guidance, coordinate the work of the team, obtain needed resources, resolve problems, and communicate with the POC. Later that day or the following day, the POC takes the team on a guided tour of the facility.

The team leader, alone or accompanied by a few selected team members, meets with facility management to explain the nature of the VA and how it will be performed at the site (see Figure 22-2). This initial briefing also serves as an opportunity for the team leader to meet face-to-face with and form first impressions of persons that can help or hinder the VA. Two other briefings of management are held: one at the midpoint of the VA and one at the conclusion.

Figure 22-2 The VA team leader briefs senior site management.

Identify the Meaningful Assets

If the team has not already done so, a first task after arriving on site will be identification of meaningful assets (see Figure 22-3).

Figure 22-3 A team member taking photographs in the company of a security officer. *(Photo Courtesy of Burns International Security Services.)*

Pencils, office chairs, pictures on the wall, brooms, and wrenches are not meaningful assets. A meaningful asset is a resource of value deserving of protection. It can be tangible (such as people, buildings, equipment, materials, and data) or intangible, such as reputation, institutional knowledge, and employee morale.

Assets most likely to be targeted by terrorists are tangible. People are a logical target because they are tangible, costly, and often irreplaceable. Even if there is an asset more valuable than people, and we are not suggesting there is, people have to be identified as an asset deserving of protection.

In the identification of assets we can and should immediately exclude nonmeaningful assets. An asset is nonmeaningful when it has no effect on life safety, has a low dollar value, or has little to do with the functioning of the facility.

Identify the Critical Assets

The focus then is on meaningful assets but only broadly. Not all meaningful assets are critical assets, which are the focal points of the VA. The difference between meaningful and critical is a matter of judgment. Judgment, however, can be aided by evaluating an asset in three dimensions.

- Impact on life
- Impact on dollars
- Impact on operations

The measurement of impact on life is answered by the question "How many people will perish if the facility is attacked?" The answer depends on the mode of attack (foot, vehicle, aircraft), weapons used (bombs, grenades, guns, chemical agents, biological agents), and intent of the attackers (infliction of casualties, theft or destruction of assets inside the facility, destruction of the entire facility).

The impact on dollars can be relative; that is, dollar value at one facility may be significantly higher or lower than at another facility, even when both facilities are comparable in size, function, and output. A facility owned by a financially secure organization may be able and willing to absorb a high dollar loss, whereas a facility that operates on the edge of bankruptcy may have no financial cushion at all and be forced to cease operations as the result of a successful attack.

Operational impact is evaluated by the probable effect of an attack on the organization's core functions and processes. It may be possible for a facility to continue functioning after sustaining severe damage. At another facility, complete shutdown could result from the loss of a single critical asset. In the latter case, a caution applies: a seemingly unimportant asset can be critical when it represents a single point of failure.

Operational impact should also be considered when loss of function at the facility can cause loss of function outside the facility. Imagine for example that the facility provides electrical power. Loss of power will impact critical outside operations such as hospitals, police and fire stations, subways, water supply and sewage disposal systems, and so on.

At about this point, which should be the midpoint of the VA, the team leader meets with facility management and presents a briefing that covers progress to date and activities remaining to be done. If significant vulnerabilities have been identified at this point, the team leader encourages management to correct them immediately if it is possible to do so.

Characterize the Potential Terrorist Group

A threat is an indication, circumstance, event, or adversary with the potential to cause loss of or damage to an asset [1]. Specific naming and characterization of potential terrorist groups relies almost entirely on information provided by news media, Department of Homeland Security (DHS), Federal Bureau of Investigation (FBI), other law enforcement agencies, and Department of State for overseas operations. DHS uses five factors to evaluate a potential terrorist group [1].

- Existence
- History
- Capability
- Intention
- Targeting

Existence addresses the questions: What terrorist groups are hostile to the facility? Are they in striking distance? If in striking distance, are they identifiable?

History addresses the questions: What has the potential threat group done in the past? Where and how many times? How recently? When was the most recent incident and where, and against what target?

Capability addresses the questions: What weapons do the terrorist groups possess? What weapons have they used in past attacks? Can such weapons be acquired or constructed in the area proximal to the facility? What tactics were used and to what degree of success? What is their manpower? Are they skilled and trained? What resources do they command? Do they have outside support?

Intention addresses the questions: What would a potential threat group hope to achieve by attacking? Has a threat group stated an intention to attack? Is the facility similar to facilities already attacked?

Targeting addresses the questions: Is the facility under surveillance in any of the numerous ways that surveillance is possible? Have any attempts been made to acquire information about the facility, particularly security-related information? Have there been any innocuous-appearing attempts to gain entry to the facility? Has security of the facility been tested in any way such as by causing an intrusion detection sensor to activate?

Identify the Site's Current Capabilities

With an understanding of the facility as a potential terrorist target and an understanding of potential terrorist groups, the VA team — with considerable input from the CSO — is able to conceptualize a security system resistant to attack. A preliminary step, however, is necessary: the capabilities of the present system must be ascertained. The assumption here is that the facility has a security system of some type already in place.

Identify the Missing Capabilities (Vulnerabilities)

The VA team's next step is to evaluate the resistance of the site to attack. For example, the potential terrorist group that may be targeting the facility has a history of attacking with vehicle bombs. The essential question to be asked is, "Does the facility currently have a capability to resist this form of attack?" If the answer is no, the VA team has identified a missing capability.

A missing capability is a vulnerability, and a vulnerability is a weakness that can be exploited by an adversary. A simple way of identifying missing capabilities is to compare current capabilities against required capabilities.

Identify and Recommend Measures That Eliminate/Reduce Vulnerabilities

Capabilities are established with countermeasures. In the vehicle bomb attack scenario a number of countermeasures are indicated: roadways that channel vehicle traffic away from the facility or key assets within, vehicle parking at a distance away from the facility or its internal assets, bollards or similar devices that prevent ramming the facility, bomb-resistant film on glass surfaces, guards that inspect approaching/entering vehicles, and guards that patrol the premises looking for suspicious activities.

Develop Countermeasures

Now comes the time to produce a set of action steps for implementing the identified countermeasures. Because many of the action steps relate directly to the facility's security system, the CSO has an important part to play. The CSO's input to the action steps can address the following:

- Use of force
- Legal restrictions and liability
- Technical feasibility of physical safeguards

- Cost and availability of security-related equipment and services
- Security manpower issues

A schedule for working through the action steps is also developed. Like the construction of a house, certain steps must be done before others, and each will have its own time frame for completion.

At a final meeting of team members, agreement is reached on the team's findings and recommendations. A rough outline of the final report might also be developed. The team leader may choose to release team members for return to their organizations or to hold them, or some of them, in the event they will be needed to answer questions that arise at the exit briefing.

EXIT BRIEFING

The exit briefing given by the team leader to facility management covers findings and recommendations, and how they will appear in the final written report. Key points of the briefing are typically explained with use of photographs, notes, sketches, and short summaries prepared by certain of the team members. The team leader should not expect the exit briefing to be a bed of roses. Vulnerabilities are weaknesses and weaknesses imply management failure, which indeed may be the case.

FINAL REPORT

The final report is prepared after the team has finished and left the site. The final report (see Figure 22-4) reflects the findings of the team leader and team members individually and collectively.

The final responsibility of the team leader is preparation of the written report. A typical report has four parts: introduction, body, conclusion, and appendices.

- Introduction
  - Sanctioning authority
  - Scope of the assessment
  - Identification of the senior manager, POC, and other site personnel that participated in the VA
  - Identification of team members and their disciplines
  - Beginning and ending dates
  - Executive summary
- Body
  - Statement of assumptions
  - Physical description of the facility in detail
  - Description of how the VA was conducted
  - Results of interviews

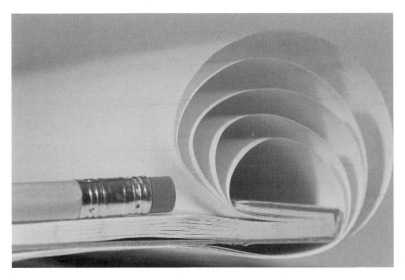

Figure 22-4 A final report requires notes, notes, and more notes.

- ○ Findings
- ○ Substantiation of findings
- • Conclusion
  - ○ Vulnerabilities
  - ○ References to documents, statements, notes, sketches, and photographs that further describe vulnerabilities
  - ○ Recommendations for correction of vulnerabilities
  - ○ Cost estimates associated with countermeasures recommended for correction of vulnerabilities
  - ○ Proposed timetable for correction
  - ○ Proposed follow-up visit to evaluate correction
- • Appendices
  - ○ Documents that proved to be pertinent to the VA
  - ○ Interview statements
  - ○ Notes and sketches
  - ○ Photographs and videotapes/disks
  - ○ Other materials

MANAGEMENT ACTIONS

Implement Recommended Measures

The VA team is long gone and essentially out of the picture when action steps are taken to implement the recommended measures. As mentioned earlier, facility management may decide to implement some measures and not others, which can be a matter of negotiation between facility management and the sanctioning authority.

The main thrust of the VA is to either construct a security system from scratch or strengthen an existing system. Action steps that relate to security usually involve:

- Improvements to physical security
- Modification of plans and procedures
- Hiring, training, and equipping security officers

But not all of management's actions will involve the security system. Many will relate to functions and processes such as HVAC systems, electrical power, water and sewage, operational equipment, and backups.

Test and Revise

This step is also management-driven. The countermeasures decided by and implemented through management are now put to the test. Testing can be done on three levels. In ascending order by difficulty are the tabletop exercise, the practical exercise, and the full-scale drill. The testing scheme might include all three, done in a series from bottom to top. (Details on how this is done can be found in the chapter on emergency management.)

Testing provides an opportunity to identify problems and learn from them. Problems in execution usually result from flaws in organizing, equipping, and training the responders. Flaws are returned to the planning table and reworked. Like the creation of a high-performance engine, the testing/revising process is ongoing, each iteration producing an improvement in performance.

CONCLUSIONS

The VA methodology is an analytical process for identifying a site's critical assets, evaluating the protective shield that surrounds the assets, determining resistance to a terrorist attack of the assets, and recommending physical and procedural measures to improve resistance (see Figure 22-5).

NOTES

1. Paraphrased from *Enhanced Threat and Risk Assessment*, pp. 1-1 and 1-2, College Station, TX: Texas A&M University System, 2002.

Steps in the SVA Process

Determine authority, scope, and leadership.

Form a multidisciplinary team.

Characterize the target site.

    In advance, obtain a full set of documents.

    Apportion documents according to disciplines on the team.

From all assets, identify the meaningful assets.

From the meaningful assets, identify the critical assets.

    Impact on life

    Impact on dollars

    Impact on operations

Characterize the potential terrorist group, i.e., the threat.

    Existence

    History

    Intentions

    Capability

    Targeting

Identify the site's current capabilities to counter the threat.

Identify the missing capabilities, i.e., the vulnerabilities.

Identify and recommend measures that eliminate/reduce vulnerabilities.

Implement the measures.

Test and revise as needed.

Figure 22-5 This document can be helpful when conducting a VA.

23. Security System Design

Terrorism has become the systematic weapon of a war that knows no borders and seldom has a face.
—Jacques Chirac

INTRODUCTION

Many references are made in this book to a security system. In the previous chapter, for example, the point was made that a vulnerability assessment is a tool for constructing a security system. In this chapter we will take a look at a system and its components, and how the components interact. We will look also at security system design features that match up against the threat of terrorism.

SECURITY SYSTEM DEFINED

Let's start with defining a system in general. A system is a combination of components that work together to perform a function. When components work together they are said to be in harmony with one another. When components fall out of harmony, the system is dysfunctional.

In the security realm, a function is made up of duties and tasks that serve a purpose. Protection exists to the extent that the duties and tasks of the function are performed as intended.

An interesting thing about systems is that every system is a component of a larger system. For example, the security system at a water plant in Houston is a component of a system of water plants in Texas, which is a component of a regional system, which is a component of a national system, and so on. The combination of physical security safeguards at the water plant in Houston is a component. The physical safeguards component is also a system because it has its own components: access control equipment, intrusion detection devices, fences, lights, and sensors. Taking it one step further, each of these components meets the definition of a system. Access control, for example, performs a function that depends on harmonious operation of various parts

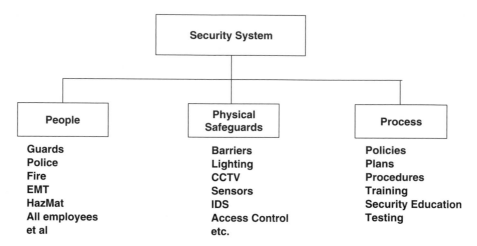

Figure 23-1 A security system rests on three pillars: people, physical safeguards, and process.

such as card keys, readers, and electronic locks. If we want to go down another level, we can say that a card key is a system consisting of three-layer plastic stock, a core of barium ferrite, and magnetic dots arranged in a readable pattern. If we wish, we can go down to the molecular level naming system after system.

The system of interest in this chapter is a security system, the major components of which are people, physical safeguards, and process. The system we have in mind is one designed to resist terrorist attack. (See Figure 23-1.)

PEOPLE COMPONENT

The people component includes any and all persons having a role to play in preventing and/or responding to a terrorist attack of a protected site.

Internal to the Site

Within the site are groups of people that discharge specific security responsibilities. The following are examples.

- Security officers
- Safety employees
- Maintenance employees
- Hazardous materials specialists
- Floor wardens
- Health professionals
- Special-designated employees (scientists, engineers, and so on)

External to the Site

Outside the site are groups of people that are not a formal part of the people component but whose participation is essential to the operation of the system as a whole. These include the following:

- First responders
  - Local law enforcement
  - Firefighting
  - Emergency medical services
  - Public safety communications
- Secondary responders
  - Healthcare
  - Public health
  - Public emergency management
  - Public works
  - Local civil defense agencies
  - The Federal Emergency Management Agency (FEMA)
  - Federal investigative agencies
  - Governmental administrative agencies

Security Officer Group

Of all the groups identified here, the security officer group is the only one that is actually part of a facility's security system. People in the other groups do not perform security tasks but are connected to security. For example, a firefighter does not perform security tasks but becomes connected to security when a fire-related incident occurs at a protected facility. Imagine that a fire-related incident resulted from a bomb explosion. Workers are trapped inside a burning building and other workers are buried under rubble. The call that brought the fire department to the scene came from a security officer. In fact, the calls made to all of the other first responders were made by security officers. And even while those calls were being made security officers were helping people to safety, rendering first aid, and dealing with the incident as best they could. The point here is that of all the job positions comprising the people component of a security system the most important position is the security officer position.

PHYSICAL SAFEGUARDS COMPONENT

Every person connected to a security system relies on tools of some type: law enforcement officers use radios, firefighters use hoses, hazmat specialists wear protective equipment, and so on. The word *tool* is a good surrogate for physical safeguard. Security officers rely on physical safeguards such as fences, access control equipment, and sensors. A fence is a tool to keep unwanted people out, access control equipment is a tool to let authorized people enter, and a sensor is a tool to detect intruders.

Physical safeguards cannot function any better than the people that use them as tools. A fence is worthless if no one inside pays attention to it, access control equipment is worthless if no one knows how to operate it, and a sensor is worthless if there is no one to respond when it activates. Conversely, people cannot function any better than the tools given to them. Think about a sagging fence with gaping holes, access control equipment that constantly breaks down, and sensors that send false alarms.

Many of the recommendations made in a vulnerability assessment will relate to physical safeguards: they are needed but don't exist, they exist but don't function properly, or they exist but serve no security purpose.

SAFEGUARD TYPES

Following are major headings of physical safeguards.

- Barriers
- Portals
- Lights
- CCTV
- Intrusion detectors
- Access controls
- Communications
- Fire detectors
- Guard enclosures
- Vehicles

Falling under each of the headings are specific items; for example, under barriers we could list chain link fences, walls, barbed wires, and bollards, and under portals we could list doors, gates, and turnstiles.

PROCESS COMPONENT

Process ties things together. It is a functional arrangement that links people with physical safeguards. Process is like the sheet of music that tells each orchestra member his/her part in a symphony. When the symphony is pleasant to hear, the orchestra is working in harmony; when the orchestra is not working together, the symphony is not as pleasant as we'd like it to be. The sheet music of process has four integral parts: policy, plans, procedures, and programs.

Policy

A policy is the management's statement of purpose and authorization. A policy that says a facility is to be protected against terrorist attacks provides direction and mandates a course of action. The CSO, for example, might be mandated by policy to mitigate the effects of a terrorist attack.

Plans

The policy mandate handed to the CSO is broad and can only be carried out by plans; for example, plans that pertain to bombing, arson, and kidnap. Plans developed by the CSO are often referred to as incident plans.

Incident plans are typically incorporated into a larger plan called the emergency operating plan (EOP). The EOP is a big picture plan that assigns command and control functions to a managerial team. Names given to such a team include emergency response team, command management team, command control team, and variations thereof. The managerial team is not to be confused with operational teams such as violence response team, hazmat team, and emergency medical team.

The primary (and possibly only) function of the managerial team is command and control, which it exercises by evaluating the incident, dispatching and coordinating the actions of response groups, keeping track of progress, recording actions taken, and communicating with external agencies.

The various incident plans are typically kept at or nearby the place where the command and control team assembles. A support staff member keeps the plans current by requiring the authors to periodically update their plans or alter them after a practical exercise has revealed problems or when the nature of the threat has changed.

The place of assembly for the command and control team can be a permanent emergency operating center (EOC) or a conference room easily converted to an EOC. In either case, the EOC is equipped with phones and phone lines, radios and antennae, status boards and maps, television sets and CCTV monitors, manuals and log books, etc. Another requirement is a backup EOC in case the incident knocks out the primary center.

Procedures

Every plan, including the EOP, has sets of procedures either in or appended to it. A procedure is a series of well-defined steps that follow a pre-determined order. A single procedure or a step in a procedure consists of one or more tasks. The author of a procedure has to ensure that the person to whom the tasks are assigned knows how to perform them. If a task requires a security officer to drive to a certain location for a certain purpose, he'd better know how to drive.

Procedures for the security group are written by the CSO or someone working for him/her. Writing procedures for maintenance employees is the job of the property manager, and those for safety employees are written by the safety manager. Because all three sets need to dovetail with one another, the CSO, the property manager, and the safety manager collaborate. In some instances, a single set of procedures can be used for more than one incident.

The procedures for evacuating premises in an arson incident can be the same as those for a bombing incident.

Programs

Programs support procedures. For example, a training program for security officers teaches the how of performing tasks related to facility evacuation. A floor warden program teaches evacuation tasks to floor wardens. In this single matter of evacuation there may be other supporting programs as well: fire safety, emergency medicine, accident prevention, and security awareness. A single procedure can be supported by multiple programs; conversely, a single program can support procedures for multiple responders.

Programs get less credit than they deserve. Here's why. A policy has no action *per se*; a plan has no action until triggered by an event; and procedures have no action until the plan goes into action. Programs, however, are active all the time.

TRAINING

Each responder group has its own training. The level of training corresponds to the knowledge and skill levels of the trainees. The person in charge of the floor warden program might attend an out-of-house workshop, while floor wardens might attend in-house training conducted by a fire inspector from the local community.

In the security group, training for the chief security officer and his/her direct reports might be obtained at security seminars, while security officers might receive training given by shift supervisors and experienced co-workers.

Security officer training has two stages: entry level and upper level. Entry level covers basic principles, followed by response procedures; upper level includes refresher and advance training. Entry level is more important than upper level because topics are foundational, capped with topics related to very serious events such as bomb incidents and arson. Also, the rate of turnover in the security officer profession is so high that only a small percentage of officers ever reach a point in time where they qualify for upper level training.

At entry level, a security officer is taught basic principles first and response procedures next. The training period begins on the day of hire and usually extends for about 100 days. (1) Training combines lecture and demonstration, films and videos, and on-the-job practice and tutorials. On-line training is gaining favor because it can be conducted anywhere, anytime, and is economical compared to other methods of instruction.

Among the basic topics taught at the entry level are the following:

- Employer Orientation and Policies
- Job Assignment and Post Orders
- Use and Operation of Equipment

- Nature of Security Operations
- Legal Aspects
- Conduct and Ethics
- Observation and Incident Reporting
- Patrol Techniques
- Interpersonal Communications
- Principles of Access Control
- Loss Prevention Principles

Upper level topics address response procedures. They might be titled:

- Fire Emergencies
- Bomb Incidents
- Workplace Violence
- Premises Evacuation
- Emergency Notifications

Training is essential because the most frequent failure in the operation of a security system is human error, and human error is most often the result of poor training or training not conducted. Training is a matter that cries out for management attention. Nearly all training deficiencies result from a failure of management to require that it be done, and the reasons behind the failure are apathy and the never-ending urge to contain costs.

TESTING THE SECURITY SYSTEM

The three components of a security system can be tested individually, along with the entire system.

People Testing

Tests that evaluate the people component can be as follows:

- Tests that assess general knowledge, aptitude, intelligence, achievement, interests, personality, honesty, integrity, drug abuse, and probability of violent behavior
- Tests conducted as part of a training program
- Cognitive tests that evaluate a security officer's knowledge of the job, post orders, special operating procedures, and incident plan procedures
- Psychomotor tests that evaluate a security officer's capacity to perform tasks that depend on body coordination such as firing a weapon, body strength such as carrying an injured person, and stamina such as working long hours
- Skill tests that evaluate a security officer's ability to perform tasks of an abstract nature such as comprehending and analyzing information

Physical Safeguards Testing

Tests that evaluate the physical safeguards component can be as follows: (2)

- Operability tests conducted daily by security group employees to evaluate operation of security system equipment
- Equipment performance tests conducted periodically (usually monthly) by security group employees and others to assess operability and sensitivity of security system equipment such as fire detectors, fire extinguishers, intrusion sensors, CCTV cameras, defibrillators, oxygen administering devices, and backup generators
- Post-maintenance tests conducted when security system equipment has been returned to use after maintenance or repair
- Limited scope tests conducted to evaluate all of the equipment comprising an entire system or one or a few major pieces of equipment
- Whole-system tests conducted to ensure the entire security system is working as designed

Process Testing

Following are tests that evaluate the process component.

- Desktop exercises are conducted by site management to evaluate the general readiness of the security system. A scenario is presented, often by the Emergency Response Team (the team of managers that perform command and control functions in an emergency operating center). A desktop exercise can call for a system-wide response to a specific incident. Working from their desks (or other non-scene locations), the responders simulate actions called for by the incident plan and procedures. An after-action assessment by management and the participants decides the workability of the plan and changes to procedures that may be required to improve the response.
- War Games evaluate the efficacy of plans and procedures in a "conflict" situation. The situation is hypothetical and typically involves a terrorist attack such as a bombing, stand-off attack, or direct assault. Following the initial attack, the terrorist group changes its tactics or reacts in some way that requires the responders to react. The war game is similar to the desk top exercise because with few exceptions the responders carry out procedures from their work stations. The differences are: the war game can be unannounced; the scenario presented by an outside group; the scenario "intense" and evolving; and the response monitored and graded.

Overall System Testing

A full-scale drill evaluates the overall security system. Everything that is done in the war game test is used in the drill, except that action is "live."

If the terrorist attack involves the use of a bomb, an explosion is simulated such as setting off a smoke grenade. Injuries are simulated, first aid is applied, a triage center is set up, mock firefighting commences, employees evacuate the site, police cordon off the area, HazMat specialists look for chemical agents, public health officials look for biological agents, etc. The drill particulars are made known to employees and local authorities in advance. The full-scale drill is a coordinated response that involves people using physical safeguards according to the procedures of a plan.

DESIGN

The design of a security system is a logical follow-on to a vulnerability assessment. Designing is more than setting lines to paper; it is melding parts and parts of parts to create or strengthen a function. For example, the function of denying access to intruders is not entirely improved by simply purchasing and installing an access control system. Adjustments of a physical/technical nature will be required within the system and at outlying points where the system joins other systems; intrusion detection devices will have to be calibrated to their external environment; console operators must be of a certain caliber and trained to operate the system; responders to intrusion detection must be equipped, trained, and drilled; and employees and guests affected by the system must be educated to accept and abide by rules.

Designing a security system is analogous to the adage that closing a door in one place opens a door in another place. Every add-on and change to a security system, whether at the micro or macro level, has a functional impact, sometimes large and obvious and sometimes small and subtle. Eliminating one glaring weakness can result in creating one or more less visible weaknesses.

NOTES

1. Guidelines developed by the American Society for Industrial Security International state that entry-level training should occur in the first 100 days of a security officer's employment.

2. These tests are paraphrased from a very useful book, *The Design and Evaluation of Physical Protection Systems*, by Mary Lynn Garcia. Boston: Butterworth-Heinemann, 2001.

24. The Nature of Terrorism

What are the threats that keep me awake at night?
—George Tenet

BACKGROUND

On 11 September 2001, terrorists hijacked four U.S. commercial passenger planes. Two crashed into the World Trade Center, a third crashed into the Pentagon, and the fourth — believed to have a target in or near Washington, D.C. — crashed into a field in Pennsylvania. The World Trade Center (see Figure 24-1) was completely destroyed, the Pentagon substantially damaged, and nearly 3,000 people killed in a matter of a few hours. Thus began the greatest shift in security the world has ever seen.

A BRIEF HISTORY

Early Events

Terrorism is hardly anything new under the sun. It has been with civilization at least since the beginning of recorded history. The following are historical highlights.

- In the sixth century B.C. Assyrians poisoned enemy wells with rye ergot, a fungus that causes convulsions if ingested.
- The Greek historian Xenophon in the fifth century B.C. wrote of the use and effectiveness of psychological warfare against enemy populations.
- Roman emperors Tiberius and Caligula used banishment, expropriation of property, and execution to discourage opposition to their rule.
- In seventh-century India, cultists called Thuggees (from whom we get the word "thug") ritually strangled travelers as sacrifices to a Hindu deity.
- Shiites in the eleventh century ate hashish (from which we get the word "assassin") to give them courage before murdering nonbelievers.
- The Spanish Inquisition used arbitrary arrest, torture, and execution to punish what it viewed as religious heresy.

Figure 24-1 The September 11, 2001 attack on the World Trade Center.

- The use of terror was openly advocated by Robespierre as a means of encouraging revolutionary virtue during the French Revolution, leading to the period of his political dominance called the Reign of Terror.
- After the end of the American Civil War in 1865, defiant Southerners formed the Ku Klux Klan to intimidate supporters of Reconstruction.
- In the latter half of the nineteenth century, terrorism was adopted by adherents of anarchism in Western Europe, Russia, and the United States. They believed that the best way to effect revolutionary political and social change was to assassinate persons in positions of power.
- From 1865 to 1905 a number of kings, presidents, prime ministers, and other government officials were killed by anarchists' guns or bombs.
- The assassination of Austrian Archduke Franz Ferdinand in 1914 by a Serb extremist touched off World War I.

Events Leading to 9-11

Today's more familiar forms of terrorism, which are often staged for a television audience, first appeared in 1968 when the Popular Front for the Liberation of Palestine conducted the first terrorist hijacking of a commercial airplane. Following are brief summations of terrorist events that preceded and possibly foreshadowed the events of 9-11 [1].

- In 1983, Hezbollah — an Iranian-backed group of Shiite Islamists — used a suicide bomber to attack the U.S. Marine barracks in Beirut, Lebanon. The bombing killed 242 Americans.
- In 1988, terrorists trained and financed by the Libyan government placed a bomb on board Pan Am flight 103. The aircraft exploded over Lockerbie, Scotland. More than 300 people died.

Figure 24-2 Bomb damage to the Edward P. Murrah Building, Oklahoma City, Oklahoma. *(Photo by Federal Emergency Management Agency.)*

- The U.S. embassies in Kenya and Tanzania were attacked in 1988 by Al Qaeda suicide bombers, killing 224 people.
- In 1993, Islamist terrorists bombed the World Trade Center, killing six and injuring about 1,000 others.
- Also in 1993, Mir Aimal Kasi killed CIA employees Frank Darling and Lansing Bennett outside CIA headquarters in Langley, Virginia.
- Timothy McVeigh killed 168 people in 1995 by bombing a federal office building in Oklahoma City (see Figure 24-2).
- In 1995, members of Aum Shinrikyo, a Japanese cult, released sarin nerve gas into the Tokyo subway, killing 12 and wounding over 3,500.
- In 1996, a truck bomb exploded outside the Khobar Towers housing complex in Saudi Arabia, killing 19 U.S. military members and wounding 515 people, including 240 U.S. citizen employees.
- In 2000, the U.S.S *Cole* — a destroyer at anchor in the port of Aden, Yemen — was rammed by a small boat carrying explosives. The resulting blast killed 17 sailors and injured 39 others. (See Figure 24.3.)

Contemporary Events

Currently, fewer terrorist attacks occur but in total they kill more people. Two reasons can be postulated: attacks motivated by religion are free of the restraints of personal conscience, and the targets of terrorism have gone on the alert and initiated enhanced security protections. The latter action, which is frequently called "target hardening," may explain why many of

Figure 24-3 Bomb damage to the U.S.S. *Cole*, Aden, Yemen.

the recent terrorist attacks have involved explosives. Bombs are relatively easy to assemble and deploy — especially when the bomber is willing to be consumed in the blast.

THE MANY FACES OF TERRORISM

People tend to think of terrorism as brutal and senseless. Brutal it is, but senseless it is not. Behind every terrorist act is a motive, if not a calculated strategy. Although the nature of the acts vary widely — from the use of kidnapping and extortion to guns and bombs — they are neither spontaneous nor random. The tactics of terrorists are intended to be spectacular. The greater the spectacle the greater the fear and the greater the intimidation. According to Brian Jenkins [2] (see Figure 24-4), "Terrorism is theater."

In recent days, Americans have begun to see terrorism in a clearer, yet differing, perspective. The organizations that exist to deal with terrorism have come up with several definitions.

DEFINITIONS OF TERRORISM

In the Code of Federal Regulations, terrorism is said to be

> The unlawful use of force and violence against persons or property to intimidate or coerce a government, the civilian population, or any segment thereof, in furtherance of political or social objectives.
>
> The FBI describes terrorism as either domestic or international, depending on the origin, base, and objectives of the terrorists [3].

Figure 24-4 Terrorism is theater.

Domestic terrorism is the unlawful use, or threatened use, of force or violence by a group or individual based and operating entirely within the United States or its territories without foreign direction committed against persons or property to intimidate or coerce a government, the civilian population, or any segment thereof, in furtherance of political or social objectives. International terrorism involves violent acts dangerous to human life that are a violation of the criminal laws of the United States or any state, or that would be a criminal violation if committed within the jurisdiction of the United States or any state. These acts appear to be intended to intimidate or coerce a civilian population, influence the policy of a government by intimidation or coercion, or affect the conduct of a government by assassination or kidnapping. International terrorist acts occur outside the United States or transcend national boundaries in terms of the means by which they are accomplished, the persons they appear intended to coerce or intimidate, or the locale in which the perpetrators operate or seek asylum.

The State Department defines terrorism as follows:

> Premeditated, politically motivated violence perpetrated against noncombatant targets by sub-national groups or clandestine agents, usually intended to influence an audience.

The Department of Defense definition of terrorism is as follows:

> The calculated use of violence or the threat of violence to inculcate fear; intended to coerce or to intimidate governments or societies in the pursuit of goals that are generally political, religious, or ideological [4].

Paul Pillar, formerly of the CIA's Counterterrorist Center, says that terrorism consists of four key elements [5]. Paraphrasing Pillar, a terrorist act is

- Premeditated and planned in advance. It is not an impulsive act of rage.
- Designed to change the existing political order. It is not violence like that used by common criminals.
- Aimed at civilians rather than military targets or combat-ready troops.
- Carried out by a subnational group, not by the legitimate army of a country.

MOTIVES OF TERRORIST GROUPS

Terrorist groups can be categorized in several ways (e.g., where they are from, where they operate, weapons and tactics they use, and the targets they attack). One categorization label that seems to work well is motivation. Terrorist groups can be seen to operate from one or any combination of politics, religion, and special interests.

Politics

Terrorist groups motivated by political considerations cover a lot of ground. First are terrorists that seek to form a separate state for their own group, which is often an ethnic minority. The group is likely to portray its activist followers as patriots (see Figure 24-5) struggling to achieve freedoms unjustly withheld by an oppressive government. Their appeal is to a world audience. They hope to win concessions at home, gain sympathy abroad, and obtain financial and logistical assistance from outside supporters.

Nationalist groups tend to calibrate their violent acts at a level high enough to maintain pressure on the established government but not so high as to alienate the group's members and outside supporters. Among the many nationalist groups are the Irish Republican Army, the Palestine

Figure 24-5 Middle East guerilla.

Liberation Organization, Basque Fatherland and Liberty, and the Kurdistan Workers' Party. Also in the political arena are state-sponsored terrorist groups that are essentially nameless. They serve as the foreign policy tools of radical governments.

What the state cannot achieve through diplomacy or conventional warfare it hopes to achieve by intimidation. Behind the intimidation are violent acts, such as assassinations and bombings, and saber rattling such as the threatened use of nuclear weapons. Groups in this category operate covertly, often hire mercenaries, and enlist no-cost services of sympathizers. These groups are capable of carrying out large-scale attacks because they can call upon resources of the state: government intelligence and weaponry, diplomatic immunity, documents that permit cross-border travel, and a cloak of legitimacy.

Religion

Religious terrorists use violence to further what they see as divinely commanded purposes. Their playing field is global as opposed to national and their targets are wide-ranging. Some terrorist groups in this category are small and cult-like, and a few exist on the ultra-radical fringe. The larger groups come from major religions and are almost always minorities within them.

One of the difficulties in assessing the intentions of religiously motivated terrorist groups is the vague and irrational statements of their leaders. For example, a leader will call for a jihad (holy war) but leave followers to use their own imagination in waging it, or leaders in subgroups will interpret the jihad in a variety of ways. By contrast, the politically motivated terrorist groups express less amorphous objectives: removal of a government or establishment of an independent nation. At least with the politically motivated groups, the protectors are able to somewhat more accurately assess the persons and groups they are dealing with, their likely targets, and the arenas of operation.

Special Interest

What the United States lacks in the way of political and religious terrorism, it makes up for in special interest terrorism. Many of the special interest groups are motivated by opposition to federal taxation and regulation, the United Nations, other international organizations, and the U.S. government generally. Much of the opposition comes from organizations, and depending on who is doing the estimates the overall membership of these groups will range from 10,000 to 100,000. Even if the total numbers are high, the extremist core of the militia movement is quite small and often out of sync with the desires of the broad majority. A strategy exercised by the leaders of some groups is to endorse violence but leave the execution of it to hard-core individuals acting on their own. An example of this strategy in action was the bombing by Timothy McVeigh (see Figure 24-6) of the Alfred P. Murrah federal building

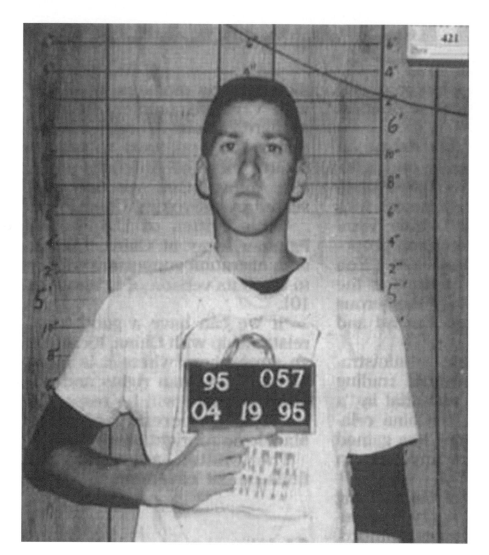

Figure 24-6 Timothy McVeigh bombed the Murrah building.

in Oklahoma City. The mailing of anthrax letters to government officials may be another.

Then there are the hate groups that terrorize in the name of race or religion, or both. The Ku Klux Klan, which used lynching to terrorize African-Americans following the Civil War, was a forerunner of today's Neo-Nazis, Skinheads, and so-called Christian Patriots. The Aryan Nation group embraces multiple issues: they hate anyone who is not white or is Jewish or is favorably disposed to the U.S. government. A similar group is the Aryan Brotherhood, which is composed of present and former prison gang members. Pro-life zealots have assassinated physicians and bombed abortion clinics, but because these individuals appear not to be members of an organized group the FBI has classified their attacks as criminal events rather than terrorist events.

The Animal Liberation Front (ALF) encourages individuals to take "direct action" against organizations that commit animal abuse such as the meat industry's practice of slaughtering cattle or the medical research industry's practice of vivisecting laboratory animals. ALF's call for action is believed to be connected to crimes that include arson, breaking and entering, and theft.

The Earth Liberation Front (ELF) is a loosely knit eco-terrorist organization whose primary agenda is protection of the environment. ELF's likely targets are new construction projects, logging sites, petroleum drilling and production facilities, and mining operations. An allied organization with a similar agenda is Earth First.

Based on what we have seen, it is correct to believe that only a very few animal-rights and environmental activists are committed to activities that kill and maim. The troubling part is that law enforcement authorities have no way of identifying them specifically. Even more troubling is the reality that one person — a Timothy McVeigh, for example — can bring about hundreds of deaths and injuries in a single act.

POLICING PRIORITIES

A consequence of 9-11 has been a nationwide shift in policing priorities. Police departments, especially those in major cities, are devoting increased resources to prevent and mitigate terrorist attacks, the effect of which is to reduce other law enforcement services. And then there is the cost of gearing up to meet extreme circumstances. Because police officers are almost always first to arrive at the scene of a disaster and first to begin rendering aid, they have to be specially trained and adequately equipped (see Figure 24-7).

The shift in law enforcement priorities varies according to a community's perception of threat, its vulnerabilities, and resources available to law enforcement. Even where great variance exists, law enforcement departments in general have done the following:

- Created new working relationships with other first-responder agencies such as fire departments and agencies responsible for delivering emergency medical treatment and hazardous materials containment
- Acquired new communication equipment and revised their methods for communicating within and outside the department
- Refined their training programs and emergency response plans to address terrorist threats, including attacks with weapons of mass destruction
- Given more patrol attention to potential target sites such as government buildings, ports of entry, transportation hubs, nuclear power plants, chemical plants, and other facilities of a symbolic or critical nature
- Increased their presence at major public events
- Reorganized and reassigned officers to perform counterterrorism duties (major city departments have joined with federal agencies to form Joint Terrorism Task Forces)

Figure 24-7 Police mobility.

- Employed new technologies in metal detection, X-ray scanning, and sensors for detecting the signals of chemical, biological, and radiological attacks

KNOWING THE ENEMY

The time-worn precept that one must know the enemy is as true today as it has ever been [6]. CSOs, whether from the private or public sector, cannot set up adequate defenses against terrorists without first gaining an understanding of them. It is one thing to define terrorists but quite another to place them in a perspective that allows us to make reasoned judgments about their intentions and capabilities.

International Terrorist Groups

Following are brief descriptions of major (but certainly not all) terrorist groups operating on the world scene [7].

Abu Nidal Organization (ANO):   The ANO has its roots in the Palestine Liberation Organization (PLO), from which it split in 1974. This group has carried out terrorist attacks in 20 countries, killing or injuring almost 900 persons. Its announced targets include the United States, the United Kingdom, France, Israel, moderate Palestinians, the PLO, and various Arab countries. Major attacks included the Rome and Vienna airports in December of 1985; the Neve Shalom synagogue in Istanbul; the Pan Am flight 73 hijacking in Karachi in September of 1986; and the City of Poros day-excursion ship attack in Greece in July of 1988. The ANO is the chief suspect in the assassination of PLO deputy chief Abu Iyad and PLO security chief Abu Hul in Tunis in January of 1991. ANO assassinated a Jordanian diplomat in Lebanon in January of 1994 and has been linked to the killing of the PLO representative there.

Al Qaeda: The name Al Qaeda literally means "the base." Like other Islamic terrorist groups, Al Qaeda has from time to time issued a fatwa, a religious commandment that Muslims must follow. The fatwa will often call for a jihad (holy war). The group holds a belief that laws outside the teachings of the Koran should not be followed because they would disrupt the total observance of Islam. Muslims that act upon this belief are called mujaheddin (holy warriors).

Al Qaeda was formed by Usama Bin Ladin in the late 1980s to bring together Arabs who fought in Afghanistan against the Soviet invasion. Bin Ladin helped finance, recruit, transport, and train Sunni Islamic extremists for the Afghan resistance. The group's current goal is to establish a pan-Islamic nation throughout the world by working with allied Islamic extremist groups to overthrow regimes it deems "non-Islamic" and expelling Westerners and non-Muslims from Muslim countries. In 1988, under the banner of The World Islamic Front for Jihad Against the Jews and Crusaders, Bin Ladin decreed that it was the duty of all Muslims to kill United States citizens (civilian or military) and their allies everywhere.

An Al Qaeda plot to kill United States and Israeli tourists visiting Jordan during millennial celebrations was thwarted by local authorities, resulting in the capture and trial of 28 suspects. In 1998, Al Qaeda bombed U.S. embassies in Nairobi, Kenya, and Dar es Salaam, Tanzania, killing more than 300 and injuring more than 5,000. The group claims to have conducted three bombings that targeted U.S. troops in Aden, Yemen, in 1992 and shot down U.S. helicopters and killed U.S. servicemen in Somalia in 1993.

Al Qaeda has been linked to various aborted plots: assassination of Pope John Paul II during his visit to Manila in 1994; simultaneous bombings of the U.S. and Israeli Embassies in Manila and other Asian capitals in 1994; midair bombing of a dozen U.S. trans-Pacific flights in 1995; and assassination of President Clinton during a visit to the Philippines in 1995. Because it acts as an umbrella organization for extremist groups world-wide, Al Qaeda may have several thousand members, including believers that operate in covert cells in Western and pro-Western nations.

Bin Ladin, son of a billionaire Saudi family, is said to have inherited approximately $300 million that he uses to finance the group. Al Qaeda also maintains moneymaking front organizations, solicits donations from supporters, and siphons funds from donations to Muslim charitable organizations.

Armed Islamic Group (GIA): A major goal of the GIA is to overthrow the secular Algerian regime and replace it with an Islamic state. The GIA began its most violent activities in 1992 after the government of Algiers voided the victory of the Islamic Salvation Front (FIS) — that nation's largest Islamic party — in the first round of legislative elections.

In the last several years, the GIA has massacred a large number of Algerian citizens, sometimes wiping out entire villages. It has also murdered journalists and more than 100 expatriate men and women. A favored weapon of assassination is the car bomb. The GIA hijacked an Air France flight to Algiers in 1994 and conducted a series of bombings in France in 1995. A splinter faction of the GIA is the Salafi Group for Call and Combat (GSPC). It is currently rated as the most effective armed group inside Algeria.

Aum Shinrikyo: More a cult than a group, the Aum Shinrikyo was established in 1987 with a proclaimed intent to take over Japan, and then the world. Approved as a religious entity in 1989 under Japanese law, the group ran candidates in a Japanese parliamentary election. Rather than softening its stance, the cult began to predict an imminent end of the world precipitated by an attack of Japan by the United States.

The Japanese government revoked its recognition of the cult as a religious organization in October of 1995, but in 1997 a government panel decided not to invoke a law that would have outlawed the cult. In 1995, a handful of Aum members simultaneously released the chemical nerve agent sarin on several Tokyo subway trains, killing 12 and injuring close to 1,300 people.

Basque Fatherland and Liberty (ETA): The area known as Basque Country sits on the border separating Spain and France. It consists of seven provinces: three under French administration and four under Spanish administration. The ETA was founded in 1959 with the aim of creating an independent homeland in the Spanish provinces. In hopes of achieving its aim, the ETA has assassinated Spanish political and judicial leaders and attacked security and military forces. In response to French operations on the border, the group has targeted French interests. The ETA finances its activities through robberies, ransom, and extortion.

The group has friendly relations with the Irish Republican Army, and with the Algerian Islamic Group, for which it has provided training in the production of explosives, guerrilla warfare, and urban terrorism. ETA has obtained weapons, safe houses, and logistics support from Islamic networks in Europe.

Al-Gama'a al-Islamiyya: The Gama'a is Egypt's largest militant group, active since the late 1970s. Until 1999, when the group issued a cease-fire, it had specialized in armed attacks against Egyptian security and other government officials, Coptic Christians, and Egyptian opponents of Islamic extremism. The Gama'a also attacked visitors, most notably an attack at Luxor in which 58 tourists were murdered. The group also claimed credit for an unsuccessful attempt in 1995 to assassinate Egyptian President Hosni Mubarak in Addis Ababa, Ethiopia. The Gama'a has threatened U.S. interests but has never specifically attacked a U.S. citizen or facility.

In 1998, the Gama'a leadership joined Usama Bin Ladin in issuing a fatwa that called for attacks against U.S. civilians. Since then, however, the main body of members has denied support for Bin Ladin and disagreed with public statements made by minority factions within the group.

Hamas: Formed in late 1987 as an outgrowth of the Palestinian branch of the Muslim Brotherhood, various Hamas elements have used both political and violent means to pursue the goal of establishing an Islamic Palestinian state in place of Israel. Hamas is loosely structured, with some elements working clandestinely and others working openly through mosques and social service institutions to recruit members, raise money, organize activities, and distribute propaganda. The group's strength is concentrated in the Gaza Strip and a few areas of the West Bank.

Hamas activists — especially those in the Izz el-Din al-Qassim Brigades — have conducted many attacks, including large-scale suicide bombings against Israeli civilian and military targets. They have also assassinated Fatah rivals and Palestinians suspected of collaboration with Israel.

Hezbollah: This radical Shia group is dedicated to the creation of an Iranian-style Islamic republic in Lebanon and the removal of all non-Islamic influences. Strongly anti-West and anti-Israel, Hezbollah is closely allied with and often directed by Iran. The group is believed to have been involved in numerous anti-U.S. terrorist attacks, including the suicide truck bombing of the U.S. Embassy and U.S. Marine barracks in Beirut in 1983 and the U.S. Embassy annex in Beirut in 1984. Elements of the group were responsible for the kidnapping and detention of U.S. and other Western hostages in Lebanon.

Japanese Red Army (JRA): This international terrorist group formed about 1970 after breaking away from the Japanese Communist League–Red Army Faction. The JRA's historical goal has been to overthrow the Japanese government and monarchy and to help foment world revolution.

In its earliest activities, the JRA carried out a series of attacks around the world, including the massacre in 1972 at Lod Airport in Israel, two Japanese airliner hijackings, and an attempted takeover of the U.S. Embassy in Kuala Lumpur. In 1988, a JRA operative was arrested on the New Jersey Turnpike while in possession of explosives that were apparently to be used in an attack on the U.S. to coincide with the bombing of a U.S.O club in Naples. In the Naples attack, five persons were killed, including a U.S. servicewoman. The JRA is small in comparison with other extremist groups but is imaginative and daring in its attacks.

Al-Jihad: An Egyptian Islamic extremist group, al-Jihad is closely allied with Al Qaeda. The group's primary goals are to overthrow the Egyptian government and replace it with an Islamic state. Al-Jihad specializes in armed attacks of high-level Egyptian government officials and car bombings directed against U.S. government officials in Egypt. In its earliest stage, Al-Jihad assassinated Egyptian President Anwar Sadat.

National Liberation Army (ELN):   This Marxist insurgent group was formed in 1965 under the direction of Cuban intellectuals inspired by Fidel Castro and Che Guevara. Following a campaign of mass kidnappings — each involving at least one U.S. citizen — the ELN demanded concessions that the Colombian government found unacceptable. To demonstrate its strength, the ELN has waged a campaign of terror that includes kidnapping, hijacking, bombing, extortion, and guerrilla warfare.

Each year the ELN conducts hundreds, if not thousands, of kidnappings for ransom — often targeting foreign employees of large corporations, especially in the petroleum industry. ELN guerrillas operating in rural and mountainous areas have inflicted major damage on petroleum pipelines and the nation's electric distribution network.

Palestine Liberation Front (PLF):   The primary target of this group is Israel. However, in 1985 it attacked the Italian cruise ship *Achille Lauro* and murdered U.S. citizen Leon Klinghoffer. A warrant for Abu Abbas's arrest, the leader of the attack, continues in effect

Revolutionary Armed Forces of Colombia (FARC):   Established in 1964 as the military wing of the Colombian Communist Party, the FARC is Colombia's oldest, largest, most capable, and best-equipped Marxist insurgency (see Figure 24-8). The FARC is organized along military lines and includes several urban fronts. In 2000, the group continued a slow-moving peace negotiation process with the Colombian government, which has gained the group several concessions, including a demilitarized zone used as a venue for negotiations.

Figure 24-8 FARC guerilla.

FARC is known for bombings, murder, kidnapping, extortion, hijacking, and guerrilla and conventional military action against Colombian political, military, and economic targets. In March of 1999 the FARC executed three U.S. Indian rights activists on Venezuelan territory after it kidnapped them in Colombia. Foreign citizens are often targets of FARC kidnapping for ransom. The FARC has well-documented ties to narcotics traffickers, principally through the provision of armed protection in exchange for financial support.

Revolutionary Organization 17 November: This radical group is named for the student uprising in Greece in November of 1973 that protested the military regime. This group is anti-Greek establishment, anti-U.S., anti-Turkey, anti-NATO, and is committed to the ouster from Greece of U.S. bases, removal of the Turkish military presence in Cyprus, and dissolution of Greece's ties to NATO and the European Union (EU). 17 November has assassinated senior U.S. and U.K. officials and Greek public figures. It has used bombs and rockets in attacks on EU facilities and foreign firms operating in Greece.

Revolutionary People's Struggle (ELA): Born from opposition to the military junta that ruled Greece from 1967 to 1974, the ELA is a self-described revolutionary, anti-capitalist, and anti-imperialist group. It has declared its opposition to "imperialist domination, exploitation, and oppression." Strongly anti-U.S., the ELA seeks the removal of U.S. military forces from Greece.

Shining Path: Also called Sendero Luminoso, this militant group adheres to a Maoist doctrine. In the 1980s, it became one of the most ruthless terrorist groups in the Western Hemisphere. Its stated goal is to destroy existing Peruvian institutions and replace them with a communist peasant revolutionary regime. It also opposes influence by foreign governments, as well as by other Latin American guerrilla groups, especially the Tupac Amaru Revolutionary Movement. Shining Path's tactics have included indiscriminate bombing campaigns and selective assassinations.

Domestic Terrorist Groups

What we now call domestic terrorism has existed for nearly a century and a half. It is seen in the lynching of freed slaves, assassinations of political leaders, fire-bombings of businesses, contamination of food and medicine, murders of abortion doctors, and the mailing of package bombs and anthrax-laced letters.

Anarchists: In the late nineteenth century, immigrants from Eastern Europe sympathetic to the international anarchist movement launched what historians consider the first wave of domestic terrorism in the United States. Anarchists tried to kill the steel tycoon Henry Clay Frick in 1892 and bombed Chicago's Haymarket in 1886. In 1901, an anarchist sympathizer assassinated President William McKinley in Buffalo, New York [8].

Anti-establishment groups: Another wave of anti-establishment terrorist activity began in the 1960s. Groups such as the Weather Underground, the Symbionese Liberation Army, and the Armed Forces for Puerto Rican National Liberation (FALN) used bombings and kidnappings to draw attention to their radical causes. The FALN tried to kill President Truman, stormed the House of Representatives, and set off bombs in New York City [9].

Pro-life, environment, and animal rights groups: As mentioned previously, special interest organizations are today's dominant domestic threats. Pro-life terrorist acts have taken the form of abortion clinic bombings and assassination of abortion doctors. The acts appear to be the work of zealots working alone. Legitimate pro-life organizations that operate on the political scene have denounced such acts.

Also mentioned earlier were Earth First, Earth Liberation Front (ELF), Animal Liberation Front (ALF). Another such group is People for the Ethical Treatment of Animals (PETA). Although active and capable of generating domestic news reports, these groups commit acts that are mild relative to international terrorist groups.

Anti-government groups: These groups share one thing in common: intense dislike of government. In addition, each has its own agenda (e.g., hatred of non-whites, non-Christians, non-Americans, and authority figures in general). The stalwarts in this category are the Neo-Nazis, Skinheads (see Figure 24.9), Christian Patriots, and Aryan Nation. Similar groups enter the scene from time to time, gain national attention, and disappear almost as quickly as they enter.

Figure 24-9 The Skinheads group hates the government, among other entities.

Possible future groups: Law enforcement officials believe the next wave of domestic terrorism will come from groups opposed to participation of the government with supranational institutions such as the International Monetary Fund and the World Trade Organization.

CONCLUSIONS

Extraordinary measures have been taken since 9-11, both in the government and private sectors. The government's efforts have moved along two tracks: destroy terrorism wherever it exists and prevent further terrorist attacks on U.S. soil. The private sector has taken a serious look at its vulnerabilities to terrorism and in substantial measure has turned to CSOs for helping in setting up protective measures.

Arising out of these efforts is a growing recognition that the public and private sectors must form a partnership and pool their separate resources and expertise. More than ever before, community leaders in law enforcement, fire-fighting, and emergency management are sitting down with CSOs and CEOs of local businesses. Vulnerability assessments are being made, new and comprehensive emergency plans developed, mutual aid agreements signed, and likely scenarios rehearsed. Federal government funding for the purchase of emergency equipment and supplies is flowing to areas where public and private sector leaders have rationally assessed and reached agreement on actual needs. It is in this context that the CSO can be an important participant in the war against terrorism.

NOTES

1. Many of the details contained in this section were drawn from *Patterns of Global Terrorism, 2003.* United States Department of State, June 2004.

2. Mr. Jenkins is a senior advisor to the president of the RAND Corporation and one of the world's leading authorities on terrorism.

3. *WMD Threat and Risk Assessment,* College Station, TX: Texas A&M University System, 2004, pp. 9–10.

4. *U.S. Army Field Manual 100-20, Stability and Support,* which can be found on-line at *www.usmilitary.about.com/od/armymanuals.*

5. *Terrorism: Questions and Answers: Council on Foreign Relations,* which can be found on-line at *www.cfrterrorism.org.*

6. Lao Tsu, writing in the *Tao Te Ching,* stated, "By underestimating the enemy, I almost lose what I value."

7. Much of what follows is based on annual reports titled *Patterns of Global Terrorism,* United States Department of State, Washington, D.C.

8. William Benton, *The Annals of America,* vol. XII. Chicago: Encyclopedia Britannica, 1968.

9. David McCullough, *Truman.* New York: Simon & Schuster, 1992, pp. 811.

25. Counterterrorism

If they can think it, they can do it.
—Anonymous

BACKGROUND

Historically, the prevailing view has been that terrorists stage their attacks to derive maximum propaganda value. Their attacks are deliberate and are calculated to achieve goals: recruit new followers, obtain financial and in-kind support, influence public opinion, force political decisions, undermine a government, and demonstrate a capacity and resolve to act. Their targets have leaned to the symbolic and are intended to deliver a message, usually political or religious.

The 9-11 attacks (see Figure 25-1) conformed to the prevailing view. They were staged, deliberate, and calculated; they influenced public opinion and demonstrated a capacity and resolve; and they targeted symbols and delivered a message. Billions of people around the globe received on television screens an impression that the United States was vulnerable.

But given the inhumanity of the 9-11 attacks, the prevailing view seems to have shifted: the primary objective, certainly of religion-based terrorist groups, may no longer be the attainment of propaganda value but the infliction of mass casualties.

EXPLOITATION OF THE MEDIA

There can be no doubt that terrorists use television, radio, newspapers, and web sites to deliver their messages. Neither can there be doubt that the media give to violent acts a high level of coverage, a circumstance that often encourages further violence. Benefits accrue to the terrorists — who want publicity — and to the media, which thrive on sensational events. A further observation of news reporting organizations is that they are nearly always motivated by profits and rarely motivated by a sense of public service.

Not all experts agree, however. They point out that media reporting of a particularly horrendous act can alienate supporters, turn away sympathizers,

Figure 25-1 The attack on the World Trade Center served as a wake-up call.

and close off the flow of essential outside financing. Of equal or greater importance can be a garbling of the terrorist message. Instead of the act defining the cause, it can make the public see only the brutality of the act.

In extortive acts, such as kidnapping or the taking of hostages, media coverage can protect lives by building sympathy for the victims and antipathy for the captors. Conversely, the victims can suffer when the media report resistance to the extortion, the effect of which can induce the captors to carry out their threats because they do not want to be seen as weak or compromising. Another negative effect of media reporting can be the pressure placed on the government (or corporation) to make a quick response when caution is the better course. To round out the negatives, the media have a knack for ferreting out and exploiting inside sources that with assurances of anonymity may reveal an intended response such as a rescue attempt.

KIDNAP AND ASSASSINATION

Kidnapping can be labeled as political and criminal. In the former, the kidnappers' adversary is a government or a prominent government figure. The kidnapping victim may be one person (e.g., a prominent government figure or other noted government official), a diplomat of another nation, and sometimes a non-government celebrity revered by the governed. The kidnappers may choose to take several hostages, usually persons that have no link to the government and do not have celebrity status.

Figure 25-2 Kidnapping is a favored tactic of terrorists and criminals.

The typical motive behind a political kidnapping is attainment of a specific objective such as amnesty or release of prisoners. Money is not a common demand. The kidnappers communicate to the government through the news media and often use videotapes of the victims to elicit public sympathy and sow discord in the government. Because the government has no direct communication channel to the kidnappers, it must reply through the media. From a propaganda standpoint, the kidnappers benefit greatly.

If the kidnappers' demands are not met, the hostages are assassinated singly, in combinations, or all at once (see Figure 25-2). Videotapes of the murders are sent to the news media and over the Internet. (Note: Technically, an assassination is the murder of a politically important person or otherwise prominent individual. In recent days, the term is being applied to the murder of people, prominent or not, when the purpose is to advance a cause or extort money.)

The criminal form of kidnapping is motivated by criminal greed or by a terrorist group's need to procure operational funds. The target is usually a profitable business or wealthy family, the demand is for money, the kidnap victim is a sole figure, selection of the victim is made on the basis of economic value and vulnerability, and communication between the kidnappers and the business or family is direct and sometimes kept secret from the media and law enforcement [1].

SUICIDE ATTACK

Suicide terror is not new. When the killing weapon was a knife, assassins of public figures rarely escaped with their own lives. The same held true for later

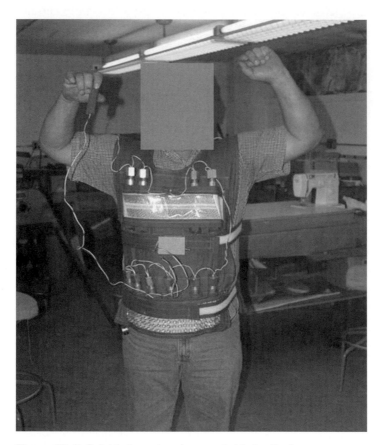

Figure 25-3 Suicide terrorism is remarkable for its frequency.

assassins firing pistols at close range or throwing makeshift bombs. Today's suicide terrorists use explosive-laden trucks and passenger airplanes. Whereas suicide terror has remained constant (see Figure 25-3), the killing methods have kept pace with weapons technology.

A knife or gun or a thrown bomb has a limit to the number of casualties, but this is not so with vehicle-laden bombs or biological, chemical, and radiological bombs. A single terrorist with a single weapon can cause mass casualties never known before. At the same time that weapons technology has evolved, the sophistication of terrorists has evolved. They are now at a level that enables them to construct rudimentary, but nonetheless effective, weapons of mass destruction. If the objective of the terrorist is to strike fear through the infliction of death and injury, the tools are at hand.

Suicide terrorism as we know it today began in 1983 when the Hezbollah blew up the Marine barracks in Lebanon. It has since been picked up by Hamas and other Palestinian groups in their attacks on Israel. Al Qaeda used it effectively in attacks on U.S. embassies in Kenya and Tanzania and U.S. military living quarters in Saudi Arabia. We have seen the same in Afghanistan and Iraq.

The notion that suicide terrorists are insane is simply too simple and not at all conducive to coming to grips with the threat. Suicide terrorists see themselves as martyrs to be glorified and rewarded in the hereafter. This is not to suggest that we should empathize but to know what we are dealing with.

Early on, Middle East suicide terrorists tended to be male, young, uneducated, and impoverished. But like the change in weapon technology, so have the users changed. They are not always male or young or uneducated or impoverished. We saw this in the events of 9-11. The terrorists were mature, intelligent, at least moderately affluent, and knew they were going to die. Terrorist bombers in Israel have been young women and mothers, as was the case with Chechen terrorists.

A suicide terrorist rarely acts without encouragement and support from a larger organization. The decision to use this tactic — as well as select the target, the time, and the place — rests not with the individual but with functionaries of the terrorist group. Moreover, the individual is often recruited, psychologically prepared, and trained well in advance. The idea that suicide terrorism is an individual act of uncontrolled rage is false. If the objective of the larger organization is to achieve dramatic results with minimum expenditure of resources, suicide terrorism is a good choice.

A question confronting the chief security officer is whether or not suicide terrorism can be prevented. The answer can be a "yes-but" only when preventive measures are in place. At a minimum, these would include a well-conducted vulnerability assessment followed by implementation of countermeasures designed to keep the suicide terrorist out of range of the target.

VEHICLE BOMB ATTACK

Compared with other weapons, vehicle bombs are inexpensive, simple to assemble, and easy to use. The number of vehicle bomb attacks around the world supports the view that vehicle bombs are the weapon of choice (see Figure 25-4). In the United States — where vehicles of all types are commonplace everywhere — it is extremely difficult, if not impossible, to differentiate between vehicles that are innocent and those that are lethal.

The challenge for the CSO is to establish procedures for keeping vehicles outside the blast zone of the protected facility. The blast zone is the area within which a high-explosive bomb will inflict death and serious injury. The size of the area is determined by the carrying capacity of the vehicle [2].

An explosion is the conversion of a solid or liquid into a gas. The rate of conversion for a bomb constructed with high explosives is much higher than the rate of conversion for a low-explosive bomb. Rapid conversion creates a blast or shockwave (see Figure 25-5). With a high explosive, the blast or shockwave can travel through air up to 27,000 feet per second; the shockwave of a low explosive moves at about 3,000 feet per second. It is the blast or shockwave that causes death, injury, and serious physical damage.

Figure 25-4 Aftermath of a vehicle bomb attack at the U.S. Embassy in Tanzania.

Vehicle Bomb Explosion Hazard and Safe-Distance Range

Vehicle Type	Carrying Capacity	Lethal Blast Range	Safe-Distance Range
Compact Car	500 pounds	100 feet	1500 feet
Full-Size Car	1,000 pounds	125 feet	1,750 feet
Passenger Van	4,000 pounds	200 feet	2,750 feet
Small Box Van	10,000 pounds	300 feet	3,750 feet
Mid-Size Truck	30,000 pounds	450 feet	6,500 feet
Semi-Trailer	60,000 pounds	600 feet	7,000 feet

Figure 25-5 Vehicle type and carrying capacity determine the lethal blast range.

Types of high explosives include the following.

- Military C-4
- PETN (pentaerythritol tetranitrate)
- TNT (trinitrotoluene)
- Dynamite
- Nitroglycerine
- ANFO (ammonium nitrate and fuel oil)

As of this date, the high explosive of choice for terrorists has been ammonium nitrate laced with diesel fuel. The ANFO-type bomb is inexpensive, easy to construct, and very effective. A terrorist-controlled aircraft with a near-full gas tank is a type of vehicle bomb, as we saw on 9-11. The same can be true of other transport vehicles such as buses, trains, and ships.

A CSO of an organization owning or contracting for vehicles ought to consider making background checks of operators, using a global positioning system (GPS), and placing within easy reach of the operator a duress alarm that annunciates at a monitoring station, security control center, or dispatcher's office when a vehicle is in jeopardy such as in a hijacking. Another step would be an engine kill switch for land-based vehicles.

DIRECT ACTION ATTACK

Direct action refers to any effort that seeks to achieve an end directly and by the most immediately effective means. Public demonstrations, boycotts, and labor strikes are nonviolent forms of direct action. In terrorism, direct action typically takes the form of armed assault in which a group, as opposed to an individual, seeks to attain a well-defined objective. The objectives tend to be assassination of opposition leaders, armed assault of government buildings, and storming prisons to obtain release of group members.

An example of direct action occurred in Munich, Germany, on 5 September 1972, when five Black September terrorists wearing sweat suits and carrying gym bags climbed over a fence surrounding the Olympic Village (see Figure 25-6). Inside the gym bags were assault rifles. Three more terrorists already inside the village joined them. They went to the dormitory housing Israeli athletes and knocked on the door of a room occupied by the wrestling team. Two Israelis who resisted were shot and killed. Nine other

Figure 25-6 A terrorist at the Olympic Village, Munich, Germany.

Israeli athletes were taken captive to be used as bargaining chips in negotiating the release of Arab terrorists held in Israel and safe passage of the terrorists and their captives from Germany to Cairo, Egypt. The German government provided helicopters to transport the terrorists and their hostages to an airfield, where German marksmen were in position. A fierce gunfight, followed by a second gunfight, ended with the deaths of all nine Israeli athletes, one policeman, and five terrorists, and the capture of three terrorists.

TERRORIST PREPARATION

An Al Qaeda training manual obtained in 2000 by U.K. authorities provides insights to terrorist preparation in targeted countries [3]. The manual suggests that up to 80 percent of information useful to a terrorist group can be collected from public sources.

Information Gathering

Much of the collected information is downloaded from

- The target's web site, where it may be possible to obtain the names of senior persons, their photographs, and biographies; physical addresses and photos of site locations and processes; phone numbers; and announcements of upcoming conferences and stockholder meetings.
- Government web sites that contain public records.
- Fact sheets and images discovered by Internet search engines.
- Chat rooms and bulletin boards.

Other open sources available and of possible interest to terrorists include

- Records available to the public at federal, state, and county agencies, with particular interest given to technical facts such as those that can be derived from maps, as-built plans, blueprints, and engineering schematics.
- Public libraries.
- News media.
- People knowledgeable about the target site — such as employees, ex-employees, contractors, and vendors — and pretext interviews conducted on the phone and in person.
- The target's trash bins.

Surveillance

Operatives will reconnoiter the areas around the target site and travel routes to and from the site (see Figure 25-7). They will look for police patrols to

Figure 25-7 Surveillance can be subtle.

determine

- Frequency and pattern.
- The number of officers in a patrol unit.
- The distance and time between the target site and the nearest police station.

Operatives will stake out the target site from several vantage points at various times: day and night, workdays and weekends, holidays, shift changes, and morning and afternoon rush hours. They will take notes and make sketches and maps. Operatives will look for vulnerabilities such as poor or nonexistent fencing and lighting, unlocked gates, and a guard service that may be stretched thin, poorly trained, or inadequately equipped.

Opportunities for surveillance are presented when the target site is open to the public, such as during an open house or a seasonal party when access control measures are relaxed. The operatives will pay attention to sign-in procedures; security posts and patrols; security communications; access control devices; intrusion detection sensors; CCTV cameras; elevators, hallways, restrooms, and similar places where bombs can be planted; and other physical aspects of the interior. Also of interest will be the physical features of the employee parking area and its proximity to people and on-site operations.

Photographs are highly prized by the planning cadre of the terrorist group. Operatives will be trained in photography and provided with cover identification such as a college student ID card or tourist visa.

Testing of Security

Operatives will want to determine the effectiveness of security at the target site. They may test security officers by attempting to gain entry using innocuous-appearing ruses. They may rattle perimeter fences to determine if they are alarmed, measure response times to alarms, or break security lights to see how long it will take for them to be replaced.

Acquisition of Needed Materials

The individuals that do the pre-attack preparation may or may not be the same individuals who carry out the attack. In either case, the attack party will acquire necessary materials; for example, firearms and ammunition, explosives and detonators, night-vision equipment, vehicles, communications gear, camouflage clothing, counterfeit identification, and funds for escape. The attack party will make several dry runs in order to identify and correct flaws in the attack plan.

COUNTERTERRORISM

Reaction to the events of 9-11 resulted in an unprecedented reorganization of the federal government and a rippling-down effect on state and local governments. In the immediate aftermath of the attacks, the U.S. Congress passed the Patriot Act (so-called because the actual title contains the words "Providing Appropriate Tools Required to Intercept and Obstruct Terrorism.") The main purposes of the law were to deter and punish terrorist acts in the United States and around the world and to give law enforcement enhanced investigative tools. The law permitted monitoring of e-mail, non-warrant searches where time is of the essence, increased surveillance, streamlined approval of phone and Internet taps, and authority for the Secretary of State to designate foreign groups as terrorist organizations and deport suspected terrorists [4].

Of greater import in counterterrorism was enactment in 2002 of the National Strategy for Homeland Security and the Homeland Security Act (the shorthand version is The Homeland Security Act). This law established the Department of Homeland Security (DHS) and gave to it the responsibility for mobilizing and organizing a national network of organizations. The overall purpose of the law was to secure the nation from terrorist attacks.

Department of Homeland Security (DHS)

Five major directorates constitute DHS. These are summarized in the following [5].

Border and Transportation Security (BTS): This directorate oversees protection of the nation's borders and transportation systems. The United States has 5,525 miles of border with Canada, 1,989 miles with Mexico, and a maritime border consisting of 95,000 miles of shoreline dotted with 350 official ports of entry. Each year, more than 500 million people — including 330 million non-citizens — enter the United States across these borders.

To carry out the border security mission (see Figure 25-8), BTS incorporated the United States Customs Service (previously part of the Department

Figure 25-8 The U.S. Customs Service is one of several federal agencies working at U.S. border entry points.

of Treasury), the enforcement division of the Immigration and Naturalization Service (Department of Justice), the Animal and Plant Health Inspection Service (Department of Agriculture), the Federal Law Enforcement Training Center (Department of Treasury), the Transportation Security Administration (Department of Transportation), and the Federal Protective Service (General Services Administration).

The BTS was also assigned the mission of securing the nation's transportation systems. The Transportation Security Administration (TSA) was created to provide security at airports.

Emergency Preparedness and Response (EP&R): This directorate was established to ensure that the United States is prepared for, and able to recover from, catastrophes — whether from terrorist attacks or natural disasters. The Federal Emergency Management Administration (FEMA) was incorporated and given the added task of moving the emergency management culture from a reactive orientation to one that is proactive (see Figure 25-9). In the matter of terrorism, for example, EP&R helps communities identify potential threats, assess their vulnerabilities, and institute security measures designed to help prevent, protect against, and mitigate the effects of terrorist acts. Key contributors to these efforts are the CSOs of companies operating within communities. CSOs are essential to the development of a comprehensive emergency management plan because they have expertise in preventive security measures and have an important say-so in the deployment of company resources when catastrophes occur.

EP&R assists communities in these efforts by managing a national training and evaluation system that designs curriculums, sets standards, and rates

Figure 25-9 FEMA aids search efforts.

emergency readiness. Allied in this effort is the Office for Domestic Preparedness (ODP), the primary office responsible for providing training, funds for the purchase of equipment, support for the planning and execution of exercises, technical assistance, and other support to assist states and local jurisdictions to prevent, plan for, and respond to acts of terrorism. The EP&R Directorate also leads the DHS response to a biological or radiological attack and coordinates the involvement of other federal response organizations, including the National Guard.

Science and Technology Directorate (S&T): The primary research and development arm of DHS is the Science and Technology Directorate. It organizes the scientific and technological resources of the United States to prevent or mitigate the effects of catastrophic terrorism. S&T coordinates much of the federal government's efforts to develop and implement scientific and technological countermeasures, including channeling the intellectual energy and capacity of important scientific institutions such as the national laboratories and academic institutions. A major priority is to sponsor research, development, and testing to invent new vaccines, antidotes, diagnostics, and therapies against biological and chemical warfare agents (see Figure 25-10).

This research and development emphasis is driven by a continuing examination of terrorist threats, the nation's vulnerabilities to them, and the security systems in place to prevent and mitigate against them. Emphasis is on catastrophic terrorist acts that could result in large-scale loss of life and major economic impact.

Information Analysis and Infrastructure Protection Directorate (IAIP): Specialists in this unit of DHS are charged with identifying and assessing a broad range of information about terrorist threats. Information that can lead to identifying or stopping terrorists before they act is essential to the

Figure 25-10 Field workers isolating suspected anthrax.

Figure 25-11 Actionable intelligence goes to high-level government officials.

DHS mission. Such information is called "actionable intelligence." It results from the timely and thorough analysis of information concerning terrorists and their likely activities. The IAIP receives information from multiple sources such as the National Security Agency, CIA, and FBI. The information is merged and processed. When the output is actionable, it is disseminated to the President of the United States and other national decision-makers holding responsibility for homeland security (see Figure 25-11).

The IAIP also administers the Homeland Security Advisory System. In advance of a real-time crisis or attack, IAIP provides threat warnings and advisories for the nation and for organizations that appear to be terrorist targets. It also releases general threat information for public consumption.

Management Directorate: This unit handles the department's budget, appropriations, expenditure of funds, accounting and finance; procurement; human resources and personnel; information technology systems; facilities, property, equipment, and other material resources; and identification and tracking of performance measurements.

The DHS Private Sector Office is of interest to a company's CSO. It provides America's business community a direct line of communication to DHS and is mandated to work directly with individual businesses, trade associations, and other professional and nongovernmental organizations to share information through partnership initiatives. Many of the nation's most critical assets (i.e., meaningful terrorist targets) are in the private sector and are looked after by private security professionals. As large as DHS is, it does not have the capacity to assume or even monitor day-to-day protection of critical private sector assets. The only sensible solution is for DHS to work with the private security industry.

Federal Bureau of Investigation (FBI)

The FBI is the lead agency and linchpin of counterterrorism within the boundaries of the United States. It has substantial resources committed to counterterrorism and is able to call upon resources of other law enforcement and intelligence agencies, the Department of Defense, and the Department of State.

The FBI's Office of Intelligence receives "raw information" from the field, distills it into meaningful intelligence, and disseminates it to users on a need-to-know basis. Counterterrorism Watch (CT Watch) is the FBI's 24-hour global command center for terrorism-prevention operations. Threat reports reaching CT Watch are given an initial review, and those deemed credible are passed on to field agents for action. CT Watch also produces daily terrorism reports for use by the President, key national security policy makers, and members of the intelligence and law enforcement communities.

Information-gathering activities since 9-11 increased to such an extent that the FBI partnered with the Central Intelligence Agency, National Security Agency, and the Defense Intelligence Agency to quickly and effectively analyze a wide range of paper documents, electronic media, photographs, and other materials. This group, called the Document Exploitation (DocEx) Working Group, generates intelligence reports and investigative leads. DocEx would not have been possible prior to the Patriot Act and a federal court decision affirming the appropriateness of information sharing by the law enforcement and intelligence communities [6].

Central Intelligence Agency (CIA)

The Central Intelligence Agency (CIA) is responsible for providing national security intelligence to senior U.S. policymakers. The Director of Central Intelligence (DCI) serves as the principal adviser to the President and the National Security Council (NSC) on matters of foreign intelligence related to national security. Both the Director and Deputy Director of Central Intelligence are appointed by the President with the advice and consent of the Senate. The CIA does not perform law enforcement functions. Prior to 9-ll, the CIA and FBI operated in separate spheres; since then, however, the two agencies have worked in tandem.

The CIA's main job is to keep top U.S. officials aware of key intelligence issues. To do this, they first have to identify an issue of national security concern such as the activities of a terrorist group or the intentions of countries that possess biological or chemical weapons. The follow-on step is collection of information about the issue.

There are several ways to collect information. Translating foreign newspaper and magazine articles and radio and television broadcasts provides open-source intelligence. Imagery satellites take pictures from space and imagery analysts write reports about what they see–for example, how many airplanes are at a foreign military base. Signals analysts work to decrypt coded messages. Operations officers recruit foreigners to obtain information of interest.

After the information is collected, intelligence analysts look it over and write reports that go to top-level officials at the White House, Pentagon, State

Department, Congress, and other government organizations. One of these reports is the President's Daily Brief (PDB), which the U.S. President and other senior officials receive each day. The CIA's analysts only report the information; they do not make policy recommendations. Policy making is left to the executive branch of the government, which includes a number of departments and offices. In the matter of terrorism, the heads of the State Department and the Department of Defense often make policy recommendations to the President. These policymakers, however, rely on information the CIA provides. The process of collecting, analyzing, and providing intelligence information ("the intelligence cycle") is carried out by the following three directorates.

Directorate of Intelligence (DI): This unit analyzes the final product of the intelligence cycle and produces reports, briefings, and papers on key foreign intelligence issues, of which terrorism is paramount.

Directorate of Operations (DO): The primary responsibility for the clandestine collection of foreign intelligence, including human source intelligence, is assigned to this unit.

Directorate of Science and Technology (DS&T): The DS&T is responsible for applying technology and technical expertise to the most critical intelligence problems (see Figure 25-12). The DS&T engages in the full range of technology activities — from applied research and development to the design, development, and operational deployment of specialized intelligence systems.

Intelligence is labeled according to the mode of acquisition, as follows.

- COMINT (Communications Intelligence) is derived from the intercept of foreign communications.

Figure 25-12 Spy planes collect raw intelligence data.

- ELINT (Electronic Intelligence) is the technical and intelligence information derived from foreign electromagnetic non-communications transmissions by other than the intended recipients.
- MASINT (Measurement and Signature Intelligence) is technically derived intelligence data, such as nuclear, optical, radio-frequency, acoustics, seismic, and materials sciences data.
- SIGINT (Signals Intelligence) is information derived from signals intercept, which comprises all COMINT, ELINT, and MASINT, however transmitted.
- HUMINT (Human Intelligence) is information acquired by human sources using covert and overt collection techniques.
- IMINT (Imagery Intelligence) includes satellite photography or other imagery that is then analyzed and processed for intelligence use.
- OPEN SOURCE is information in the public domain, such as periodicals, news broadcasts, and information on the Internet.

Defense Intelligence Agency (DIA)

The DIA is a Department of Defense combat-support agency and a major producer of foreign military intelligence. The principal users of DIA-collected information are military units operating in the field, Pentagon planners, and Department of Defense policy makers. Because the DIA and CIA have global assignments, they often work together. About 80 percent of the national budget for intelligence operations goes to the DIA.

DIA is headquartered at the Pentagon in Arlington, Virginia, with major operational activities at the Defense Intelligence Analysis Center (DIAC) in Washington, D.C.; the Armed Forces Medical Intelligence Center (AFMIC) at Frederick, Maryland; and the Missile and Space Intelligence Center (MSIC) at Huntsville, Alabama. In addition, DIA has more than a hundred sites around the globe, including U.S. embassies and combatant commands. Of particular interest to the DIA in the war against terrorism is the proliferation of advanced conventional weapons and weapons of mass destruction.

U.S. Coast Guard (USCG)

The Homeland Security Act placed the USCG in the Homeland Security Department, yet kept it as a separate military service. Upon declaration of war or when the President so directs, the Coast Guard reverts to an element of the U.S. Navy. Its current role is to work closely with the DHS's Border and Transportation Security Directorate in providing security on inland waterways, harbors, seaports, and coastlines. The Coast Guard's counterterrorism role is to

- Protect ports, the flow of commerce, and the marine transportation system.
- Maintain maritime border security against illegal entry of potential terrorists, conventional weapons, and weapons of mass destruction.

Figure 25-13 Protection of the President is the primary mission of the Secret Service.

- Keep marine transportation routes open for the movement of military assets.

United States Secret Service (USSS)

The Secret Service is another of the several separate agencies that fall under the umbrella of the Homeland Security Department. The primary mission of the Secret Service has been and continues to be protection of the President and other government leaders — a mission that clearly includes protection against the terrorist threat (see Figure 25-13).

The secondary mission is to deflect or neutralize cyber-terrorist attacks, which if successful would seriously damage major information systems, telecommunication networks, and other technology-based operations essential to meeting the routine needs of people, business and industry, and the national economy.

At a different level, but still operating under the DHS aegis, is the National Infrastructure Advisory Council (NIAC). It provides the President with advice on the security of critical information systems that support various economy sectors such as banking and finance, transportation, energy, manufacturing, and emergency government services.

Counterterrorism in the Private Sector

The private sector owns and is responsible for protecting close to 85 percent of all assets located in the United States. The government sector, although

Anti-Terrorist Measures

Little or No Cost Measures

Maintain situational awareness of world events and ongoing threats.

Ensure all levels of personnel are notified via briefings, email, voice mail and signage of any changes in threat conditions and protective measures.

Encourage personnel to be alert and immediately report any situation that may constitute a threat or suspicious activity.

Post emergency telephone numbers for police, fire, and rescue. Encourage personnel to memorize important numbers.

Know the location of the closest police stations, hospitals, schools, etc.

Encourage personnel to avoid routines, vary times and routes, pre-plan, and keep a low profile, especially during periods of high threat.

Encourage personnel to take notice and report suspicious packages, devices, unattended briefcases, or other unusual materials immediately; inform them not to handle or attempt to remove any such object.

Take any threatening or malicious telephone call, facsimile, or bomb threat seriously. If such a call is received, obtain and record as much information as possible to assist in identification of the caller. Record the time of the call, the exact words, any distinguishing features of the caller, and any background noise. Develop bomb threat information forms to assist if not already in place.

Encourage personnel to keep their family members and supervisors apprised of their whereabouts.

Encourage personnel to know emergency exits and stairwells.

Increase the number of visible security personnel wherever possible.

Rearrange exterior vehicle barriers, traffic cones, and road blocks to alter traffic patterns near facilities and cover by alert security forces.

Institute/increase vehicle, foot and roving security patrols varying in size, timing and routes. Implement random security guard shift changes.

Arrange for law enforcement vehicles to be parked randomly near entrances and exits.

Review current contingency plans and if not already in place, develop and implement procedures for receiving and acting on threat information, alert notification procedures, terrorist incident response procedures, evacuation procedures, bomb threat procedures, hostage and barricade procedures, chemical, biological, radiological and nuclear (CBRN) procedures, consequence and crisis management procedures, accountability procedures, and media procedures.

When the aforementioned plans and procedures have been implemented, conduct internal training exercises and invite local emergency responders (fire, rescue, medical and bomb squads) to participate in joint exercises.

Coordinate and establish partnerships with local authorities to develop intelligence and information sharing relationships.

Place personnel on standby for contingency planning.

Limit the number of access points and strictly enforce access control procedures.

Implement stringent identification procedures to include conducting 100 percent "hands on" checks of security badges for all personnel, if badges are required.

Remind personnel to properly display badges, if applicable, and enforce visibility.

Require two forms of photo identification for all visitors.

Escort all visitors entering and departing.

X-ray all packages, if possible, prior to entry, and inspect all handbags, and briefcases.

Validate vendor lists of all routine emergency deliveries and repair services.

Approach all illegally parked vehicles in and around facilities, question drivers and direct them to move immediately; if owner can not be identified, have vehicle towed by law enforcement.

Figure 25-14 Measures that may be of use to businesses.

Measures That May Bear Cost
Install telephone caller ID and record phone calls as needed.
Increase perimeter lighting.
Deploy visible security cameras and motion sensors.
Remove vegetation in and around perimeters; maintain regularly.
Institute a robust vehicle inspection program to include checking under the undercarriage of vehicles, under the hood, and in the trunk. Provide vehicle inspection training to security personnel.
Deploy explosive detection devices and explosive detection canine teams.
Conduct vulnerability studies focusing on physical security, structural engineering, infrastructure engineering, power, water, and air infiltration, if feasible.
Initiate a system to enhance mail and package screening procedures (both announced and unannounced).
Install special locking devices on manhole covers in and around facilities.
Implement a counter-surveillance detection program.

Figure 25-14 *continued*

playing a leadership role in countering terrorism, cannot possibly protect assets in both sectors. For the most part, it is up to the private sector to provide protection for its owned assets, particularly those of a nature critical to the safety of the public and defense of the nation. To be sure, a viable partnership between sectors is absolutely essential but there cannot be any doubt as to the security responsibilities of business leadership. Business leaders look to their CSOs for identifying potential threats, setting up countermeasures, and mitigating the consequences of adverse situations. They also rely on CSOs to be active in helping cement the partnership between business and government (see Figure 25-14).

CONCLUSIONS

The overall goals of terrorist groups vary: promote a religion, destroy an adversary, coerce or topple a government, aid brothers-in-arms, or advance a social cause or special interest. To meet their goals, terrorists employ a common strategy: intimidate by inflicting terror. The tactics they employ also vary: propagandize, exploit the media, threaten, maim, and kill. Their weapons and attack modes are relatively simple: kidnap, assassination, suicide bombs, vehicle bombs, armed assault, and cyber attack. Their targets are people, critical assets essential to an economy and government, and symbols. Terrorists are intelligent and dedicated. They choose targets that have high value to their immediate purpose; plan and prepare carefully; and act with determination.

NOTES

1. Brian M. Jenkins, "Terrorism: Communicating with Kidnappers," in *Encyclopedia of Security Management*, Boston: Butterworth-Heinemann, 1993, pp. 712.

2. *Vehicle Bomb Explosion Hazard and Evacuation Distance*, Washington: Bureau of Alcohol, Tobacco, Firearms and Explosives, undated, unnumbered.

3. *FBI Intelligence Bulletin Number 148*, Washington: Federal Bureau of Investigation, 2004, unnumbered.

4. Details of the Patriot Act can be found at *www.legal-database.com/patriot-act*.

5. Further information regarding the Department of Homeland Security can be obtained on-line at *www.dhs.gov/dhspublic/*.

6. For further information on the FBI's role in countering terrorism go to *www.fbi.gov/publications/terror/terror*.

26. Weapons of Mass Destruction

I don't know with what weapons World War III will be fought, but World War IV will be fought with sticks and stones.
—Albert Einstein

BACKGROUND

Weapons of mass destruction (WMD) are designed to kill large numbers of people, civilians and members of the military alike. WMDs are generally considered to have more of a psychological value than military usefulness. In some circles, however, there exists a growing belief that Islamic terrorists, which comprise the main source of world-wide terrorism, simply wish to inflict mass casualties on non-Islamic societies. Psychological value may be a side issue.

Several definitions have been given to WMD over the past 20 years or so. The definition most used in the United States today comes from the U.S. Code, which says that a weapon of mass destruction is:

Any explosive, incendiary or poison gas, bomb, grenade or rocket having a propellant charge of more than four ounces; missile having an explosive or incendiary charge or device similar to the above; poison gas; any weapon involving a disease organism; or any weapon that is designed to release radiation or radioactivity at a level dangerous to human life. [1]

Derived from this statutory definition is the acronym CBRNE, a grouping of five types of weapons as follows.

- Chemical
- Biological
- Radiological
- Nuclear
- Explosive

The first three of these take effect in the human body through

- Ingestion.
- Inhalation.
- Absorption.
- Injection.

The effects of the last two weapons require no further explanation.

CHEMICAL WEAPONS

The following are also definitions from the U.S Code:

> A chemical warfare agent is any chemical substance, whether gaseous, liquid or solid, which might be employed because of its direct toxic effects on man, animals and plants.
>   A toxic chemical is any chemical which, through its chemical effect on living processes may cause death, temporary loss of performance, or permanent injury to people and animals.

Included within these understandings of chemical warfare agents are dispersal mechanisms such as ammunition, projectiles, and aerosolizing devices.

Toxins

Although produced by living organisms or their synthetic equivalents, toxins fall into the chemical warfare agent classification. Thousands of toxic substances exist but only a few are amenable to chemical warfare. This is because a number of rigorous demands must be met before a toxic substance can be used as a chemical warfare agent. Mainly, these are

- The agent cannot be so toxic as to affect the persons preparing to use it.
- The agent must be capable of being stored for a long period without degradation and without corroding the packaging material.
- The agent must be relatively resistant to atmospheric water and oxygen so that it does not lose effect when dispersed.
- The agent must withstand heat that is generated during dispersal.

Chemical warfare agents, at least the way they are produced today, are liquids or solids of which a certain amount is in a volatile form. Both solid and liquid substances can be dispersed in the air in an aerosolized form. As such, they enter the human body through the respiratory organs.
    Some chemical warfare agents can also penetrate the skin. The penetration of a solid substance is slow except when it is mixed with a penetrating solvent. Within the chemical warfare classification are the following:

- Volatiles, which are mainly air borne
- Penetrating substances, which mainly cover surfaces

- Lethal substances
- Incapacitating substances

To achieve good ground coverage when dispersed from high altitude, a chemical warfare agent must be in the form of droplets sufficiently large to ensure they fall within the target area. This can be achieved by making the chemical warfare agent viscous by the addition of polymers. In this form, the chemical warfare agent lasts longer and complicates decontamination.

Nerve Agents

Nerve agents are so called because they affect the transmission of nerve impulses in the nervous system. All nerve agents belong chemically to the group of organo-phosphorus compounds. They are stable and easily dispersed, highly toxic, and have rapid effects both when absorbed through the skin and inhaled into the lungs. Nerve agents can be manufactured by means of fairly simple chemical techniques. The raw materials are inexpensive and generally readily available.

In 1936, Dr. Gerhard Schrader, a chemist at IG Farben, developed a phosphorus compound for use as an insecticide. Named tabun, the compound was later adapted for use as a nerve agent. In 1938, Schrader produced a second nerve agent called sarin, and in 1944 a third agent called soman. These three compounds are known as G agents.

Sarin is one of the world's most dangerous chemical warfare agents (see Figure 26-1). When inhaled as a gas or absorbed through the skin, sarin disrupts the nervous system and overstimulates muscles and vital organs.

Figure 26-1 Cleanup of a Tokyo subway car following release of the nerve agent sarin by the Aum Shinrikyo cult.

In high doses, sarin suffocates its victims by paralyzing the muscles around their lungs. One hundred milligrams of sarin, which is about one drop, can kill the average person in a few minutes. Experts say sarin is more than 500 times as toxic as cyanide.

In 1945 research began to find protections against the G agents, and in the process of that study even more toxic agents were discovered. These are known as V agents and are about 10 times as toxic as sarin.

In 1958, discovery was made of an even more effective nerve agent known by its U.S. Army code name VX. This is a persistent substance that can remain on material, equipment, and terrain for long periods. Penetration is mainly through the skin but also through inhalation when dispersed as a gas or aerosol.

VX is the deadliest nerve agent ever created. It is a clear, colorless liquid with the consistency of motor oil. A fraction of a drop of VX, absorbed through the skin, can kill by severely disrupting the nervous system. Although a cocktail of drugs can serve as an antidote, VX acts so quickly that victims would have to be injected with the antidote almost immediately to have a chance of survival. VX is the only significant nerve agent created since World War II.

The use of VX by terrorists is unlikely but possible. Synthesizing the agent is complicated and extremely dangerous. It requires the use of toxic and corrosive chemicals and high temperatures in a sophisticated chemical laboratory. Still, the Japanese doomsday cult Aum Shinrikyo, which recruited trained chemists from Japanese universities, managed to synthesize small quantities of VX to use for assassinations. Terrorists lacking access to trained organic chemists might be more likely to steal a weapon containing VX from a poorly guarded chemical weapons depot in a country such as Russia.

If terrorists obtained or produced a significant quantity of VX without killing themselves in the process, they might try to spread VX over a large area, such as a city. But experts say that because of the hazards involved in handling VX terrorists might turn first to other forms of attack.

VX enters the body primarily through the skin and secondarily through inhalation. Like all nerve agents, VX disrupts the transmission of communications between nerve cells. Symptoms of exposure include increased heart rate and salivation, nausea, and vomiting. A fatal dose of VX causes convulsions, respiratory paralysis, and death within several minutes.

VX and sarin have similar effects on the body, but VX is about a hundred times more deadly when absorbed through the skin and about twice as deadly when inhaled. VX is oil based, extremely adhesive, and long lasting, whereas sarin evaporates at about the same rate as water.

Mustard Agent

Mustard agent is often called a "blistering agent" because the wounds it causes resemble burns and blisters (see Figure 26-2). It also causes severe damage to the eyes, respiratory system, and internal organs.

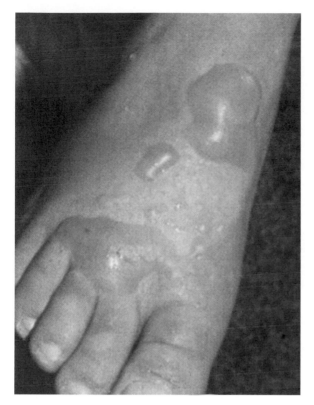

Figure 26-2 Mustard agent burn.

Mustard agent was first produced in 1822, but its harmful effects were not discovered until 1860. It was first used as a chemical warfare agent during the latter part of World War I and caused lung and eye injuries to a very large number of soldiers. During the war between Iran and Iraq from 1979 to 1988, Iraq used large quantities of chemical agents. About 5,000 Iranian soldiers were reportedly killed, 10 to 20 percent of them by mustard agent, plus 40,000 to 50,000 injured.

Mustard agent is very simple to manufacture, which makes it a weapon of preference by unsophisticated terror groups. It is also effective in concentrations so low that the victim senses no immediate symptoms upon contact. Up to 24 hours may elapse before pain is felt, and by then cell damage has already occurred. In the form of gas or liquid, mustard agent attacks the skin, eyes, lungs, gastrointestinal tract, and internal organs (mainly blood-generating organs).

Hydrogen Cyanide

Hydrogen cyanide is usually included among the chemical warfare agents, but there is no solid proof it has been used in chemical warfare. Iraq is suspected, however, of using hydrogen cyanide in its war against Iran and against Kurds in northern Iraq. During World War II, a form of hydrogen cyanide (Zyklon B) was used in Nazi gas chambers. For hydrogen cyanide to be effective in the outdoors environment it has to be dispersed in high concentrations. In confined spaces, this is not a problem.

Chlorine

Chlorine is widely used in industry and found in some household products. As a gas, it can be converted to liquid form by pressurizing and cooling. In liquid form it can be shipped and stored. When liquid chlorine is released, it quickly turns into a gas that is heavier than air. In this form, it stays close to the ground and spreads rapidly. Chlorine is recognizable by its pungent, irritating odor, which is like the odor of bleach. The strong smell may provide warning to people that have been exposed. Chlorine gas is yellow-green in color. It is not flammable, but can react explosively or form explosive compounds when combined with other chemicals such as turpentine and ammonia.

Phosgene is an industrial chemical similar to chlorine. Both are transported in multi-ton shipments by road and rail. Rupturing a transport container can easily disseminate these gases over a fairly wide area. For this reason, these gases while in transit can have particular appeal to terrorists because the transport vehicle is a weapon in itself.

BIOLOGICAL WEAPONS

Discussion of the possible use of bio-weapons by terrorists began even earlier than 11 September 2001, during the break-up of the Soviet Union. The specter of Russia's biological agents covertly migrating into the weapons inventory of terrorist groups moved the issue from discussion to prevention and response [2].

CSOs need to consider the possibility of a biological attack and have security personnel and others of the organization's first-responders prepared to respond rapidly and properly. Experts in the health community have concluded that major reductions in illness, death, and costs can be achieved with early intervention. Preparing for a biological attack, as with any other form of attack, involves planning, training, and rehearsing.

Criminals, the traditional adversary of the CSO, can to a large extent be deterred from carrying out their crimes. However, the same cannot be said for terrorists. A determined terrorist group is not easily deterred, is skilled at evading detection, and may succeed in releasing an aerosol of a virulent bacterium, virus, or toxin in a susceptible target area such as the intake of a heating, ventilation, and air conditioning (HVAC) system or the organization's water supply.

In general, security groups lack the capacity to protect employees from biological attack. The responsibility for dealing with the use of bio-weapons falls on multiple federal, state, and municipal agencies and the civilian health care community. A good part of the responsibility for integrating an organization's emergency operating plan (EOP) with the various government plans falls on the shoulders of the CSO.

The CSO's responsibilities, as spelled out in the EOP, can be daunting. The training aspect of preparation is a major effort alone, and for the training to take hold requires acceptance and participation within the organization and by the involved external agencies.

Biological weapons are mysterious, unfamiliar, indiscriminate, uncontrollable, inequitable, and invisible — all of which are characteristics associated with heightened fear. [3]. To the extent terrorists believe a bio-attack would help their cause the greater the likelihood of it.

A case can be made for anticipating the use of a bio-weapon. At some point the magnitude of terrorist attacks using conventional weapons will plateau. The next logical step in escalation will be the use of chemical and bio-weapons. Unlike conventional weapons, biological agents would be effective in destroying crops, poisoning foods, or contaminating pharmaceutical products.

Terrorists might use biological agents to attack corporations perceived to be national icons, such as Coca-Cola and Gerber baby food. In addition to the fear factor, such an act would place enormous demands on the medical system, require large cleanup expenditures, and damage the economy. On the other side of the coin, a terrorist group contemplating use of a bio-weapon will face several problems:

- Formidable political risk and loss of private support
- Acquisition or construction of a dispersal device
- The ability to deliver or disperse the agent covertly
- The risk of infection to themselves and to others they do not wish to infect

Biological weapons are any infectious agent such as a bacteria or virus when used intentionally to inflict harm upon others. This definition is often expanded to include biologically derived toxins and poisons.

Biological warfare agents include both living microorganisms (bacteria and viruses) and toxins (chemicals). Some of these agents are highly lethal; others would serve mainly in an incapacitating role. Since 9-11, considerable speculation has arisen concerning possible terrorist use of new, genetically engineered agents designed to defeat conventional methods of treatment or to attack specific ethnic groups. Biological agents with a potential for use by terrorists can be placed into three groups and their subgroups [4] as follows.

- Bacteria
  - Anthrax
  - Brucellosis
  - Plague

- ○ Tularemia
- ○ Q Fever
- Viruses
  - ○ Smallpox
  - ○ Viral hemorrhagic fevers
- Toxins
  - ○ Botulism
  - ○ Ricin

Bacterial agent is a general term. In the current context it means any bacteria that has been or can be used by terrorists to kill people. Lethal bacteria are numerous. In this section, we will address those that are amenable to use as a weapon of mass destruction.

Anthrax: Anthrax is an acute, specific, infectious, febrile disease of animals, including humans, and is caused by an organism that under certain conditions will form highly resistant spores capable of persisting and retaining their virulence in contaminated soil or other material for many years. The anthrax bacterium is often found naturally in the soil of rural Texas and Oklahoma and in areas near the Mississippi. It is also produced in research laboratories — but not easily. Significant scientific training is needed (see Figure 26-3).

This is a disease chiefly of herbivores (grass eaters). Humans can be infected by handling the wool, hair, hide, bones, or carcasses of afflicted animals. Veterinarians and workers exposed to infected animals or animal parts are at risk, but not everyone exposed to anthrax comes down with the disease. According to the Centers for Disease Control, anthrax cannot be passed from one person to another. Anthrax spores can enter the human body in any of three ways.

- *Through the skin:* Microscopic anthrax spores (the inactive form of the bacteria) can get into the body through cuts in the skin, even tiny ones, after contact with diseased animal tissue (or, in the case of terrorism, a tainted letter). Skin anthrax starts with an itch. Later, small pimples form on the skin and sometimes turn into black sores within two to six days. Skin anthrax is the least dangerous form. Untreated, doctors think it would kill only 5 to 20 percent of its victims. If treated effectively with antibiotics, few deaths would occur.
- *Through the lungs:* Spores can enter the body by breathing them into the lungs. From there, spores make their way to the lymph nodes, where they turn into bacteria that release poisons into the surrounding tissue. Inhalation anthrax leads to early symptoms much like those of the flu, the common cold, or other respiratory diseases. Lung anthrax is genuinely life-threatening. Before the anthrax letters attack, the medical community estimated the disease would kill more than 80 percent of victims if left untreated. Since then, however, we have learned that people who inhale spores can recover even if treatment starts after their symptoms appear.

Figure 26-3 Field workers wear special protective equipment handling material suspected of coming in contact with anthrax.

- *Through the stomach:* Spores can wind up in the digestive system after the meat of a contaminated animal is eaten. Ingested anthrax may cause loss of appetite, nausea, fever, vomiting (sometimes with blood), and abdominal pain. Untreated, doctors think it would kill between 25 and 70 percent of its victims.

Probably because so little is known about anthrax, opinions of it as a terrorist weapon vary widely. On the one hand, it is touted as the terrorist's preferred biological warfare agent because a single gram of anthrax material is believed capable of producing 100 million lethal doses and that a single dose is 100,000 times deadlier than the deadliest chemical warfare agent. It is also considered a silent, invisible killer because the symptoms of infection mimic nonlethal ailments.

This view also holds that the barriers to production of anthrax are minimal because production costs are low, large quantities can be produced and stockpiled without great difficulty, and production know-how, although technical, is in the public domain. On the other hand, there is evidence pointing to difficulties in acquiring, making, and deploying anthrax. The Japanese cult Aum Shinrikyo, which used the sarin nerve agent to attack the Tokyo subway system, failed completely when it attempted two years earlier to spread anthrax from its Tokyo office building. There is also little agreement on the extent of damage to human health if anthrax were introduced — for example, into an office building's ventilation system, a crowded bus, or a football stadium filled to capacity.

But among the experts there is a shared belief that anthrax can be weaponized. Because anthrax is stable it can be stored almost indefinitely as a dry powder. When freeze-dried, it can be loaded into munitions and with limited technology can be disseminated as an aerosol. With a little more expertise, the spores can be made smaller so that they are more easily inhaled and made lighter so that they float in the air longer. In addition, it is possible to alter the genetic makeup of the spore so that it is resistant to medical treatment.

Brucellosis: This is an infectious disease primarily passed among animals and that causes disease in many different vertebrates. Humans become infected by coming in contact with animals or animal products contaminated with these bacteria. In humans, brucellosis can cause a range of symptoms that are similar to the flu and may include fever, sweats, headaches, back pains, and physical weakness. Severe infections of the central nervous systems or lining of the heart may occur. Brucellosis can also cause long-lasting or chronic symptoms that include recurrent fevers, joint pain, and fatigue. It is not very common in the United States, where 100 to 200 cases occur each year, but it can be very common in countries where animal disease control programs have not reduced the amount of disease among animals. Humans are generally infected in one of three ways.

- *Eating or drinking something that is contaminated with Brucella:* The most common way is by eating or drinking contaminated milk products. When sheep, goats, cows, or camels are infected, their milk is contaminated with the bacteria. If the milk is not pasteurized, these bacteria can be transmitted to persons who drink the milk or eat cheeses or other products made of it.
- *Inhaling the organism:* Inhalation of Brucella organisms is not a common route of infection, but it can be a significant hazard for people in certain occupations such as those working in laboratories where the organism is cultured. Inhalation is often responsible for a significant percentage of cases in abattoir employees.
- *Having the bacteria enter the body through skin wounds:* Contamination of skin wounds may be a problem for persons working in slaughterhouses

or meat packing plants or for veterinarians. Hunters may be infected through skin wounds or by accidentally ingesting the bacteria after cleaning such animals as deer, elk, moose, or wild pigs.

Direct person-to-person spread of brucellosis is extremely rare. As a terrorist weapon, it would be most effective if it were introduced into food ingested by cattle.

Plague: This disease appears in two variants: bubonic and pneumonic. Bubonic plague is carried by rodents and transmitted to humans via flea bites. It cannot spread from person to person. This form of plague (see Figure 26-4) caused the Black Death that devastated China, the Middle East, and Europe in the fourteenth century, killing a larger proportion of the world's population than any single war or epidemic since.

During World War II, the Japanese army spread bubonic plague by dropping infected fleas over China with lethal results. In 1346, plague broke out in the Tartar army during its siege of Kaffa (now Feodosia in Crimea). Attackers hurled the corpses of plague victims over the city walls, causing an epidemic that forced the city to surrender. Some infected Kaffa residents who left the city may have inadvertently started the Black Death pandemic that raged all across Europe.

The pneumonic plague infects the lungs, travels through the air, and is highly contagious. It is also rarer and more lethal than bubonic plague. If those infected do not receive treatment, their mortality rate can approach 100 percent. Peumonic plague in an aerosolized form has a potential for use as a terrorist weapon.

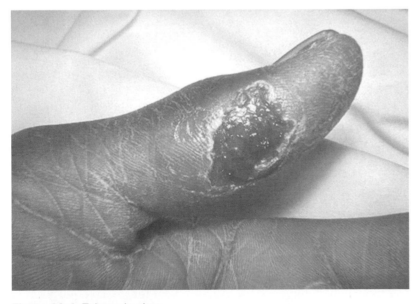

Figure 26-4 Tularemia ulcer.

Tularemia: This is one of the world's most contagious diseases. It is caused by a rare bacterium carried by small mammals such as rabbits and squirrels. Humans can get the disease from contact with the tissues or body fluids of infected animals or from the bites of infected insects, but they cannot get it from person-to-person contact.

Some experts believe that if tularemia bacterium were used as a weapon, it would probably be aerosolized, thereby causing an especially serious inhaled form of the disease. Although tularemia is less lethal than other bio-weapons, death rates for those infected with the inhaled form of the disease can still climb as high as 30 to 60 percent if left untreated. Ken Alibek, a former top Soviet bio-weapons scientist, contends that an outbreak of tularemia among German troops during the 1942 Battle of Stalingrad resulted from the deliberate spraying of the agent by the Soviet defenders.

Q fever: This is a disease caused by a species of bacteria that exists globally. Because the disease is underreported, scientists cannot reliably assess how many cases of Q fever have actually occurred worldwide. Human infections are often unnoticed.

Cattle, sheep, and goats are the primary reservoirs of the bacteria. Infection has been noted in a wide variety of other animals, including other species of livestock and domesticated pets. The Q fever bacterium is highly infectious and somewhat resistant to heat and drying. It can become airborne and inhaled by humans. A single organism may cause disease in a susceptible person. This agent could be developed for use in biological warfare and is considered a potential terrorist threat.

Viruses

A virus is an extremely tiny infectious agent that is only able to live within a cell. Basically, viruses are composed of just two parts. The outer part is a protective shell and the inner part is made of genetic material (see Figure 26-5).

A virus cannot reproduce by itself. To reproduce, a virus invades a cell within the body of a human or other creature, called the host. Each type of virus has particular types of host creatures and host cells it will invade successfully.

Once within the host cell, the virus uses the cell's own properties to produce more viruses. In essence, the virus forces the cell to replicate the virus's own genetic material and protective shell. Once replicated, the new viruses leave the host cell and are ready to invade others [5].

Smallpox: The most common and deadly form of smallpox is *variola major*. Smallpox is ancient; descriptions of the disease have been found dating from as far back as the fourth century A.D. in China. The World Health Organization officially declared smallpox eradicated in 1979, after a painstaking vaccination campaign. Samples of the virus are kept for research purposes at the Centers for Disease Control in Atlanta and in laboratories in Russia.

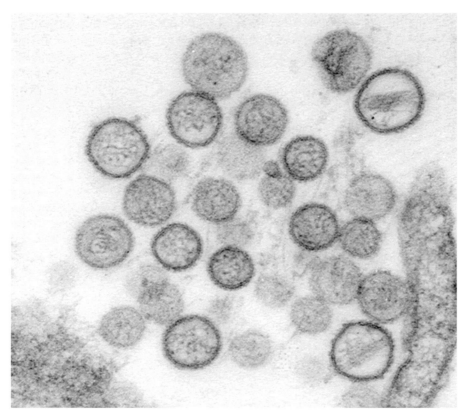

Figure 26-5 A microscopic view of a virus.

Smallpox is extremely contagious. It can spread like the common cold, through person-to-person contact and through the air. Historically, smallpox killed about 30 percent of those infected. The mortality rate varied with age and with the strength of a person's immune system. Smallpox is one of the most devastating diseases known to humankind, having killed between 300 and 500 million people in the twentieth century alone.

The use of smallpox as a weapon of war is not new. British forces in North America gave blankets used by smallpox patients to Native Americans during the French and Indian War of 1754 to 1767. Some tribes lost up to half their populations. The threat of smallpox as a bio-weapon greatly diminished when a vaccine was developed in 1796.

Smallpox is small enough to be inhaled, and thus could be spread in aerosol form. The virus is very stable, which means it isn't easy to destroy, and it retains its potency for days outside a human host. Smallpox can be freeze-dried and stored at room temperature for months or years, and remain potent when revived with water. American scientists in the 1960s were able to turn dried smallpox into a fine powder and to create tiny aerosol generators that could disseminate the virus.

Smallpox is less readily available than many other agents such as anthrax or the bacterium that causes plague. Special skills are required to grow the virus in large quantities and to preserve it for dispersion as an aerosol. Due to the personal risks associated with weaponizing smallpox, it would seem unlikely it would have appeal for extremist groups, especially if they are small, technically unsophisticated groups. On the other hand, fanatics unconcerned with personal risk may prefer it over less lethal bio-weapons.

Viral hemorrhagic fever: The term *viral hemorrhagic fever* (VHF) refers to a group of illnesses caused by several distinct families of viruses. In general, the term describes a severe syndrome that impairs the body's ability to regulate itself. These symptoms are often accompanied by hemorrhage or bleeding. With a few noteworthy exceptions, there is no cure or established drug treatment for VHFs.

Some viruses that cause hemorrhagic fever can spread from one person to another, once an initial person has become infected. Ebola, Marburg, Lassa, and Crimean-Congo hemorrhagic fever viruses are examples. Compared to anthrax and smallpox, VHFs are less stable; are more vulnerable to heat, light, and disinfectants; and once released into the air have shorter life spans than either anthrax or smallpox. Some experts, with good evidence, argue that terrorists would sooner turn to anthrax or smallpox than VHFs.

VHFs are especially gruesome. They produce high fever and leakage from blood vessels, ultimately causing bleeding from internal organs as well as the eyes, ears, nose, and mouth. VHFs are carried by animals in Africa, Asia, the Middle East, and South America. We don't know exactly how these diseases spread from animals to humans, but once they do they can be transmitted from person to person via contact with blood or other body fluids. There are four VHF families, of which filoviruses — including the notorious Ebola and Marburg viruses, and arenaviruses, such as the Lassa virus — are considered the most serious bio-terror threats. There is no treatment for Ebola, and up to 90 percent of those who contract the disease die.

Toxins

A toxin is a poisonous substance produced by a living organism, which can include bacteria, fungi, algae, and plants. Many toxins are extremely poisonous, with toxicity several orders of magnitude greater than nerve agents (see Figure 26-6).

Rapid development of gene technology during the 1970s stirred interest in creating bio-weapons using toxins, both natural and synthetic. Later research in cancer treatment discovered a way to target toxins to different body organs. Still, toxins are considered to be less suitable as a bio-weapon because they cannot be dispersed on a large scale. However, they could be used for sabotage of a specific location or assassination of specific persons.

Botulism: The botulinum nerve toxin is the single most toxic substance known to science. Its extraordinary potency has made it one of the most

Figure 26-6 Field workers examining a possible toxic substance.

widely researched bio-weapons. If a lethal dose were administered to each person individually, a single gram of botulinum toxin would theoretically be enough to kill more than a million people. There are three main types of botulism.

- Food-borne botulism is caused by eating foods that contain the botulism toxin.
- Wound botulism is caused by a toxin produced from a wound that has been infected with botulinum.
- Infant botulism is caused by consuming the spores of the botulinum bacteria, which then grow in the intestines and release toxin.

All forms of botulism can be fatal and are considered medical emergencies. Food-borne botulism can be especially dangerous because many people can be poisoned by eating a contaminated food. It is for this very reason that terrorists would seek to use botulism as a weapon.

Iraq, North Korea, Iran, and Syria are believed to have developed botulinum toxin as a weapon. After the 1991 Gulf War, Iraq told U.N. weapons inspectors that it had produced 19,000 liters of concentrated botulinum toxin, enough theoretically to kill everyone on earth three times over.

Botulinum toxin is the first biological toxin to be approved for medical treatment. It is used to treat neuromuscular disorders, lower back pain, and cerebral palsy. It is also an ingredient in Botox, a product that temporarily eliminates wrinkles by paralyzing the facial muscles.

Ricin: This toxin is found in the mash-like waste left over from the processing of castor beans, which are used to make castor oil. The ricin in the

Ricin

In 1978, Georgi Markov, a Bulgarian writer and journalist living in London, died after he was shot in the leg by a pellet gun concealed in the tip of an umbrella. The pellet contained ricin.

Figure 26-7 The effects of ricin.

waste can be made into the form of a powder, pellet, or mist and can be dissolved in water or a weak acid. Ricin is only minimally affected by extreme temperature conditions and is stable in aerosolized form (see Figure 26-7).

Ricin is produced easily and inexpensively, is highly toxic, and has no treatment or vaccine. When compared to some of the other biological agents that could be used to produce the desired effect of a WMD, ricin ranks relatively low. For example, to achieve the same damaging effect produced by one kilogram of anthrax would require four metric tons of ricin. Ricin, however, would have efficacy as a disabling agent. Its use as a food and water contaminant easily could incapacitate many and overwhelm local healthcare resources.

RADIOLOGICAL WEAPONS

A radiological dispersion device (RDD), commonly known as a dirty bomb, is a device that combines a radioactive material and a conventional explosive. The explosive is used to disperse the radiological material. The area of dispersal is conditioned by the type and amount of explosive, the nature of the container, the detonation height, and weather/wind factors such as rain, wind velocity, and air currents.

The harmful effects of an RDD include radiation burns, acute poisoning, and contamination of the environment. The tasks of first responders are complex and very much different in an RDD incident than in a conventional bomb incident.

The radiological material in an RDD is not weapons-grade fissionable material such as that contained in a nuclear weapon. The more likely terrorist attack involving radiological material is by use of the RDD rather than a nuclear weapon. This is the case because construction of a nuclear weapon is enormously difficult, whereas the RDD can be constructed simply and with types of radiological material that are routinely used in health care, research, metal structure evaluation, and a variety of industrial applications. These materials include cobalt, cesium, strontium, and others [6]. CSOs at facilities that contain radiological materials are obligated to implement and enforce highly stringent security measures.

NUCLEAR WEAPONS

As already stated, a terrorist-attack scenario involving a nuclear weapon is less likely than one involving an RDD. Although relatively remote, the possibility does exist. In the case of a nuclear weapon being stolen or purchased by a terrorist group, the possibility rises to a very dangerous level. The doctrine of mutual-assured destruction (MAD) becomes irrelevant when the adversary is a terrorist group. (The MAD doctrine holds that a nuclear weapon attack by one nation state upon another nation state that also has a nuclear weapon capability would cause the defending state to launch a nuclear weapon counterattack, thus assuring the destruction of both states. MAD is therefore considered a deterrent to nuclear weapons warfare.) The amorphous nature of terrorist groups renders MAD ineffective as a deterrent.

Loose Nukes

A loose nuke is a nuclear weapon that has left control of its original owner. The term can also refer to weapons-grade uranium and plutonium. Since the collapse of the Soviet Union in 1991, concern has been raised that unpaid and embittered nuclear scientists may have sold Russian nuclear weapons to terrorist or criminal groups. Also of concern is poor security at Russia's nuclear storage facilities and evidence that enriched uranium has been sold and purchased on Europe's black market. Evidence also exists that terrorist groups have attempted to acquire loose nukes.

Improvised Nuclear Device

A type of loose nuke is the improvised nuclear device (IND). It is constructed entirely of covertly obtained or manufactured components. The IND contains fissile material (highly enriched uranium or plutonium) and is designed to cause a nuclear explosion. The IND can be constructed "from scratch" or with nuclear weapons components or an actual nuclear weapon that has been modified (see Figure 26-8).

If successfully detonated, a small nuclear weapon would cause the sort of destruction seen at Hiroshima or Nagasaki. With larger, more modern weapons — which are hundreds to thousands of times more powerful — the results would be much worse. Experts predict that human casualties would vary dramatically depending on the bomb's yield, the height above the ground at which it was detonated, and weather conditions. One worst-case scenario simulation estimated that a 1-megaton explosion in Detroit could kill 250,000 people, injure half a million more, and flatten all buildings within a 1.7-mile radius [7].

Figure 26-8 An improvised nuclear device inside a brief case.

EXPLOSIVE WEAPONS

The most frequently used terrorist weapon is the explosive bomb. The materials for constructing a bomb are not difficult to obtain and the know-how of construction is relatively simple. For the totally uninformed potential bomber, do-it-yourself information is available on the Internet and in bookstores.

Explosion Dynamics

An explosion is an extremely rapid release of energy in the form of light, heat, sound, and a shock wave. The shock wave consists of highly compressed air that travels outward from the source at supersonic velocities. When the shock wave encounters a surface the wave is reflected, resulting in a tremendous amplification of pressure.

Late in the explosive event, the shock wave is followed by a partial vacuum, which creates suction behind the shock wave. Immediately following the vacuum, air rushes in, creating a powerful wind or drag pressure. This wind picks up and carries flying debris in the vicinity of the detonation. In an external explosion, a portion of the energy is also imparted to the ground, creating a crater and generating a ground shock wave analogous to a high-intensity, short-duration earthquake [8].

Explosives are categorized as high and low. The primary distinguishing characteristic is the pressure wave. A high-explosive detonation can produce a pressure wave ranging from 50,000 to 4 million pounds per square inch

Figure 26-9 Damage caused by a fire bomb.

(psi), whereas a low-explosive detonation will produce a pressure wave under 50,000 psi.

Among the high explosives are military compositions 3, 4, and B, TNT, nitroglycerin, dynamite, RDX, semtex, amatol, ednatol, picric acid, pentolite, and tetrytol. The low explosives are fewer in number: black powder, ammonium nitrate, and the pyrotechnics (see Figure 26-9).

Although not accurate technically, incendiaries are often considered explosives. An incendiary is any device used to start a fire. It is generally man-made, hand-held, and thrown or propelled a short distance. The Molotov cocktail is an incendiary device, typically a glass bottle filled with gasoline. At the mouth of the bottle is a piece of gasoline-soaked cloth. The tip of the cloth is ignited and the bottle is thrown. The bottle breaks upon impact and the gasoline is dispersed and ignited by the flaming cloth. The burn component of an incendiary device can be any highly flammable liquid such as gasoline, kerosene, lantern fuel, and lighter fluid.

Bomb-related Structural Damage

From the standpoint of structural design, the vehicle bomb is the most important consideration for the CSO. Vehicle bombs are able to deliver a sufficiently large quantity of explosive to cause devastating structural damage. Security design intended to limit or mitigate damage from a vehicle bomb assumes that the bomb is detonated at a so-called critical location. The critical location is a function of the site, the building layout, and the security measures in place. The critical location is taken to be the closest point a vehicle can approach, assuming that all security measures are in place. This may be a parking area directly beneath the occupied building, the loading dock, the curb directly outside the facility, or at a vehicle-access control gate where inspection takes place, depending on the level of protection incorporated into the design.

Another explosive attack threat is the small bomb that is hand delivered. Small weapons can cause the greatest damage when brought into vulnerable, unsecured areas of the building interior, such as the building lobby, mail room, and retail spaces. Events around the world make it clear that bombs will be delivered by persons who are willing to sacrifice their own lives. Hand-carried explosives are typically on the order of 5 to 10 pounds of TNT equivalent. However, larger charge weights, in the 50- to 100-pound TNT equivalent range, can be readily carried in rolling cases. Mail bombs are typically less than 10 pounds of TNT equivalent.

In general, the largest credible explosive size is a function of the security measures in place. Each line of security may be thought of as a sieve, reducing the size of the weapon that may gain access. Therefore, the largest weapons are considered in totally unsecured public space (e.g., in a vehicle on the nearest public street), and the smallest weapons are considered in the most secured areas of the building (e.g., in a briefcase smuggled past the screening station).

Two parameters define the design threat: the weapon size, measured in equivalent pounds of TNT, and the standoff. The standoff is the distance measured from the center of gravity of the charge to the component of interest (target). The likely target can be a high-risk building near the attack location. Historically, more building damage has been done by collateral effect than direct attack.

It is difficult to quantify the risk of terrorist-style bombings. However, qualitatively it may be stated that the chance of a large-scale terrorist attack occurring is extremely low. A smaller explosive attack is far more likely [9].

NOTES

1. United States Code, Title 18, USC 2332a.

2. From a paper titled, "Emerging Infectious Diseases" delivered by Philip K. Russell, Johns Hopkins University, Baltimore, MD, to the Centers for Disease Control and Prevention, Atlanta, GA.

3. From a paper titled, "The Prospect of Domestic Bioterrorism," by Jessica Stern for the Centers for Disease Control and Prevention, Atlanta, GA.

4. From a fact sheet produced by the Emergency Preparedness and Response Office, Centers for Disease Control and Prevention, Atlanta, GA.

5. From a fact sheet titled, "Viruses," Centers for Disease Control and Prevention, Atlanta, GA.

6. *WMD Threat and Risk Assessment*, (College Station, TX: Texas A&M University System, 2004) p. 55.

7. *The Effects of Nuclear War*, (Washington: United States Office of Technology Assessment, 2002) unnumbered.

8. *Providing Protection to People and Buildings*, (Washington: Federal Emergency Management Agency, 2002) unnumbered.

9. *Terrorist Threats*, (Washington: Federal Emergency Management Agency, 2003) unnumbered.

27. Assessment of the Terrorist Threat

We have learned that terrorist attacks are not caused by the use of strength; they are invited by the perception of weakness.

—George W. Bush

DETERMINING RISK

Integral to the protection of assets against terrorism is the determination of risk. Risk is the potential for loss of or damage to an asset. Risk is determined by comparing the asset's value against the probability of a threat occurrence and identifying vulnerabilities in the asset's protective screen. Thus, we have the following three interrelated factors.

- An asset
- The probability of a threat occurrence
- Vulnerability of the asset to the threat

Asset value is expressed in dollars because nearly everything can be measured in dollars — for example, replacement cost, repair cost, collateral damage, loss of function, reputation, and even lives. The Federal Security Risk Management approach holds that a human life is worth $2.7 million [1].

An asset can be discrete — such as a nuclear weapon — or it can be less so such as data, institutional knowledge, or morale. Threat is measured by the probability that the threat will occur and will bring about adverse consequences. Determining probability is essentially making an educated guess. Determining the consequences of the occurrence is more than making a guess. An estimate of consequences relies on assumptions that can range from marginal damage to complete destruction.

Measuring vulnerabilities is also subjective. Examples of vulnerabilities can be untrained security officers, a fence that is needed but missing, or a malfunctioning access control system. In terms of risk, vulnerability is not a cost such as the purchase of a CCTV system or the hiring of additional security officers; vulnerability is an exposure to a defined threat.

Because a threat and its associated vulnerabilities cannot be expressed in dollars, they are expressed as ratings. Risk, then, is dollar value impacted by two ratings. It is sometimes computed with the following equation:

Asset Value X Threat Probability X Vulnerabilities = Risk.

ASSET VALUE

The dollar value of an asset and its importance to operations are two different things. An asset can have a low dollar value yet play a critical role in the functioning of an organization, and vice versa. During the Vietnam War, for example, certain radios used in combat operations relied on D-cell batteries. The Army's logistics command could not get enough D-cell batteries to the forward areas because the batteries were being stolen at the Port of Saigon and then sold on the black market. Although the batteries were low cost, they were essential to the mission. The point here is that a seemingly unimportant asset can be critical when it represents a single point of failure.

Figure 27-1 shows an example of how to rate an asset for the purpose of determining its exposure to risk. Note that points are assigned on a 0-to-5 scale [2].

Asset Rating

Characterization	Arbitrary Dollar Value	Operational Impact	Points
Catastrophic	$100 million or more	Complete and permanent shutdown of operations. Death of the organization.	5
Highly Serious	$50 million to $100 million	Very negative impact on operations over an extended period of time.	4
Very Serious	$10 million to 50 million	Negative impact on operations over an extended period of time.	3
Serious	$1 million to $10 million	Appreciable negative impact on operations over an endurable period.	2
Moderately Serious	$100,000 to $1 million	Appreciable negative impact on operations over a short period of time.	1
Not Important	Less than $100,000	A negative impact but of no appreciable effect on operations.	0

Figure 27-1 The owner/possessor of an asset can characterize loss-producing events, set the levels for dollar value, and describe operational impacts in whatever terms are suitable to the rater/organization.

THREAT PROBABILITY

A threat occurrence is a possibility — nothing more, nothing less. We can believe that a certain threat does in fact exist but we cannot be sure of it, and we can believe that the threat will impact the organization but we cannot be sure of that either. We can believe that should the threat occur we will experience loss of some type. We can gain a better understanding of threat probability by answering three simple questions.

- Are there facts that would cause us to believe the threat exists?
- Has the organization ever been impacted by this particular threat?
- Does the threat have the capacity to damage the organization?

Let's label these questions, respectively, *existence*, *history*, and *capacity*. These labels are appropriate when the threat is something we are powerless to prevent. Examples of such threats are earthquake, severe weather, and flooding. When the threat is terror related, we ask two more questions.

- Are there facts to indicate that a terrorist or terrorist group (i.e., the threat) intends to commit an act of terrorism?
- Are there facts to indicate that the organization is the intended target?

Unlike the first three questions, these last two represent factors we can do something about. We cannot prevent an earthquake but we can prevent or mitigate a terrorist attack. We now have five factors that characterize a potential terrorist threat.

- Existence
- History
- Capacity
- Intention
- Target

We can use these factors to rate a particular threat. (We use the term *particular threat* to differentiate between terrorism in general and a terrorist group specifically.) We rate a threat in the same way we rate an asset: we use a rating scale to evaluate factors (see Figure 27-2). Again, the rating scale is 0 to 5. (Note: If the existence factor is 0, all other factors must be 0. You cannot rate a threat if it doesn't exist.)

If we wish to compare asset value against threat probability, we can create a chart. In the example shown in Figure 27-3, asset value is on the vertical axis and threat probability is on the horizontal. Using the 0-to-5 scale on both axes we produce 25 blocks, each of which has a shorthand designation. The designation for an asset rated 3 and having a threat probability of 2 is shown in the block marked A3/P2.

The chart presents a graphical view of asset value juxtaposed against threat probability. In the upper right-hand corner is A5/P5, meaning that the asset

Threat Rating Matrix

Threat Factors	Point Values
Existence. A threat to the asset exists.	1
History. A threat event involving a like asset has occurred in the past.	1
Capability. The threat has a capacity to destroy or severely damage the asset.	2
Intention. The threat shows an intent to destroy or severely damage the asset.	2
Targeting. The asset has been identified as a target of the threat.	4
Maximum Possible Points	10

Figure 27-2 In some risk analysis methodologies, threat is weighted higher or lower than asset value and vulnerabilities.

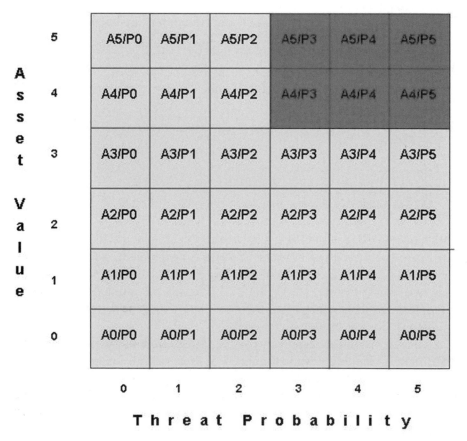

Figure 27-3 This approach can also be used to compare asset value against vulnerabilities.

has maximum value and has maximum threat probability. In short, this asset requires maximum protection. It may be that the asset already has such protection, but if not something needs to be done about it — the sooner the better. The blocks also in a darkened color and surrounding the A5/P5 block indicate a need for protection as well, but not to the same extent.

VULNERABILITIES

A vulnerability rating involves the following seven factors, which pertain to the location of the asset (i.e., the target site).

- Visibility of the target site
- Importance of the target site to the organization's overall operations
- Importance of the target site to persons, entities, and operations external to the target site
- Ease of access to the target site and assets within it
- Potential for significant damage to the site resulting from the terrorists' use of material or process located at the site
- Potential for casualties at the target site
- Potential for casualties outside the target site

Visibility of the Target Site

In rating visibility, the following questions apply.

- Is the existence of the target site known to the public?
- Is the location of the target site known to the public?
- Is the target site recognizable?
- Is the target site iconic or symbolic?
- Is the target site in close proximity to another possible target site?

From the answers to these questions, a CSO would estimate the visibility of the target site and assign points from 0 to 5. The rating scale starts with no visibility (0 points) and tops out with very high visibility (5 points).

Importance of the Target Site

The importance of the target site will be fairly well established if the rating of all assets (including identification of critical assets) was properly done. Importance in this context relates to the criticality of one or more assets to the owner or operator of the target site.

A target site that contains no critical assets is rated 0. Technically, a site that has no critical assets cannot be a target site. However, the site at one time may have contained critical assets that later were moved to a different site. The terrorists may not be aware that the site no longer contains critical assets, a circumstance that makes the site a target. In such a case, the importance of the site is rated 0. A rating of 1 is given to a target site that contains extremely low critical assets; low is 2; 3 is medium; 4 is high; and 5 is extremely high.

Importance of the Target Site Outside the Target Site

Think about the value of the target site in terms of its relationship to the immediately surrounding community, the region, or a sector of the critical national infrastructure such as energy, agriculture, transportation, or finance. Importance is high when damage to or destruction of the target will have an effect on external agencies or operations. Again, the rating scheme is from 0 to 5, with the highest rating at the upper end.

Ease of Access

Access means penetration of the target by an adversary. Ease of access (and conversely, difficulty of access) is basically a matter of three protective components.

- Physical security safeguards such as barriers, lighting, intrusion sensors, access control devices, locks, and so on.
- People such as security officers and other site personnel in general.
- Procedures such as guard orders and actions to be taken by designated persons in various contingency plans, plus an overall emergency operating plan.

When the three components function very well according to design, it can be said that the adversary's ease of access is low. Because we are assessing vulnerability (a negative circumstance), we assign a high score when access is difficult, and a low score when access is easy. In other words, we get high marks when the security system is effective in denying unauthorized access to the site. Figure 27-4 shows a matrix that can be used.

Weapon-like Material or Process at the Target Site

Assigning a value to this factor can be helped by asking this question: "Is there anything at the target site that can be used as a weapon to destroy or significantly damage the target site?" The answer would be yes if the target site contains any WMD material (i.e., chemical and biological agents, radioactive substances, explosives, or nuclear weapons). Examples of such target sites would be a plant containing toxic chemicals, a research lab containing dangerous viruses or radioactive substances, a nuclear weapons storage site, or an ammunition plant. The following is a possible rating scheme.

- Very High (5 points) can apply when
  - The target site contains large quantities or large concentrations of any WMD material.

Difficulty of Access

Physical Security Safeguards, People, and Procedures	Points
Perimeter fencing; security lighting; intrusion detection; CCTV monitoring; security response force 24/7; controlled parking outside of blast zone; control of vehicles, persons, and property into, within, and from the site; restricted areas within the site; security clearance required; HVAC protection; security posts and patrols 24/7	5
Perimeter fencing; security lighting; intrusion detection; CCTV monitoring; controlled parking; control of vehicles, persons, and property into, within, and from the site; restricted areas within the site; security posts and patrols 24/7.	4
Perimeter fencing; security lighting; access control at entry gates; security posts and patrols operating less than 24/7.	3
Access control at entry gates; security posts and patrols operating less than 24/7.	2
Access control at entry gates.	1
No security measures in place.	0

Figure 27-4 A security system is often conceptualized as a combination of physical security safeguards that are used and operated by people in accordance with well-defined procedures.

- ○ Access to the WMD material is uncontrolled.
- ○ Access to the target site is uncontrolled.
- High (4 points) can apply when
  - ○ The target site contains moderate quantities or moderate concentrations of any WMD material.
  - ○ Access to the WMD material is uncontrolled.
  - ○ Access to the target site is uncontrolled.
- Medium (3 points) can apply when
  - ○ The target site contains small quantities or small concentrations of any WMD material.
  - ○ Access to the WMD material is controlled.
  - ○ Access to the target site is uncontrolled.
- Low (2 points) can apply when
  - ○ The target site contains small quantities or small concentrations of any WMD material.
  - ○ Access to the WMD material is controlled.
  - ○ Access to the target site is controlled.
- Very Low (1) can apply when
  - ○ The target site contains small quantities or small concentrations of any WMD material.
  - ○ Access to the WMD material is controlled.
  - ○ Access to the target site is controlled.
  - ○ Extraordinary security measures are in place such as the two-man rule, security clearance required, exterior and interior dual-technology sensors, and a 24/7 response force.
- Not Applicable (0 points) can apply when the target site does not contain any WMD materials.

Target Site Population	
Number of Persons at the Site At Any Given Time	**Points**
0	0
1 to 250	1
251 to 5,000	2
5,001 to 15,000	3
15,001 to 50,000	4
More than 50,000	5

Note that a target site can be a town, city, metropolitan area or other large jurisdiction.

Figure 27-5 The population numbers in this chart are illustrative; for example, 1 to 100 instead of 1 to 250.

Potential for Casualties at the Target Site

This factor is fairly simple to rate. All that needs to be known is the population of the target site (see Figure 27-5). Note that, although most often a facility or facilities, a target site can also be a town, city, metropolitan area, or region.

Potential for Casualties Outside the Target Site

Again, we are talking about numbers of persons, but in this case the number will usually be higher except when the target site is far away from a populated area. An example might be an oil production facility on Alaska's North Slope or a weapons testing facility in the middle of a New Mexico desert.

We are concerned here with potential mass casualties in the area around the target site. The number of potential casualties will vary according to population density. Industrial, commercial, and residential areas have different population densities.

A rule of thumb, or at least a starting point, in determining potential human casualties is to include every person living, working, or passing through within a one-mile radius around the site. But the radius, whatever it might be, is not carved in stone. For example, if the site contains chlorine the lethal zone would not be a radius but a shape that represents the prevailing wind and air currents.

Computing a Vulnerability Rating

The points assigned to each of the seven vulnerability factors can now be added up. The lowest possible score is 0, an impossible number in that vulnerability factors are beyond the control of the target site's management. The highest possible score is 35, which represents maximum vulnerability. The sum of the numbers is a raw score. To convert the raw score to the scale

Vulnerability Rating		

Vulnerability Factors	Possible Points	Actual Points
Visibility of the Target Site	0-5	
Importance of the Target Site	0-5	
Importance of the Target Site to Outside Persons, Entities	0-5	
Ease of Access	0-5	
WMD Material on the Target Site	0-5	
Potential Casualties at the Target Site	0-5	
Potential Casualties Outside the Target Site	0-5	
Sum of Points (Raw Score)		
Raw Score Converted to a Scale of 0 to 5		

Figure 27-6 In this chart, the rater is required to choose a number between 0 and 5 for each factor.

of 0 to 5, which is the scale we used in rating assets and threat probability (see Figure 27-6), we can say that

- 0 to 7 points equals a value of 1.
- 8 to 14 points equals a value of 2.
- 15 to 21 points equals a value of 3.
- 22 to 28 points equals a value of 4.
- 29 to 35 points equals a value of 5.

Computing Risk

At the outset of this section, we said:

Asset Value X Threat Probability X Vulnerabilities = Risk

Let's assume that our rating of asset value is 5, threat probability is 5, and vulnerability is 5. The risk rating is therefore 5 x 5 x 5 = 125. This is the greatest risk for the asset being measured. The asset value is highest, the threat probability is highest, and the vulnerabilities are highest. The lowest rating can be 0, but only when the asset is rated 0. This is the case because zero times any number, times any number, is still zero.

CONCLUSIONS

Presented in this chapter is one of several methodologies that can be used to analyze the terrorist risk. Other methodologies of various complexities can be found in the security literature. The one used here is based in part on a methodology developed by the Federal Emergency Management Agency (FEMA) [3].

NOTES

1. The Federal Security Risk Management approach was developed by Applied Research Associates (Waltham, MA) for use by the Department of Defense.

2. Any scale will work.

3. See *Reference Manual to Mitigate Potential Terrorist Attacks Against Buildings* (FEMA 426) and *Primer for Design of Commercial Buildings* (FEMA 427), both of which can be found at *www.fema.gov*.

28. Critical National Infrastructure

History does not long entrust the care of freedom to the weak or the timid.
—Dwight D. Eisenhower

SECTORS OF THE CRITICAL NATIONAL INFRASTRUCTURE

Our society and modern way of life depend on the availability of life-essential products and services. The sectors that deliver these products and services are bound together in a complex arrangement called the critical national infrastructure. The infrastructure consists of the following sectors [1].

- Agriculture and food
- Water
- Public health
- Emergency services
- Defense industrial base
- Information and telecommunications
- Energy
- Transportation
- Finance
- Chemicals
- Postal and shipping

AGRICULTURE AND FOOD SECTOR

From farm to table, our nation's agriculture and food systems are among the most efficient and productive in the world. These industries are a source of essential commodities in the United States, and they account for close to one-fifth of the gross domestic product (GDP). A significant percentage of that figure also contributes to our export economy [2]. The agriculture and food sector includes the following.

- The supply chains for feed, animals, and animal products
- Crop production and the supply chains of seed, fertilizer, and other related materials

- The post-harvesting components of the food supply chain, from processing, production, and packaging through storage and distribution to retail sales, institutional food services, and restaurant or home consumption

Changes in the ways food is produced, distributed, and consumed present new challenges for ensuring its security. More of our food is grown abroad, many foods are transported long distances, and we eat away from home frequently.

The destruction of domestically cultivated crops or livestock or introduction of poisons into the food supply system is a tactic that cannot be ignored. According to the Centers for Disease Control, food-borne diseases cause about 5,000 deaths and 325,000 hospitalizations each year, and those figures have nothing at all to do with terrorism.

Agro-terrorism is difficult to detect and prevent. The number and types of illnesses make it difficult to distinguish between what has been caused in nature or by accident and what has been caused by a malicious human act. Prevention is difficult because it requires safeguards at farms and ranches and along the numerous pathways between farms and ranches and the dining table.

Food — whether imported or domestically grown, and whether procured at a supermarket or consumed in a restaurant — can be tainted with biological or chemical agents; toxins can be mixed with products at food-processing and packaging plants; infectious agents can be implanted in or fed to livestock; and destructive contaminants can be placed in ground soil, animal feed, and water. Another form of attack is the use of disinformation to cast doubt on the safety of food, resulting in consumer fear and damage to the economy — especially in the matter of food exporting.

The U.S. Department of Agriculture estimates that an attack on livestock using an agent of the contagious hoof-and-mouth disease could cause up to $30 billion in damage to the national economy. Public confidence in the security of agricultural and food-processing and packaging systems represents a key part of sustaining economic viability. America's reputation as a reliable supplier of safe, high-quality foodstuffs is essential to maintaining the confidence of foreign customers who are important to the national economy as a whole.

The greatest threats to crops and food are disease and contamination (see Figure 28-1). Because the food system has many points of entry, detection of bio-terrorist agents is critical and difficult at the same time. Although a security issue, detection cannot be made using guards and physical security safeguards. The only rational approach is detection in the laboratory using advanced analytical methods specifically designed to detect disease and contamination resulting from bio-terroristic acts. However, many of the public health and agriculture laboratories are able only to detect the presence of traditional human pathogens that occasionally and unintentionally contaminate foods.

The Food and Drug Administration (FDA) and the Food Safety and Inspection Service (FSIS) are the watchdogs of food safety. The FDA can inspect only

Figure 28-1 A crop destroyed by a contaminant.

1 percent of the 30 billion tons of food imported into the United States annually. Their inspections consist mainly of smelling and looking. The FSIS does the same, but also conducts a small number of laboratory tests. The FDA and FSIS both have emergency response units that deal with food-contamination incidents and coordinate activities with their respective field offices, the Department of Homeland Security, public health officials, hospitals, and other federal, state, and local agencies.

Moving and processing crops and animals require transporting them over long distances. During transport and in-transit storage, these resources are vulnerable. Dependence is upon transportation system owners and operators, particularly regarding trucks and containers, to provide security. In addition to security, a need exists to pinpoint where an outbreak or contamination originated.

Rapid acquisition and use of threat information can help prevent an attack from spreading beyond individual facilities or local communities. Unfortunately, serious institutional barriers and disincentives for sharing such information exist. For instance, there are economic disincentives associated with reporting problems or suspected contamination in food processing. In addition, the agriculture and food markets are highly competitive, and many parts of the food system operate within slim profit margins. As a result, some companies have reason to hold onto information related to incidents involving suspected contamination.

- Deliberate contaminations by terrorists serve two purposes: to harm people to the greatest extent possible and to inflict economic damage. Protecting the public requires timely reporting of information for prompt decision making and action. When crops or animals must be culled or preventively killed to deal with disease or contamination, the fear of a negative public response and attendant economic implications may impede the needed level of response.

WATER SECTOR

Water is critical from both a public health and an economic standpoint. The water sector consists of two basic, yet vital, components: fresh water supply and wastewater collection and treatment. The water component is diverse, complex, and distributed, ranging from systems that serve a few customers to those that serve millions. On the supply side, the primary focus of protection is the nation's 170,000 public water systems. These utilities depend on reservoirs, dams, wells, and aquifers, as well as treatment facilities, pumping stations, aqueducts, and transmission pipelines.

The wastewater component's emphasis is on the 19,500 municipal sanitary sewer systems, including an estimated 800,000 miles of sewer lines. Wastewater utilities collect and treat sewage and process water from domestic, commercial, and industrial sources. The wastewater component also includes storm water systems that collect and sometimes treat storm water runoff.

The water sector has taken steps to protect its critical facilities and systems (see Figure 28-2). For instance, government and industry have developed vulnerability assessment methodologies for both drinking water and wastewater facilities and have trained thousands of utility operators to conduct them.

The Public Health Security and Bioterrorism Preparedness and Response Act of 2002 requires many drinking water systems to conduct vulnerability assessments and prepare or revise emergency response plans. These documents are submitted to the Environmental Protection Agency (EPA). The EPA has developed baseline threat information to use in conjunction with vulnerability assessments.

To improve the flow of information among water-sector organizations, the industry operates a secure forum for gathering, analyzing, and sharing security-related information. Additionally, several federal agencies outside the water sector collect and warehouse information regarding contamination threats such as the release of biological, chemical, and radiological substances into the water supply and how to respond to their presence in drinking water. For example, the EPA verifies monitoring technologies that may be useful in detecting or avoiding biological or chemical threats.

Figure 28-2 Water is essential to daily life.

The water sector is focused on preventing and mitigating attacks that could result in significant human casualties and property damage or widespread economic consequences. In general, there are four areas of primary concentration.

- Physical damage or destruction of critical assets, including intentional release of toxic chemicals
- Actual or threatened contamination of the water supply
- Cyber-attack on information management systems or other electronic systems
- Interruption of services

The water sector also requires increased monitoring and analytic capabilities to enhance detection of contaminants that could be intentionally introduced into the water supply. Approaches to emergency response and the handling of security incidents at water facilities vary according to state and local policies and procedures. With regard to the public reaction associated with contamination or perceived contamination, local, state, and federal agencies coordinate their protection and response efforts. Suspected events concerning water systems can elicit responses that involve taking systems out of service until their integrity can be verified, announcing the incident to the public, and issuing "boil water" orders.

The operations of the water sector depend extensively on other sectors. The heaviest dependence is on the energy sector. For example, running pumps to move water and wastewater and operating drinking water and wastewater treatment plants require large amounts of electricity.

- To a lesser extent, the water sector also depends on the transportation system for supplies of water treatment chemicals, on natural gas pipelines for the energy used in operational activities, and on the telecommunications sector for automated control of operations at remote locations.

PUBLIC HEALTH SECTOR

The public health sector is vast and diverse. It consists of state and local health departments, hospitals, health clinics, mental health facilities, nursing homes, blood-supply facilities, laboratories, mortuaries, and pharmaceutical stockpiles.

Hospitals, clinics, and public health systems play a critical role in mitigating and recovering from the effects of deliberate attacks. Physical damage to one of these facilities or disruption of its operations could prevent a full, effective response to a terrorist attack and exacerbate the outcome. Even if a hospital or public health facility were not the direct target of a terrorist strike, it could be significantly impacted by secondary contamination involving chemical, radiological, or biological agents (see Figure 28-3).

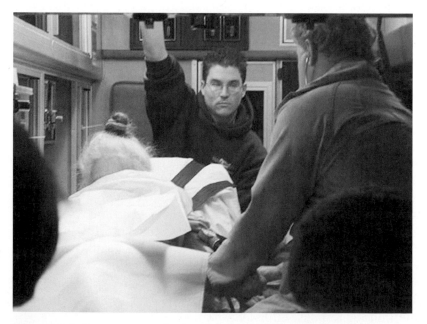

Figure 28-3 Emergency medical teams provide essential services.

In addition to established medical networks, the nation depends on several highly specialized laboratory facilities and assets, especially those related to disease control and vaccine development and storage. Although public health workers are accustomed to placing themselves in harm's way during an emergency, they may be unlikely to view themselves as potential targets of terrorist acts. Most hospitals and clinics are freely accessible to the public, which makes it difficult to prevent malicious entry. This fact can have a substantially negative impact on facility security.

Another significant challenge is the variation in structural and systems design of hospitals and clinics. On one hand, so-called "immune buildings" have built-in structural design elements that help prevent contamination and the spread of infectious agents. Such features include controlled airflow systems, isolation rooms, and special surfaces that eliminate infectious agents on contact.

At the other extreme are buildings with little built-in protection against infectious agents. During a terrorist-initiated epidemic, infectious individuals who continue to operate in the community at large may pose a significant public health risk. Protection of this type of facility presents a daunting security challenge. An additional challenge is protection of medical supplies and materials stockpiled at locations apart from the using facility.

Security is an issue at specialized medical and pharmaceutical laboratories that handle highly toxic or infectious agents. These facilities are mission critical with respect to identifying hazardous agents and containing, neutralizing, and destroying hazardous materials.

EMERGENCY SERVICES SECTOR

The emergency services sector consists of fire, rescue, emergency medical service (EMS), and law enforcement organizations that have a mission to save lives and property in the event of a terrorist incident. Lessons learned from the September 11 attacks indicate that the most pressing problems to be addressed in this sector are as follows.

- Inadequate information sharing between different organizations — particularly between law enforcement and other first responders
- Telecommunications problems such as a lack of redundant systems
- Lack of control at the scene
- Lack of security to mitigate a secondary attack

Terrorists pose a major challenge to our national emergency response network. Although existing resources are sufficient for dealing with routine accidents and regional disasters, the September 11 attacks revealed short-falls in specific capabilities of local, state, and federal emergency response organizations. Most pressing among the shortfalls has been the inability of multiple first-responder units to coordinate their efforts — even when they originate from the same jurisdiction (see Figure 28-4).

Figure 28-4 A terrorist bombing requires a fire service response.

In many jurisdictions, first responders are trained to deal with incidents that are unique to their areas of operation — not to incidents that are out of the ordinary or that occur in nearby jurisdictions. Interoperability is thereby made complicated. Various first-responder units are unable to effectively communicate and coordinate their responses. This problem impedes the speed of response and puts the lives of responders at risk.

Another important issue is the extent to which emergency response communications depend on key linkages such as central dispatch units, firehouses, and 911 call centers. Destruction of these facilities immediately prior to or during a terrorist attack could be disastrous to the response effort. For this reason, guards and physical security safeguards are essential for their protection, which is made difficult by personnel and vehicle traffic in and around these facilities during the emergency.

- Faced with the threat of a major terrorist attack, no single jurisdiction has the ability to maintain or assemble all of the resources necessary to provide an effective response. This truth is a driving force for preparedness exercises and mutual aid agreements. Various state and local governments and federal agencies regularly conduct multijurisdictional preparedness exercises. However, the response methodologies tend to vary widely — a fact that could impede effectiveness. Mutual aid agreements can iron out some of the wrinkles. Specifications of an agreement can require the agreeing parties to perform certain actions in certain ways, the effect of which can be standardization of response actions.

DEFENSE INDUSTRIAL SECTOR

Our nation's defense and military strength rely primarily on the Department of Defense (DoD) and the private sector defense industry that supports it. Without the important contributions of the private sector, the DoD cannot effectively execute its core defense missions, including mobilization and deployment of our nation's military forces abroad. Conversely, private industry and the public at large rely on the federal government to provide for the common defense of our nation and protect our interests both domestically and abroad.

Success in the war on terrorism depends on the ability of the United States military to mount swift, calculated offensive and defensive operations. Ensuring that our military is well trained and properly equipped is critical to maintaining that capability. Private industry manufactures and provides the majority of the equipment, materials, services, and weaponry used by our armed forces. For several decades, the DoD has worked to identify its own critical assets and its dependency on the defense industrial base (see Figure 28-5).

Market competition, consolidations, globalization, and attrition have reduced or eliminated redundant sources of products and services. Outsourcing and complex domestic and foreign corporate mergers and acquisitions have made it difficult for the DoD to be assured that backup products and services will be available when needed.

Figure 28-5 Fighter aircraft are products of the defense industrial base.

Functions that support many of the nation's important military installations have been privatized. A good example is employment of contract security officers that perform nonenforcement duties. Of equal concern is the extent to which the DoD's security requirements are met by private companies that provide services and products of a classified nature. With respect to military installation security, the DoD is unrivaled. Nearly every security concept used in the private sector originated in the military services.

INFORMATION AND TELECOMMUNICATIONS SECTOR

The information and telecommunications sector evolves in step with technology advances, business and competitive pressures, and changes in the regulatory environment. Despite its dynamic nature, this sector has consistently provided robust and reliable communications and processes to meet the needs of businesses and governments.

In the terrorist threat environment, the users of information and telecommunications systems face significant challenges to protect their vast and dispersed critical assets, both cyber and physical (see Figure 28-6). Protection of this

Figure 28-6 Data backup may not be enough to counter a cyber attack.

sector is essential because government and businesses rely heavily on it for processing, sending, and receiving information that ranges from routine to ultrasensitive.

Voice and data services to public and private users pass through a complex and diverse network that encompasses the Public Switched Telecommunications Network (PSTN), the Internet, and private enterprise networks. The PSTN provides switched circuits for telephone, data, and leased point-to-point services. It consists of physical facilities, including over 20,000 switches, access tandems, and other equipment. These components are connected by nearly two billion miles of fiber and copper cable. The PSTN is clearly the backbone of telecommunications.

Advances in data network technology and the increasing demand for data services have spawned rapid proliferation of Internet use. The Internet is a global network made up of many networks that use a common suite of protocols. Internet Service Providers (ISPs) provide end users with access to the Internet. Larger ISPs use network operation centers (NOCs), which connect their high-capacity networks to the Internet's access points. International PSTN and Internet traffic travels via underwater cables that connect to the United States at various cable landing points.

In addition to the PSTN and the Internet are enterprise networks that support the voice and data needs of large enterprises. An enterprise network is a combination of lines leased from the PSTN or Internet providers.

Telecommunications networks allow us to use the telephone, watch television, send and receive e-mail, and surf the Internet. They connect us individually to entities for services both routine and emergency, such as the bank, the power company, the boss, clients and customers, the doctor, the police and fire departments, and other contacts essential to our daily lives.

The information and telecommunications sector is an important resource in peacetime and a vital one during times of crisis, making protection of it a key goal. Very important among the components of this sector is the Internet. The Internet is also an asset for terrorists. They can use it in four ways.

- Communicate among their members and cells
- Obtain information useful to attack planning
- Spread propaganda
- Damage data assets

The Internet makes possible the movement of terrorist-owned information, often ciphered, across great distances and at real-time speed. Such communication facilitates good organization, cohesiveness, and coordination of terrorist activities.

Terrorists also use the Internet to acquire information, such as details about a potential target. Attack planning requires knowledge, even more than material resources, skill, and resolve. The amount of information accessible through the Internet is astounding, and some of it very useful to people intent upon misusing it.

Figure 28-7 Damage to a telecommunications network can knock out emergency response centers.

The Internet provides a platform for propaganda that is intended to convince people of the righteousness of the terrorist cause, recruit members, gain empathetic support, and elicit funds. The audience for propaganda delivered on the Internet is wide and diverse.

Terrorists can use the Internet to destroy or at least damage U.S. information systems and their content. This is more than just hacking, and the targets are not necessarily the Pentagon and other entities of government. At great risk are critical services that American society has come to depend on, such as power grids, financial networks, telecommunication and transportation systems, and emergency services (see Figure 28-7).

The information and telecommunications sector is a logical and inviting terrorist target. Attempted and actual cyber sabotage occurs every day at one location or another. The government places high priority on consistent application of security across the entire sector. However, private enterprises have a different perspective on what constitutes acceptable risk and how to achieve security. As a result, the two parties sometimes disagree.

Because of growing interdependencies among the various systems comprising this sector, a successful terrorist attack on any one of them could result in cascading damage to the others. Interdependencies increase the need to identify critical assets and secure them against both physical and cyber threats.

ENERGY SECTOR

Energy drives the foundation of sophisticated processes at work in American society today. Energy is essential to our economy, national defense, and quality of life. In the context of protection, the energy sector has two segments: (1) electricity and (2) oil and natural gas.

Electricity Segment

This segment services almost 130 million households and institutions. The United States consumes in the range of 4 trillion kilowatt hours per year. Almost every form of productive activity — whether in businesses, manufacturing plants, schools, hospitals, or homes — requires electricity (see Figure 28-8). Electricity is also necessary to produce other forms of energy such as refined oil. A widespread or long-term disruption of the electricity segment would have a devastating effect on activities critical to our economy and national defense, including those associated with response and recovery.

The North American electric system is an interconnected, multinodal distribution system that accounts for virtually all electricity supplied to the United States, Canada, and a portion of northern Mexico. The physical system consists of three major parts.

- Generation assets that include fossil fuel plants, hydroelectric dams, and nuclear power plants
- Transmission and distribution systems that link areas of the national grid and deliver electricity to homes and businesses
- Control and communications systems that operate and monitor critical components

In addition to these components, the electricity segment encompasses ancillary facilities and systems that guarantee fuel supplies necessary to support

Figure 28-8 Power stations link generating plants to a multitude of electricity users.

electricity generation, some of which involve the handling of hazardous materials. This segment also depends heavily on other critical sectors for power generation.

The Federal Energy Regulatory Commission (FERC) and state utility commissions regulate some of the activities and operations of certain electricity industry participants. An example is the Nuclear Regulatory Commission (NRC), which regulates nuclear power reactors and other civilian nuclear facilities.

Oil and Natural Gas Segment

Oil and natural gas facilities and assets are widely distributed, consisting of more than 300,000 producing sites, 4,000 off-shore platforms, more than 600 natural gas processing plants, 153 refineries, more than 1,400 product terminals, and 7,500 bulk stations. The oil industry has five components.

- Crude oil production
- Crude oil transport
- Refining
- Product transport and distribution
- Control and other external support systems

The production component includes exploration, field development, onshore and offshore production, field collection systems, and their supporting infrastructures (see Figure 28-9).

Figure 28-9 Refined oil is an input to power generating plants.

Crude oil transport includes pipelines (160,000 miles), storage terminals, ports, and ships. The refinement component consists of about 150 refineries that range in size and production capabilities from 5,000 to over 500,000 barrels per day. Transport and distribution of oil includes pipelines, trains, ships, ports, terminals and storage, trucks, and retail stations. The natural gas industry consists of three major components.

- Exploration and production
- Transmission
- Distribution

The United States produces roughly 20 percent of the world's natural gas supply. There are 278,000 miles of natural gas pipelines and 1,119,000 miles of natural gas distribution lines. Distribution includes storage facilities, gas processing, liquid natural gas facilities, pipelines, liquefied petroleum gas storage facilities, and citygates. (A citygate is a pipeline node through which gas passes from interstate pipelines to a local distribution system.) Underground aquifers, depleted oil and gas fields, and salt caverns provide storage of natural gas.

- The first responders to a terrorist attack on most oil and natural gas sector facilities are local police and fire departments. In general, these responders are constantly improving their capabilities and preparedness to confront well-planned, sophisticated attacks, particularly those involving chemical, biological, and radiological (CBR) weapons.

TRANSPORTATION SECTOR

The transportation sector embraces the aviation, maritime, rail, pipeline, highway, trucking and busing, and public mass transit industries. The diversity and size of this sector makes it vital to our economy and national security, including military mobilization and deployment. As a whole, the transportation sector is robust, having been developed over decades of both private and public investment. Together, the various transportation modes provide mobility of our population and contribute to our much-cherished individual freedom.

The transportation sector is also convenient. Americans rely on its easy access and reliability in their daily lives. Interdependencies exist between transportation and nearly every other sector of the nation's critical infrastructure.

Aviation Mode

This component of the transportation sector is vast, consisting of thousands of possible terrorist entry points. Aircraft have symbolic value, representing the freedom of movement Americans value so highly. The aviation mode consists of two main parts.

- Airports and the associated assets needed to support their operations, including the aircraft they serve
- Aviation command, control, communications, and information systems that support and maintain safe use of airspace

The terrorist attacks on the World Trade center and the Pentagon demonstrated vulnerabilities of the nation's air transportation system (see Figure 28-10). Repeat attacks are possible despite major security measures put in place following 9-11.

The Aviation and Transportation Security Act, which became law in November of 2001, mandated the following.

- Creation of the Transportation Security Administration (TSA)
- The use of explosive-detection devices to screen checked bags for bombs and explosives
- The use of federal employees to perform airport security duties
- Fortified cockpit doors
- An increase in the number of sky marshals
- Training of flight crews in how to respond to a hijacking

TSA screeners must undergo background checks, pass a training course, and speak English. To attract and retain quality employees, the pay and benefits

Figure 28-10 Aircraft are visible reminders of advanced technology and industrial prowess.

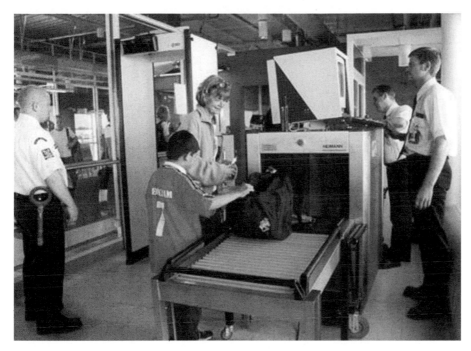

Figure 28-11 Baggage screening is tedious and attention sensitive.

of TSA employees are substantially higher than for their counterparts in the private security industry (see Figure 28-11).

Despite the unprecedented number of security measures put into place since 9-11, there is little assurance that determined terrorists willing to give up their lives will not find a way to destroy passenger aircraft or use them as flying bombs. Two issues make protection difficult. First, there are simply too many attack points and vulnerabilities to establish an adequate level of security. Second, we tend to rule out attack methods until they occur, even when early signals are present. For example, in the case of 9-11 we observed the hijacking of an Air France flight in 1994. The hijackers, members of the Armed Islamic Group, said they intended to blow up the plane over Paris or crash it into the Eiffel Tower. In that same year, a disgruntled FedEx employee tried to hijack a DC-10 so that he could nosedive it into a FedEx facility in Memphis. A year later, Philippine authorities uncovered an Al Qaeda plot to hijack an airliner and crash it into CIA headquarters. Aviation faces several protection challenges.

- *Heavy volume:* U.S. air carriers transport millions of passengers every day and at least twice as many bags and other cargo.
- *Limited capabilities and available space:* Current detection equipment and methods are limited in number, capability, and ease of use.
- *Time-sensitive cargo:* Just-in-time delivery of cargo is essential for many businesses. Any significant time delay in processing and transporting cargo would negatively affect business operations.

- *Security versus convenience:* Maintaining security while limiting congestion and delays complicates the task of security and has important financial implications.
- *Accessibility:* Most airports are open to the public and are near public roadways.
- Another concern for the aviation industry is the additional cost of increased security during sustained periods of heightened alert.

Rail Mode

More so than airlines, where security officers screen passengers and luggage, ground transportation modes (including railways) are wide open to attack. Boarding points are constructed to be easily accessible, and for that reason difficult to protect. The most likely form of attack would involve the use of conventional bombs, either at the boarding points or within conveyances. Jerusalem, Moscow, Paris, London, and Madrid have experienced such attacks.

During every hour of every day, trains traverse the United States, linking producers of raw materials to manufacturers and retailers. Trains carry mining, manufacturing, and agriculture products; liquid chemicals and fuels; and consumer goods (see Figure 28-12). They carry 40 percent of intercity freight, which includes coal, a critical resource for the generation of electricity. More than 20 million intercity travelers use the rail system annually, and 45 million passengers ride trains and subways operated by local transit authorities.

Securing rail mode assets is critical to protecting U.S. commerce and the safety of travelers. Differences in design, structure, and purpose of railway stations complicate overall protection, and the size and breadth of the rail

Figure 28-12 Freight trains carry goods from ports and factories to truck distribution points.

mode makes it difficult to prevent or react to terrorist attacks. This fact complicates protection efforts, but also offers certain advantages in the event of a terrorist attack. For example, trains are confined to specific routes and are highly controllable. If hijacked, a train can be shunted off the main line and rendered less of a threat.

Similarly, the loss of a bridge or tunnel can impact traffic along major corridors. However, the potential for national-level disruptions is limited. The greater risk is associated with rail transport of hazardous materials. Freight railways often carry hazardous materials essential to manufacturing and national defense industries.

Freight trains transporting hazardous cargo are logical targets. The release of chlorine, for example, would be lethal to people living or working anywhere nearby. A bomb placed on a freight train, on its tracks, or under a trestle is a possibility.

Rail transport is complex and requires close coordination between industry and government. A sector-wide information-sharing process can help prevent overreactive security measures such as restricting rail movement of hazardous materials critical to business operations. A shutdown of this type can create unintentional negative consequences.

An additional area of concern is the marking of container cars to indicate the specific type of hazardous materials being transported. During an emergency response, placards on rail cars help to alert first responders to hazardous materials they may encounter.

- Following 9-11, the rail sector adopted heightened security levels that are now the new "normal" state. But not all is rosy: some cash-strapped operators face tradeoffs between providing increased levels of security and going out of business.

Trucking and Busing Mode

The trucking and busing industry is a fundamental component of our national transportation infrastructure. Without this sector's resources, the movement of people, goods, and services around the country would be greatly impeded. Components of this mode include highways, roads, intermodal terminals, bridges, tunnels, trucks, buses, maintenance facilities, and roadway border crossings. Transportation choke points (e.g., bridges and tunnels, intermodal terminals, border crossings, and highway interchanges) present unique security challenges (see Figure 28-13).

Although many states have conducted risk assessments of their respective highway systems, no true basis for comparison among them exists to determine relative criticality, identify vulnerabilities, and decide mitigation measures. A reason for this lack of synchronization is a paucity of funds. As a result, the mode as a whole has neither a coherent picture of industry-wide risks nor a set of appropriate security criteria on which to baseline its protection planning efforts.

Figure 28-13 Bridges are choke points for ground transportation.

Given the number of public and private small-business owners and operators, the cost of protection is prohibitive. Highway, trucking, and busing organizations regard the possibility of security-related delays at border crossings a problem of major financial significance.

Pipelines Mode

The United States has a vast pipeline industry, consisting of many hundreds of thousands of miles of pipelines, many of which are buried underground. These lines move a variety of substances such as crude oil, refined petroleum products, and natural gas.

Pipeline facilities already incorporate a variety of stringent safety precautions that account for the potential effects a disaster could have on surrounding areas. Moreover, most elements of pipeline infrastructures can be quickly repaired or bypassed to mitigate localized disruptions.

As a whole, the response and recovery capabilities of the pipeline industry are well proven, and most large control-center operators have established extensive contingency plans and backup protocols. Pipelines are not independent entities, but rather integral parts of industrial and public service networks. Loss of a pipeline could impact a wide array of facilities and industrial factories that depend on reliable fuel delivery to operate (see Figure 28-14).

Many of the products that pipelines deliver are inherently volatile. Hence, their protection is a significant security issue. Pipelines cross numerous state and local jurisdictions. Operators face a confusing, and sometimes conflicting, array of regulations and mandatory security programs. In addition, the

Figure 28-14 Pipelines transport hydrocarbons to refineries and processing plants.

pipeline industry's dependence on the energy and telecommunications sectors necessitates coordination that transcends jurisdictional boundaries. This creates problems in assessing broad implications of an attack on a major pipeline segment.

- Historically, individual enterprises within the pipeline mode have invested in security. However, the new terrorist risk environment calls for different and stronger security measures. The Department of Transportation, which regulates this mode, has developed a methodology for determining a pipeline facility's criticality and identifying protective measures. The measures are synchronized with the Department of Homeland Security's threat levels.

Maritime Mode

Security in the maritime shipping industry is conditioned by ports and their associated assets, ships and passenger transportation systems, coastal and inland waterways, locks, dams and canals, and a network of railroads and pipelines that connect to other transportation modes.

Figure 28-15 Ships, both cargo and passenger, are difficult to protect.

The 300-plus seaports in the United States range widely in size, characteristics, and operations. Most ports have diverse waterside facilities that are owned, operated, and accessed by diverse entities. State and local governments control some port authority facilities, whereas others are owned and operated by private corporations. Most ships are privately owned and operated (see Figure 28-15). Cargo is stored in terminals at ports and loaded onto ships or other vehicles that pass through on their way to domestic and international destinations.

The DoD has designated certain commercial seaports as strategic seaports because they provide facilities and services needed for military deployment. U.S. seaports could be tempting targets for terrorists bent on killing large numbers of people and disrupting the economy. Port, ferry, and cruise-ship terminals are often filled with workers and passengers embarking and disembarking. The locales tend to be in congested areas. Likely to be nearby are bulk storage tanks containing volatile liquids waiting to be transported or taken aboard ships for use as fuels. An attack on a seaport could take many lives and shut down the regional economy.

Even with a high number of inspectors and wide use of inspection technologies, only a fraction of incoming cargo ships can be examined. Close to 8,000 foreign-flag ships make 51,000 calls at U.S. seaports each year. They carry about 890 million tons of goods, 8 million containers, and 175 billion gallons of liquid petroleum. On average, it takes five persons working three hours to adequately inspect a single shipping container. When reason exists to believe that a container may contain explosives or lethal chemical, biological, or radiological material the inspection can require thirty or more experts working three weeks or longer with the aid of scientific equipment.

Security is also frustrated at inland ports reachable along narrow channels where terrorists would be able to "jump ship." In addition, a ship sunk in a narrow waterway could close down a port for weeks or months. Owners and operators of foreign vessels are required to make notice of a vessel's planned arrival at a U.S. port. When a ship arrives outside the port, it is boarded by a sea marshal. After docking, a portion of the cargo is inspected.

Vessel and cargo inspections are tedious, difficult, and expensive despite recent introduction of technology-based inspection methods. Given the demonstrable inability of port managements to prevent smuggling and drug trafficking, there is little reason to expect reliability in detecting entry of terrorists and/or their weapons.

CSOs employed by importers/exporters, freight companies, ship owners, and other organizations in the private side of marine transportation can improve port security through enhanced communication with a port's public sector agencies. The matters of interest include agreement on common objectives, information sharing, mutual aid, and memorandums of understanding.

On the port security horizon is better use of available technology such as global positioning and radio frequency identification. Complexity of the maritime industry's operations is compounded by international agreements and multinational rules that are beyond the purview of the DoT to negotiate. The negotiating entity is the Department of State, whose efforts involve extended discussions.

The maritime industry continually looks for cost-effective technologies that can rapidly and reliably detect explosives and other hazardous substances. Physical security and operating procedures have undergone a comprehensive review since 11 September 2001. Findings of risk assessments conducted at all ports helped define key asset designations, identify vulnerabilities, develop mitigation strategies, and highlight best practices. From these efforts came new ideas for controlling movement of high-risk vessels carrying high-consequence cargoes and large numbers of passengers.

The U.S. Coast Guard, an element of DoT, operates a Sea Marshal program that deploys Maritime Safety and Security Teams to enforce security rules. DoT also works with multinational authorities to develop and enforce security standards for vessels and ports. Shippers that fail to comply are subject to greater scrutiny and delays when entering U.S. ports. DoT and DHS collaborate to enhance security of the maritime mode. Collaboration includes efforts to

- Identify vulnerabilities, interdependencies, best practices, and remediation measures.
- Develop an industry-wide plan for implementing security measures that correspond to varying threats.
- Develop processes to enhance maritime domain awareness and gain international cooperation.
- Develop a template for improving physical and operational port security.
- Develop security and protection guidelines and technologies for cargo and passenger ships.
- Improve waterway security such as monitoring waterway traffic using electronic monitoring systems.

Public Mass Transit Mode

Each year passengers take approximately 9.5 billion trips on public transit. In fact, mass transit carries more passengers in a single day than the air and rail transportation modes combined. Mass transit systems are designed to be publicly accessible, and most are owned and operated by state and local agencies. A city relies on its mass transit system to serve a significant portion of its workforce in addition to being a means of evacuation in case of emergency (see Figure 28-16). Protection of mass transit systems is therefore an important requirement.

Not far from the realm of possibility would be the release of a chemical or biological agent in a subway or other enclosed area of a transit system. Just such an attack occurred in a Tokyo subway.

A subway draws outside air in and expels inside air out. An air intake that is accessible, as many are, presents opportunities for the release of aerosolized agents that would be literally sucked into the underground station. The contaminated air would further spread on air currents generated by moving trains, and as contaminated air is expelled from the subway it too would reach people at ground level and higher.

A mass transit entity is funded and managed at the local level, and operated as a not-for-profit organization. It is regulated by various agencies that work together to bring separate mass transit entities into a single region-wide system.

- A mass transit system is designed for openness and ease of public access, which makes security monitoring difficult at points of entry and exit.

Figure 28-16 Commuter trains carry people between work and home and evacuate them away from danger.

Protecting the overall system is expensive. The cost of implementing new security requirements can result in significant financial consequences. Standardization of security can reduce costs but this is not an option because mass transit systems vary widely in size and operating methods. Despite differences, basic planning factors are relatively consistent from system to system.

FINANCE SECTOR

The financial services sector has a variety of large commercial office buildings that enclose retail and wholesale banking operations, financial market operations, regulatory agencies, and repositories for documents and financial assets (see Figure 28-17). Financial utilities, such as payment and clearing and settlement systems, are primarily electronic, using computers, data storing and retrieving equipment, and telecommunication networks.

The financial industry cannot exist absent public confidence. Confidence is eroded when the public perceives that financial assets are subject to loss resulting from inadequate security protection. Risk of loss can be reduced when an organization keeps on hand a small fraction of cash and convertibles.

In a time of crisis, such as during and following a terrorist attack, public confidence demands that financial institutions, financial markets, and payment systems remain operational or immediately restorable (see Figure 28-18). The sector operates according to security plans and procedures developed by the Department of the Treasury and federal and state regulatory agen-

Figure 28-17 Banking institutions are an important segment of the financial sector.

cies. These groups regularly engage in identifying sector vulnerabilities and take appropriate protective measures, including penalties for institutions that consistently fail to meet standards.

The sector's retail niche is characterized by a high degree of substitutability, meaning that one form of payment is replaceable by another payment form. For example, retailers can accept payments in cash, checks, or credit cards.

The finance sector relies on other sectors for continuity of operations: the energy sector provides electric power, the transportation sector provides means for transporting assets and human capital, the emergency services sector provides public safety services, and the information and telecommunications sector provides services for processing data and moving them to multiple points and over great distances. Disruption in other sectors is an important concern. For instance, the equity securities markets remained closed for four business days following September 11, not because market systems were inoperable but because the telecommunications lines in lower

Figure 28-18 Wall Street is the center of the nation's financial sector.

Manhattan that connect key market participants were heavily damaged and could not be restored immediately. To deal with problems such as this, many financial institutions have added redundancy and backups to their systems.

After the September 11 attacks, the industry and its associations initiated lessons-learned reviews to identify needed improvement to security, and established a forum for sharing best practices. Other protection initiatives include efforts to identify and address the risks of sector dependencies on electronic networks and telecommunications, and enhance the exchange of security-related information.

CHEMICALS SECTOR

The chemical industry manufactures products that are indispensable to other sectors. For example, it produces fertilizer for agriculture, chlorine for water purification, and ingredients of products used in the public health sector.

The chemical industry is the nation's top exporter, accounting for ten cents of every export dollar. One out of every seven patents issued in the U.S. is acquired by the chemical industry. Chemicals production is highly diverse; companies vary in size, operations, and geographic dispersion. Product manufacture and delivery depends on research and development, raw materials, manufacturing plants and processes, and distribution networks.

Uncertainty regarding the safety of chemical-based products impacts producers as well as users (see Figure 28-19). Malicious product contamination

Figure 28-19 Chemical containers of one type or another are situated close to end users.

is a safety and security issue. Risk of contamination is present at the place of production, in storage areas, aboard transport vehicles, and on retail shelves. Clearly, security under this circumstance is problematic at best.

In addition to the potential for human injury and death, there is the potential for damage to the environment and the economy. The industry's ability to protect and ensure the quality and safety of chemical stockpiles is also important. Chemicals are the raw materials for the manufacture of countless products. Contamination of chemicals in storage can impact a wide range of industries. In addition to the contamination risk is the fact that many chemicals are inherently hazardous to people and the environment.

For all of the previous reasons, protection of chemicals is paramount. Yet with respect to security there is currently no clear, unambiguous legal or regulatory authority at the federal level to ensure comprehensive uniform security standards for chemical facilities.

Improving security can be expensive. No single, specific security regime can be effective for all environments where chemicals are present. Further, many current statutes related to the handling of highly toxic substances were created decades ago and may no longer be correct for monitoring and controlling access. For example, distributors of pesticides must be licensed, but almost anyone can obtain a license.

As in most other industries, the chemical industry relies on the availability, continuity, and quality of supplies obtained from other critical sectors. The most critical of other sectors is energy; the chemical industry is the nation's third largest consumer of electricity.

- Despite some progress in establishing security, a significant percentage of companies that operate major hazardous chemical facilities do not abide by security standards voluntarily developed by the industry as a whole.

POSTAL AND SHIPPING SECTOR

Each day, U.S. citizens place more than two-thirds of a billion pieces of mail into the U.S. postal system; and each day more than 300,000 city and rural postal carriers deliver that mail to more than 137 million delivery addresses nationwide (see Figure 28-20). In all, the vast network operated by the United States Postal Service (USPS) is comprised of a headquarters in Washington, D.C., tens of thousands of postal offices, and hundreds of thousands of drop-box locations.

The USPS employs more than 749,000 full-time personnel in rural and urban locations across the country and generates more than $60 billion in revenues each year. Together, the USPS and private-industry mailing and shipping revenues exceed $200 billion annually.

The postal system is highly dependent on and interconnected with other key infrastructure systems, especially the transportation system. USPS depends on a transportation fleet composed of both service-owned and contractor-operated vehicles and equipment. Mail also travels daily by commercial aircraft, truck, railroad, and ship. Because of these dependencies, many key postal facilities are co-located with transportation hubs.

Figure 28-20 The U.S. Postal system is a conduit for moving lethal items from terrorists to victims.

The expansiveness of the national postal facilities network presents a significant direct protection challenge. Additionally, the size and pervasiveness of the system as a whole have important implications in terms of the potential secondary effects of a malicious attack. The 2001 anthrax attacks underscore this concern. In addition to localized mail stoppages across the United States, the tainted mail caused widespread anxiety that translated into significant economic impact.

Historically, the American public has placed great trust, confidence, and reliance on the integrity of the postal sector. This trust and confidence are at risk when the public considers the mail service to be a potential threat to its health and safety. Consequently, the USPS continues to focus on the specific protection issues facing its sector and is trying to find solutions to increase postal security without hampering its ability to provide fast, reliable mail service. The USPS has identified five areas of concern for the postal system.

- Points of entry and locations of key facilities
- The mail's chain of custody
- Unique constitutional and legal issues
- Interagency coordination
- Ability to respond in emergency situations

The large number of postal offices and their geographical dispersion complicate protection. The location of a postal office can also be a problem when the office is co-located with or adjacent to another facility that may be a terrorist target. Relocating to mitigate risk is often constrained by limited resources or a lack of alternative sites.

A perfect system has not been found to provide early warning of hazards during mail scanning. Related to this shortcoming is the fact that mail often moves in and out of USPS control during its movement from sender to addressee. To offset this risk, USPS requires contractors to vet their employees for criminal history and drug abuse.

USPS security efforts face constitutional and legal challenges that are unique to the postal and shipping sector. Specifically, the Fourth Amendment (unreasonable search and seizure) prohibits opening and looking into the mail without probable cause. The alternative is to X-ray mail suspected of containing a bomb or other hazardous items or materials.

Discovery of mail containing a toxic substance, such as anthrax, presents a logistical nightmare. The USPS does not have a stockpile of decontaminants sufficient to get through a sustained period of danger. The problem is not with the USPS but with a paucity of companies that manufacture the decontaminants.

- The federal authority to implement protective and response measures related to the actual or potential transmission of certain biological agents across state lines is not widely understood. Not knowing or not understanding the authority to act can get in the way of a rapid and coordinated response.

CONCLUSIONS

Our society is very much dependent on the functioning of sectors that comprise the critical national infrastructure. We depend on these sectors for the provision of basic necessities such as food, water, power, communications, transportation, and public health services. Damage to any of the critical sectors can alter the routines of our daily lives. More importantly, our ability to defend ourselves against our enemies can be seriously impaired.

NOTES

1. Much of the information contained in this chapter was drawn from material published by the Department of Homeland Security.

2. The United States exports approximately a quarter of its farm and ranch products.

Index